Writing Effectively in BUSINESS

Beth S. Neman
Wilmington College of Ohio

Sandra Smythe
Smythe & Marrs

HarperCollins*Publishers*

To David, Dan, and Mark,
and especially Albert, without whom . . .

Project Coordination: Carnes-Lachina Publication Services, Inc.
Text Design: Sona Blakeslee
Cover Design: Susan D'Angelo
Cover Photo: Fernando Bueno/The Image Bank
Production Manager: Michael Weinstein
Compositor: Omegatype Typography, Inc.
Printer and Binder: R. R. Donnelley & Sons Company
Cover Printer: The Lehigh Press, Inc.

WRITING EFFECTIVELY IN BUSINESS

Library of Congress Cataloging-in-Publication Data

Neman, Beth.
    Writing effectively in business / Beth S. Neman and Sandra H.
Smythe.
        p.   cm.
    Includes index.
    ISBN 0-06-044809-1 (student ed.)   ISBN 0-06-044817-2 (instructor ed.)
    1. Business writing.   I. Smythe, Sandra.   II. Title.
HF5718.3.N46   1991
658.4'5—dc20
                                                                91-19950
                                                                CIP

91 92 93 94 9 8 7 6 5 4 3 2 1

CONTENTS

Writing Effectively in Business is not like other business communications texts. It brings a hard-edged business perspective necessary for business writing in the decade of the nineties.

Like any good business-writing text, *WEB* is firmly grounded in sound principles of process rhetoric. (One author has taught university rhetoric and composition courses for more than 20 years.) Unlike other texts, however, *WEB* teaches techniques heavily influenced by free-market business imperatives—action, profit, and the constraints of time and competition. (The other author, who has also taught writing professionally, is currently a corporate communications consultant and has been a business communications manager for more than 20 years, 10 in a Fortune 500 company.)

In the 1980s the authors combined their teaching and business skills to design a business-writing course that would accurately reflect the communications demands of the contemporary workplace. *Writing Effectively in Business* grew out of that successful course.

BUSINESS FOCUSED

Writing Effectively in Business has a distinctively business point of view. It acknowledges the complex nature of business communications problems and provides practical strategies for problems particular to business. The text offers authentic problems for students to work on—simulations of real business situations. In fact, almost all of the examples—both good and bad—are real business problems that business writers have faced. Only the names have been changed and the situations disguised. With these experiential exercises, the authors have aimed to equip students to handle effectively most of the business thinking, planning, and writing assignments likely to come their way in their first years at work.

The book models an effective business style—brief, simple, and clear. The vocabulary is for the most part nontechnical, and definitions are supplied where needed. The syntax is simple, as business prefers, and relies heavily on simple and compound structures. Headlines and other signposts guide the reader. Chapters are preceded by *Executive Summaries* to give students and instructors the same kinds of communications support top business executives are accustomed to. As in business writing, the approach is straightforward and uncluttered. Scholarly comment and other interesting sidelights are relegated to sidebars, and most sidebars have a business focus. One important sequence offers practical suggestions for using word processors to expedite business writing and organization.

PEDAGOGICALLY USEFUL

Writing Effectively in Business also takes into account the realities of the classroom. Research shows that experiential learning is effective. Throughout the book, assignments permit students to interact with business problems and participate in their solution. Further, because examples and models are important to skills acquisition, the text has an abundance of them. In addition, *WEB*'s structure is designed to meet academic needs for sequential learning, scheduling flexibility, and guided revision.

SEQUENTIAL LEARNING. *WEB* offers a lesson sequence that has been classroom tested for graduated difficulty.

Part 1: The Process of Effective Business Writing teaches in Chapter 1 the fundamental principles of purpose and empathy. These principles underlie all effective business writing and support the applications in the rest of the book. Chapters 2 and 3 clear away stylistic and mechanical questions so that students are free to deal with substance. This style review also acts as a diagnostic tool and permits students who need help with basics to get such assistance early.

Part 2: Applications of Effective Business Writing discusses business letters, memos, and reports. But writing complex business communications is like playing three-dimensional chess: problems must be viewed from many angles and at many levels. And this situation presents serious pedagogical problems, because it's not possible to teach everything at once. To address this teaching problem, Part 2 permits the student to accumulate the multi-dimensional skills necessary to deal with complex business problems, but sequences the work so that there are opportunities for success at each stage. Then each chapter adds one more level of complexity.

Chapters 4 and 5, for instance, consider business letters and organizations from a psychological point of view. Chapter 6 begins a seven-chapter sequence on the closely related forms of internal communication. And here we add political awareness to the psychological sensitivity already emphasized. Chapter 6 teaches simple memos, and Chapter 7 builds on those skills to teach the more complex recommendation memo. Chapter 8 suggests realistic strategies for business research (which is markedly different from academic research). Then the newly acquired business research skills can be applied to the writing of both recommendation memos and reports, studied in Chapter 9. Chapter 10 completes the sequence by adding graphic illustration to the skills already mastered.

FLEXIBILITY. The text is paced to accommodate varying academic schedules and individual teaching strategies.

Part 3: Special Types of Effective Business Writing is designed to provide flexibility and accommodate various academic schedules and individual teaching strategies. For instance, Chapter 11 offers comprehensive and practical advice on the job application process. Graduating seniors and other job seekers could use this information early in the term.

Similarly, the chapters on proposal writing, brochures, meetings, and oral presentations—Chapters 12, 13, 14, and 15—could be used to satisfy special course demands. Some courses might include one or more of these chapters early in the term. In a brief general course, an instructor might choose to omit some of them altogether.

The three *Focus Segments* give an instructor further scheduling flexibility. They offer a fully developed midterm project to evaluate the students' progress as competent and independent communicators; complex research and writing assignments for the individual student; and collaborative assignments—authentic case studies to give students research and writing experience as members of a business team or task force.

GUIDED REVISION. *WEB* concludes with the *Painless Usage Guide,* a quick, accessible, alphabetical guide to the mechanics of English syntax, usage, punctuation, capitalization, and spelling. Students can use the PUG comfortably to revise their assignments and, later in their business careers, as a handy desk reference.

LEARNING WITH PLEASURE

Working in business is lively and stimulating. And because the problems and situations in *WEB* are authentic to business, students find the coursework stimulating and interesting too.

Wherever we have taught *Writing Effectively in Business,* students have enjoyed the cases and problems, and we have enjoyed watching them achieve competence as business writers. We hope that you who study this text and you who teach it will find the experience equally rewarding.

ACKNOWLEDGMENTS

In the writing of this book we have been lucky beyond all deserving in the advice and help we have been given. Warm thanks are due to all those who helped us, but especially to Sheila Bell, Dick Boynton, Joyce Braude, Carol Burke, Robin Dias, Wilma Dumas, Allison, Hartley, and John Flege, Pat Ikeda, John Landsman, Hank Loudermilk, Susan Marrs, Jim Michaux, Daniel Neman, Ingrid and Hans Nuetzel, Roger Rassche, Carol Sanger, Jim Sluzewski, Mark C. Smythe, Stephen Weisbrod, Lowell Wenger, and Klaus Ziermaier, who generously gave us the benefit of their experience and accomplishment.

This book also benefited from the guidance of a distinguished senior executive whose business acumen is exceeded only by his modesty. Though he remains anonymous by choice, his excellent sense and elegant business judgment made an enormous contribution, and we acknowledge that with admiration.

For unstintingly sharing their technical knowledge, we are heavily indebted to Norman Bates, Nick Carey, William Hershey, John Nuetzel, James Suchan, Klaus and Audrone Willeke, and most especially David Neman, without whom this enterprise would surely have foundered early on. We also thank Wendy Allen and Lois Frankel for contributing art work. And at Wilmington College—one of the laboratories in which the book was tested—we thank Iris Kelsen and William Guthrie for helpful support, and business professors Alan Goldstein and Michael Jancovic for reading the text and making useful suggestions.

For additional suggestions that shaped the text in important ways, we thank readers across the country: Lecia Archer, San Diego State University; Susan Aylworth, California State University–Chico; Joseph Cosenza, St. John's University; Eugene Cunnar, New Mexico State University; Earl Dvorak, Indiana University; Gretchen Flesher, Gustavus Adolphus College; Robert Grieselman, University of Illinois at Urbana-Champaign; John Hagge, Iowa State University; George Haich, Georgia State University; Kelsie Harder, SUNY-Potsdam; Edwina Jordan, Illinois Central College; Kimball King, University of North Carolina; Carl Kropf, Georgia State University; Harvey Lillywhite, Towson State University; Thomas Means, Louisiana Tech University; Nancy Mower, University of Hawaii at Manoa; Layne Neeper, Pennsylvania State University; and Karen Quinn, University of Illinois at Chicago.

We are mindful of the skill and hard work of the many people at HarperCollins in New York, Scott, Foresman in Chicago, and Carnes-Lachina in Cleveland, who produced the book. At HarperCollins, we are particularly grateful to Paula Cousin, whose kindness and good sense guided the enterprise smoothly, and Anne Smith for her unwavering confidence in this project.

Beth S. Neman
Sandra Smythe

MEMO

To: Reader
From: Beth Neman and Sandra Smythe
Re: Executive Summaries

Most business communications are kept brief because of urgent time constraints, as we demonstrate in Chapters 1 and 2. When brevity is not possible, as in reports or book chapters, business writers usually precede their work with brief executive summaries.

Writing Effectively in Business adopts this practice. Before each chapter you will find an Executive Summary that sets out the chapter's main points and introduces the chapter's most significant concepts and vocabulary.

How to Use the Executive Summaries

- Read the Executive Summary before you read the chapter. Use the summary for prereading preparation as you would a list of learning objectives.
- Read the summary after you've completed the chapter to refresh your memory before class.
- You will find the summaries particularly useful in reviewing for quizzes or examinations.

For a discussion of how to write executive summaries, see page 251.

Part 1

THE PROCESS OF EFFECTIVE BUSINESS WRITING

PRINCIPLES OF EFFECTIVE BUSINESS WRITING

EXECUTIVE SUMMARY

You already know much of what you need to know to be an effective business writer. Your college writing skills are based on sound principles of rhetoric—the art of persuading the reader or listener. So are business writing skills. But they are modified by three important factors:

- **Profit motive.** Business is a competitive pursuit. It must take into account the cost to produce and distribute communications, as well as how the messages themselves are likely to influence company profit or loss.

- **Time constraints.** Information must be made quickly available to facilitate time-critical decisions. In addition, the business must pay for every minute of employee writing or reading time.

- **Hierarchy.** Businesses are organized hierarchically. Efficiency—and your success—depend on observing unwritten but powerful rules of rank.

These are the realities of the business world and, taken together with time-tested rhetorical principles, they suggest a single fundamental axiom for effective business writing:

Consider your reader in light of your purpose.

This simple rule will help you use the practical writing skills you have already mastered and apply the political and psychological insights the text suggests to write successfully in a business environment.

Business writers work in a highly charged, goal-directed environment. Every action, every thought—and every written communication— reflect a preoccupation with competition. Some have called everything about this competitive world cold and impersonal, more involved with profit than with people. Whatever the general merits of such a view, when it comes to business communication nothing could be further from the truth. *Because* business writers are involved in profit making, they need to be interested in people.

An expository essay ought to persuade its readers of the value of the ideas it expresses. But a piece of business writing ought to get something done, to make something happen. Because the need to persuade its readers is urgent, effective business writing must be even more reader-centered than other kinds of communication. For sound, pragmatic reasons, you as a business writer can write most effectively when you understand and empathize with your readers—that is, when you literally "feel with," imaginatively identify with, them.

CHARACTERISTICS OF BUSINESS

To understand why empathy is central to business communication, we need first to examine how business differs from other pursuits. Business, the business-writing process, and its final product are shaped by three forces:

- The profit motive.
- Time constraints.
- Hierarchical organization.

PROFIT

The purpose of business is to provide society with needed goods or services. To do so it must survive and succeed. And in business, succeeding means making a profit. Even nonprofit organizations must control costs and stay within budgets. Businesses base decisions about which goods to buy or salaries to pay on whether their costs can be justified by the profit attributable to them.

TIME

Time is money. In the business world this statement is not a cliché; it is a simple operating truth. Making a profit in a competitive environment demands quick decisions, and so the entire communications process is time-critical.

Time is quite literally money when every minute of employee writing or reading time must be paid for by the business. The cost of sending a letter, for instance, includes the time the writer requires to draft it, the time the secretary takes to type it, and the cost of stationery and postage. For a memo, which is sent in-house, the total cost includes the time required for the reader to read it, understand it, and make a decision based on it.

Most of us understand that time is valuable, but it is sobering to calculate the cost of time in a modern business. Try the boxed problem below.

HIERARCHY   Business uses hierarchy (ranked order) both to structure its organization and to motivate its people. Good performance is rewarded by promotion—to a higher rank with higher pay.

A CEO's Time per Minute

Chief executive officers (CEOs) of publicly owned corporations are highly compensated, and their annual salaries must be publicly disclosed. In 1989, 372 American corporations paid their CEOs more than a million dollars. The top executive salary was $53,944,000. But consider even a typical CEO, whose 1989 average salary and bonus alone ran to about $1.2 million (excluding benefits and stock options). Taking this number, we can figure the cost of the CEO's time per minute.

37.5 hours per week × 48 work weeks	= _____ hours per year.
_____ hours per year × 60 minutes per hour	= _____ minutes per year.
CEO salary: $1,200,000 ÷ _____ minutes per year	= _____ per minute.

Did you get $11.11 per minute? That's the cost for every minute an averagely compensated CEO takes to read a memo. A 12-minute memo would cost $133.33.

Considering the 1989 salary of the top-paid corporate executive in America, each minute of time would cost $499.48. If it took him or her even five minutes to read and act on a memo, the cost would be $2,497.40. With 25 or 30 such communications in a morning, the cost would be more than $12,000 just for that phase of work. And this figure does not include the cost of writing the memo or the cost of the time of other senior and middle-level managers who might also have read and considered it.

The figures in this exercise are taken from the May 7, 1990, issue of *Business Week*, which publishes an annual survey of CEO's salaries.

Hierarchy in business works much as it does in the military services. Business executives do not wear insignia or salute superior officers. Yet distinctions of rank in a corporate culture are just as important as in the military. And the consequences of disregarding rank can be equally disastrous to a business career. It is not just a matter of being polite or obeying a manager's orders. Rather it is a matter of observing ranked order in complex ways, including in communications. Hierarchy permeates every aspect of business.

BUSINESS PEOPLE—WITH THE EMPHASIS ON PEOPLE.   In spite of different imperatives, however, you can count on certain human verities. Business writers are not radically different from other writers. Business executives are themselves human beings with the same good qualities and flaws, the same needs and desires, as human beings in general. Therefore, although there are special political and psychological aspects to business communication which must be observed (and which we will discuss later in detail), business writing is based on the same principles that apply to writing in general. And so you will be able to use the familiar principles of rhetoric that you have learned through your academic years. To write effectively in business, you just have to learn to put a new spin on the ball.

BUILDING ON WHAT YOU ALREADY KNOW ABOUT RHETORIC

The principles of rhetoric that serve you well in your college writing are even more important in business, because rhetoric is the art of *persuasive* communication. For instance, when you write a history or biology paper, your purpose is to persuade your reader that your ideas are sound or at least worth considering. In business writing, your purpose coincides exactly with the classic goal of rhetoric—to influence the thought and actions of the reader (or listener). The purpose of almost everything written in the business setting is clearly and openly persuasive: you want to get something done by persuading someone to do it or approve it.

You will remember that rhetoric is concerned with an interlocking relationship between *writer* and *reader* and *writer's purpose*. That relationship is often pictured as a triangle (see Figure 1.1).

FIGURE 1.1
The Rhetorical Triangle

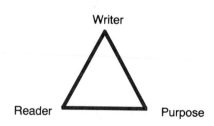

Business rhetoric is also concerned with this triad. But because of the special nature of the business world, each member of the triad takes on additional significance, and the relationship between them becomes intensified.

- Take *purpose,* for instance. In a business communication the persuasive purpose is more apt to be laden with economic or monetary consequences than other writing. You write, for example:

  A business letter, to get a shipment of disposable diapers across the country in time for a special sale.
  A memo, to announce a major management restructuring before the rumor mill distorts it and it gets out to the press.
  A report, to analyze the profitability of a plant your management is considering closing.

  The profits of the company are, to some extent, always involved.

- The stakes are higher for the *writer* too. Every piece of writing is linked potentially to the writer's livelihood, because the writer's competence—or lack of it—is always reflected in it.

- And, if considering your *reader* is important in academic writing, in business writing this consideration becomes crucial. For in business your relationship with each person to whom your communications are addressed has greater consequences. The person on the receiving end of everything you write can affect your career.

Thus the rhetorical perspective is especially applicable to business writing.

Furthermore, most writing-process strategies that you already use in *prewriting, writing,* and *revising* your college papers also will be useful in business. In fact, in writing for business you will need to keep in mind everything you've learned about rhetoric and then be even more aware of its principles and techniques. Let's review the most significant strategies. (See also "Expedite the Writing Process with the Word Processor," pages 60–67, for ways a word processor can help you implement these strategies.)

━━━━━━━━━━━━━━ **GUIDELINES** ━━━━━━━

Review of the Process of Effective Writing

Prewrite

- Purpose is central. You must be very clear about exactly what you mean to accomplish before you write.
- Gather all the relevant information available to you.
  Read.
  Interview.

Discuss.

Think.

- Then put together or "invent" (as Aristotle says in his *Rhetoric*) the ideas you will need to support your purposes. To do so, try one or both of these brainstorming strategies:

  Free-write. With your purpose in mind, just begin writing. Don't stop to think. Don't take your fingers off the keyboard (keep your pen moving). If you can't think what to say, write "I can't think what to say. I can't . . ." until you can. Let these humdrum mechanical processes lull your conscious mind so you can pull out ideas from your unconscious and your thoughtful imagination.

  Inventory or list. Inventory all the ideas you have gathered on the subject. List them. Relate them or subordinate them to one another. Order them into categories.

  Or if brainstorming alone is not enough to stir your creative juices, try to generate ideas by using *heuristics,* that is, more formal discovery procedures. Try, for instance, directing at your subject the well-known five "*W* Questions" of journalism: Who? What? Where? When? Why?

  Other heuristic techniques suggest exploring your topic through the six perspectives of "cubing": describing, comparing, associating, analyzing, applying, and arguing. Or you could ask questions associated with Aristotle's *topoi* (topics): definition, comparison, classification, cause and effect, etc. You could also combine free-writing with heuristics by free-writing through a series of categories.

- Structure your ideas in the order best suited to carrying out your purpose. If your writing is to be of any length, it is a good idea to jot down a plan (a mini-outline) for organization. In making your plan, choose whatever brief format is most comfortable for you—a simple list, a traditional outline, or a balloon cluster or web configuration.[1] Use whatever works best for you.

Write

- Follow your plan (but change it as needed), and support your purpose in paragraphs. State each supporting or amplifying point clearly in a sentence (or heading) at or near the beginning of your paragraphs (or paragraph clusters).
- Be sure to demonstrate and/or develop each point concretely and specifically.
- Write in your own voice and in a way that will present your purpose most persuasively. Try to imagine your reader and put yourself in his or her shoes. What will be of interest? What will persuade?

---

1. Traditional outlines usually include subordinated items indicated by indentation and marked by Roman and Arabic numbers and by letters. Bullet outlines are simple lists, sometimes with a single level of subordination; the items are indicated by bullets, checks, asterisks, etc. Balloon clusters or web configurations are diagrams with horizontal as well as vertical dimensions. To make them, circle your ideas and connect them with lines or hang subordinate ideas from them.

Rewrite or Revise

- As you write, don't hesitate to work *recursively,* to pause and rethink and even revise as you go along.
- When you finish your draft, check your work for *clarity, unity,* and *coherence.* Edit as necessary. (For assistance, see pages 34–35; 64–65.)
- Reconsider your work from your reader's point of view. Does it persuade? Revise as necessary.
- Correct errors and problems with syntax (sentence structure) or diction (word choice).
- Proofread.

THE BUSINESS DIFFERENCE

The process steps shown in the Guidelines are as fundamental to business writing as to any other kind. We urge you to follow them.

And yet they are not enough. The interplay of profit, time, and hierarchy generates pressures for those who work in business. Like everyone else, businessmen and businesswomen are self-involved, ambitious, and never completely secure. And they cannot help but react to these pervasive pressures in human ways. For this reason, whenever you write in a business situation, you need something besides your knowledge of how to write well. You need a thorough understanding of the politics of the situation and an empathetic awareness of the psychology of the other participants.

Examine, for instance, the following generally well written memo and evaluate it in terms of how effective it is likely to be.

```
TO:    Henry C. Hendrikson
       [Director of State Affairs, XYZ Corporation]²
FROM:  James C. Greene
       [Assistant Manager, Tax Compliance, Southwest Region]
RE:    Management of XYZ's state tax legislation monitoring
DATE:  October 28, 19—


    I have just returned from the annual meeting in Memphis of
the National Society of Tax Administrators, which I attended in
Joanna Blank's absence.

    The presentations at that meeting were informative, and many
of them would, I believe, be worth considering to make sure that
we do not again lose track of important tax legislation under
```

---

2. Identifying business titles are included here and elsewhere throughout the text to help you assess rank relationships. But since business memos ordinarily do not give such titles, we have enclosed them in brackets.

consideration by a state legislature—as occurred, you will
remember, in September in Georgia.

The seminar on legislative tracking presented by George
Sinton, of ABC Products, was particularly interesting. There was
also a presentation on tax depreciation, and knowing of your
interest in that, I have attached my notes and the materials
from that session.

I will follow up with you next week to discuss any reactions
you may have.

cc: Joanna Y. Blank [Vice President, Tax][3]
    Ellery M. Badham [Senior Vice President, Public Affairs]

At first glance this memo may strike you as a good example of business writing. Brief. Informative. Courteous. Its syntax is correct, its diction clear, and its purpose well defined. Nicely worded, it indicates that its author is paying attention to problems and using initiative to find solutions. And yet, when judged by the psychology and politics peculiar to the business context, this memo is not only ineffective but it actually could create the kind of repercussions that might put its writer's next promotion in jeopardy.

Where did Jim go wrong? To answer that question we have to read his memo as it would appear to Hendrikson, to whom it is addressed, and to Blank and Badham, who receive copies.

HENDRIKSON'S VIEW OF JIM'S MEMO

1. In reading Jim's memo, Hendrikson would be keenly aware of the discrepancy in their rank in the corporate structure. Jim is an *assistant* manager in the Tax Department, several steps below Hendrikson's rank as Director of State Affairs. Jim also works in another department (sometimes known as a function or pyramid or line of reporting) in the organization.

2. Because of the organizational considerations, Hendrikson might be amused—or perhaps even annoyed—by the presumptuousness of Jim's offer of his "notes and materials" on tax depreciation legislation. On the one hand, he might be miffed at the waste of his time. On the other, he might read an inappropriate condescension into the offer. He would suppose that as Director of State Affairs, especially with his "particular interest" in the subject, he should be expected to know more about such matters than an assistant manager for tax compliance. He would ask

---

3. Copy lines, always following the notation *cc:* or *c:* in the lower left corner, give the names of the people, besides the addressee, to whom copies of the communication have been sent.

himself why Greene should think he would have the time—or desire—to plow through reams of undigested material from a conference he has not attended.

3. More seriously, Hendrikson would feel a deep and urgent concern about Jim's reference to "[our having] los[t] track of important tax legislation . . . in September in Georgia." He would believe that in letting this cat out of the bag Jim meant to criticize, and thus embarrass, him. He would be particularly uncomfortable to see from the indicated copies that a copy of the memo has gone to Badham, to whom he reports.

4. Hendrikson would wonder whether Joanna Blank, Jim's supervisor, knew that Jim was sending this memo. The tone of the memo and the copy lines at the bottom suggest that she did. Such a notation implies that Blank has approved the action or would do so. Hendrikson would speculate on possible causes for what he could only read as Blank's hostile act. Angry, he would decide to call Blank to find out why one of her people is out to "get" him and embarrass Badham. (He would not know that Blank, at home recovering from the flu that prevented her attendance at the meeting, is completely ignorant of her assistant's memo.)

BADHAM'S VIEW OF JIM'S MEMO

1. Badham might be interested to learn that Hendrikson hadn't known about the Georgia legislation before it was too late, and might decide to "discuss" the matter with him.

2. Speculating that the Tax Department might be trying to take over some of the turf of the Public Affairs Department's function, Badham would likely also decide to call his counterpart—the Senior Vice President for Finance, and Joanna Blank's superior—to find out who's trying to deflate whom and why.

BLANK'S VIEW OF JIM'S MEMO

1. Blank, of course, would not see the memo until she returned after her illness. But as soon as she read it, she would understand all the implications and begin to worry about how to set thing things right with Hendrikson, Badham, and her own supervisor.

2. Her respect for Jim would inevitably decline.

Jim clearly meant well, but with that memo he would manage not only to offend both a director and a senior vice president but also roundly to embarrass his own supervisor.

AVOIDING THE HAZARDS

Jim's main mistake was his failure to put himself in his readers' shoes, to look at his memo through their eyes. He did not remember that his readers would be much influenced by considerations of time and profit and, especially, of hierarchy. Had he done so, he would have foreseen the problems the memo could cause, and would have substituted something like the following:

```
TO:    Henry C. Hendrikson
       [Director of State Affairs, XYZ Corporation]
FROM:  James C. Greene
       [Assistant Manager, Tax Compliance, Southwest Region]
RE:    State tax legislation
DATE:  October 28, 19——
```

At Joanna Blank's request, I attended the annual meeting of the
National Society of Tax Administrators last week in Memphis.

George Sinton of ABC Products chaired the first two sessions,
and his own presentation of legislative tracking was
particularly interesting. He remembered you very well from the
work you did together last year on tax depreciation and said you
had also been extremely helpful to the coalition effort when
legislation came up unexpectedly in Georgia in September and
caught everyone by surprise. He asked to be remembered to you.

I have not yet had a chance to talk to Joanna about how we can
use the information I brought back from the meeting, but my
report will be on her desk on Monday when she returns. I am
attaching the summary that will go with the report, as well as
Sinton's chart of currently pending legislation.

When Joanna has had a chance to review the report, she may want
us all to meet to discuss how we can coordinate our programs
more closely next year—a year that Sinton certainly believes
will be an active one for state tax legislation.

I am also attaching for your information a summary of NSTA's
assessment of the outlook for tax depreciation changes that I
know you have a particular interest in.

I would be glad to answer any question you might have.

cc: Joanna Y. Blank [Vice President, Tax—Jim Green's supervisor]
```

In syntax, diction, and courtesy, this memo may not be any better than
the earlier draft, but it is a far more effective piece of business writing in
many subtle ways. Hendrikson will get help in avoiding problems like the
September situation, without risk of embarrassment. And he will under-
stand that Jim and Joanna bear him no malice. The interests of the
flu-vanquished Joanna have been looked after. And Jim will have made a
friend, not an enemy. Furthermore, he will have shown his own promise
as a sophisticated communicator in the business hierarchy. If you are
```

relatively inexperienced in business, you may think this example is too subtle to be believable or even to communicate clearly. But business is exactly this subtle.

Since every business problem, every company, every political situation, is different, Jim Greene's redraft cannot serve you as a model memo. But we hope it might sensitize you to the techniques competent business writers use to smooth relations among their ranks—and to get things done.

THE KEY TO WRITING EFFECTIVELY IN BUSINESS

The key to effective business writing, then, is rhetorical after all:

Consider your reader in light of your purpose.

The rest of *Writing Effectively in Business* consists of specific strategies for implementing this axiom. Whatever the situation and whatever the kind of business writing—letter, memo, or report—this axiom will serve you well. It will help you develop strategies to confront the psychology and the politics of any writing situation. And it offers a unifying focus for structuring all types of business communication (see the sidebar).

Every situation is, of course, distinctive. Nevertheless, if you adopt the axiom and apply its principles thoughtfully, you cannot go far astray when you write any communication. This technique is embodied in the Guidelines on page 14.

The Structure of Business Communications

Business communications conventionally have a three-part structure, which is based on the principles of reader empathy and purpose, and varies according to the goal of the specific piece of writing.

Business Letter	*Memo*	*Recommendation Memo*	*Short Report*
Empathetic Opening (combined with Point in Good-News Letters)	Orienting Opening	Purpose Statement	Purpose Statement
The Point	The Point	Recommendations	Recommendations
Empathetic Close	"Next Step" Close	"Request for Approval to Implement" Close	"Request for Approval to Implement" (included in Transmittal Memo)

--- **GUIDELINES** ---

Think—and Think Again

Before you begin to write and *again* before you revise, ask yourself these questions:

1. What do I really want to do with this piece of writing?
2. How can I best achieve this result? That is, if I were _____ (the recipient of this communication), what approach would be most likely to make me perform the desired action or to adopt the desired opinion?
3. If I were _____ , how would I react to the various approaches under consideration (or in the draft)? Is there anything else I would need to know to make a sound decision?
4. What would others who are likely to read this communication infer from it? What would I infer from it if I were in their shoes?

When your final draft is complete, ask yourself Questions 3 and 4 again. And when you have satisfied yourself that you can answer them positively, you can send off your communication with confidence.

--- **AUTHENTIC BUSINESS PROBLEMS** ---

1. Analyze and evaluate Jim Greene's memos. The following hints may be useful.

   - Compare the introductory paragraphs of the two drafts. How does the revision give Jim more clout?
   - In what ways does Jim use his mention of George Sinton (who, as seminar chair, is clearly a senior tax administrator) to his advantage?
   - Jim's first memo left him open to charges of presumptuousness. How does the revision eliminate this problem?
   - In what ways does Jim's revised memo give due deference to Joanna Blank? How does it screen her?
   - How does Jim's change in the copy lines protect Hendrikson? In what other ways does he do so?
   - What is the departmental purpose behind Jim's memo? That is, what action does the Tax Department expect of the Public Affairs Department? Which memo better accomplishes this purpose? Why?

2. It's time for your company's annual holiday party, and you have been asked by your supervisor, the Director of Employee Relations, to draft the invitation memo for his or her signature. Your memo should announce the date, time, and arrangements for the affair, and should encourage attendance.

   At first glance, this assignment looks like a simple, nonpolitical task. Upon careful investigation, however, you find out that the job is not so simple. The problem is not merely to plan a party. The CEO is keen on having full, or close to full, attendance. The holiday party is one of the two major employee get-togethers each year; and the CEO, who is a member of the firm's founding family, believes it is important to the morale of the work force. As nominal host, he plans to drop by to see how things are going. He is also a backer of civil libertarian causes, however, and any hint of coercion would be repugnant to him.

Just for your information: Last year, the date of the party was unfortunate—so near the actual holiday that many people had already left. In fact, so few people turned up that the party was dreary and an embarrassment to the CEO.

It is up to you to meet with the Employee Committee in charge of arrangements and set the date, time, and theme. Draft a memo. Remember that it will bear your supervisor's signature, not yours. Get a better turnout this year. That would be the best holiday present you could give your supervisor and your CEO. It wouldn't hurt your career either.

 a. Think through the assignment by answering the four questions on page 14.
 b. Write the memo.

3. You've been working at LMNT Industries for 14 months, and you're doing well. You got a good first-year review and a raise. Last Tuesday, your favorite Aunt Josie sent you a note and enclosed a résumé for her goddaughter, Allison Seymour.

    Allison has just graduated from Michigan State University with a Bachelor's in Business Administration and a concentration in Communications. She had about a 3.25 GPA (grade-point average). Aunt Josie wants you to send Allison's résumé to somebody who might consider her for her first professional job.

    You have a good friend, Alonzo Smits, at your level in Customer Service. You have met your friend's supervisor, Adeline Harris, who is the Customer Service manager for your division, several times, but you do not know her well. You've checked with your friend, and he says his manager is nice and would probably look at Allison's résumé, but there is no opening at present.

    You have not met Allison and know very little about her capabilities. Aunt Josie's enthusiastic praise may or may not be reliable: Aunt Josie loves everybody. You would like to oblige Aunt Josie—and Allison—by at least passing the résumé along, but you cannot in good conscience recommend someone you don't know.

    Your Assignment. Write the cover letter to accompany Allison's résumé.

4. Alternatively, if you have recently been asked to write a memo in your professional life, you might substitute that assignment for one of the others.
 a. Think through the assignment by answering the four questions on page 14.
 b. Write the memo according to the principles suggested in this chapter.

COMPOSING EFFECTIVE BUSINESS PROSE

EXECUTIVE SUMMARY

In business every internal memo you write reflects upon your personal competence; every external communication reflects upon the business you represent. And you and your company will not be judged on the quality of your ideas alone. Your prose style is crucial. A competent business prose is founded on the basic axiom of effective business writing:

Consider your reader in light of your purpose.

Considering your reader in this way suggests two major strategies:

- Be brief, be simple, be clear.

- Do not offend in any way: observe the requirements of errorless Standard English, accurate diction, appropriate tone, and the courtesies of business rank.

To ensure that your ideas receive a fair hearing, revise all letters, memos, and reports in light of these strategies. Don't waste the reader's time: edit for conciseness. Weed out wordiness, untangle convoluted sentences, and exchange any pompous jargon for expressions that are direct and precise. Aim especially for clarity—in text and in format. Proofread to ensure errorless Standard English. Edit everything you write for courtesy; exclude anything that might offend your reader.

These strategies will help you earn a reputation for competence. The people who read what you write will understand it. They will decide that they are smart and that you are too.

SECTION A: *Be Brief, Be Simple, Be Clear*

HOW IMPORTANT IS YOUR PROSE STYLE?

Most of us believe that substance is more important than style. That belief ought to be especially true in business. But style—difficult to define and hard to pin down—is equally critical in business writing.

What is style actually but words and sentences (diction and syntax)? Or the way the words are arranged on the page? Yet, in business writing, a style that is inappropriate, slovenly, obscure, or badly formatted can distract from substance and rob even the most impressive content of its effect. Worse yet. Since every piece of business writing is potentially a political document, an ineffective style can make the writer seem incompetent.

Fortunately, however, the reverse is also true. Effective business prose can create the impression of competence. Every letter, memo, or report you write in a courteous, accurate, correct, clear style reflects good business judgment and demonstrates your competence.

WHAT CONSTITUTES EFFECTIVE BUSINESS PROSE?

To gain some understanding of your own sense of business style, try the Diagnostic Quiz on pages 20–21. The answers, some of which may surprise you, are listed upside down at the end.

If you missed some of the answers on the Diagnostic Quiz, you are not alone. The wrong answers largely exemplify Bureaucratic Style. Research[1] has shown such style to be ineffectual, and business people know from experience that prose of this kind confuses and does not communicate efficiently. It does not take either reader or purpose into account and thus violates the basic axiom of effective business writing:

Consider your reader in light of your purpose.

Nevertheless, this mechanical, often pompous way of writing continues to afflict business communication to this day.

---

1. See, for instance, the sidebar on page 23.

Because *your* purpose in business writing is to get your message across effectively and to impress your reader with your competence, we suggest that you make all your communications clear, concise, and easily interpreted. In short:

- Be brief.
- Be simple.
- Be clear.

This strategy is logical and reasonable. Yet, if you missed some of the answers on the quiz, you may find it hard to accept its application to *business* writing. For the strategy contradicts some widely held myths—myths you yourself may take for granted.

DISCARDING MYTHS

LONGER IS NOT BETTER. In the Diagnostic Quiz you compared these sentences:

A. Due to a fortuitous combination of unforeseen circumstances and unpredictable occurrences, it is my pleasant duty to inform you that the order you charged us with Tuesday, the fifth, with the expectation of accomplishment and subsequent delivery no earlier than Thursday, the fourteenth, has been duly executed and will be implemented by Friday, the eighth day of the current month.

B. We are pleased to be able to complete your order by Friday, the 8th, four days ahead of schedule.

Answer B is preferable to Answer A primarily because it is briefer. In the academic world it sometimes seems as if the 20-page paper gets an A

Too Long. Too Long.

Recently a Fortune 500 company was suddenly the subject of an unwanted takeover bid. An employee trusted for her experience and judgment was assigned to research the background of the bidding company and to make an assessment.

She studied hundreds of documents and news clips, interviewed dozens of specialists, and made more than 600 phone calls. Then she analyzed the information, condensed it, and returned a five-page report to her supervisor. "Fine work, but too long," the supervisor said. The researcher struggled and, feeling finally rather pleased, condensed the report to two pages. "Still too long," she was told. "The CEO wants a single-page report." The information was critical; the issue was vital; but a one-page report was all that was wanted.

Diagnostic Quiz

For each item, choose the sentence that best represents effective business prose.

___ 1. (a) Due to a fortuitous combination of unforeseen circumstances and unpredictable occurrences, it is my pleasant duty to inform you that the order you charged us with Tuesday, the fifth, with the expectation of accomplishment and subsequent delivery no earlier than Thursday, the fourteenth, has been duly executed and will be implemented by Friday, the eighth day of the current month.

   (b) We are pleased to be able to complete your order by Friday, the 8th, four days ahead of schedule.

___ 2. (a) Please be advised that the Hollings merger has been discussed with the LMO top staff in accordance with your request, in a meeting, which, for all intents and purposes, was so successful that at this point in time the possibility exists for another such meeting in the near future in which we may be able to close the deal and reach final agreement in the approximate amount of $3 million, a deal which, in addition, meets each and every one of the individual concerns we had anticipated in advance.

   (b) We have discussed the Hollings merger with the LMO top staff, as you suggested. The meeting was successful. In fact, it now appears that another meeting could bring agreement, providing us with about $3 million and meeting all of our anticipated concerns.

___ 3. (a) Business executives do not wear insignia or salute superior officers. Yet distinctions of rank in a corporate culture are just as important as they are in the military. And the consequences of disregarding them can be equally disastrous to a business career.

   (b) While business executives do not wear insignia or salute superior officers, distinctions of rank in a corporate culture are just as important as they are in the military, and the consequences of disregarding them are equally disastrous to a business career.

while the 6-page paper gets a C, and the student who can throw in the most multisyllable words and the longest sentences wins the instructor's approval. Thus, you may be hard to convince that the standards in business are often quite the opposite. But it is so. Why? Because in business, as we have said, time is money. At the rates we calculated in Chapter 1, every extra minute needed to read and understand a long or complex communication costs the company significantly. Therefore, the main thing a busy business reader requires of any piece of writing is that it get its information and point across as quickly as possible.

COMPLEX IS NOT MORE IMPRESSIVE. Which of the following sentences from the Diagnostic Quiz did you choose?

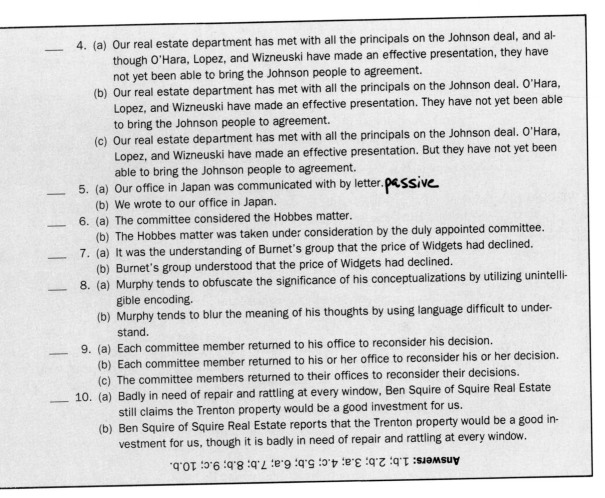

____ 4. (a) Our real estate department has met with all the principals on the Johnson deal, and although O'Hara, Lopez, and Wizneuski have made an effective presentation, they have not yet been able to bring the Johnson people to agreement.

    (b) Our real estate department has met with all the principals on the Johnson deal. O'Hara, Lopez, and Wizneuski have made an effective presentation. They have not yet been able to bring the Johnson people to agreement.

    (c) Our real estate department has met with all the principals on the Johnson deal. O'Hara, Lopez, and Wizneuski have made an effective presentation. But they have not yet been able to bring the Johnson people to agreement.

____ 5. (a) Our office in Japan was communicated with by letter. *passive*

    (b) We wrote to our office in Japan.

____ 6. (a) The committee considered the Hobbes matter.

    (b) The Hobbes matter was taken under consideration by the duly appointed committee.

____ 7. (a) It was the understanding of Burnet's group that the price of Widgets had declined.

    (b) Burnet's group understood that the price of Widgets had declined.

____ 8. (a) Murphy tends to obfuscate the significance of his conceptualizations by utilizing unintelligible encoding.

    (b) Murphy tends to blur the meaning of his thoughts by using language difficult to understand.

____ 9. (a) Each committee member returned to his office to reconsider his decision.

    (b) Each committee member returned to his or her office to reconsider his or her decision.

    (c) The committee members returned to their offices to reconsider their decisions.

____ 10. (a) Badly in need of repair and rattling at every window, Ben Squire of Squire Real Estate still claims the Trenton property would be a good investment for us.

    (b) Ben Squire of Squire Real Estate reports that the Trenton property would be a good investment for us, though it is badly in need of repair and rattling at every window.

Answers: 1.b; 2.b; 3.a; 4.c; 5.b; 6.a; 7.b; 8.b; 9.c; 10.b.

A. Please be advised that the Hollings merger has been discussed with the LMO top staff in accordance with your request, in a meeting, which, for all intents and purposes, was so successful that at this point in time the possibility exists for another such meeting in the near future in which we may be able to close the deal and reach final agreement in the approximate amount of $3 million, a deal which, in addition, meets each and every one of the individual concerns we had anticipated in advance.

B. We have discussed the Hollings merger with the LMO top staff, as you suggested. The meeting was successful. In fact, it now appears that another meeting could bring agreement, providing us with about $3 million and meeting all of our anticipated concerns.

Sentence B is preferable to Sentence A not only because it is briefer, but also because it is less complex. Research into "readability" factors[2] has demonstrated that length is only one determiner of reading time. More complex sentences and paragraphs, fewer familiar words, and less familiar syntax also make reading harder and slower. The eye takes in the shorter word, phrase, sentence, and paragraph more quickly than the longer. The mind decodes and processes the familiar faster than the unusual. And a less complex style speeds up the reading process. Long and complex wording does *not* impress. In fact, by impeding reading, it actually can annoy business readers.

BE CONCISE

In business, a brief, simple, clear style can help you advance. You can find examples of this style in well-written periodicals such as *The Wall Street Journal, Forbes, Fortune,* and the business section of *The New York Times.* We suggest that you familiarize yourself with this style by regularly reading these publications. Simply put, effective business prose is concise.

How do you make your own writing concise? Conciseness is primarily an editing problem. To edit for conciseness, try this helpful mental trick: Ration your space.

- Pretend that the space available to you has been strictly rationed.
- To make the needed economies, eliminate any sentence that adds nothing new to your presentation.
- Combine where there is overlap. Cross out any word that does not contribute to your meaning.

Edit as if every word costs money because . . . it does.

TRIM THE FAT. As you edit, eliminate what Richard A. Lanham[3] calls the "lard." Unlike the suet on red meat, verbal fat may not be instantly recognizable. But the Guidelines on pages 23–25 should help you locate trimmable words and phrases, so that you can make your writing the strong, lean prose prized in the business world.

---

2. For a discussion of the research up to 1974, see G. Klare, "Assessing Readability," *Reading Research Quarterly* 10 (1974): 62–102. For a more recent thoughtful analysis, see Richard Bamberger and Annette T. Rabin, "New Approaches to Readability," *Reading Teacher* 37 (Feb. 1984): 512–519. And see especially the impressive research of James Suchan and Robert Colucci (sidebars, pages 23 and 37); the information cited has been published in "The High Cost of Bureaucratic Written Communication," *Business Horizons* (Mar.–Apr. 1991): 1–6, and in "An Analysis of Communication Efficiency Between High Impact and Bureaucratic Writing Communities," *Management Communication Quarterly* 2 (May 1989): 454–484.

3. *Revising Business Prose,* 2d ed. (New York: Macmillan, 1987).

Research Proves Brief, Clear, Simple Style Cost Effective

Researchers James Suchan and Robert Colucci,* professors at the Naval Postgraduate School in Monterey, California, distinguish a brief, clear, simple style from a bureaucratic style by two organizational cues (early statement of purpose and an organizational sentence) and the following stylistic characteristics:

Clear Business Style

1. Short, simple sentences
2. Active verbs
3. Concrete, "easy" language
4. Short paragraphs, headings
5. Use of *I* and *you.*

Bureaucratic Style

1. Long, complex sentences
2. Passive verbs; implied subjects
3. Abstract, "difficult" language
4. Long paragraphs; no headings
5. No personal pronouns

Having prepared a one-page, well-written memo of identical content in each style, the researchers surveyed 255 naval officers and compared the two memos on reading rate and comprehension, with these clear-cut results:

Clear Business Style

17.2%–23% less reading time
92.5% comprehension of purpose
57.5%–95.8% general comprehension
11% perceived rereading need

Bureaucratic Style

17.2%–23% more reading time
65.4% comprehension of purpose
24.8%–89.5% general comprehension
22% perceived rereading need

Using complex formulas, the researchers determined that substitution of the Clear Style for the Bureaucratic Style would save the Navy $37 million each year in first-reading time. With the addition of the second-reading time required by prose that is hard to comprehend, the total annual savings would amount to $53 million.

Only one conclusion is possible: brevity, clarity, and simplicity are the marks of a competent, efficient, and ultimately cost-effective writing style.

---

*"The High Cost of Bureaucratic Written Communication," *Business Horizons* (Mar.–Apr. 1991): 1–6.

GUIDELINES

Trimmable Words and Phrases

1. **Redundancies.** Redundancies are words that can be omitted without any change in meaning. To edit such phrases as these, cross out one half, since both halves often mean the same.

   at this point in time
   true and accurate

   eight A.M. in the morning
   full and complete

each and every	any and all
falsely misrepresent	advance forward
adequate enough	past history
circle around	disappear from sight
consensus of opinion	my own personal
few in number	usual custom
anticipate in advance	popular with the people
each individual	and so on and so forth

2. **Wordiness.** When you edit, substitute the single word for the cliché, wordy phrase.

in spite of the fact that	(although)
due to the fact that	(because)
in order to	(to)
have need for	(need)
during the time that	(while)
by means of	(by)
concerning the nature of	(about)
in light of the fact that	(because)
at the present writing	(now)
at your earliest convenience	(as soon as you can)
in the event that	(if)
in the near future	(soon)
with regard to	(about)
inasmuch as	(because)
the possibility exists for	(can)
in the approximate amount of	(about)

3. **Conventional space fillers.** Phrases like those in the next set can be cut drastically, often altogether excised, without changing the substance of your message.

please be advised	to all intents and purposes
permit me to say	please don't hesitate to . . .
in closing, I remain	enclosed please find
more or less	in accordance with your request
in this day and age	when all is said and done
as luck would have it	in the society of today
aforementioned	hitherto

4. **Excess qualifiers and intensifiers.** The following have meaning, but they are frequently used meaninglessly. And so, before permitting them in your final draft, consider twice whether you intend them literally. Intensifiers can even boomerang, because a thought often appears stronger without *very, so,* or *quite.* For example, note which is stronger: "Lee Iacocca is quite well known" or "Lee Iacocca is well known."

actually	very
basically	so
generally	quite
really	really
virtually	kind of
definitely	sort of
ultimately	somewhat

USE SPECIAL TRIMMING TACTICS. To achieve the concise prose desirable in business writing, business writers have adopted certain conventions. The next set of Guidelines lists some of them.

■■■■■■■■■■■■■■■■■■■■■■■■ **GUIDELINES** ■■■■■■■■

How Business Keeps It Brief

1. **Avoid repeating lengthy titles.** In business writing, it is conventional to give a full name or title only on first mention; later use the shortened form. When the shortened form is an abbreviation, include it parenthetically at first mention. Some examples:

First Mention	Later Mentions
Sears, Roebuck and Company	Sears
Professor Mary Jo O'Connor	O'Connor or Professor O'Connor
Internal Revenue Service (IRS)	IRS

   Try, however, not to use *this* or *that* without a single clear referent. That is, don't use *that* to mean "All I've just said." For example, avoid:

   > Jones said pay and hours would remain negotiable, but the rank and file would not consider negotiating working conditions or benefits. <u>They are not likely to accept that.</u>

2. **Omit unneeded *whiches* or *thats*.** Business writing conventionally contracts a brief *which* clause into an adjective.

The company, which was successful, ...	(The successful company)
The meeting, which had been brief, ...	(The brief meeting)

   Further, the *that* introducing brief *that* clauses is also generally deleted.

```
He told her that he was        (He told her he was
  lunching with Smith.           lunching...)
Jones did not think that        (Jones did not think Allen
  Allen was up to the task.      up to the task.)
```

3. **Eliminate surplus prepositions.** Effective business writing is also short on prepositions. Descriptive prepositional phrases, like the descriptive *which* clauses discussed above, are conventionally compacted into adjectives.

```
Procedures of accounting       Accounting procedures
XYZ Company, based in New       The New York-based XYZ
  York                           Company
```

For another method of removing unnecessary prepositional phrases, see pages 38–40.

 ◼◼◼◼◼◼ **PROSE WORKOUT** ◼◼◼◼◼◼

Some of the examples in these problems (and in others later in the chapter) are quoted from early drafts of business communications. Some, we are sorry to say, are derived from faulty writing that has actually circulated. All are wordy, and the meanings are sometimes obscured by the wordiness. Edit for conciseness and clarity.

1. Due to the fact that we did not anticipate in advance that the color which you selected would be so very popular with the people who are our customers, the amount which we ordered has not been adequate enough in order to cover the full and complete demand of all who have a need and/or a desire for it at this point in time.
2. Enclosed please find a copy of the information concerning the nature of our current offer which we are sending at the present writing in accordance with our request inasmuch as the possibility still exists for you actually to take full and complete advantage of the given offer.

LIMIT EACH SENTENCE TO ONE MAJOR IDEA.   Consider the following sentences from the Quiz again:

A. Business executives do not wear insignia or salute superior officers. Yet distinctions of rank in a corporate culture are just as important as they are in the military. And the consequences of disregarding them can be equally disastrous to a business career.
B. While business executives do not wear insignia or salute superior officers, distinctions of rank in a corporate culture are just as

important as they are in the military, and the consequences of disregarding them equally disastrous to a business career.

Answer A is a quotation from Chapter 1 of this book. You will find it on page 6. Answer B was our first draft of the passage. You may find Answer B more pleasing to the ear. But we edited it to the A phrasing because the ideas it contains come through more clearly this way, each in its own sentence. This procedure makes each sentence shorter and less complex. Most important, it permits the reader to process one idea at a time. Comprehension is thus quicker—and surer.

Subordinate minor related ideas. The rule "Limit each of your sentences to a single major idea" is sound, but we need to expand it to include certain lesser concepts closely related to that major idea. In fact, there is even another satisfactory way to handle the sample construction. The following sentence is almost as effective: *Although business executives do not wear insignia or salute superior officers, the distinctions of rank in a corporate culture are just as important as they are in the military.* The first idea does not necessarily demand its own sentence, because it is both clearly connected with and clearly subordinate to the second. The following Guidelines on subordinating ideas suggest tactics for when you wish to include a minor idea or two with the single major one.

━━━━━━━━━━━━━━━━━━━━━━ **GUIDELINES** ━━━━━━━

Subordinating Ideas

If you wish to use the subordinate construction, here is the three-part rule:

- Limit each sentence to a single *major* idea.
- Add only secondary concepts that are closely related to that idea.
- For any sentence, limit severely the number of secondary concepts.

For example:

```
Major idea: This month's sales are necessary for projecting
  this quarter's profit.
Minor idea: We do not yet know this month's sales.
```

You can attach less important concepts to the major idea (that is to say, subordinate them) in any of these three ways:

1. With a *who, which, whom* word.

```
This month's sales, which we do not yet know, will
help us project this quarter's profit.
```

2. With a *because, when, although, if, since* word.

> <u>Because we do not yet know this month's sales</u>, we can-
> not project this quarter's profit.

> <u>When we know this month's sales</u>, we will be better
> able to project this quarter's profit.

3. With a *that* or *what* word.

> <u>What this month's sales will be</u> should largely deter-
> mine this quarter's profit.

BEWARE OF OVERLOADED SENTENCES. Researchers into cognitive learning have confirmed that our minds work much more efficiently when they process one concept at a time. If you overload your sentences, some of your ideas may escape the reader's notice. Study this sentence, for example:

> Our company's final decision not to purchase the thus
> far unimproved Johnson property with its access to the
> highway and its view of the river, despite our substan-
> tial preliminary investment in it in time and money, was
> based on the surveyor's negative report emphasizing a
> public sewer located underground in the central portion
> of the property, where it cannot escape interfering with
> our building plans.

The sentence is cumbersome (though not ungrammatical). But what does it mean? Its writer, Cliff Meyer, has packed it so full of ideas that even if you reread it a time or two, you will probably miss some of them. Though he doesn't give all ideas equal weight, Cliff clearly wants us to glean the following facts from the sentence:

- Our company has decided not to purchase the Johnson property.
- The decision is final.
- The decision was taken despite a substantial preliminary invest-ment.
- The Johnson property is not yet improved.
- It has access to the highway.
- It has a view of the river.
- The decision was taken because of a surveyor's negative report.
- The report was negative because the surveyor found a public sewer.

- The sewer was under the central part of the property.
- The sewer's central position will interfere with our purposes for the property.
- We had planned to build on the property.

Since we cannot take in all these ideas at once, the sentence clearly needs revising. How should Cliff revise? He has a number of options. What he decides on, of course, depends upon which of the ideas are major to his purpose. He needs to put each of the major ideas in a sentence of its own and to subordinate less important related material to them in subordinate clauses. How would you do it? This is what Cliff did:

> (1) Despite substantial preliminary investment in investigating the Johnson properties, the company has decided not to purchase them. (2) Although the properties are as yet unimproved, their access to the highway and their view of the river could have made them suitable for our building purposes. (3) However, a surveyor's negative report changed our plans. (4) The surveyor discovered a public sewer in the central portion of the property, directly under the spot where we would have had to place our building. (5) Our decision against the project is final.

Cliff divided his original overloaded sentence with its obscure meaning into five sentences that convey his points clearly. And he specified the relationships between his ideas by using such precise signals as *despite, although,* and *however* (see the Guidelines on page 35). Although his new message is a few words longer, what it gains in clarity is well worth the additional length.

Overloaded sentences may be hard for you to discover in your own work because, after all, *you* know what *you* meant when you wrote them. To find them, let some time go by between your writing and your editing so that you can approach your work as a reader rather than as a writer. Then make sure each sentence makes one major point perfectly clear.

IT'S OKAY TO START SENTENCES WITH *AND* OR *BUT*. Granted, you might say, too lengthy sentences slow down reading and delay comprehension. But how can we shorten them without making the reading choppy? The answer often is to divide the sentences into two or more, but retain the *and*s and *but*s that made for smooth transitions.

<table>
<tr><td>**Too
Long**</td><td>Although our real estate department has met with all the principals on the Johnson deal, and O'Hara, Lopez, and Wizneuski have made an effective presentation, they have not yet been able to bring the Johnson people to agreement.</td></tr>
</table>

Contemporary Professionals Use Initial *And*s and *But*s
(Grundys, Are You Listening?)

American style-authority Joseph M. Williams writes:

> Some rules . . . are not rules at all, but a species of folklore, widely enforced by editors and school-teachers, but largely ignored by most educated and careful writers. . . . [These] so-called rules . . . are violated so consistently that, unless we indict for bad grammar just about every serious writer of modern English, we have to reject as misinformed anyone who would try to enforce them.*

The following examples of introductory *and* or *but* usage are selected randomly from articles by business experts in well-regarded publications. (Emphasis supplied.)

- Jane Bryant Quinn, economist and writer on business issues:

  > [T]he stock market crash brought the market for high-priced houses to a dead halt. *But* reports of the death of real estate were premature. . . . To buy, however, you pretty much have to own a house already. . . . Closing costs . . . are now running more than 2 percent. . . . *And* in many markets, the low 5 percent down payment has gone the way of the dodo.†

- Daniel Yergin, author and president of Cambridge Energy Research Associates, an international consulting firm:

  > Since the days of the czars, Russia's petroleum industry has had a far-reaching impact on the global economy. *And* that history holds clues to what may happen in the next decade.‡

- Graefe S. Crystal, professor at the Haas School of Business at the University of California, Berkeley:

  > Steven J. Ross, co-CEO of Time Warner (parent of *Fortune*'s publisher), is not included in this survey. . . . *But* writing an article on executive compensation without mentioning Ross would be like writing an article on baseball's greatest heroes and omitting Babe Ruth.§

This usage goes back a long way:

> The Declaration of Independence (final sentence): *And* for the support of this declaration, we mutually pledge to each other our lives, our fortunes, and our sacred honor.

Style: Ten Lessons in Clarity and Grace. 2d ed. (Glenview, Ill.: Scott, Foresman, 1985): 177.
†*Newsweek* 111 (11 Apr. 1988): 65.
‡*The New York Times Magazine*, Part 2: *The Business World* (2 Dec. 1990): 8.
§*Fortune* 121, no. 14 (18 June 1990): 96.

Too Choppy
```
Our real estate department has met with all
the principals on the Johnson deal. O'Hara,
Lopez, and Wizneuski have made an effective
presentation. They have not yet been able to
bring the Johnson people to agreement.
```

Just Fine
```
Our real estate department has met with all
the principals on the Johnson deal. O'Hara,
Lopez, and Wizneuski have made an effective
presentation. But they have not yet been able
to bring the Johnson people to agreement.
```

Sounds fine, you say. But what about the unbreakable rule that you should not begin a sentence with an *and* or a *but*? The Grundys (whether Ms. or Mr.), those rigid grammarians of our school days, used to subtract points every time they caught such a sentence on our seventh-grade papers.

We would answer that, with due respect for the Grundys, they were mistaken on this point. Professional authors, including business writers, follow this practice as a matter of course (see the sidebar).

When overused, initial *and*s and *but*s can of course give your style a breathless, unfinished quality. But their use is now completely conventional in Standard English. And, employed in moderation, they can help smooth out a shortened-sentence style.

▬▬ PROSE WORKOUT ▬▬

Edit the following overloaded sentences into meaningful passages. Remember:

- Limit each sentence to one major idea.
- Subordinate related lesser ideas.
- Don't be concerned if you need to begin a sentence with *and* or *but*.

1. Having investigated the claim of your customer, Mrs. Stanley Blum, that the china cabinet she ordered from our Schenectady store on June 5th arrived on June 28th in battered condition with two panes of glass broken, a gash completely through the veneer on the middle drawer, and a crushed pedestal, we have determined that the damage must have occurred while the merchandise was in transit (carried by a newly employed delivery service), and we have begun negotiations with the service for restitution.

2. Since November when we last surveyed usage of electronic office equipment throughout the company, we have discovered a 65% increase in use of word processors—a 25% increase in the Chillicothe office alone, a 35% increase in use of telephone services—most of

which is concentrated in overseas lines, and a 15% increase in use of telemetric equipment, indicating, according to our interpretation of the information, that we will need, at least, to double our present word-processing capability, to install 12 new cable connections (the number arrived at in consultation with AT&T representatives), and to purchase selected telemetric equipment.

KEEP PARAGRAPHS BRIEF. You may be wondering about another Grundy rule. Remember? The Grundys always insisted that paragraphs have at least X number of sentences. (The length varies with each particular Mr. or Ms. Grundy.) That rule would seem to argue for a longer, less comprehensible style. But time and custom have left the Grundys behind. The truth is that no unbreakable rule can be made about the size of a paragraph. Paragraph size is purely arbitrary, dependent as much on the size of type and columns as on an author's rhetorical intent. If, for example, a book paragraph of some 200 words must be printed in a narrow newspaper column, it will probably be divided into several brief segments strictly for visual reasons. The content remains the same: two paragraphs or six (see Figure 2.1).

How do you decide what to put into your paragraphs? Think of your material and apply the life-and-death test to it:

> If I had to tell this crucial information to somebody in the time he had left before he had to get into his life jacket as the ship is going down, what things would I choose to tell him?

Throw out almost everything else in your first draft. If you've left out an essential, you can always put it back in when you revise.

There are good reasons for keeping business paragraphs brief. A brief paragraph is more easily read and understood. Since the reader's mind processes content in "chunks," short paragraphs will supply ready-made chunks. Occasionally, for emphasis, you may even wish to include a paragraph of only a sentence or two—as many effective business writers do. A very brief paragraph, among those of ordinary length, calls the reader's attention to its contents.

Use topic sentences. Don't forget to alert your reader to your meaning by incorporating topic sentences at or near the beginning of your paragraphs (or paragraph clusters). The Grundys *were* right about topic sentences. In these organizing sentences, you signal in a nutshell what your paragraph is going to be about, as we do, for example, in the paragraph immediately above.

There are good reasons for keeping business paragraphs brief. A brief paragraph is more easily read and under-stood. Since the reader's mind processes content in

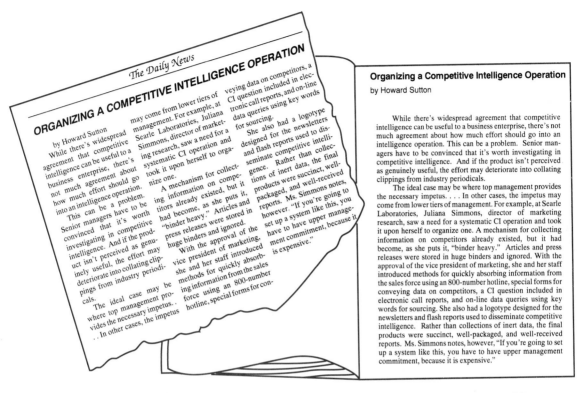

FIGURE 2.1: *As the drawing illustrates, paragraph length is arbitrary. Business uses paragraphing as a visual aid for rapid comprehension.*

"chunks," short paragraphs will supply ready-made chunks. Occasionally, for emphasis, you may even wish to include a paragraph of only a sentence or two--as many effective business writers do. A very brief paragraph, among those of ordinary length, calls the reader's attention to its contents.

Business writers, in fact, find topic sentences so helpful that they sometimes distinguish them, or their more important portions, as topic heads. Such typographical devices (sometimes called signposting) promote clarity, and we recommend them to you (see page 71).

KEEP PARAGRAPHS COHERENT: LINKAGES AND TRANSITIONS

What if your topic sentences and your supporting material are all in order, but your paragraphs still do not read as clearly and coherently as you would like? The problem then might be a lack of appropriate linkage between your ideas. Besides providing a clear underlying structure, you have to give your readers surface clues to help them connect your ideas. You can give these clues in two basic ways: *repetition* and *transitional devices*.

REPETITION OF IDEAS. If you analyze most sentences in a well-written paragraph, you'll find that they consist of both old material and new material. The old material provides continuity of thought and thus prevents confusion. The new material develops the ideas. Examine, for example, the sentences in the paragraph preceding this one, the one headed "Keep Paragraphs Coherent: Linkages and Transitions" (or, for that matter, almost any professionally written paragraph), and you will see that this principle holds true.

Old, Linking Material	New Ideas
1. What if your topic sentences and your supporting material are all in order,	
	but your paragraphs still do not read as clearly and coherently as you would like?
2. The problem then	
	might be a lack of appropriate linkage between your ideas.
3. Besides providing a clear underlying structure,	
	you have to give your readers surface clues to help them connect your ideas.
4. You can give these clues	
	in two basic ways: *repetition* and *transitional devices.*

REPETITIONAL LINKS. To achieve coherence by reinforcing what the readers already know requires some repetition.

- You can repeat words or phrases, as we did, for instance, in repeating *clues* and *clearly* and *clear* in the sample paragraph.
- You can tie your ideas even closer together by using linking pronouns such as *these,* in *these clues.*
- You can keep the connection and yet avoid monotony by changing the wording of a repeated idea, as we did by interchanging *link[age]* and *connect.*
- You can substitute an appropriate pronoun, as we did in substituting *them* for *readers.*

TRANSITIONAL DEVICES. To write coherently you should also make use of the rich variety of transitional devices that the English language affords. These words and phrases link ideas to each other. They also point the reader to the particular relationships between the ideas. Even our brief paragraph on linkages and transitions offers a number of instances of these devices. *What if,* for instance, implies speculative possibility. *But* suggests a mild contradiction of the preceding idea. *Then* suggests a logical summation. And *besides* denotes an addition to what has gone before.

Transitional devices help tie your work together and thus make it read more smoothly. But you must select such words carefully. Since these phrases point to very specific relationships, they cannot easily be interchanged. Wrong choices will lead your reader to make a connection you do not intend. There are, for example, significant differences in meaning among the following:

```
We signed the contract.    Moreover, Jones & Co. stock
                              declined.
                           Consequently, Jones & Co. stock
                              declined.
                           Nonetheless, Jones & Co. stock
                              declined.
```

The following Guidelines list some useful transitional words and phrases and specify the general relationship to which each points.

GUIDELINES

Transitional Words and Phrases

Sequence: first, second, third . . . ; first, then; after, afterward, since, before, when, whenever, until, as soon as, as long as, while, in (1923, in the summer, . . .), at (Christmastime, the end of term, . . .), finally

Affirmation: in fact, actually, indeed, certainly

Negation: nevertheless, on the contrary, notwithstanding, on the other hand, despite, still, however, but, yet, conversely

Concession: although, though, granted that, no doubt, to be sure, whereas, of course, doubtless, certainly

Illustration: for example, for instance, to illustrate, in particular, specifically

Addition: and, also, moreover, furthermore, next, again, too, second, third, . . . , another, finally

Qualification: frequently, often, usually, in general, occasionally, provided, in case, unless, when, since, because, for, if

Causation: consequently, because, since

Summation: therefore, thus, in conclusion, to sum up, so, consequently, accordingly, all in all, in short, on the whole, in other words, then

---

AVOID ROBOTIC WRITING

PERSONALIZE YOUR WRITING. Reconsider the following sentences from the Quiz:

A. Our office in Japan was communicated with by letter.
B. We wrote a letter to our office in Japan.

Example B is much better than Example A because it has a human voice. Underpersonalized writing speaks to its readers in the dehumanized drone of a machine, with no identifiable human author addressing the human reader. Nobody really does anything in such writing, or at least nobody seems willing to take responsibility for doing anything. It is as if everything that happens is propelled by some vague, nameless force.

```
It has been thought that...
It has been brought to our attention that...
There can be no doubt that...
```

Nobody ever complains:

```
Complaints have been made.
```

Nobody receives letters:

```
Letters are received.
```

Nobody conducts business:

```
Business is conducted.
Yours of the fifth inst. received and contents
duly noted.
```

Occasionally you may think it prudent to neglect including an *I* or *we* subject in order to obscure who actually did the deed. That practice is legitimate and can sometimes be useful in business. For example, when blame might be unnecessarily allocated, such concealment might be wise. But whether deliberate or not, impersonal writing can sound as if you might have something to hide. And surely that is not a message you want to send frequently.

Even so, impersonal writing may still exert an appeal for you. It might seem objective—almost scientific—and, therefore, businesslike. Yet, as we have shown, since the business writer ordinarily knows the specific person

Do Brevity, Simplicity, and Clarity Really Promote Readability?

Try your own research. Get a partner and, using a stopwatch or a watch with a second hand, ask your partner to time your reading of each of the following two passages excerpted from the research materials used by Suchan and Colucci.* Confirm your results by timing your partner's reading.

Be sure to read at a speed that permits you fully to comprehend each sample and enables you to write an answer to the question at its close.

Your Time: Sample A. _____   Sample B. _____

Your Partner's Time: Sample A. _____   Sample B. _____

Conclusion: _____

The Research Material

Sample A. Flextime

As is suggested by the term flextime, staff members are given the choice of determining when they commence and terminate work rather than being confined to a rigid 9 A.M. to 5 P.M. schedule. It has been determined that hospitals are a particularly good environment to implement this plan because they remain open 24 hours per day. However, the following ground rules are needed so that the flextime plan will run smoothly.

The clerical staff should be allowed to work their eight hours any time between 6 A.M. and 9 P.M.; in addition, the staff should be given the opportunity to segment their eight-hour shifts into four-hour blocks. Four clerical staff members must be required to be on duty from 8 A.M. to 5 P.M. to handle internal and external information requests. The scheduling arrangements needed to handle this requirement should be made by the staff. A sign-up sheet should be provided so that the clerical staff can log their hours. Finally, the flextime schedule must be adopted by yourself so as to reflect support of the plan and to ensure that all workers are supervised during the course of the work week.

Question: Briefly, what is flextime?

Sample B. How Flextime Works

Flextime scheduling lets your staff choose a wide range of starting and quitting times rather than locking them into a rigid 9–5 schedule. Because hospitals are open 24 hours, you can easily implement the plan. But you do need to set up some ground rules so that flextime runs smoothly. Here's what I suggest:

1. Allow your staff to put in their eight hours between 6 A.M. and 9 P.M.
2. Enable them to break their eight-hour shifts into four-hour blocks.
3. Require that at least four staff members be in the office between 8 A.M. and 5 P.M. to handle phone calls and information requests. Let your staff make the arrangements to meet this requirement.
4. Provide a sign-in sheet so that your staff can log its hours.
5. Adopt a flextime schedule for yourself. By doing so you can show your staff you believe in the plan. Also, you can "manage" all your workers during the course of a week.

Question: Briefly, how can flextime be made to work?

---

*James Suchan and Robert Colucci, "An Analysis of Communication Efficiency Between High Impact and Bureaucratic Writing Communities," *Management Communication Quarterly* 2 (May 1989): 454–484.

or people who will receive the communication, business writing is inherently the most personal of all expository writing. All the world's business is communicated by a thoroughly human "I" or "we" to an equally human "you." Put yourself in the place of the "you" who will receive your letter or memo. Aren't you more likely to be persuaded by a message addressed to you personally than one that does not acknowledge your existence? Certainly in business correspondence, consultant Rudolf Flesch is right when he speaks of the "Indispensable You."

We urge you not to let Mr. or Ms. Grundy's injunction against personal pronouns keep you from the psychological—and often political—advantage of a personal business style.

PROSE WORKOUT

Edit the following memo to make it less mechanical, more direct, more human, and less cumbersome. Do not be afraid to use proper names or personal pronouns.

```
To:   Henry Hooper [Senior Vice President,
      Planning and Accounting]
From: John Young [Director, Planning Projects]

In light of unavoidable reasons advanced by
Accounting for delays in closing the books, there
would seem to be reason to suppose that the entire
project might not be able to be finalized in this
section either until some future date to be
determined mutually by the two department heads.
The current writer awaits further direction.

cc: Joe Johnson [Supervisor, Accounting Department]
    Jim Clay [Head, Accounting Department]
    Patricia Andress [Head, Planning Department]
```

ACTIVATE MOST PASSIVE STRUCTURES. Which of the following sentences from the Quiz did you think put the point across better?

A. The committee considered the Hobbes matter.
B. The Hobbes matter was taken under consideration by the duly appointed committee.

Example A is the better choice, not only because its syntax is less cumbersome but also because its verb, *considered,* is alive and active, not passive and ponderous like *was taken under consideration.* Much of the unappealing, nonpersonal quality in writing discussed earlier stems from structuring too many sentences in the passive voice.

In English, the basic sentence has what is called an *active* structure. In Professor Lanham's terms, a good sentence tells "who is kicking who":

```
Smith called the adjuster.
```

Most sentences can also be given a *passive* structure by switching object for subject and turning the verb passive:

```
The adjuster was called (by Smith).
```

But now the new subject remains passive, being acted upon; and the actor, relegated to a phrase at the end, no longer seems necessary. As a matter of fact, the actor is often dropped from the sentence.

Of course, there are times when passive sentences—though on the whole less interesting—can convey your meaning more precisely. Sometimes it is not Smith but the adjuster you want to concentrate on:

```
The adjuster was called. She came immediately.
```

Sometimes the active construction is simply inappropriate. Only the passive can get across what you wish to say:

```
The mail was delivered on time.
The president was elected by a large plurality.
```

Nevertheless, if you use the passive habitually, your writing will probably become both mechanical and awkward. It will sound as if a robot were writing, because:

1. The passive encourages that curious absence of an agent or actor, of a human being in charge.
2. The passive, not the most natural construction in English, often leads to long and convoluted (twisted) sentence structures. Compare:

Passive	**Active**
A question is raised whether...	I question whether...
It was recommended by the committee that...	The committee recommended that...

3. The kind of twisted prose that passive sentences produce often involves turning verbs into elongated and pretentious nouns. Such words give writing a tone of pompous clutter. Compare:

```
A reduction in paperwork would be brought about by this
plan. (long passive phrasing)
```

> This plan <u>would reduce</u> paperwork. (short, direct *active* phrasing)

Habitual users of the passive form pile up such constructions in awkward abundance. The convolutions in the following example are typical.

> <u>The suggestion is made</u> (1) <u>that the utilization of company money</u> (2) to pay for executive vacations in Hawaii <u>could be construed as suspicious to the Internal Revenue Service</u> (3) and make them think that <u>an improper accountancy of these items may have been made</u>. (4)

To edit this sentence you would first turn all of the passive verb constructions into active ones.

> <u>We suggest</u> (1) that if <u>the company uses its money</u> (2) to pay for executive vacations in Hawaii, <u>the IRS might suspect</u> (3) that the <u>company has accounted improperly for its expenses</u>. (4)

Next, you would compare your new sentence with the original one and decide whether it conveys the meaning you intended in a more direct way. In the case of the sample sentence, the revised version clears up the awkwardness, indirectness, and pretension of the original without changing its meaning.

When you activate passive verbs, you make your writing more active and powerful. You also get an added dividend. Notice that the improved example eliminates those long, heavy verb-nouns (*utilization* and *accountancy*) and the chains of prepositional phrases (*of company money, of these items*) that dangle from them. Transforming passive structures typically results in such trimming and strengthening.

LIMIT SENTENCES HEADED BY *THERE* AND *IT*. Which of the following sentences from the Quiz is more effective?

> **A.** It was the understanding of Burnet's group that the price of Widgets had declined.

> **B.** Burnet's group understood that the price of Widgets had declined.

Example B is clearly superior because it is straightforward (rather than roundabout), and because, having cut out the lard in *It, was, the,* and *of,* it is briefer and neater.

You may have noticed that sentences headed by *There* or *It* often have a rather limp and passive flavor. For instance:

```
There exists a reason that...
It has been brought to our attention that...
```

Nothing seems quite as mechanical or as awkward as this sort of construction, and we recommend that you keep a sharp eye out for such sentences. Revise those you find in the way suggested.

A caveat. The recommendation to limit your use of *It* and *There* sentences gives us an opportunity to emphasize an idea we firmly believe in:

In writing (as, perhaps, in life) there are very few *always*es and almost no *never*s.

If you try to revise that sentence to eliminate the *there,* you will see what we mean. *There* and *It* constructions are a part of English syntax because they serve useful purposes.

- They throw the emphasis to the end of the sentence (as the *there* does in the example).
- And a *There* sentence, especially, can, in its generality, sometimes provide a good sentence to introduce specific support.

Having said this, we still caution you not to use such constructions often—first, because they are subject to all the problems of passive sentences; and, second, because they can lead you into a style that is all introduction and no support.

PROSE WORKOUT

1. Eliminate the awkwardness of the impersonal style in the following passages. How? By looking in every clause for the answer to: Who is doing what? ("Who is kicking who?") Then try to get most of the sentences into an appropriate subject-verb-object relationship. In the process, prune any unnecessary words or phrases. By doing so, you will have edited out the unnecessary passive constructions.
   a. The findings of the survey have been announced and have resulted in concern that increased market availability would have implications of a weakening in demand and a softening in price.
   b. It has been brought to my attention that there has been a recurrence of investment opportunities in electronics; and although these opportunities have not met with universal agreement by the Board, an effort is being made to search out those members

> who are reluctant so that their opposition may be answered by the reasoning of the Investment Department.
>
> **2.** Without using a single passive, write a paragraph explaining why profits do not meet expectations this quarter.

AVOID ROBOTIC DICTION. A mechanistic choice of words also lends an unappealing, robotic tone to business writing. It also obscures rather than enhances meaning. Lately, the user of such language has become something of a figure of fun, as the Goosemyer cartoon demonstrates.

Whatever could possess anybody to write such nonsense as "A logistical interface of management referendums"? Only a desire to impress and a misguided notion of what is impressive.

Resist the urge to choose "impressive" mechanized words. Although business writing is often effectively motivated by a desire to demonstrate competence, showing off for the express purpose of being impressive is misguided and can backfire. Using long, complicated, or obscure words is almost sure to backfire. Our advice to be simple and brief applies to word choice as well. Therefore:

- Avoid piling on prefixes and suffixes to create such unnecessary monstrosities as *directionality* and *scrutinization,* as in "Our goal is to establish directionality in the development of financial programs" or "He gave the summary careful scrutinization." (To get a word like *directionality,* the writer had to begin with the perfectly good noun *direction*—which is already an extension of the verb *direct*—add a suffix to turn it into the adjective *directional,* and add yet another suffix to turn it back into a noun.

GOOSEMYER   by parker and wilder

Reprinted with special permission of North America Syndicate, Inc.

Don't Use Hydrochloric Acid

Professors Herta A. Murphy and Herbert W. Hildebrandt tell the story of the plumber who was vastly pleased by the response he received from a bureaucrat at a Government agency, to whom he had written to request approval for his discovery of hydrochloric acid as an effective pipe cleanser. The reply said:

> The efficacy of hydrochloric acid is indisputable, but the corrosive residue is incompatible with metallic permanence.

The plumber answered that he was glad the agency had found his discovery helpful. The bureaucrat, concerned about the plumber's misunderstanding, replied:

> We cannot assume responsibility for the production of toxic and noxious residue with hydrochloric acid and suggest you use an alternative procedure.

The plumber, delighted with his perception of the governmental response, thanked the bureaucrat again and added that he would now use hydrochloric regularly on all of his jobs. The now apprehensive bureaucrat replied by express mail:

> Don't use hydrochloric acid. It eats hell out of the pipes.

Adapted from Herta A. Murphy and Herbert W. Hildebrandt, *Effective Business Communications*, 5th ed. (New York: McGraw-Hill, 1988): 59–60. Other texts have slightly different versions of this old favorite.

- Avoid using nonessential verb-nouns. Nominalizations are not only unnecessarily long, but they often make an active sentence passive and more difficult to understand. Write:

`We recommend that...`	`NOT: It is our recommendation that...`
`She will consider it.`	`NOT: She will take it under consideration.`
`He referred to the plan.`	`NOT: He made reference to the plan.`

- Avoid ornamenting your writing with jargon. There are few occasions when *utilize* would convey your meaning more precisely than *use;* when *transmit* would be more meaningful than *send;* or when *terminate* would be preferable to *end.*

Vanquish gobbledy-jargon. Business cannot escape the use of some jargon. Every trade or profession has terminology that serves as shorthand for technical communication within the field. When jargon is used in this technical sense and confined to communication between those who share the technical knowledge, it performs a useful function and speeds up communication. (See, for example, the memo to Clarence Dawson on page 162.)

Jargon, however, has a way of leaking into more general use. One sees, for instance, such terms as *peer group, fixation, goal-directed,* and *function* in contexts far from the field of psychology, and *feedback, input, breakthrough,* and *interface* in writing that has nothing to do with computer science. (See the sidebar for further examples.) When this sort of jargon is combined with the pseudoimpressive language discussed earlier, the result is a pompous nonsense commonly called "gobbledygook." Such "technospeak" can produce the most outrageous noncommunication. Take, for instance, an item in the Diagnostic Quiz:

A. Murphy tends to obfuscate the significance of his conceptualizations by utilizing unintelligible encoding.

B. Murphy tends to blur the meaning of his thoughts by using language difficult to understand.

Some Typical Gobbledygook Diction and Better Ways to Say It

Don't say	Say instead
prioritize	rank
utilize	use
render operative	implement (or better: carry out)
take cognizance of	note
maximize	get the best results you can
potentiality	possibility
visualization	picture
causative factor	cause
energize	motivate
synergize	(omit altogether)
utilization	use
transmit	send
finalize	conclude
impact on	affect

Why is Example B the better sentence? Because Example A is sheer gobbledygook. The purpose of business writing is to communicate efficiently. And such gobbledy-jargon doesn't communicate clearly and directly to anyone. Therefore, except to express technical ideas within a specialized field, edit out a specialized term when a nontechnical word will convey all you mean to say.

Technology, too, has fostered the growth of gobbledygook. Edward Tenner, a Princeton University Press editor, satirized this tendency in his usage spoof, *Tech Speak*. In it he refers, for instance, to coffee as "psychoactive, high-temperature botanical filtrate." (See Figure 2.2 for other examples.)

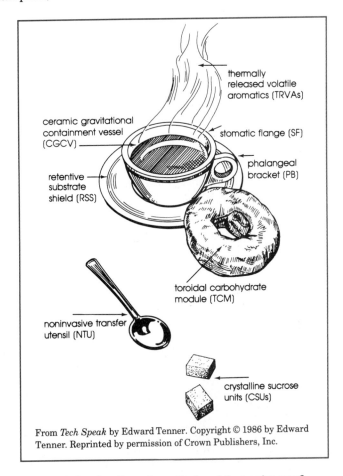

From *Tech Speak* by Edward Tenner. Copyright © 1986 by Edward Tenner. Reprinted by permission of Crown Publishers, Inc.

FIGURE 2.2: *Can't you hear the breakfast order now? "One CGCV of psychoactive high-temperature botanical filtrate, with two CSUs and a TCM, please." It's enough to make you give up coffee and doughnuts. Well, almost enough.*

To prevent readers having this sort of fun with your writing, resolve to eliminate all gobbledygook.

IN SUMMARY

Readers who find their minds confused and their time wasted by long-winded writing are likely to see its writer not as an impressive achiever but rather as an inconsiderate show-off. Sadly, even the best-chosen diction that aims at being impressive tends to divert the readers' attention and thus to distract them from the writer's purpose. In general, therefore, good writing, like good acting, should move its audience without calling too much attention to itself.

PROSE WORKOUT

Edit the following sentences. Eliminate the gobbledygook and rephrase in a clear, meaningful way.

Sample Problem
Insofar as Jones's excessive trepidation will incapacitate his vocational advancement, I will endeavor to confer with him concerning this inadequacy at my earliest convenience.

Sample Solution
Because Jones's shyness may harm his career, I will talk to him about it as soon as possible.

1. From the Goosemyer cartoon: Mr. Farnestock, I believe at this point in time that a logistical interface of management referendums would be of significant manifestation.
2. There are no clear *indicia* of a recession potential just now, but that is not to say that a resurgence of countercyclical indications could not bring such an eventuality to fruition.
3. As I enumerate the unpalatable consequences of your proposed endeavor, I begin to abhor the entire prevailing circumstance.
4. Consequently, the operator of the motor vehicle determined that it would be advantageous to maneuver his conveyance to a position perpendicular to where it was now located.
5. There is an intensive necessity for an annual personnel department executive relocation program reevaluation.

SECTION B: *Be Sure You Do Not Offend*

BEWARE OF OFFENDING YOUR READER

Business prose that is brief, simple, and clear will always serve you well. But, unfortunately, it is possible for you to write an intelligent communication in a brisk, professional style and still have it get you into trouble. You can, indeed, offend your reader. Therefore, in addition to the rules we have already suggested, we need to add:

> **Be careful that nothing in your writing style—in your words, your sentences, or your tone—can offend your reader.**

What can offend?

- Stereotypical—especially racist or sexist or ageist—language.
- Obscenity.
- Writing that does not conform to the conventions of Standard English.
- Writing that is offensive in tone.

Let's look at them more closely.

OFFENSES AGAINST TASTE

RACIAL SLURS. Quite simply, acceptable business writing does not permit racial, religious, sexist, or ageist slurs. We can think of no occasion when the use of an ugly slang term for a member of a racial, religious, national, or age group would be appropriate. Nor are there many times when a legitimate rhetorical purpose is served by including stereotypical details about any group. No group has a monopoly on any characteristic, either good or bad, and implying that it does is not only false but can also be damaging to the writer. You may know for a fact that the person you address does not belong to a group that might take offense at a stereotypical word or phrase, but what about his brother-in-law? What about her cousin? The wise businessperson avoids *all* such references, for each represents a pitfall that can in a minute overturn even a lifetime of exemplary service (see the sidebar on page 48).

SEXIST SLURS. The sorts of stereotypes claiming that all politicians take bribes and that all athletes are dumb are offensive, but we need not take up each kind individually. However, one sort of stereotypical thinking must be singled out for special mention, because more than half the population is involved. We refer, of course, to stereotypes about women. Our society is coming to understand more and more how offensive sexist references can

---

Bigotry Does Not Pay

Jimmy the Greek's Bizarre Excursion into Racial History Costs Him His Job at CBS

It was Martin Luther King's birthday, and Ed Hotaling, a local TV reporter, approached Jimmy "The Greek" Snyder for a comment on the progress blacks had made in athletics.

It was as if he had "touched a button," Hotaling said later. Spewing forth came some of the most bizarre and dunderheaded social analysis since Los Angeles Dodgers vice-president Al Campanis passed judgment last April on *Nightline* concerning blacks' buoyancy and intellectual prowess. Claiming that blacks dominate most major sports, Snyder added facetiously, "If they take over coaching like everybody wants them to, there's not going to be anything left for the white people." Plunging ahead, Snyder suggested that blacks owe their superiority on the playing fields to the genetic engineering of their former oppressors, the slave owners. . . .

The reaction from his employers was instant and drastic. CBS Sports fired the 69-year-old prognosticator from his estimated $500,000-a-year spot on the network's *The NFL Today* even as the press flayed him for boorishness, bias and ignorance. . . .

[*P.S. Al Campanis got fired too.*]

People Weekly (1 Feb. 1988): 35. Reprinted by permission.

---

be. We need not dwell on the boorishness of such terms as *broad* or *chick* or of such contradictory notions as "all women are weak and helpless" and "all women are domineering nags." Such lapses are easily rooted out. Unfortunately, some sexist thinking seems to be built into the language itself. And it is here that it is possible for you to offend unawares. Take the ninth item in our Diagnostic Quiz, for example:

A. Each committee member returned to his office to reconsider his decision.

B. Each committee member returned to his or her office to reconsider his or her decision.

C. The committee members returned to their offices to reconsider their decisions.

Answer A would probably have been considered correct 30 or 40 years ago. But now the use of *his* is understood to reinforce a silent assumption about the subordinate position of women. Such usage is offensive, so A is no longer an acceptable answer. Answer B is acceptable, but awkward. Answer C is, therefore, the best.

The hints in the following Guidelines may be helpful.

GUIDELINES

Avoiding Sexist Language

1. Use plurals when you want to avoid a sex-marked pronoun. Or avoid raising the issue altogether. Try to construct the sentence so it won't require the gender-marked pronoun. If a singular subject is unavoidable, you may use the awkward *his or her* or *his/her.* For example, you could write: "A worker must be careful not to antagonize his or her superiors." (The old rule that suggested turning all neuter pronouns masculine is now outdated, and the practice is offensive to many.)

2. Avoid the use of expressions such as *lady lawyer.* These carry the insulting implication that a professional who is a woman is somehow less of a professional than a man, since it assumes that the occupational term by itself refers exclusively to men. When you write simply "Susan Jones is an engineer," there is no lack of clarity.

3. Choose the more general term, not the male term. For example, use *humankind* rather than *mankind, chair* instead of *chairman,* and *person* or one of its synonyms instead of *man* (as in "We had a five-*person* delegation" or "a five-*member* team").

PROFANITY AND OBSCENITY. Business norms are largely conservative. Even though profanity and obscenity are common currency in business conversation, they are simply not acceptable in business prose. Those who might be offended by such language make up a sizable group. So think carefully before you commit to writing even a mild expression that somebody could consider profane or obscene. The communication might, after all, become part of a permanent impression of you.

PROSE WORKOUT

Revise the following to edit out offenses against taste:

1. Every employee will receive his W2 form by Monday.

2. To: Bruce Jerome [Head, Public Relations Department]
   From: Chris Peterson [Project Manager, Public Relations]

   This has been a bitch of a day. I had to spend the whole morning arguing with that bastard in Finance, before I could even begin to tackle the bozos over at L&L Inc. But if those creeps will get off their duffs, it looks as though the Foundation will fund part of the L&L project.

3. The local hospitality committee has invited the famous Negress Poetess Gwendolyn Brooks to address the spouse luncheon on the last day of the convention.

4. The old gal who runs the Senior Center has been after us for a donation to support the geezers' musical comedy. I guess we have to do our bit for our fellow man—even if he is over the hill.

OFFENSES AGAINST STANDARD WRITTEN ENGLISH

A. Badly in need of repair and rattling at every window, Ben Squire of Squire Real Estate still claims the Trenton property would be a good investment for us.

B. Ben Squire of Squire Real Estate reports that the Trenton property would be a good investment for us, though it is badly in need of repair and rattling at every window.

The dangling modifier in Example A says that Ben Squire is badly in need of repair—not to mention "rattling at every window." It does not *mean* to say so, but it does. By placing the modifier next to the word it describes (that is, *it,* meaning the Trenton property), Example B corrects the error and is, of course, a better sentence.

And here, right in the midst of a book that we hope reflects the exciting world of business, we find ourselves talking about grammar. But many

---

Don't Dangle Your Modifiers

```
Mr. Albert H. Norton
Attorney at Law
800 Lawyers' Building
St. Paul, Minnesota

Re: Kenneth C. Plummer
    vs. Andrew L. Miller, et al.
    Case No. 97-DB-2064

Dear Al:
    Due to the illness and death of Mr. Plummer's father-
in-law, he has not had time to get together the informa-
tion to answer the interrogatories you forwarded to
me....
```

[We don't suppose he would have had—under the circumstances.]

people in that exciting world are offended by lapses from the writing conventions of Standard English. That this is so has long been understood intuitively and through experience. And research by Professor Maxine Hairston of the University of Texas[5] has confirmed this understanding. It seems clear that those who are offended by nonstandard English believe it reflects the general incompetence of the writer. Hairston specifies which lapses the business executives and professional people she surveyed find most offensive. The particular mistakes they singled out are listed in the box on page 52, in the order in which they ranked them.

ERRORS OF THE SENTENCE. If we examine the results of Professor Hairston's survey, we find that almost all the lapses that offend businesspeople fall into two categories: *errors of the sentence* and *nonstandard-dialect usage.* The errors of the sentence that business readers find especially troubling include sentence fragments, run-on sentences, and commas that interrupt the sentence flow.

To edit out these problems you need a clear sense of the shape of the English sentence. We do not think you will find the old definition of the sentence as "a complete thought" useful in this regard. Think rather of a sentence as *a subject verbing,* something doing or being; or, more often, *a subject verbing an object,* something doing or being something.

```
Leslie writes.       Leslie writes a memo.
(subj.) (verb)       (subj.) (verb) (object)
```

Sentences always have a subject and a verb, but since dependent clauses also have both of these (and phrases often one or the other), we have to add to our definition, so that you can always distinguish a sentence from a nonsentence:

> A sentence has a subject and a verb (and usually an object), often with their various modifiers, and *nothing attached to keep it from standing on its own.*

Some examples of nonsentences follow. (The words that make the clauses dependent are underlined.)

```
Writing a memo.              No subject, no verb
Leslie writing a memo.       No verb (only a verbal derivative)
```

---

5. *Successful Writing: A Rhetoric for Advanced Composition* (New York: Norton, 1981): 245. In quoting Hairston's list we have adjusted the wording of some items to make them alphabetically accessible and have supplied examples where they were lacking.

Extremely Serious Lapses from the Standard

Nonstandard verb forms. For example: *he done, we was, he don't.*

Double negatives. For example: *He hasn't got none.*

Fragmented sentences. For example: *When she went home.*

Pronoun objects used as subjects. For example: *Him and Jones are going.*

Run-on sentences. For example: *He loved his job he never took holidays.*

Capitalization fault (especially failure to capitalize proper names referring to people and places).

Comma error (intrusion between the verb and complement of the sentence). For example: *Cox cannot predict, that street crime will diminish.*

Serious Lapses from the Standard

Parallelism fault. For example: *The politician's tour included munching on such ethnic delights as pizza, bagels, and gyros and some adorable Chinese-American babies whom he kissed.*

Subject-verb disagreement. For example: *The box of stamps were on the desk.*

Adjectives used as adverbs. For example: *He treats his men bad.*

Comma error (not setting off interrupters such as *however* with commas). For example: *Jones however treats his staff cruelly.*

Pronoun subjects used as objects. For example: *The Army sent my husband and I to Japan.*

Sit and *set* usage confused. For example: *Sit your papers down and set back in that chair and relax.*

Hairston's research also distinguished "Lapses that seem to matter very little," and "Lapses that do not seem to matter"; and these lapses need not matter much to us either. Her list of "Moderately serious lapses," however, should give us some concern. It includes:

Tense shifting.

Dangling modifiers.

Quotation mark omission.

This and *these* confusion; for example: *these* kind.

Comma error: omission in a series.

Faulty word choice.

Which ambiguously used.

Pronoun object errors; for example: *That is her.*

Affect and *effect* confusion.

<u>Because</u> Leslie wrote a memo.	Dependent clause
The memo <u>which</u> Leslie wrote.	Including a dependent clause
<u>That</u> Leslie wrote a memo.	Dependent clause

See the following Guidelines for other examples of nonsentences and ways to correct them. Once you can confidently distinguish sentences from nonsentences, you can edit out the errors some find so distressing by following the rules.

━━━━━━━━━━━━━━━━━━━━━━ **GUIDELINES** ━━━━━━━

Editing Errors Out of a Sentence

Edit Out Fragments

1. Add subjects or verbs necessary to turn discovered fragments (indicated by quotation marks) into full sentences:

    <u>Leslie was</u> "writing a memo."
     (subj.) (verb)
    "Leslie, writing a memo," <u>thought</u> carefully.
                               (verb)

2. Attach dependent clauses (indicated by quotation marks) to appropriate sentences:

    <u>The contract was secured</u> "because Leslie wrote a memo."
       (subj.)   (verb)
    <u>The contract was secured</u> by the memo "which Leslie wrote."
       (subj.)   (verb)
    <u>The supervisor mentioned</u> "that Leslie wrote a memo."
       (subj.)   (verb)

Note, however, that many professional writers deliberately use fragments for stylistic effect. We use them occasionally ourselves (see page 230, for example).

Edit Out Run-ons and Comma Splices

Having determined that you are dealing with genuine sentences, do not run them together without punctuation or connect them with commas. Choose one of the four other alternatives.

1. Keep the sentences separate:	Leslie wrote. The phone rang.
2. Attach them with a semicolon:	Leslie wrote; the phone rang.
3. Attach with a comma/*and:*	Leslie wrote, <u>and</u> the phone rang.
or a comma/*but:*	The phone rang, <u>but</u> Leslie still wrote.

4. Subordinate one sentence to
the other:

```
While Leslie wrote, the phone
rang.
```

Edit Out Interrupting Commas

With commas, the best general rule is: When in doubt, leave them out!
Most business writing these days uses what is referred to as an "open
style"—that is, the fewest possible commas and other punctuation
marks.

1. Make sure that in your editing you have not placed a single comma
between a sentence's subject and its verb. Cross out the comma in,
for instance:

```
Leslie, still wrote.
Leslie still, wrote.
```

2. Make equally sure that you have not placed a single comma between a sentence's verb and its object. Cross out these commas:

```
Leslie wrote, the memo.
Leslie wrote, that Jones had called.
```

3. Be sure to surround any interrupting word or phrase with *two* commas (except, of course, at the beginning or end of the sentence) so
that the interrupter can be imaginatively lifted out by its commas
and not interrupt at all.

```
Leslie wrote  ,however,  that Jones had called.
```

NONSTANDARD DIALECT USAGE. A second category of stylistic offenses uncov-
ered by Hairston's survey is dialectal. Although linguists have been unable
to identify any qualities that make one language or dialect inherently more
beautiful, more understandable, or even more logical than another, every
society singles out the dialect of its most powerful citizens as standard and
calls it "correct." And as the heavily dialectal cast of the survey's stylistic
offenses makes clear, a culture also subtly penalizes those who do not
conform to that standard.

Scholars tell us that the double negative construction of many Appa-
lachian dialects ("He doesn't know nothing") has an honorable history
dating to medieval times and is still a standard construction in, for
example, contemporary Spanish. Further, Black English constructions
such as "I be thinking" are not corruptions of Standard English, but rather
a remnant of a complex West African verb tense.

Even so, because the notion equating standard dialect with "right" and nonstandard with "wrong" is so deep-seated in the business community, you cannot expect a sympathetic audience for such usage. So if you speak a nonstandard dialect, we encourage you to cherish it and retain it for conversing with other members of your dialect community. But we strongly recommend that you *use only the standard dialect in the business world.* For to write effectively in business as it exists today, you must carefully observe the conventions of Standard English and of standard written prose.

Where you can obtain help. You can find help for many of the problems Hairston's survey has singled out in the Painless Usage Guide (PUG) in this book, where they are listed alphabetically. The Guide is designed to answer these and other usage problems that may puzzle you as you edit your work. If your difficulties are more deep-seated—and you can judge this by how easily you are able to edit the following problematic first draft—we urge you to seek out the more extensive treatment of writing mechanics in handbooks available in libraries or bookstores or to obtain tutorial help.

━━━━━ **PROSE WORKOUT** ━━━━━

Edit this mechanically flawed draft memo.

To: Employees of SMS Corporation
From: Nelson Hodges, Personnel Department
Re: Insurance Plans

Having advertised for bids and having interviewed representatives of the Six Insurance Companys who responded. Our Personnel Committee, narowed the choice to the Green mutual co. and to Life, health, & Accident, inc. Myself and the committee thought that, you would like these best except for Johnson who don't agree. (Johnson doesn't hardly ever agree.)

You can meet with the Green Agent, on thursday, at 2:30, in room 406. If you are interested or if you have questions you would like to have answered. Two sales-reps of the LH&H company is coming here on friday morning at 10:00, the room will be the same.

A brochure of each of the plans are available in the Personnel offices on the third floor. Which you'll find setting on the table. Don't hessitate to ask the comittee and I if you want more information. We hope this way of reaching all of you works good. Because insurance effects each and every one of us.

Advice for Closet Bad Spellers

Research-based fact: There is no correlation between intelligence and spelling ability. The IQs of spelling champions are not unusually high.

Business-world reality: Andrew Jackson said he had nothing but contempt for a man who only knows one way to spell a word. But misspelled words almost invariably mark their writer as stupid. It's not fair. But there it is. It's okay to *be a bad speller,* but NOT *to spell badly* when you write for business.

Advice for closet bad spellers: Stay in the closet. Spell every word correctly.

1. If you compose on a word processor, use the spell-checker to spell as you write and correct as you go along. Pay attention to every blip or activate the corrector frequently.
2. Proofread! Check every word you are less sure of than C-A-T with the spell-checker or your dictionary. For sound-alike words (*their, there, they're; accept, except;* and the like), consult the Painless Usage Guide (PUG) for fast relief.
3. For general rules that will make you a better speller and save some of this bother, look in the PUG under "Spelling."

Spelling mistakes are another kind of error that can count against you, particularly if they occur in any number. If you have problems spelling correctly, see the sidebar above and the Painless Usage Guide.

CONCLUDING THOUGHTS

Now that you've read this chapter, we suggest that you keep its information on the back burner of your mind while you compose your first drafts. Concentrating on mechanics can block your creative thought and tangle you in details. But we want you to have the information ahead of time—at hand when you need it to revise.

AUTHENTIC BUSINESS PROBLEM

Edit the following memo according to the principles suggested in this chapter. Be brief, be simple, be clear. And be sure the memo does not offend by tone or by errors in diction, syntax, punctuation, capitalization, or spelling.

Hint: Be bold. Don't be afraid to cut drastically.

```
TO:      Marion Fine
From:    M.F. Witless
Re:      The mixup over Over Time
```

In regards to what still needs to be ascertained with respect to the problems disgussed by us at the most recent employee grievance Committee meeting which was attended by myself with Airhead and the girls from the typing pool, let me say first of all, that it looks like, it is finally up to you and I what decision will be made in regard to insuring the equitable dipensation of available over time.

But this is not what the union thinks. Bloated with over-time, the girls in the Typing Pool's schedule has got out of hand, with the unfortunate result, of which the discussion was had at the meeting.

During the time that the possibility existed for implementation of the increase in productiveness, the excessive overtime charges in the approximate amount of 50% or thereabouts could have been justified to be needed by a consensus of Managerial opinion. In spite of the fact that it was known at the time of the first Schedule reprioritization, that the possibility existed that they should have been able to anticpate in advance if there configuration of secreterial support then in use would be adequate enough.

If three more typists are offered positions of employment, there would be no need for the schedulization of any more Over Time for all!

Three of the minority ladies in the pool whom didn't concider that they got they're fare share of the over time. And complaints, have been maid. Which were not kept confidential by Personnal. And also two of the girls even had evidenced objections to being reffered to in terms of Manhours as well. This is not all there complaint's either. Needless to say.

Please call me right away if I shouldnt do this because of the union interferrence when they wrote the Work rules as I mentioned.

It would be impossible to underestimate the value of your Contribution in this Problem, and I as just one of the Team, are very apreciative.

Chapter 3

EXPEDITING YOUR BUSINESS PROSE

EXECUTIVE SUMMARY

Composing on a word processor and formatting effectively are powerful techniques in business communication.

Compose on a Word Processor

The computer can help you accomplish more efficiently many of the business writing tasks you must perform. It can help you:

- "Invent" your text through listing or free-writing.

- Outline (with special software or word-processor features that structure your ideas).

- Invent and revise as you go along, recursively.

- Revise.

- Edit.

- Check your spelling.

- Check your diction.

Format Your Business Communications

If your written message is to get from your mind to your reader's, it must first be processed by your reader's eyes. Effective format makes a tremendous difference in expediting this process. To format effectively:

- Give your message prominence by surrounding it with the space offered by generous margins.

- Segment your material into readable "chunks," paragraphed and separated by white space.

- Headline the chunks for quick comprehension.

- Underline to call attention to the most significant information.

- Highlight material by breaking up the conventional pattern of the page with bulleted or numbered lists.

- Where appropriate, arrange information into charted columns.

SECTION A: *Expedite the Writing Process with a Word Processor*

The watchword in business is *expedite*. Get it done. Get it out. The two techniques discussed here—composing on the word processor and formatting—will expedite your work. You will write more efficiently and you will make your reader's job easier.

WORD-PROCESSING YOUR BUSINESS WRITING

The word processor, now almost universally available in the business world, offers the potential for expediting the whole process of writing. It can facilitate the writing process at every step. In this section we will review the process and point out ways a word processor can help smooth out the difficulties you might encounter.

WHEN YOU DON'T KNOW WHAT TO WRITE

A customer has posed a problem, and you have to write an answering letter suggesting a solution. Or you've completed your work on an important project, and now you have to write a memo making your recommendations. Your knowledge of your subject, reader, and purpose will either spontaneously suggest a structure and a phrasing, or it won't. If it does, all is well; and your first draft is underway. But if you can't think how to start or what to say, turn to your word processor.

INVENTING ON A WORD PROCESSOR.   A word processor can help you "invent" your ideas, to use Aristotle's term. Actually, people really do not invent ideas; they discover them. They bring ideas out of their own subconscious mind into the light, where their conscious mind can examine and work with them. Our research shows that writers "invent" in either of two ways:

- *By listing.* Some writers take an inventory of all the ideas the brain might be harboring on a subject and list them. Then they relate them to each other and organize them into a purposeful structure before starting to write.
- *By the act of writing itself.* For other writers, the process of finding words and formulating sentences helps to discover ideas and strategies they didn't know they had. These writers report that once they bring their subconscious ideas to the surface through free-writing, their letters and memos seem almost to structure themselves.

Whichever way is more effective for you, your word processor can help.

LISTING ON A WORK PROCESSOR. If you are a lister, jot down your ideas with a word processor. Make one long list, and analyze it. Or if your word processor has *column* or *window* capabilities, use them to make a number of lists until you've inventoried all your ideas and strategies. Then relate your ideas to one another. Move them from list to list. Combine lists. Add headings and turn the lists into categories. Experiment. Subordinate some ideas to others in a variety of ways.

Outline. Organize your ideas according to one strategy. Then, saving your first version, organize them according to a different strategy.

Compare. Try again if you are still not satisfied. When you have a structural plan (or an outline) that you think will work, print it and keep it by your computer as you write your draft. Keep a pencil handy, though, so you can make changes as you go along. A useful structural plan is flexible in this way.

Software for listers. A number of companies have developed programs especially to help listers organize their ideas. These programs, known as "outliners," permit you to subordinate your ideas and write a conventional outline easily. They also can convert your outline to a tree, bullet, or other outline format. Type a line of outline and the outliner will indent or move items left or right, up or down, to place your thought at whatever level of subordination you choose. These programs also automatically adjust your outline to take in new material or to omit deleted material. They will even let you reshuffle or resort your ideas.

You can also use an outline to begin writing. Each point on the outline can be expanded, allowing additional text under the heading. You can hide or view the extra material as you choose.

Special outlining software packages include More and MindWrite. Among the word-processing programs with outlining capabilities are Microsoft Word, Word Perfect, Word Star, Perfect Writer, and Textra.

Advantages of using an outliner. How can you make use of these outliner capabilities in your writing? William Hershey, systems engineer and university lecturer, suggests five ways:

- *Modularize ideas.* By encouraging you to begin new ideas on new lines, in list format, an outliner circumvents the snakelike tendency of sentences to slither from one idea to the next.
- *Subordinate ideas to a broader idea.* When you subordinate certain ideas to other broader ones, your information becomes manageable. Reorganize as often as necessary to get the best hierarchy. The very process will clarify your thinking.
- *Rearrange ideas.* You can sort your lists of ideas in a variety of orders—by time, relative importance, or deductive reasoning, for example. By trying alternative sequences of ideas, you can arrive at

the best order before taking the time to add the rhetorical links—the *howevers, therefores,* and *furthermores*—that bind the finished paragraphs together.

- *Develop ideas in parallel.* When a new idea pops into your head just when you are recording another idea, the outliner's capacity for hierarchical structure and its expand/collapse capability (that is, its ability to hide and reveal subordinate material) comes to your aid. It lets you find the appropriate location for the new idea and lets you record it with minimal interference.[1]

Outlining and listing help you identify patterns and relationships among ideas and build a structure that can serve as a skeleton for your final document.

FREE-WRITING ON A WORD PROCESSOR. About half of all writers brainstorm more fruitfully through free-writing. Free-writing is, as its name implies, totally unrestricted writing. Free-writers need to give themselves a free rein intellectually, and a word processor makes it easier. For many, a computer turns out to be much less intimidating than a blank page.

━━━━━━━━━━━━━━━━━━━━━━━━━━━━━━ **GUIDELINES** ━━━━━━━

Some Hints for Computer Free-Writing

- Begin by typing in the idea (or ideas) that seem central. Let the wording of the topic suggest ideas to you, and follow those ideas wherever they might lead you.
- Then relax and let your ideas flow through your fingers. To get at the ideas in your subconscious, don't stop to think, to rest your fingers, to relax your muscles; just keep typing.
- Don't look back at what you've written. Don't make corrections. Turn off your spell-checker.
- If you cannot think what to say, just repeat the last phrase over and over until a new idea comes.
- When you have completed your initial free-writing—or after a set time, say, 10 minutes, has elapsed—study what you have written on the screen. Or run it off and examine it. Underline or circle ideas that might be worth pursuing.
- Then organize and write.
- Sometimes it is helpful to try another free-writing session as a follow-up to the first. The second attempt will probably turn out to be more structured. Usually you will be able to work out a plan from this free-writing that will lead directly to your draft memo or report. If not, there is no harm in yet another round of free-writing.

---

1. Adapted from "Computer Programs: Outliners" by William Hershey, in *Encyclopedia of Microcomputers,* vol. 3, edited by Allen Kent and James G. Williams (New York: Marcel Dekker, 1988). Reprinted by permission of Marcel Dekker Inc.

Free-writing is not for everybody at all times. It is a good technique to try, however, if your mind feels blank or if you are confused about the subject. And many people find free-writing a useful way to begin on those days when even the thought of writing seems disagreeable.

WRITING RECURSIVELY ON A WORD PROCESSOR

Research shows that the most effective writers write recursively. That is, they do not start at the beginning and steam-roller straight through to the end. Rather, they work in fits and starts.[2]

- They will write a sentence or two or a paragraph or two and then read over what they've written to make revisions.
- While creating one section, they will return often to what they have already written.
- Far from getting all their inventing out of the way before they write, and doing all their revising afterward, they will both invent and revise as they go along.

With its easy "page ups" and "page downs," the word processor seems almost invented for recursive writing.

━━━━━━━━━━━━━━━━━━━━━━━━━━ **GUIDELINES** ━━━━━━━

Some Strategies for Writing Recursively on the Computer

1. Work until you run out of ideas and then go back, reread, and revise. This very act stimulates new ideas or better ways of arranging those you have.
2. Recall a key word from where you were working and enter a search command to return you there. If you have been working at the end of the writing, your word processor has a way of advancing you back to the end rapidly.
3. If a useful change for an earlier section occurs to you as you write, recall a key word or phrase from that section and use it for a back-search command. Within seconds, your cursor is right at the spot where you can try out the change.
4. When one change necessitates another—and this complication happens often—use the search commands to help find those places.
5. If you have a section that needs to be completed at a later date, you may find it useful to mark the text at that point with a string of symbols. Use a string (such as $$$) that you're not likely to require in your ordinary text.
6. You can also use such a string to mark your place when you're working in the middle of a document and are called away.

---

2. Students of rhetoric and composition pedagogy define *recursive* in this way. The term has a different meaning in computer science.

TACTICS FOR REVISING AND EDITING

A word processor is extraordinarily useful in the revision process. All the techniques that help in recursive revising also help in final revising. And most word processors give additional assistance with editing as well.

USING A WORD PROCESSOR FOR STRUCTURAL REVISION. The best way to go about revising is to work from large to small. Don't start with the commas. Think through the overall structure of your work. Then consider revising your paragraphs. Don't worry about mechanics and style until last. This ordering saves a good deal of effort, for in making major revisions you may very well eliminate material where smaller revisions would have been needed. Furthermore, research has shown that when a writer clarifies the thinking behind an awkwardly worded passage, more often than not the syntactical problems take care of themselves. The word processor is at its most useful in the major revisions through its cut-and-paste capabilities.

Cut and paste. The phrase *cut and paste,* computer jargon for revising, recalls a time when large-scale editing was a matter of scissoring out a portion of writing and pasting or taping it elsewhere in the manuscript. The problem then was that once you made the change, your original structure and phrasing were gone.

"OH, HOW I HATE THE RE-WRITING!"

But a word processor lets you save your thoughts while you rearrange them. If yours has window capability, use it to view various versions of a troublesome passage simultaneously. If it lacks such capability, duplicate the pesky portion in a space you have cleared beneath it. While keeping your original sentences or paragraphs, take them apart in the duplicate and recombine them. If the section you want to revise is lengthy, duplicate it in a scratch file you can open for the purpose. Whichever method you use, try out a variety of phrasings or organizations and find the one that best achieves your purpose.

EDITING WITH A WORD PROCESSOR. In Chapter 2 we demonstrated the importance of a clear, correct, inoffensive stylistic surface to your business prose. We urge you to edit every final draft until you are completely sure it is clear and correct and then to proofread to make certain you have missed nothing. Your word processor will expedite your editing.

Read your screen carefully. If a paragraph needs focus, add a topic sentence. If you decide that your bulleted points would be more effective in a different order, switch them. If a paragraph is too wordy, delete all nonessential words, phrases, or sentences. Or move the paragraph to a place where it can help achieve greater unity, coherence, or emphasis. If a passage adds nothing relevant to your purpose, delete it entirely.

Making global corrections. If you find a word or phrase you have misspelled, miscapitalized, or misused throughout a document, your word processor can speed up the necessary repeated changes. Say, for example, you have referred a number of times to a Dennis *Pizonka* in a memo you are writing. You had no way of knowing until today when you saw the name in writing that the correct spelling is really *Pieczonka*. Use the command that will correct the spelling wherever it appears throughout the document.

A $25,000 Punctuation Mark

- The company needed 10 foot-long pipes.
- The order said "10-foot-long pipes."
- The pipe was cut and the order was filled.
- The result: The company paid an extra $25,000.

All for the want of a . . . well-placed hyphen!

Discovered by Gary Blake, Language Skills Consultant; cited by Rick Burnham in *Investor's Daily*.

Using a spell-checker and thesaurus. If your word processor has an interactive spell-checker, it will prevent you from making an inadvertent spelling error as you work. Listen for the beep. The speller will also help you find the correct spelling to substitute when you are not sure. If your speller is noninteractive, remember to spell-check your work at regular intervals.

If your word processor has a thesaurus, consult it (or its printed equivalent) whenever you want to find a word to express precisely the meaning you have in mind. Use it to bring greater accuracy to your diction or to find a synonym when you have repeated a word too many times.

You will find a thesaurus a helpful tool. But since it also has some limitations, the following Guidelines provide a number of usage hints.

GUIDELINES

Using a Thesaurus

1. Use a thesaurus to spur your memory when you have a word on the "tip of your tongue" but aren't able to bring it to your conscious mind.
2. Try the thesaurus when you have used a word several times and feel you are beginning to establish a repetitive pattern.
3. Do NOT use the thesaurus to find a word that will seem more impressive than your original term.
4. And, most important, NEVER replace a word you know with one whose meaning you're not sure of. Do NOT gamble with semiblind substitution.

   Synonyms cannot always be interchanged, and a wrong choice can be downright embarrassing. One new employee, for example, after a working visit at another company, wrote to express his thanks. Looking up *continually* in his thesaurus, he chose a grander-sounder synonym and wrote:

   "Please thank Ms. Jackson especially for me. She was <u>interminably</u> helpful."

COMPUTER WORKOUT

Here is an exercise that we hope will help make writing a more comfortable process for you. The best writers experiment and use and discard all kinds of inventing strategies. This exercise should help you experience the two major ways of focusing in on your topic.

Take any writing problem you are presently confronting in either your academic or professional work. Using this material:

1. Search your mind with free-writing for 10 minutes. Save and print.
2. Structure your ideas with a plan, list, or outline.
   - Study your free-writing.

- If your work is a business project, decide what your purpose is. If the work is an expository paper, decide what your thesis is.
- What support can you find for your purpose or your thesis?
- Structure your supporting points to guide your writing.
- Save and print.

3. Now take a look at what you've done and answer these questions:
   - Are you comfortable with this two-step process?
   - Were you impatient with the free-writing and eager to get to a more structured approach?
   - Were you impatient with the outlining and ready to begin your draft as soon as you had finished the free-writing?

In your future writing, use the technique—or combination—that suits your own way of thinking.

SECTION B: *Expedite Your Message: Format for Instant Clarity*

Your word processor can help expedite the entire writing process. But once your message is composed, the most important way you can expedite it for your reader is to format it effectively. In fact, formatting is the fastest, easiest way to be brief, simple, and clear.

FORMATTING CAN MAKE A DIFFERENCE

Format is the way information is arranged on the page. White space and indentation, headings, and lists help organize your message and make it clear. To appreciate the difference effective formatting can make, compare the following two memos.

To: John Sealand [SVP, Marketing, Glotz's Department Stores, Inc.]
From: Denise Jones [Director of Consumer Marketing]
Subject: Budget, Fall Harvest Sale
Date: July 17, 19—

As you know, last year's Fall Harvest promotional event was not as well attended as we had hoped. Nor did the sales justify what we spent on its promotion. We would like to recommend a change in the amount of money being spent on the event this year, as well as a major change in the allocation of the dollars.

Last year's budget of $0,000,000 was allocated in this way: Direct mail—$000,000; Newspaper inserts—$000,000; Broadcast effort—$000,000.

We suggest allocating $1,000,000 to this year's budget to be spent as follows: $450M for a newspaper insert (preprint) to be run in major city newspapers in our various markets on Sunday, October 17, 76 pages, 4 color, consisting of promotional merchandise from every department in the store, specific items to be cleared with the merchants involved and presentation in line with the fall nature of the promotion. In addition, $300M for direct mailing of some of the material from the newspaper insert. And $250M for broadcast support of the print pieces.

The bulk of the money should be spent on the newspaper insert because, according to our latest marketing survey, this is currently the best way to reach our buying oriented customers. We can cut our normal budget for direct mail in half since we now have a system that enables us to identify the most productive portion of our credit customer list. We should send only to the 30% that research shows most likely to respond.

The $1 million represents a 20% decrease from last year's event. That could cause some apprehension on the part of the merchants that they are not receiving adequate support for this promotion. To speak to their concerns: The united focus of this campaign plus the new direct mail system should result in maximum benefit from our resources.

The numbers in this memo are only approximate. Different allocations could be made based on discussions with Jim and Martin, which we should have promptly. If you could let me have your response by Tuesday, I would be able to set up the necessary meetings in time for the publication deadline.

The following memo is identical in content to the one above and differs only in format.

To: John Sealand [SVP, Marketing, Glotz's Department Stores, Inc.]
From: Denise Jones [Director of Consumer Marketing]
Re: Budget, Fall Harvest Sale
Date: July 17, 19—

As you know, last year's Fall Harvest promotional event was not as well attended as we had hoped. Nor did the sales justify what we spent on its promotion. We would like to recommend a change in the amount of money being spent on the event this year, as well as a major change in the allocation of the dollars.

BACKGROUND
Last year's budget of $0,000,000 was allocated in this way:

Direct mail	$000,000
Newspaper inserts	$000,000
Broadcast effort	$000,000

RECOMMENDATIONS
- Allocate $1,000,000 to this year's budget.
- $450M for a newspaper insert (preprint). To be run in major city newspapers in our various markets on Sunday, October 17, 76 pages, 4 color, consisting of promotional merchandise from every department in the store, specific items to be cleared with the merchants involved and presentation in line with the fall nature of the promotion.
- $300M for direct mailing of some of the material from the newspaper insert.
- $250M for broadcast support of the print pieces.

ANALYSIS
1. The bulk of the money should be spent on the newspaper insert because, according to our latest marketing survey, this is currently the best way to reach our buying oriented customers.

2. We can cut our normal budget for direct mail in half since we now have a system that enables us to identify the most productive portion of our credit customer list. We should send only to the 30% that research shows most likely to respond.

3. The $1 million represents a 20% decrease from last year's event. That could cause some apprehension on the part of the merchants that they are not receiving adequate support for this promotion. To speak to their concerns: The united focus of this campaign plus the new direct mail system should result in maximum benefit from our resources.

The numbers in this memo are only approximate. Different allocations could be made based on discussions with Jim and Martin, which we should have promptly.

If you could let me have your response by Tuesday, I would be able to set up the necessary meetings in time for the publication deadline.

For all practical purposes, the message remains the same in both versions of the Harvest Sale memo. But which do you find easier to understand? By how much? And which version would you rather read? You can be sure that a busy executive would agree. The second version can be mentally processed much faster.

CHUNKING AND HIGHLIGHTING

The second version is easier to understand because it directs the reader's attention through the techniques of *chunking* and *highlighting*. Cognitive psychologists tell us that although our minds are capable of comprehending an almost unlimited amount of material, they cannot take in much unbroken content at once.

We learn in "chunks," segments of related material, and then relate the chunks of knowledge to each other and assimilate them into our accumulated knowledge.

You can use this principle to format your own message in comprehensible chunks.

- First, make sure your paragraphs are short enough for your reader to take in as a single chunk.
- Then highlight the most significant portions to bring them directly to the reader's notice. Such highlighting will help your reader understand the chunks more readily and integrate them more quickly.

The revised Harvest Sale memo is easier to read and understand because of chunking and highlighting.

INDENTING AND SPACING. When we learn to read, our eyes are trained to notice only the print on a page. But actually a printed page consists of both print and white space. To make your writing most effective, allocate your space purposefully. Within limits, the more surrounding space, the easier it is to read the print. Thus, to achieve maximum clarity in business letters, we recommend that you:

- Provide generous margins.
- Divide your text into short paragraphs.
- List information where appropriate and bullet or number your lists.
- Consider using a chart for complex data.

CHARTING. Charts and lists both break the conventional pattern of writing on the page. They shift margins and open up the page with additional white space. The chart format clarifies and dramatizes sets of figures. Compare the "Background" segment from the two versions of the Harvest Sale memo:

```
Last year's budget of $0,000,000 was allocated in this
way: Direct mail--$000,000; Newspaper inserts--$000,000;
Broadcast effort--$000,000.

Last year's budget of $0,000,000 was allocated in this
way:

Direct mail              $000,000
Newspaper inserts        $000,000
Broadcast effort         $000,000
```

Arranging the information into charted columns makes comparison of the figures easier and faster.

LISTING. Use lists to help you format. You can number, letter, or bullet items you want to emphasize individually. The bulleted list is considered particularly useful in business because it does not require the serial order that numbers or letters imply. You can order listed items:

- Chronologically.
- Serially.
- Circumstantially.

Or you can arrange them in an inverted pyramid to present your information in a decreasing order of importance. (See pages 199–202 for a more detailed discussion of structuring.)

SIGNPOSTING

You can also increase clarity by *signposting*—that is, by using headings and underlinings judiciously.

HEADINGS AND TOPLININGS. When you place headings or toplinings on your paragraphs, you define chunks of subject matter and put the subchunks under them into categories that mean something. With this technique you help your readers preview a chunk of substance for content and sequence.

The most useful headings are those that sum up their subject matter. Write, for example, "Request to Purchase a New Fax Machine" rather than the less explanatory "New Fax Machine."

UNDERLINING. Underlining is another way to highlight the most important material and attract the reader's eye to it. In most cases the underlined sentence heads the chunk, just the way the topic sentence usually heads a paragraph. For example:

```
Lease a second fax machine, to be housed in the market-
ing office and designated primarily for marketing busi-
ness. One fax machine clearly can no longer handle our
increased communications volume.
```

Occasionally you can direct your reader's eye by underlining the significant portion as it takes shape throughout the segment. For instance:

```
A plant manager who has identified problems early in the
manufacturing schedule may also, at his or her discre-
tion, request the services of a corporate troubleshooter.
```

━━━━━━━━ **FORMATTING WORKOUT** ━━━━━━━━

1. Format the following memo to make its message as clear as possible to the reader. Then write a brief memo to your instructor, giving a rationale for the formatting devices you selected.

```
DATE:
TO:       All Department Heads
FROM:     [You]
RE:       Techniques for improving meeting
          effectiveness*
```

```
At Tom's request, I am sharing with you the
techniques for better meeting management that I
brought back from last week's seminar. These
guidelines are adapted from a U.S. Department of
State pilot program, "Chairing Effective
Meetings." Generate alternatives to meeting: Make
the decision; hold a conference call; postpone;
use electronic mail; cancel; send a repre-
sentative.  Clearly define the meeting's purpose
(to analyze, decide, inform or coordinate).  Limit
attendance (only those needed should attend).
Stagger attendance (attend only for time needed to
make a contribution).  Pick the right time
(strategic timing: can people and information be
present?).  Pick the right place (remote to avoid
interruptions; geographically accessible).  Send
an advance agenda and required information (no
surprises, all people prepared).  Compute cost per
minute (measure the costs of a late start or
specific agenda items).  Set time limits per
meeting (establish starting and ending times).
Start on time (don't penalize those arriving on
time or reward latecomers).  End on time (respect
participants' other commitments).  Expedite
minutes (concise minutes should include any
decisions, individual assignments, and deadlines;
distribute within 48 hours after the meeting).
Follow up with (A) progress reports (B) execution
of decisions.  Tom believes that we should try
this program for eight weeks.  At the end of that
time, we will send you an evaluation form that you
should both fill out yourself and administer to
those who report to you.  Please let Tom know by
memo the list of meetings you anticipate holding
over the next two months and who will be
responsible for implementing these guidelines.
```

---

*From "21 Rules for Getting More Out of Meetings," *Meeting Management News,* vol. 1, no. 4. Reprinted by permission of 3M Management Institute.

```
You might need to keep notes or a log on each
meeting to use as a source for the evaluation
form.  Feel free to call if you have questions
about any part of the plan.  We appreciate your
cooperation.
```

2. Alternatively, if you have had to write a memo recently in the course of your work, submit a copy of it. And write a brief memo to your instructor, giving a rationale for the formatting devices you selected.

Word Processing Your Business Writing:
Formatting Strategies

Find the right format for your business message by experimenting with the variety of possibilities available on most word processors. Word-processing programs are increasingly WYSIWYG (an abbreviation of "What You See Is What You Get"), permitting the screen to reflect accurately the appearance the type will take on the printed page. This capability can help expedite your format decisions. So try out various formats. Adjust the system's code, for example, to:

- Vary the number of lines per page.
- Vary the space between lines and between paragraphs.
- Vary the number of sentences in a paragraph.
- Change the margins—both left and right.
- Try out a variety of hanging-indent positions.
- Try out bullets, numbers, or other hanging-indent markers.
- Try center or side headlines.
- Vary the headline type: roman or italic, capitals or lowercase.
- Try underlined regular or bold heads.
- Highlight by varying type weight: bold, medium, or light.
- Highlight by underlining or underlining in bold.

If your software or your system permits you to change type fonts (for instance, to change from Times Roman to Helvetica), ordinarily choose a type having serifs, the fine lines projecting from the main strokes of letters. Research shows that readers find type with serifs more readable than type without serifs (sans-serif).

This is a sample of serif type.

This is a sample of sans-serif type.

AUTHENTIC BUSINESS PROBLEM

You work for Smoothlin Products, a company that manufactures lotions, handcreams, and toiletries. It is among the 20 companies the local Chamber of Commerce has invited to a meeting to prepare for the North American Figure Skating Competition to be held in your city next February. Your supervisor, Carl Mechem, Vice President for Public Affairs, has been called out of town unexpectedly, and in his absence you have covered the June 8 meeting at the Chamber office. *Your job is to write a brief memo giving him the information you picked up at the meeting.* Since the meeting is only a preliminary one, you can make your memo strictly informational and need not make recommendations.

John Brooklin, of the Anderson Drug Chain and Chair of the Chamber committee, called and chaired the meeting. For all his accomplishments, he has an absentminded manner and makes a rather disorganized presentation. Your meeting notes, therefore, are necessarily a bit jumbled (see page 75).

Your Assignment. Use your word processor to work through the problem and write the memo. Since we are studying process in this chapter, please (for this assignment only) turn in written work for every step of the writing process.

1. Study the notes. Then, use the prewriting technique you are most comfortable with: free-write or make a list, plan, or outline. (For help in deciding, see Computer Workout, pages 66–67.) Save and print.
2. Study your prewriting. Write your first draft. Save and print.
3. Revise your draft for clarity. Save and print.
4. Format for effective communication. Save and print.
5. Edit for mechanics and style. Save and print.

Your Notes

- Only potential sponsors invited
- Some pretty important folks here: I recognized Jim Arnold from Ledco Steel, Andrea Serviss from Agon Computers, Edith Anderson from the Anderson Drugs Conglomerate, Matt O'Neil from Slurpa Jams and Jellies, Marty Rusko from JMJM Realty Development, Carol Lasky of Barnabus Department Stores, Edward Joao—president— of the Summit Imported Auto Sales chain; and people I didn't recognize from Spiritus Distillers and Petersen's Bakery chain.
- The media came in force: The Morning Beacon, KYWW-ET (Public Television), KUOY (national public radio), KEZY radio and Channel 9.
- Edith Anderson of Anderson Drugs (a big customer of ours) asked me if we were interested in the event because Anna Campion (former North American champion skater, now turned professional) sponsors our SilkSkin Lotion. I didn't see any harm in saying yes, probably.
- Just a general meeting to organize the event.
- The Chamber hopes every company will consider underwriting some projects and events.
- They're going to need funding for a new Zamboni machine to resurface the ice rink.
- They plan to commission a sculpture from a regional artist to become a permanent part of the planned hospitality garden.
- The committee will also be asking for volunteer help from corporate employees and hopes companies will consider giving employees work time to participate.
- They're going to need help with lodging and hospitality for skaters, competition judges and other officials — people to pick up officials at the airport, house them and escort them during the event.
- They're going to need publicity (Brooklin would like to have a team of seasoned public relations people manage this aspect; that committee needs to be up and running within the month.)
- The present press facility is inadequate to handle the expected national and international attention.
- Need sponsors for a new press facility and hospitality garden.
- There might be plaques on the new facilities with sponsors' names.
- The Chamber wouldn't mind a little friendly competition among the underwriters. After all the new sculpture is supposed to represent the Spirit of Competition.
- The sponsor for the Zamboni could get their name on a banner on the machine, which would appear periodically on the ice during the competition.
- The sponsor of a new cafeteria that they're contemplating could have name attached. Since there is presently no food service other than the hot dog concession stands, they're suggesting a new cafeteria for competitors and officials. This would be a lasting contribution to the city, Brooklin said.
- They're also going to need help with organizing receptions and other hospitality for competitors.
- Jim Arnold mentioned the need to renovate the changing rooms.
- And Marty Rusko urged us not to forget the really major funds needed to upgrade the ice rink at Yurcity Gardens to bring it up to standard for a national competition.
- Edith Anderson asked if they would need some help with financial control — accounting, auditing, cash management and the like.

Part 2

APPLICATIONS OF EFFECTIVE BUSINESS WRITING

WRITING EFFECTIVE BUSINESS LETTERS

EXECUTIVE SUMMARY

The purpose of a business letter is to get something done. The best way to accomplish this purpose is to put yourself in the place of the person who will receive your letter. Empathy—that is, identifying and feeling with your reader—is the first principle of business-letter writing and the heart of our basic axiom:

Consider your reader in light of your purpose.

When you draft a letter, begin and end with an empathetic statement.

- If your message is a welcome one, begin with that. The pleasing message *itself* is an empathetic statement.

- If your message is not likely to be welcomed or if it is a request, *precede* it with an empathetic statement.

- End all letters with an empathetic close, one that reaches out to your correspondent and speaks as one human being to another.

When you revise a letter, revise empathetically.

- Read the draft through your correspondent's eyes. Try to experience every sentence—every word—as your correspondent would.

- Edit out anything that makes you as reader less likely to want to help accomplish the letter's goal.

- Rewrite with empathy to influence the reader toward your purpose.

Businesspeople write all sorts of letters: letters of acceptance, acknowledgment, adjustment, application, complaint, and congratulations; cover letters; customer relations letters; letters of inquiry, marketing, order, reference, and request; refusal letters, sales letters; letters of transmittal and of technical information. And this list does not exhaust all the categories. You could learn a specific pattern for each of these kinds of letters (and many texts adopt that approach).

But we think that such an approach is impractical. For when you sit down actually to write a letter in the business world, you likely will discover that the situation in which you find yourself does not precisely fit any of the models. For this reason, we think some psychological insight and a few overall strategies, coupled with the good judgment you will develop, will serve you better.

These insights and strategies can all be derived from the general axiom of business writing:

Consider your reader in light of your purpose.

When we analyze the axiom, we see that it focuses on two concepts: purpose and reader.

- **Purpose.** No one ever writes a business letter without a purpose. Business is active. It aims to get things done. Writing letters is one major way that it gets things done. In successful business letters the writer communicates with the recipient so that the purpose is achieved and the things get done.
- **Reader.** The recipients are also important. After all, they are the ones who must be persuaded to do what needs to be done. How can you persuade your readers? By trying to understand their psychology. By empathizing—that is, by actually trying to imagine yourself in your reader's place.

A PSYCHOLOGICAL APPROACH TO BUSINESS CORRESPONDENCE

To understand the value of the psychological approach, the value of considering your reader, try this experimental simulation.[1] The idea is to

---

1. The concept is similar to one Professor Paul V. Anderson uses in his consulting work and with his classes at Miami University in Ohio.

experience the following letter for yourself just as it would be perceived by its addressee, Bill Ace. Use a blank paper and cover the letter so that only one line at a time is visible. Then read it through Bill Ace's eyes. Try to really get into Ace's mind, just as you would if you were playing his part in a play. Once you have "become" Bill Ace, monitor your reactions sentence by sentence as you read the letter:

June 12, 19——

Mr. William P. Ace
President
Ace Janitorial Services
123 Sunshine Blvd.
Paterson, New Jersey 00000

Re: Cleaning Contract Noncompliance

Dear Mr. Ace:

1 I have personally inspected the Dreadnought Corporation Board Room which Ace Janitorial Services "cleaned" yesterday morning.

2 Our fully paid contract with you, which runs through September, is for weekly, thorough cleaning of both the headquarters offices and the Board Room. However, this

3 morning's inspection showed that the Board Room, which you claim to have cleaned, clearly has not received

4 proper attention. There were carry-out food service car-

5 tons strewn about. There also were ashes on the carpet.

6 Moreover, there is a long and deep scratch on the board table for which I intend to hold you responsible, and the restoration cost for which we will expect compensation.

7 I consider that you have not lived up to the terms and

8 conditions of the contract. This negligence is particularly unfortunate at this time because I need to be able to trust you to do a better than usual job for the June 20th cleaning, since our annual meeting is scheduled for

9 the 25th. Although the service contract does not specify cleaning of the Board Room every week, we will require you to make an extra inspection the week of the meeting and assure us that the Board Room does in fact meet our standards.

10 Because the office cleaning has in general been satisfactory, I have not until now thought it necessary to

11 make my own inspection. That is your job. If I have to

12 assign one of my own employees to do it, I will expect

you to reimburse Dreadnought for the cost of her super-
visory time.

13 Please contact Miss Kennedy in my office. We need your
14 assurance that both cleaning dates we have indicated
will be attended to.

Your very truly,

H. Claude Andrews
Office Manager
Dreadnought Corporation

HCA: j

HOW DOES THE READER RESPOND?	In your role as Bill Ace, what goes through your mind as you read? Let's look at the letter sentence by sentence. (The parenthetical comments represent the responses of most "Bill Aces.")

Re: How do you feel about the reference line? What's this about "contract noncompliance"? (The phrase suggests bad performance and bad faith, and hints in its legalistic tone that legal action could be taken.) All this before you even have a chance to hear what the problem is. Do you begin to be on your guard?

1. "I have *personally* inspected the Dreadnought Corporation Board Room." (The tone is unpleasant.) How do you react to *cleaned* in quotation marks? (Read "so-called cleaned.") Do you find yourself bristling even before you finish sentence 1?

2. "*Thorough* cleaning"? (Why, we always clean thoroughly. That's the basis of our reputation.)

3. "*Claim* to have cleaned." (There's that nasty sarcasm again. We don't just *claim* to clean; we really clean.) Do you find yourself becoming genuinely annoyed—pride in your work turning into anger as you feel your company's reputation questioned?

4, 5, 6. What comes to your mind as Andrews brings in the evidence? Cartons, ashes, and a scratched table. (Could it be that the new crew isn't up to par? No, George is foreman, and he's always been reliable—except for that one time last year when he didn't show up.) Does the possibility of some culpability make you feel a bit defensive and perhaps even more annoyed?

"Expect compensation." (Let me think. Our guys were there yesterday. Maybe someone else came in in the meantime. And besides, if George didn't show and the crew didn't do the room, they couldn't have made the scratch. Why didn't Claude think of *that*?)

7, 8, 9. Do you read disdain in these sentences? Does it raise your hackles? (*We* haven't lived up to *our* contract?) "I need to be able to trust you to do a better than usual job for the June 20th cleaning, since our annual meeting is scheduled for the 25th." (Note that.) Perhaps the possibility of getting back at Andrews even begins to take on a certain appeal? "Although the service contract does not specify cleaning of the Board Room every week, we will require . . ." (Now he's talking about *their* breaking the contract to "require" us to make an extra cleaning and inspection. Well, *he* said it in the second paragraph: we've *already* been paid.)

10. "The cleaning has . . . been satisfactory." Does the compliment strike you as grudging? (Too little and too late.)

11. "That is your job." Do you find that condescending? Even offensive?

12. How do you react to Andrews's tone here? (*He's* going to have someone supervise *me*? Who does he think he is to patronize me?) "I will expect you to reimburse Dreadnought." (He'll have to wait a long time on that one.)

13. "Contact Miss Kennedy." (More condescension. This office manager can't speak to me himself! Does he expect the president of a company to deal only with his secretary?)

14. "We need your assurance that both cleaning dates we have indicated will be attended to." Here, where the request finally comes, how do you respond? (In a pig's eye!)

PRAGMATIC ANALYSIS

We've looked at Andrews's letter from the point of view of the recipient. Now let's analyze it in terms of Andrews's purpose, what he wants to get done. Why does Claude Andrews write to Bill Ace? What does he hope to accomplish by the letter?

"And what salutation do you want to use with this letter, Mr. Dubbins?"

From *Do You Want to Talk About It?* by Edward Koren, ©1968 by Edward Koren. Published by Pantheon Books, New York.

If all Andrews wants to do is to work off his indignation, then his letter succeeds in its purpose. On the contrary, however, it seems most likely that his aim is rather:

- To get better supervision of the cleaning crew, so that they will never again leave the board room in an unsatisfactory condition.
- To have Ace provide an extra-contractual cleaning of the board room before the annual meeting.

When it comes to getting the board room properly prepared for that meeting, Andrews starts out with two major disadvantages:

1. Ace Janitorial is not contractually obligated to render the service.
2. Since Dreadnought has paid Ace Janitorial in advance, Andrews cannot hire another company without duplicating his expenditures. Ace has him over the proverbial barrel. And if our visceral reaction to the letter is any indication of Bill Ace's, then Andrews's letter has failed. It is not likely to net him anything except a supplier with high blood pressure— and little inclination to be helpful.

APPLICATION. We, however, can learn from Andrews's mistakes. (At the end of the chapter, you will have an opportunity to provide Andrews with a more effective letter.) Analyzing Andrews's failure reinforces the universal business-writing axiom:

Consider your reader in light of your purpose.

Such analysis also suggests two fundamental principles for writing business letters that we can derive from the axiom:

Empathetic Principle: Consider your reader; put yourself in your reader's place.

Purpose Principle: Never lose track of your purpose.

Let's consider these principles in a practical way.

EMPATHETIC PRINCIPLE

KNOW YOURSELF. How can you make your letter achieve the desired impression? Put yourself in your reader's shoes. People are enough alike emotionally that there is almost always something to be gained by this strategy. Read over your letter before you send it, and consider. If you are pleased, chances are good—though not guaranteed—that your reader will be pleased too. If you are annoyed, chances are your reader will be. If, for example, Andrews's letter to Ace made you angry, the odds are that it would make Ace angry too. And if you annoy your readers or make them angry, what will you have accomplished? Tact and diplomacy always work best.

KNOW YOUR READER. Your own reactions as a fellow vulnerable human being are your strongest guide. But when it comes to writing a business letter, they need not be your only guide. Ordinarily, you will have some knowledge of your correspondents as well. You or one of your colleagues (with whom you can confer) may have had personal or phone contact with them or, if you are answering a letter, the clues are there before you. How, for instance, do you characterize the writer of the handwritten letter on the following page? It's a letter actually received by a company doing business in the midwestern United States.

Although Mrs. Schmidtmeyer's purpose is far from biographical, this letter paints a fairly full portrait of its author. It tells us that she is elderly, somewhat infirm, and intelligent—though not very well educated. This sort of information can be enormously helpful as you try to compose an answer that will best win her goodwill and that of her friends, clearly good customers all.

Adapt your letter to what your reader is like. The more solid the information you have about your correspondents, the more accurately you can put yourself in their place and the more dependable will be your analysis. If you imagine yourself elderly and infirm like Mrs. Schmidtmeyer, you can guess how she might take any suggestion of yours that she use the lavatories on the sixth floor—just three departments straight ahead from the escalators, then turn right at china, please. Your knowledge of her may also give you an idea for a solution to her problem: You could tell her that the stalls reserved for the handicapped, where the difficulty she complains of could be met, are available to the general public as well.

To go back to the case of the janitorial services, Claude Andrews might have observed that Bill Ace's company bears his name. This observation should have made him aware of the special pride Ace would take in the company's reputation. Thus Andrews might have expected a particularly strong reaction to what Ace could only view as unwarranted condemnation. Had Andrews thought about Ace in this way, he would have written a completely different letter.

Adapt your letter to what your reader knows. Base the wording of your letter on what your reader knows. When you write to those whose knowledge of your area of expertise is limited or nonexistent, avoid technical jargon altogether (see pages 43–45). If you are writing to a colleague who shares your understanding of the subject at hand, feel free to use technical terms—or even jargon—if they will convey your message efficiently. But if you are not sure your colleague completely shares your knowledge, diplomatically explain all technical terms. This approach permits you to include the information without embarrassing the reader about a lack of knowledge. It is particularly useful if you are writing to a person

The Management
Fashion Wear Department Stores
St. Louis, Missouri

Dear Sirs:

I hope I am writing to the right place for a very much needed project in your stores. One which will help the elderly ladies who come to your stores.

I hope it isn't asking too much, you know the elderly love to shop, or even just look.

Here is my problem, and I'll bet many another old gal's problem.

The toilets in your restrooms, they are so very low, almost to the floor some of them seem. And when we ladies get old and stiff in our joints, their lowness makes life harder for us.

So would it be possible to have just one or two of them replaced with a high bowl which would be more convenient. Then too maybe one larger in width, to fit a walker, many people use walkers while in town.

So many restaurants have put these high bowls in, so I have wanted to write and ask if it would be possible to put them in at your stores.

If so, I thank you very much, and I know all the old Senior Citizens will do the same.

Thanks for Listening
Sincerely,
Mrs. Blitha Schmidtmeyer

of high rank. The portion we have underlined in the following excerpt exemplifies this tactful strategy:

> ... The bill you inquired about is expected to go to <u>full committee markup</u> next Thursday. At that time--<u>when they actually draft the legislative language for final consideration</u>--they will incorporate the changes Senator Noyes's staff negotiated with our trade association representatives.

Some otherwise sophisticated business executives might be unsure about what is entailed in the legislative markup process. The approach in the sample informs tactfully, without any hint of patronizing.

PURPOSE PRINCIPLE

In every letter you are trying to get something done. Do not let lesser satisfactions—expressing your annoyance, giving vent even to a well-deserved telling-off—interfere with achieving your goal. In other words, keep your eye on the ball.

Your purpose in every business communication is twofold. One is general, the other particular:

- General purpose: to influence your reader favorably; to win goodwill for yourself and your business.
- Specific purpose: to meet the needs of the specific situation.

ALWAYS TRY TO INFLUENCE YOUR READER FAVORABLY. This cartoon may exaggerate the case a little—but only a little. Your company's business is dependent upon pleasing the people you serve. And so, although customers may not

"Here's what we'll do. We'll exchange the merchandise, refund your money, shoot the manager, and go out of business. Would you consider that a satisfactory adjustment, madam?"

actually always be right, in their own eyes they always have a case. Your treatment of them must recognize that fact. Thus, no matter what the specific purpose of your letter, one of its major goals must always be to influence your reader in a favorable way. No matter whether your message affirms or denies your correspondent's desires, your letter should make him or her think well of you and your business.

KEEP YOUR SPECIFIC PURPOSE UPPERMOST IN MIND. Before you begin your letter, ask yourself: "Just what do I want to accomplish by this letter? What do I want it to get done?" Don't be satisfied with a vague sense of purpose. Formulate your answer in actual words. It is even a good idea to write down your objectives and refer to them as you compose your letter.

If you were answering Mrs. Schmidtmeyer, you would want to suggest a practical solution to her very real problem, one necessarily not involving much company investment. You would want to keep her and her friends as satisfied customers, for you'd know full well that only stores which answered those needs would retain their patronage. If you were Claude Andrews, you would want to insure thorough cleaning in the future and obtain an extra-contractual cleaning next week.

STRATEGIES FOR WRITING EFFECTIVE BUSINESS LETTERS

The Empathetic Principle and the Purpose Principle are so powerful that they generate strategies which can be applied to *all* business-letter-writing situations. You can follow these strategies confidently:

Strategy 1: Begin with an empathetic statement.
Strategy 2: In every letter there is an ideal place to make your point. Make your point there.
Strategy 3: Relate to your reader again at the close.

Sample Letters 4A through 4G show how business writers have solved some typical problems effectively by using these strategies. The situations, as you can see, could hardly be more dissimilar. Yet each writer found an effective solution in this way.

The letters are not meant as models, but rather as samples. But you should find the strategies they use and the principles they embody useful in your own business-writing problems, however diverse.

STRATEGY 1: BEGIN WITH EMPATHY

Once you formulate your purpose, decide how you are going to approach it with your reader. Only one approach is effective in a business letter. And that is the empathetic approach. *Empathy* means "feeling with." Begin

▪ *R. G. Smith, Inc.*
◻ *Educational Software Programs* ◻ ◻ ◻
_____

1 East Liberty Bell Plaza ▪ *Boston, Massachusetts 00000-0000* ▪ *Tel.: 000 000-0000*
Fax: 000 000-0000

J. M. Woodruff   February 13, 19--
Apt. 3A
1322 West Bridge Street
Fort Lee, New Jersey 00000

Dear Woodie:

We are pleased to offer you the position of Assistant Sales
Manager for the Western Region.

Both John Paloma and Jennifer Chang were favorably impressed
with your track record and the proposals you submitted. They
appreciated your willingness to meet with them over several
weeks to work out final details.

Should you accept, we would suggest that we meet again before
the end of the month to discuss final salary and incentives, as
well as benefits and a starting date. As we have already
discussed, however, the salary range is $35 to $45M in addition
to the bonus program. The starting date will be governed both
by your own needs to give your present employer notice and our
needs to have the programs underway before September 1.

Everyone here very much hopes you will be able to accept our
offer, and we would appreciate knowing your decision by the end
of next week at the latest. I look forward to hearing from you
and hope to welcome you to R. G. Smith, Inc.

Very truly yours,

Leslie M. Klaus

Leslie M. Klaus
Director of Human Resources

LMK: lbn

SAMPLE LETTER 4A: *Good News—Offering A Job*

P.J. Jennings & Sons
Labor Consultants
800 Vine Street
St. Louis, Missouri 00000

May 22, 19—

Ms. Erica Headley
Senior Research Fellow
American Association of Demographers
1923 North Countyline Road
Boston, Massachusetts 00000

Dear Ms. Headley:

Thank you for the interesting reference notes on the growth of the
contract work force in this country since 1982. I had not, in fact,
seen that clip; and I am sure it will be useful to us as we continue
to track this issue.

I very much enjoyed meeting you and Tom Rivers during the conference
and will wait for the publication of our joint article with interest.

Certainly, I would be glad to discuss any of this company's findings
with you for inclusion in your data. Feel free to call.

Sincerely,

Jamala Jefferson

Jamala Jefferson

JJ: pz

SAMPLE LETTER 4B: *Good News—A Letter of Thanks*

■ *R. G. Smith, Inc.*
▫ *Educational Software Programs* ▫ ▫ ▫

1 East Liberty Bell Plaza   ■   _Boston, Massachusetts 00000-0000_   ■   *Tel.: 000 000-0000*
Fax: 000 000-0000

February 13, 19--

Robin Browne
1101 Lois Drive
Cincinnati, Ohio 00000

Dear Robin Browne:

    Both Jennifer Chang and John Paloma appreciated your coming
to Boston last week to meet with us and discuss our needs for
the Western Region. They were favorably impressed with both
your background and your proposed plans. In spite of all that,
however, they felt that the technical requirements of the job--
which you so forthrightly indicated were not part of your own
experience--were such that they must offer the position to the
other candidate.

    Both they and I appreciated your interest and the fine
preparation you had clearly made for your meeting with them.
We all wish you very good luck with your continued job search.

With best wishes.

Leslie M. Klaus

Leslie M. Klaus
Director of Human Resources

LMK: bb

SAMPLE LETTER 4C: *Bad News—Turning Down a Job Applicant*

ALONZO'S DEPARTMENT STORES
1 ROYALE PLAZA
HOUSTON, TEXAS 00000-0000

TEL.: 000 000-0000
FAX: 000 000-0000

Mrs Sarah Wallace   February 17, 19—
003 Longhorn Road
Dallas, Texas 00000

Dear Mrs. Wallace,

Thank you for your inquiry. Our customers sometimes misunderstand
the charges we are required to make for late payment. Because of the
way our credit policies are structured, these charges may accrue if
payment is received after the closing of the next billing cycle.

To avoid late charges in the future, I would suggest that you check
the lower left-hand corner of your statement for that closing date.
So long as a payment is received in our Dallas offices prior to that
date, no late charges will be assessed.

We have recomputed the list of figures that you sent and have found
no errors if we take into consideration the arrival of payments after
the due dates. The numbers in the third of your accounting columns
should be reexamined for calculation errors.

We trust this will answer your questions and clear up the confusion.
We appreciate your patronage.

Sincerely,

Willie Amico

Willie Amico
Manager of Credit Services

WA: n

SAMPLE LETTER 4D: *Bad News—Insisting a Customer Pay the Full Charge*

January 22, 19—

CCC
Carmen Candy
Corporation
415 North L Street
Tacoma, Washington
00000-0000
Tel.: 000 000-0000
Fax: 000 000-0000

Mr. Henry Stuyvesant
Vice President and Director of Manufacturing
Stuyvesant Spice and Essence, Inc.
10224 Del Coronado Blvd.
San Diego, California 00000

Dear Mr. Stuyvesant:

As I mentioned in my conversation with Andy Henson this morning, we value our eleven-year relationship with your firm. It has been, on the whole, free from problems.

On March 6, however, we took delivery on two drums of vanilla flavoring, which has been the source of major difficulties. According to our ordering department, our order was placed for #126 pure vanilla extract, which we have been ordering from you for more than three years. This flavoring is used only in the manufacture of our vanilla caramels.

Since putting these two drums on line, we have been getting nothing but rejected batches from our quality-control people, who have, in fact, recommended shutting down the line on this product completely. According to their test procedures, the two lines with these two drums of product feeding into them have produced <u>only</u> rejects.

I talked with your own quality-control people last week. They suggested that we send back a sample from each drum for them to test. They called this morning to say that the samples test exactly on spec with their quality-control standards.

We are, of course, running our own tests on your product, as well as on our equipment, to check for contamination here.

Nevertheless, we would like to ask that you authorize us to return the remainder of the product we have on hand and to have your people replace the two drums in question. We would also very much appreciate having one of your representatives here to confer with our production staff on site. It was my understanding from Andy Henson that an adjustment along these lines might be made.

We have never before experienced any problems with your flavorings, and we look forward to working with you to get this problem solved as expeditiously as possible. Please may I hear from you at the earliest possible time?

Very truly yours,

B. G. Girard

B. G. Girard
Manager of Production

BGG: lb

SAMPLE LETTER 4E: *A Complaint*

XYZ, Inc.
32540 Industrial Parkway
Elgin, Illinois 00000

Daniel L. MacMurray   October 17, 19--
Manager, Parts and Maintenance
Kapocketa Machine Company
Kapocketa, Wisconsin 00000

Dear Mr. MacMurray:

XYZ, Inc., has installed 33 of your Kapocketa machines since
1986. Because we operate such a large number of these machines,
our maintenance crew keeps a full line of supplies in inventory.
Last year our parts purchases exceeded $25,000.

With this sort of volume, our crew would like to have on hand a
copy of your Kapocketa Parts Manual (DIST/6666, most recent
edition).

I understand that this manual is usually provided to Kapocketa
distributors only and sold to others at $500. But since most of
our orders are factory-direct, we believe that having the full
manual readily available would expedite your procedures as well
as ours. We believe that this procedural streamlining for the
quantity of orders you process for us would warrant waiving of
the customary charge for the manual.

We feel certain that our having the manual will work to our
mutual benefit and would appreciate your sending it within the
next two weeks.

Yours truly,

Alec M. Polanski

Alec M. Polanski
Foreman
XYZ, Inc.

AMP: ss

SAMPLE LETTER 4F: *A Request*

Cola Producers Council

127 M Street, NE   Washington, DC 00000-0000   Tel.: 000 000-0000   Fax: 000 000-0000

Ms. Hannah Adams   April 26, 19—
Vice President
Squeegee Cola Corporation
6106 Kincaid Street
Chicago, Illinois 00000

Dear Ms. Adams:

    We know that in the course of the approval process, it is easy
for an invoice to be lost or set aside and a payment to be delayed.
Accordingly, we are enclosing a copy of the invoice we sent to you
four weeks ago for the annual renewal of your trade association dues.

    We are glad we have been able to serve your company over the
years, and we very much value your company's support of our programs.

    We look forward to hearing from you as soon as possible. If your
payment has been sent within the past week, please disregard this
reminder and thank you.

    If, however, I can assist you in any way to expedite approval of
the invoice, please do not hesitate to call.

Sincerely,

Henrietta Langford

Henrietta Langford

HL: cb

SAMPLE LETTER 4G: *A Request for Funds (Initial Collection Attempt)*

each letter by saying something appropriate to the matter at hand that shows you are "feeling with" the human being who is your reader. In a sentence or two, identify your interests with those of your reader. Always start with an empathetic statement. The sample letters exemplify a wide variety of purposes, but every one of them begins with an empathetic statement:

- We are pleased to offer you the position of Assistant Sales Manager for the Western Region.

  Both John Paloma and Jennifer Chang were favorably impressed with your track record and the proposals you submitted. They appreciated your willingness to meet with them over several weeks to work out final details. (Sample Letter 4A)

- Thank you for the interesting reference notes on the growth of the contract work force in this country since 1982. I had not, in fact, seen that clip; and I am sure it will be useful to us as we continue to track this issue. (Sample Letter 4B)

- Both Jennifer Chang and John Paloma appreciated your coming to Boston last week to meet with us and discuss our needs for the Western Region. They were favorably impressed with both your background and your proposed plans. (Sample Letter 4C)

- Thank you for your inquiry. (Sample Letter 4D)

- ... We value our eleven-year relationship with your firm. It has been, on the whole, free from problems. (Sample Letter 4E)

- XYZ, Inc., has installed 33 of your Kapocketa machines since 1986. Because we operate such a large number of these machines, our maintenance crew keeps a full line of supplies in inventory. Last year our parts purchases exceeded $25,000. (Sample Letter 4F)

- We know that in the course of the approval process, it is easy for an invoice to be lost or set aside and a payment to be delayed. (Sample Letter 4G)

Whatever your purpose in writing, both simple courtesy and shrewd business judgment demand that your first approach to your reader should somehow recognize your common humanity.

STRATEGY 2: FIND THE IDEAL PLACE TO MAKE YOUR POINT

When should you get to the real point of your letter? The answer varies with what you have to say. If the point of your letter makes a request of your reader or will probably disappoint, the point should follow your empathetic statement. If the request is difficult or the disappointment likely to be great, take even more care with the preliminary empathy.

But if your letter's point will please your correspondent, then your expression of the point *is itself* an empathetic statement and thus rightly comes first. For example, the opening sentence of Sample Letter 4A:

```
We are pleased to offer you the position of Assistant
Sales Manager for the Western Region.
```

Or of Sample Letter 4B:

```
Thank you for the interesting reference notes....
```

Or consider the question of timing from your reader's viewpoint:

- Would you want to wait to hear good news?
- Would you want to be bluntly confronted with the bad?

STRATEGY 3: END WITH EMPATHY

Whatever business you have transacted within your letter, relate to your reader again as human being to human being as you take your leave. The diverse letters on pages 89–95 again offer examples:

- ```
  Everyone here very much hopes you will be able to ac-
  cept our offer.... I look forward to hearing from you
  and hope to welcome you to R. G. Smith, Inc. (Sample
  Letter 4A)
  ```

- ```
  Certainly, I would be glad to discuss...with you. Feel
  free to call. (Sample Letter 4B)
  ```

- ```
  Both they and I appreciated your interest and the fine
  preparation you had clearly made for your meeting with
  them. We all wish you very good luck with your contin-
  ued job search. (Sample Letter 4C)
  ```

- ```
  We trust this will answer your questions and clear up
  the confusion. We appreciate your patronage. (Sample
  Letter 4D)
  ```

- ```
  We have never before experienced any problem with your
  flavorings, and we look forward to working with you to
  get this problem solved as expeditiously as possible.
  (Sample Letter 4E)
  ```
  ```

- We feel certain that our having the manual will work to our mutual benefit.... (Sample Letter 4F)
- If, however, I can assist you in any way to expedite approval of the invoice, please do not hesitate to call. (Sample Letter 4G)

Some communications texts call this sort of ending a "sweetener." Others discuss it in terms of "reselling." But from a psychological or human point of view, it is the final touch of empathetic approach, upon which principle all effective business writing is based.

APPLY THE PRINCIPLES

GOOD-NEWS LETTERS

To communicate good news, apply the principles and the strategies. If you were, for instance, the writer offering a job in Sample Letter 4A,[2] what would your purpose be? Your general purpose would be to create goodwill for your specific purpose. In this case, you would want to persuade your correspondent to accept the offered position. How should you go about it? Put yourself in your reader's shoes.

Would you want to wait very long to hear the news if you were getting this kind of good news? No? Well, then, start right out with it, as Leslie Klaus did in Sample Letter 4A:

Dear Woodie:

We are pleased to offer you the position of Assistant Sales Manager for the Western Region.

Continue thinking as your reader. It would be nice to know just why they decided to make the offer, wouldn't it? Even if you chose not to accept, it always makes you feel good to hear yourself sincerely praised.

Both John Paloma and Jennifer Chang were favorably impressed with your track record and the proposals you submitted. They appreciated your willingness to meet with them over several weeks to work out final details.

Should you accept....

If you were thinking about accepting, what now? Wouldn't you want some practical details?

---

2. Although in your first years in business you probably will not yourself be in a position to write such a letter over your own signature, you may well be asked to write such a letter for your supervisor to sign.

Should you accept, we would suggest that we meet again before the end of the month to discuss final salary and incentives, as well as benefits and a starting date. As we have already discussed, however, the salary range is $35 to $45M in addition to the bonus program. The starting date will be governed both by your own needs to give your present employer notice and our needs to have the programs underway before September 1.

But whether or not you choose to go with the company, you would appreciate a warm conclusion on the human level.

Everyone here very much hopes you will be able to accept our offer, and we would appreciate knowing your decision by the end of next week at the latest. I look forward to hearing from you and hope to welcome you to R. G. Smith, Inc.

Very truly yours,

THANK-YOU NOTES. Among letters always bound to please their recipients are thank-you's. By its very nature, a thank-you should fulfill the universal business communication purpose. It should establish goodwill. If we again generalize from our own feelings, we know that everyone likes to be appreciated, and most people feel they are not appreciated enough. For these very human reasons, always *write* your thanks where courtesy requires it, and don't hesitate to find other opportunities to express your gratitude. Never neglect an appreciative follow-up when you have been given a gift, been treated to a meal, or have received some other special attention or service. How to write an effective thank-you note? Apply the principles and strategies. Look back at page 90 and note how they motivate Sample Letter 4B.

Sample Letter 4B is a full-dress thank-you for some clippings that Ms. Headley and Ms. Jefferson apparently discussed at a conference and that Ms. Headley must have sent on to Ms. Jefferson when she got home. As you can see, the thank-you letter is more than just a thank-you. It can help you, as this one does Ms. Jefferson, to establish contacts—here setting up an information exchange—that may enhance your own work. Business courtesies *are* for purposes of good manners. But they also serve another practical purpose by setting up such mutually helpful networks.

BAD-NEWS LETTERS

The principles and strategies suggested here are even more important when the news your letter must impart will not be received happily by your correspondent. In all bad-news letters your job is to get across your company's position, while still offering your correspondent what satisfaction is possible.

Your ability to succeed at the universal letter-writing purpose of establishing or maintaining your reader's goodwill may sometimes be pushed to the limit. But even if your letter's purpose is disagreeable, don't lose heart. Rather, consider such letters a challenge. What should you do when you must turn down a request, issue a complaint, or disappoint a contractor, supplier, customer, or job-seeker? The answer is: Follow the principles, but follow them with additional courtesy and tact.

Sample Letter 4C, for example (page 91), turns down an applicant and still maintains goodwill and good feeling. How does it manage to do so? It follows the strategies we have suggested:

- It has an empathetic beginning and close.
- It accomplishes its purpose by sandwiching difficult information between the two.
- Its language conveys the fact that the writer identified closely enough with the reader to really understand.

These principles also help the writer of Sample Letter 4D (page 92) achieve her quite different purpose. The strategies help the writer tactfully answer a customer's complaint about a perceived overcharge. The goal in Sample Letter 4D is for the customer to (1) understand that the bill is fair and pay it, and (2) feel comfortable enough about her mistaken inquiry to continue as a satisfied customer.

HOW TO REJECT WITHOUT REJECTING. In writing such letters, the trick is to discover an approach that permits the correspondent to accept a rejection without losing self-esteem. The following Guidelines offer techniques that you may find helpful.

■■■■■■■■■■■■■■■■■■■■■■■■■■■■■ **GUIDELINES** ■■■■■■■■■

Bad-News Letters

1. Bad-news letters, by their nature, disappoint and reject. But make the rejection as impersonal as possible. Separate your reader's personal qualities from the reason for the rejection. *It's the match that's wrong, not the applicant. Though the bill must be paid, the customer is not at fault.* (Sample Letter 4C insists that Robin Browne did not lose out because of any personal defects, but because of a lack of technical experience. Sample Letter 4D implicitly commends Sarah Wallace for her intelligent inquiry.)

2. When the rejection *is* based directly on the reader's qualities, make sure that you mention something that can be mended. And keep the door open—at least a crack—in case the desired change takes place. For example:

- As much as we admire your company's work, the close connection of one of our important clients with the AFL mandates our employing only firms with a union shop.

- We appreciate your bid. However, the nature of our business necessitates occasional overtime work.

- Should your policy change, we would welcome another bid.

3. Sometimes personally identifying with your reader involves taking an impersonal line. Praise is more pleasing when it is personal (for instance, the phrase: "which you so forthrightly indicated" in Sample Letter 4C). Criticism, however, is more acceptable when it is diffuse. In Sample Letter D, for instance, the writer makes the correspondent more comfortable (note the portion we have underlined) by identifying her with a general lack of understanding on the subject:

- Thank you for your inquiry. <u>Our customers sometimes misunderstand</u> the charges we are required to make for late payment.

Ordinarily you should resist passive constructions, as we caution in Chapter 2. Nevertheless, the generality of passive syntax can sometimes help when you want to avoid saying, "You have made a mistake." For example, in Sample Letter 4D:

- The numbers in the third of your accounting columns <u>should be reexamined</u> for calculation errors.

4. You could also follow the well-known formula for Bad-News Letters: Sandwich the bad news between two slices of good. But that's just another way of saying put disappointing information *after* your empathetic opening and *before* your empathetic close.

Why bother? You may be thinking: Why go to all this bother? No reason to be needlessly cruel, but what's the point in worrying so much about how we turn people down? The answer is that your letters can have ramifications far beyond the immediate situation. Circumstances change and memories are long. Sample Letter 4C's Robin Browne—or a friend or a cousin—may one day become *the* expert that all the companies in the field are vying for. Or Robin Browne may head, or be a decision-maker within, a firm with which your company would very much want to do business or even where you personally might seek employment. The customer whose complaints you turn down or whose claims you are unable to adjust today may well be in a position to give important favors or withhold them from your company tomorrow. So, quite aside from the personal satisfaction you will gain from turning your reader down as painlessly as possible, there are sound business reasons for you to do so.

COMPLAINTS. If there are shrewd reasons to empathize with those correspondents whose services or ideas or selves you must reject, there are even more pragmatic reasons to deal empathetically with those correspondents whose work you must criticize or complain about. In these equally unwelcome letters your purpose is to ameliorate the situation you are criticizing. You may even hope for help from these correspondents. If you review the problems of Claude Andrews and Bill Ace, presented earlier in this chapter, you will see that following the principles is especially important in letters of complaint. Sample Letter 4E, a written confirmation of a telephone conversation (page 93), is a complaint letter that works well. Why is this letter effective?

- B. G. Girard empathizes with the position of the reader-supplier, and, without recrimination, understands that both parties will benefit by getting the problem settled expeditiously.
- Clearly and unemotionally, Girard explains exactly what happened and what has been done about it.
- The letter does not blame. Girard presents the evidence fairly but makes the tacit assumption that it is the vanilla which is causing the problem.
- Since this assumption has not yet been conclusively proved, Girard requests replacement tactfully.
- The letter's opening and the conclusion offer both a friendly approach based upon longtime profitable association and a latent incentive for satisfactory solution of the problem.

REQUEST LETTERS

All business letters are, in a manner of speaking, request letters—since all business letters are written to someone to get something done. But some business letters make requests overtly. In such letters, it is even more important to establish a mutuality of interest with your reader. When you are making a request, it is not enough to empathize with your correspondent's situation; you need to show why it is in your correspondent's interest to empathize with yours. In Sample Letter 4F, for instance (page 94), Alec Polanski's chances of getting his request granted are good. Polanski puts the principles into action. First, knowing himself and understanding the value of being addressed by name, he went to the trouble to find the name of the parts manager. (Names of key personnel are almost always available from the company switchboard operator.) Then, in his empathetic opening, he reminded Daniel MacMurray of the long and profitable association of their firms.

In the next paragraph he comes right to the point and states his request specifically. He does not risk being misunderstood. Finally, in approaching the more delicate part of his petition, the waiving of the fee, he looks at the situation through MacMurray's eyes and puts his request in terms of Kapocketa's benefit as well as his own. (See the sidebar.)

REQUESTS FOR PAYMENT. Collection letters are particularly unpleasant request letters to receive because they ask for money. The trick, then, is to make your initial request for payment sound as little like a collection letter as possible. And even the first follow-up letter should assume the correspondent's good intentions. Sample Letter 4G (page 95) is an effective example. In this letter Ms. Langford empathizes with her correspondent and simultaneously offers both a graceful excuse for the delayed payment and a solid reason for including another bill:

> We know that in the course of the approval process it is easy for an invoice to be lost or set aside and a payment to be delayed. Accordingly, we are enclosing a copy of the invoice....

In the second paragraph she identifies her reader's interest with her own as she points out the mutual benefit of their association. Only later, in the third paragraph, does she get to her point, carefully including an apology—in case even this gentle dunning had been unnecessary. In the last paragraph, she concludes with a helpfully courteous and empathetic close.

How can you make your request letters effective? How can you better the chances that your correspondent will accede to your requests? The

---

Psychological Rhetoric

The psychologist Carl Rogers has added modern psychological insights to the question of writer-reader relationships. Rogers advises us to reach readers through those areas where agreement might be worked out, to try for some commonality of ideas as a start. He writes:

> Mutual communication . . . leads to a situation in which I see how the problem appears to you, as well as to me, and you see how it appears to me as well as to you.*

---

*"Communication: Its Blocking, Its Facilitation," in *On Becoming a Person* (Boston: Houghton Mifflin, 1961), 336.

following Guidelines, derived from the principles, provide some practical help.

━━━━━━━━━━━━━━━━━━━━━━━━━━ **GUIDELINES** ━━━━━━━━

Request Letters

- Keep your purpose in mind, and approach it empathetically.
- Show why fulfilling your request is in your reader's interest.
- Ask. Don't demand (even if you've got the leverage—certainly not otherwise).
- If you have reason to think there may be opposition to your request, begin with areas of agreement. (See the sidebar on psychologist Carl Rogers, page 103.)
- Be clear and specific in describing what you want your correspondent to do. You don't want to miss out just because he or she isn't sure exactly what you want and doesn't want to bother with another exchange of letters to find out.

━━━━━━━━━━━━━━ **LETTER WORKOUT** ━━━━━━━━━━━━

The models in this chapter are typical of business letters, but the number we could include is necessarily limited. So we urge you to examine some other business letters that you or business friends of yours have received.

1. Select at least two such business letters. (Try to choose letters that differ in purpose.) Evaluate them by deciding for each:
   a. If I were the recipient of this letter, how likely would I be:
      - To do what the writer suggests?
      - To adopt the writer's thinking on the subject?
      Why?
   b. How does this letter influence my opinion of the writer and/or the company he or she represents?
      Does it increase my goodwill?
      Why or why not?
2. Analyze each letter to see if the writer employed the three letter-writing strategies. If not, could you make the letter more effective by employing the strategies to revise? How?

USING THE STRATEGIES

However complicated or delicate the situation—and many business problems *are* complicated or delicate—the strategies outlined here will see you through. Keep in mind the cautionary things we told you in Chapter 2 about never offending. Then remember to:

- Begin with empathy.
- Consider carefully at what place in your letter you should make your point.
- End with empathy and courtesy.

Your letter should then accomplish the thing you are trying to get done. When you get it done smoothly again and again, your supervisors will notice and will be impressed with your skill.

AUTHENTIC BUSINESS PROBLEMS

Let's begin this series of exercises by editing letters already written and then proceed to the more difficult task of drafting fresh material.

1. Edit business letters effectively.
   a. Revise Claude Andrews's letter to William Ace (pages 81–82) so that Andrews can achieve his objective.
   b. You are a travel agent for a large concern. There has been a foul-up in the reservations for a nationally advertised, expensive African safari trip. You have been assigned to write those passengers whose accommodations must be changed. You have written the following draft. But as you read it over, it seems negative to you. Think carefully about what you want to achieve by the letter. And rewrite to give it a more positive thrust.

Dear Mr. and Mrs. Brady:

I am writing to those customers whose checks for the Cameroon Camera Safari have been received only in the last three weeks. I am sorry to tell you that a number of the accommodations pictured in our brochure are unable to accept any more reservations.

However, if you are still willing to take the trip, I can suggest some alternative accommodations. The Biltonian has canceled your room, but we could put you up at the Coastal Hotel, which may not have quite as good views of the bay but is still supposed to be pretty nice. Similarly, the Yaounde Plaza has over-booked, but the Yaounde Villa is willing to take a few of our travelers. Actually, you'll be so tired after you return from the Cameroon Mountain excursion that any bed should satisfy you.

There may also be some shift in flight scheduling. But don't worry. We will keep you informed.

We hope you will not cancel your Safari plans.

Yours for worry-free journeys,

c. Put yourself in the shoes of K. L. Irate, an executive with City-ton (Illinois) Gas and Electric. Since 1974, you and your family have had a charge account with Apparelers, which you consider the finest department store in Cityton. Your relations with the store have been satisfactory during this time; and, in fact, you find the telephone-ordering feature of the charge account particularly useful.

But last January you were billed instead of credited for a knit hat from Aunt Tillie that you returned after Christmas. Your note on the statement stub, which should have rectified the mistake and subtracted $24.95 (plus tax) from your bill, led rather to the addition of *another* $24.95 charge. When you subsequently withheld $49.90 from your otherwise full monthly payment, you got a series of dunning letters that culminated in a threat to cut off your charging privileges and turn the account over to a collection agency.

In May, business takes you to Chicago, where the Apparelers chain has its central office. Before your appointments, you call Apparelers' office and ask to speak to your correspondents in this matter. But you are put on hold, and after what seems an interminable wait, you are told that the parties "haven't come in yet." Naturally, you are angry and, in a white heat, you write the following letter:

```
                                        May 7, 19—
                                        Acct. #4172.734A


Apparelers Department Stores
P.O. Box 789
Chicago, Illinois 60606

To Whom It May Concern:

It is about time some of the so-called managers with
this company get off their collective rear-ends and
start taking care of customers. I am one customer who
will never do business with Apparelers again.

On Friday, May 5, I called from Cityton and left a
message for Mr. Jones to call me Friday P.M. or Mon-
day A.M. He never did. I called again from Chicago
when I got off the plane at 9:10 on Wednesday and was
told that neither Mr. Jones nor Ms. Sanders nor any
other manager was in so early.

Until such time as I either receive a phone call or,
better still, get a letter telling when these "prize"
executives are in, I am not sending you one dime to
correct an account that you screwed up!

K.L. Irate
P.O. Box 123
```

```
Cityton, Illinois 60066
(555) 717-7864

cc: Mr. Jones
    Ms. Sanders
    Apparelers' President (if he works)
```

This letter (which is, by the way, a real one, with only names and key facts changed to protect the guilty) may have given you a chance to vent some well-justified anger, but it needs thorough editing before it can help you accomplish your ends.

2. Write effective business letters.

a. Write a letter answering Mrs. Bertha Schmidtmeyer's complaint (page 86).

b. The Chairman of your Board has been invited to become Honorary Chair of the County Cure Vicious Diseases Campaign. If he accepts, he will be given a plaque at a dinner in his honor and be named County "Man of the Year."

    He has no inclination to accept either the honor or the obligation (he is already heavily committed to other charities) and has asked you—as his aide—to write a tactful refusal.

c. Let's reverse the scenario posited in Problem 1c. This time you are not K. L. Irate, the writer of that angry—but authentic—letter. You are instead the trainee in the Public Relations Department of the home office of Apparelers Department Stores who has been asked to reply to it. Your supervisor put a copy of Irate's letter on your desk.

    Responding to the undisguised antagonism of that letter, you find yourself becoming indignant. A call to the Delinquent Accounts Department only increases your indignation when you are told: "Irate? Let me look him up. Oh, that's the guy in Cityton. He's owed us $37.70 since Christmas. We're about to give up on him." But just before you blast off a letter in kind to Mr. Irate, something tells you to make one more check, so you call Customer Records. There you find out that the Irates have been charge customers in good standing since 1974, with an average yearly expenditure of about $6,500.

    This, then, is your assignment:

(i) Explain: What, precisely, do you want to accomplish by your letter to K. L. Irate?

(ii) Write a letter which will help you accomplish those aims.

d. Or, if your own business currently requires you to write a problematic letter, take advantage of this assignment:

(i) Write the letter according to the principles suggested in this text.

(ii) Write a brief memo to your instructor, explaining the problem that initiated the letter and showing how your letter solves it.

WRITING EFFECTIVE BUSINESS LETTERS: SPECIAL CASES

EXECUTIVE SUMMARY

You can write effective sales and international correspondence by following the principles and strategies that apply to all business letters. But these kinds of letters demand some extra finesse.

Sales Letters

In writing sales letters you run into the paradox of having to empathize personally with an unknown person. You can surmount this difficulty if you:

■ Investigate the demographic groups to which your customers belong and try to understand the people in these groups by thorough research.

■ Then personalize your letters. Make them fit the recipients. Give them a human voice.

To write a sales letter, modify the traditional three-part structure. Its empathetic opening should get the reader's attention and interest. Its point, the presentation of your product or service, should awaken the reader's desire. Its empathetic close involves the reader and calls on him or her to take action.

International Correspondence

When you write to foreign readers, you face a similar problem. Differences in language, culture, and values can prevent you from accurately anticipating your readers' response.

What can you do?

■ Research, for information is power.

■ Be sensitive to the norms of each reader's culture.

■ Investigate *before* you communicate.

The principles and strategies outlined in Chapter 4 should help you compose an effective letter in any business situation. Nevertheless, there are two kinds of business correspondence where these strategies and principles need to be applied in specialized ways: sales letters and international correspondence. This chapter will consider these special kinds of writing.

SECTION A: *Sales Letters*

In one sense, most business letters are sales letters. Whatever you write to a potential customer, for instance, may help or hinder sales. Even an answer to an information request should make your company's goods and services seem desirable. And all sales letters are based upon the principles we advocate in this text. Nevertheless, direct-mail sales strategy is a special science beyond the scope of this text. Marketing departments or outside agencies usually handle sales campaigns of any magnitude.

This text does not attempt to deal comprehensively with written sales communication. However, the following discussion should help you to write the occasional sales letter you may be assigned, as well as to participate in and evaluate wider sales campaigns.

THE SALES LETTER PARADOX

Sales letters are, of course, request letters: when you write one, you request that your reader purchase your product or service. Everything we have said about writing request letters applies to sales letters. These are more difficult to write, however, because it may be harder for you to establish mutual interest. And the whole point of sales letters is to show your correspondents that buying your product or service is in their interest.

To meet this challenge, remember the principles and strategies—though they are more difficult to apply in this context too. You, the writer, must empathize with your individual correspondents. However, sales letters are typically written not to particular individuals but to members of groups. The problem, though, suggests its own solutions:

1. *Select your recipients carefully* and learn all you can about their group so that you can make even a mass mailing personal to some degree. The more solid the information you have about your prospects, the more effective your letter will be.
2. *Personalize your letter* in every way you can: make the message fit the reader; give the sender a human voice.

SELECTING THE RECIPIENTS OF YOUR SALES LETTER

The best list—made up of prospects most likely to be interested and prospects you know most about—is a list of those who are already your customers or clients.

If you are to go beyond that list, even with a letter intended only to expand it, you need to consult experienced opinion. Speak to an expert if possible. At least, look up what you need to know in a good reference work. Two good ones are:

- Richard S. Hodgson, *The Dartnell Direct Mail and Mail Order Handbook,* 3d ed. (Chicago: The Dartnell Corp., 1980), 1538 pages. This book, which includes a full bibliography of reference works, an address list of 22 direct-marketing associations, and an 18-page annotated bibliography of principal business directories, is a comprehensive collection of the available information on direct mail.
- Ed Burnett, *The Complete Direct Mail List Handbook: Everything You Need to Know About Lists and How to Use Them for Greater Profit* (Englewood Cliffs, N.J.: Prentice-Hall, 1988), 744 pages. This text, which is limited to material about finding and using mailing lists, is accurately summed up by its subtitle.

PERSONALIZING YOUR SALES LETTER

KNOW YOUR MAILING LIST. Social scientists have extensively researched the size, growth, density, distribution, vital statistics, and other demographic characteristics of various human populations. They also have studied these populations psychologically and have accumulated considerable information, which they term "psychographic" data. Such material is available to commercial enterprises.

Once you have determined the particular list of potential customers or clients you will address in your sales letter, carefully study the demographic and psychographic characteristics of the groups they represent. When you have done so, you may want to break down a too-diverse list into categories of reasonably homogeneous people. For example, you might want to break down a list of new homeowners by locale, by age, by income, or by the presence or absence of children and to compose a different letter for each new group.

Pay attention to the implications of such demographic information when you make your marketing decisions on:

- Number of mailings in a series.
- Length of letters. (Research shows a wide diversity of optimum lengths; the length you choose should be governed by demographic and psychographic factors.)
- Quality and color of paper. (Would your group be favorably enough impressed by high quality to make it worth the price? Would they think expensive paper wasteful?)
- Type of print or ink.
- Color. (Would color add persuasiveness? Which color or colors?)
- Enclosures. (What kind?)

You can find an impressive array of market research to help guide you in making these specific decisions and similar ones. There is scarcely a group you could choose to correspond with that has not been studied.

WRITE TO AN INDIVIDUAL CUSTOMER OR CLIENT. Consider your research data and try to understand the people on your mailing lists thoroughly. But remember that your letter will be read not by a group but by a single individual. And so try to imagine an individual from the group and empathize with him or her as you compose your letter.

What is she like? What are his ambitions? What are her problems? What are his needs? How can your product or service help to achieve these ambitions, solve these problems, meet these needs? What does she need to know about your product or service that will help her understand that it can help her? The writer of Sample Letter 5A successfully answered these questions for the presidents of newly incorporated small businesses.

An analysis of Sample Letter 5A: Why it works. Why would Washington's letter be successful? He is selling a service, an especially difficult task because it is intangible and depends heavily on reputation. But his thoughtful approach in providing the kinds of advice a corporate client might not have without professional guidance is a powerful selling technique.

What strategies does Washington employ? He has selected as his correspondents presidents of new, small corporations who may well be needing services like this. Understanding that his correspondents may be somewhat overwhelmed by the tangled and changing array of tax law, he begins by presenting, as a sort of gift sample, information many of his correspondents might find useful. He follows up with another free offer that, if accepted, will bring the correspondents into his office. The letter works because it is so closely tailored to the particular needs of the readers.

WRITE PERSONALLY TO YOUR INDIVIDUAL CUSTOMER OR CLIENT. Personalizing also means that you write a sales letter as if it were part of a private correspondence between you and your prospective customer or client. The letter should not sound like a pitch addressed to a crowd. Your study of the

J.D. Horton & Company
1918 Maisie Drive
Milwaukee, Wisconsin 00000-0000

January 10, 19--

Cynthia Morris, President
Lyle and Morris, Inc.
3404 Observatory Lane
Milwaukee, Wisconsin 00000

Dear Corporate President,

As a new corporation, you will be required to file several annual tax returns. Two filing deadlines which you should be aware of are:

   1. Personal Property Tax Return. This return must be filed within ninety (90) days of your incorporation. There can be a large penalty if this return is not filed on time.
   2. Election to be an S-Corporation. This election must generally be filed within two and one-half (2-1/2) months of incorporation. This is an important election to consider, since the right choice could save much tax expense.

If you would like our firm to assist you with your tax matters, please call our office closest to you to arrange an appointment. We will provide one-half hour of consultation at no charge. Our accountants have many years' experience in business tax preparation as well as in helping businesses structure their financial affairs to provide the largest tax savings.

We would be happy to meet with you and provide assistance to your new corporation.

Yours truly,

Steven L. Washington

Steven L. Washington, CPA

SLW: na

SAMPLE SALES LETTER 5A: *Addressing a Particular Need*

available demographic and psychographic information on the members of your mailing list and your imaginative identification with an individual correspondent should help you find the right tone in which to write.

Let's examine another effective sales letter, Sample Letter 5B, from this point of view.

An analysis of Sample Letter 5B: Why it works. F. J. Bookbinder begins by including Loft in an exclusive group. In doing so he flatters: "We wouldn't be writing to just anyone" is strongly implied. He also personalizes the letter, perhaps taking Loft beyond the urge to discard triggered by "Pre-SORT" on the envelope. And, by presumably including himself and his company also within the exclusive group, he may kindle the empathetic oneness of interest he aims for. There is a more subtle flattery here too. Conventional thinking has it that "Everybody is doing it" advertising has strong appeal. But the same research that identified Loft as a longtime subscriber to *Egghead Review* gave Bookbinder to understand that such subscribers could be stoutly unconventional in this respect.

Bookbinder also imagines *Egghead Review* subscribers as likely to be tempted by an opportunity to be among the first to read well-reviewed books. The central appeal of the letter plays on this desire, by offering the pleasure and then making it financially attractive. He concludes by giving his reader a plan of action. And even that is personalized. He gives Loft a second chance to order, figuring in both general human absentmindedness and the preoccupation that a busy, thoughtful intellectual might be subject to.

MAKE YOUR READER EMPATHIZE WITH YOU. You can make empathy work both ways. Where it is appropriate, you can address your reader in a personal way and have him or her identify with you as one human being to another. Take, for example, Sample Letter 5C, a letter the John Plain mail-order-catalog company used successfully to entice orders from former customers.[1]

An analysis of Sample Letter 5C: Why it works. Hale's John Plain letter is effective primarily because it reads as if the recipient is a treasured friend. Hale begins by getting his reader to commiserate with an experience most of us have shared, having to work late all alone. He then explains his problem, using the homey bread-and-butter metaphor. He seems like such a nice fellow that most readers will wish him well in solving his dilemma. And so when he suggests that he and the reader could solve it together, the reader is favorably disposed toward him and his predicament.

The paragraph about searching for the reader's order is a nice touch. With it Hale manages to suggest both his special interest in the reader and his amazement that the reader could have gone so long without an order.

---

1. John Plain letter, Bankers Life excerpt on page 119, and American Heritage excerpt on page 121 from *The Dartnell Direct Mail and Mail Order Handbook,* 3d ed. Copyright © 1980 by the Dartnell Corporation. Reprinted by permission.

F. J. Bookbinder
SmartBooks, Inc.
Garden City, New Jersey 00000-0000

October 14, 19—

Mr. Samuel J. Loft
1023 Ivorytower Drive
San Francisco, California

Dear Mr. Loft:

Not everybody is interested in the kind of books we publish—serious, scholarly works on history, politics, and economics. We believe, however, that you are, because we know that you have been a subscriber to <u>Egghead Review</u> for more than five years.

The enclosed list of newly published works includes four that have already received major and favorable reviews by <u>The Wall Street Journal</u>, <u>The New York Times</u>, <u>Foreign Policy Magazine</u>, and the <u>British Journal of Economics</u>.

Our special introductory offer will give you two of these important titles for the price of one. And the price for that one is the publisher's price of 40% off.

If, as we have supposed, you like to be just one step behind the reviews in reading new works of this kind, we hope you will send the enclosed order card before this offer expires on May 31. After that date, the first-book discount will be 20%, but the books will be just as timely, just as provocative for seminal thinkers.

Sincerely,

F. J. Bookbinder

F. J. Bookbinder
SmartBooks, Inc.

FJB: ns

John Plain

JOHN PLAIN & COMPANY • 444 W. WASHINGTON STREET • CHICAGO 60606

Please forgive me for not addressing this to you personally — too little time.
D. H.

Dear Friend and Customer:

I'm sitting here in my office — long after everyone else has gone home — wrestling with a problem, and I need your help.

I'm trying to stretch the dollars that my boss has allowed me for publishing our handsome new John Plain book far enough to send one to every one of our customers — but it doesn't appear as though I'm going to make it. It's sort of like trying to make the butter come out even with the bread.

I have a list before me that has your name on it, but it tells me that you have not placed an order in over a year. I've tried to find your name elsewhere on the list, perhaps at another address, showing you've ordered, but so far no luck.

So there's my problem . . . and here is my solution.

If I want you to have the new 700-page John Plain Catalog next August when it comes off the press, the two of us must find a way to do so.

If you will send me an order — <u>just one</u> — in the next sixty days, <u>I can send you that catalog</u>, and I've had an order form printed with your name and customer number, just to make it easier for you.

If you'll do your part, I'll do mine.

Will you send me that one order (and to my attention, please) so that I can put a green check after your name and send you your 19— John Plain Book?

Sincerely,

Denzell Hale

Denzell Hale
Circulation Manager

P.S. If you've ordered from us recently, please disregard this letter — you <u>will</u> be getting your catalog. (But save the order form and use it for your next order.)

DH: sm

SAMPLE SALES LETTER 5C: *Using a Personal Voice*

This paragraph reinforces the intimacy of the first one and of the hand-written note hastily scrawled in the top margin.

The tone of a personal relationship established in the letter's beginning continues into the action paragraphs. Hale says he's had an order form specially printed in the customer's name and urges him or her to send the order to his particular attention. Notice how specifying the color green lends credence to the letter. "I know I can trust this company; Hale will expedite my order himself—with his green pen."

The intimacy makes the easy action—just one order and the filled-out form already supplied—seem easier still. Hale does not neglect the "what's in it for me" factor: the customer will get a new catalog by taking this action. But he constructs the letter so effectively that this factor hardly matters in the end. Many of Hale's readers will be feeling they want to take the action just to help him out and have him place that green check mark after their names.

EXTERNAL PERSONALIZING DEVICES

The best sales letters read as if they were a personal communication with the reader, a difficult achievement on a large scale. But, perhaps paradoxically, technology has provided means to humanize and personalize sales letters meant for mass mailings.

AUTOTYPE. Automatic typewriters produce multiple letters indistinguishable from those individually typed. This process involves some secretarial time to set up the individualized letter and thus can be expensive. But if your list is limited, individualizing can also be remarkably successful. American Mail Advertising (Waltham, Massachusetts) cites the example of a college alumni association that used autotyped letters to solicit for membership 400 alumni who had not been in touch since their graduation; 80 joined by return mail. Another membership organization's form letter to 16,000 business executives had over a period of years run its course. The last mailing had produced only one new membership. But when the organization sent an automatically typed letter to 500 of those who had already turned it down, it received $8000 in new memberships.[2]

COMPUTER PERSONALIZATION. Computer-personalized letters are useful when your solicitation is large-scale. This technique permits you to personalize a form letter by inserting, where appropriate, such items as the reader's own name and hometown or college or other demographic details. Such letters go a long way toward solving the paradox of the sales letter: the need to establish a person-to-person empathy in a communication sent to hundreds (or thousands) of strangers. Personalized letters seem to speak

---

2. Examples from American Mail Advertising's pamphlet quoted in Hodgson, *The Dartnell Direct Mail and Mail Order Handbook*, page 693.

individually to each recipient. Even if you write the same letter to each addressee and change nothing but the address and salutation, you have the beginning, at least, of personal contact.

Some critics, however, believe that such letters have been overused. Still, they have achieved results. Professionals in the field agree almost unanimously that, in the words of Ed Burnett, owner of a successful direct-mail business: "As long as human beings value their own names and their own activities, computerized, personalized pieces will be a continuing and increasing part of the mail flow."[3]

Some caveats. Nevertheless, certain computer-personalizing practices can be counterproductive. So we would caution you to:

- Use personalizations *only* where you would naturally do so in an individually written letter. Your aim is to simulate personal correspondence, to make each reader feel you are writing directly to him or her, not to show off the capabilities of your computer.
- Keep your style warm and human. In computerized letters especially, avoid mechanized, clichéd diction.
- Be sure your personalized information is accurate and consistent. Your letter will not succeed if, for instance, it misspells the recipient's name or town or gets the gender of the pronouns wrong.

MERGE MAIL. Merge mail describes letters that look as though they had been individually written and addressed but are really one letter, personalized or particularized by a computer program. This technique, which is standard on many word-processing programs, is an invaluable tool for mass mailings.

After you draft your letter, individualize it by *merging* items from a separate list into the "shell" letter you have created. You would make one list, for example, of the full names and addresses of prospective customers. Follow the directions of your merge mail software, and most such program features will fill in the designated slots to personalize the letter.

You may wonder what efficiency is gained by typing this material on a separate list. After all, one typing is the same as another, you might think. The efficiency comes with the program's automatic insertion. Instead of you or your secretary taking the time to find the appropriate slots in your shell letter, the program automatically fills them.

Furthermore, merge mail permits you to address the recipient by name internally and to fill designated slots with other personal data. For example:

---

3. *The Complete Direct Mail List Handbook,* pages 81–82.

```
And, Mrs. Jones, we fully understand the discomfort of a
Texas summer, and that is why we are writing you about
our special offer.
```

```
And, Mrs. Brown, we fully understand the discomfort of
an Alabama summer, and that is why....
```

Note how effectively Bankers Life and Casualty Company used information from automobile purchase lists to personalize this award-winning merged-mail letter:

```
You've read how hospital costs in the _____ [recipient's
city] area have been skyrocketing--as they have all over
the country. The American Hospital Association says that
the average cost of just a single day in _____ (recipi-
ent's locale: city, county or state] hospitals is now
more than $_____ [actual amount]--and going up!...
```

```
It's a dangerous financial situation to be in, _____ [re-
cipient]--especially if you're buying your new _____
[make of car] on time, or have other financial obliga-
tions that you'd find hard to handle if you also had to
shell out money for hospital bills.
```

The following are practical hints for using merge mail:

- *Pay close attention to how you set up the slots in your base letter.* Your sentences need to read smoothly whatever lists you merge with it. Notice, for instance, that in the Mrs. Jones/Mrs. Brown example the base-letter slot leaves room for, and the fill-in includes, the article *a* or *an*. This detail permits the natural insertion of "a Texas summer" or "an Alabama summer" into the sentence.
- *Proofread your fill-in list before merging.* You may know some details unknown to the list typist. You would, for instance, find it embarrassing if the list of names automatically generated a "Dear Mr. Smith:" salutation for an old friend of the family, whom you've always known as Jim. Or the list typist might logically type a *Mr.* in front of *Bradford Blayne*, whom you know to be a woman. It is easier to proof and amend the list than to correct the letter later.
- *Proofread the merge letters themselves.* Never send the letters out without checking them, and don't leave the checking job to somebody else. In some cases, you may want to reedit. But even in a sales mass mailing, strange things can happen to lists. For instance,

every so often your list may include a name with a *Jr.* after it; and unless your matrix and list have been adjusted for that factor, you can end up with a letter whose salutation reads absurdly: "Dear Mr. Combs, Jr.:"

STRUCTURING YOUR SALES LETTER

When it comes to structure, successful sales letters are again both like and unlike other effective business letters. Like all business letters, successful sales letters must begin with an empathetic opening, follow up with a strong presentation of the point, and conclude with an empathetic close. But in sales letters the thrust of each portion is sharpened and in some measure changed. Your sales letter aims to:

- Attract your correspondent's interest.
- Motivate a desire for your product or service.
- Stimulate action.

This purpose translates into the three-part structure of the business letter. Your letter's empathetic opening gets and holds your prospective customer's attention and gains the goodwill needed to awaken customer interest in your product or service. When you present your point—the features of your product or service that will fit your customer's needs—your aim is to arouse desire for that product or service. And in your empathetic close, instead of again expressing your identification with your reader, you aim to identify and involve your reader with what you have to sell. To achieve involvement, you offer some action for your customer to take, an action that precedes and anticipates commitment.

Let's discuss each of these parts of your letter in more detail.

ATTRACT THE READER'S INTEREST

To make your sales letter succeed, you need to take great care with the initial empathetic approach. Here you do not have the advantage of the instant reader attention that an individually addressed letter usually provides. Consequently, you have to strive to gain your reader's attention and the sense that you have something to say that will be in his or her personal interest to read. How? Here are some of the strategies business has found effective:

FOCUS ON A SINGLE CHARACTERISTIC. Your preliminary research on the group addressed has identified at least one characteristic that should make its members a good market for your product or service. Approach your readers through that characteristic. It might be a time of life. Your letter could begin: "Congratulations on your graduation" or "Welcome to the new little person in your life." Note how F. J. Bookbinder plays on the characteristic of intellectual independence in Sample Letter 5B:

```
Not everybody is interested in the kind of books we pub-
lish--serious, scholarly works on history, politics, and
economics. We believe, however, that you are, because we
know that you have been a subscriber to Egghead Review
for more than five years.
```

INVOLVE YOUR READER THROUGH A QUESTION. The question might be one that engages the reader's curiosity. For instance: "Have you ever wondered what the real difference is between genuine and cultured pearls?" (to sell cultured pearls). Or use a question that involves your reader in a personal way. For example: "While shoveling out from the latest snowstorm, have you given any thought to the Bahamian sands?" (for a letter selling tropical cruises).

START WITH AN INTRIGUING THOUGHT. Gain your reader's interest through a striking image, a seeming paradox, or a witty allusion. The American Heritage Publishing Company, for instance, attracted prospective buyers for a volume on architecture with this opening paragraph:

```
If your house is much more than a century old, the odds
are its bathrooms are an afterthought--because its build-
ers knew that "if a person should bathe in warm water
every day, debility would inevitably follow."
```

TRY HUMOR OR AN INTRODUCTORY ANNOUNCEMENT. But exercise caution. A genuinely funny opening can work for you because almost everyone likes to laugh. But if you try for humor, be sure that most of your readers will consider what you say funny. Unappreciated wit can backfire. What is comic to one person may be offensive or even painful to another.

Similarly, announcements of a striking development in your product or service, of a sale, or of a new product all make for good openings. But such announcements can also arouse a bored "so what?" Thus if you choose to begin in this way, quickly establish empathy with your reader. Write, for example:

```
I'm proud to be able to announce _____ and to notify you,
an especially valued customer, of your opportunity to....
```

```
We are pleased to announce the private sale of a deluxe
limited edition of....
```

```
Reserved for you--the new _____, which you will find par-
ticularly useful in your favorite hobby....
```

MOTIVATE CUSTOMER DESIRE

Having gained your readers' attention and interest, arouse their desire for your product or service. To sell them, you must convince your readers that they need or would benefit by what you are offering. And you must persuade them to overcome their natural skepticism and the human inertia that could make them discard your letter rather than take the steps necessary to acquire your product or service. Again, the personal touch is essential. Your research has shown you why this particular group would find your product or service useful. Your letter's job is to convince them that what you have to sell is useful. Here are some approaches that have proved effective:

- *Focus on one benefit* and show why it would help your *particular* reader. (In selling a vacation in Florida, for instance, you might emphasize sun and relaxation for hard-driving executives, supervised swimming for parents of young children, and opportunities to meet people for single adults.) You might briefly mention other advantages in a follow-up paragraph. Sample Letter 5A, from the CPA, uses this strategy effectively when it concentrates on the tax problems sure to trouble executives of newly established businesses. Sample Letter 5B refers openly to this strategy:

  ```
  If, as we have supposed, you like to be just one
  step behind the reviews in reading new works of
  this kind ...
  ```

- *Describe the product or service in a way that stimulates customer desire.* Be vivid in your language. And, where it is appropriate, use words that appeal to the reader's senses. Harry and David, successful mail-order fruit merchants, for example, write:

  ```
  Have you ever seen a pear you had to eat with a
  spoon?
  ```

Instead of just saying your product is beautiful, use words that will show your reader that it is indeed beautiful (as, for instance, in this entry adapted from the Rose & Gerard Mail Order Catalogue, Mill Valley, California):

```
Whether this terra cotta pitcher is filled with
lemonade or fresh-cut daffodils, its earthy
tones add warmth to a table and serve as a foil
to rich, bright colors.
```

- *Anticipate and answer reader objections.* Some customer needs are almost universal. For instance, most new babies need special equipment and special food. Most homeowners need help with repairs and refurbishing. In such cases, your problem is not so much convincing prospective customers of their desire for your product or service as making them sure of their safety in using it. If you are offering a handy-person service, for example, you need to address the home-owner's not unfounded fears of the unfamiliar. You would do well to offer evidence that you are not a fly-by-night concern that will take the money and run, that your workers will not make off with the silverware, and that your paint job won't hang in peelings a week or two later. But you should convince them in a positive rather than a negative way. One enterprising concern sent letters listing the services they offered (plumbing repair, electrical repair, painting, papering, windows, etc.) on the sides of the stationery while the central message itself cited their 14 years of successful business, offered references for their work, and mentioned that all employees were bonded and that their work was guaranteed.
- *Present evidence that what you are claiming is true.* You might, for example, include testimonials from satisfied customers or clients. If these are not from well-known people or firms, it is a good idea to offer addresses upon request. Or you might include verifiable statistics from named laboratories or testing services. You might even include samples and let your customers test the product for themselves. Or give a free-trial period. Or offer a guarantee.

GIVE AN OPPORTUNITY FOR ACTION

If your sales letter has been successful, before the concluding portion you will have attracted your correspondents to your product or service and created a desire for it. As you conclude, you need to direct this desire into meaningful action. Ask yourself: "What do I want my readers to do?" Then suggest that they do it and *clearly* tell them how.

Effective sales letters explicitly inform their readers:

1. What they will get.
2. What they will have to do to get it.

Clearly tell your readers exactly what they will have to do to acquire what you are selling. They should not have to exert themselves too much or, of course, they won't. But they should have to take some action. For your empathetic close to work, your readers must be personally involved. Here's how the writers of our sample letters handle the problem (emphasis ours):

> <u>If you would like our firm to assist you</u> with your tax matters, <u>please call our office</u> closest to you to arrange an appointment. We will provide one-half hour of consultation at no charge. (Sample Letter 5A)

> If, as we have supposed, you like to be just one step behind the reviews in reading new works of this kind, we hope you will <u>send the enclosed order card before this offer expires</u> on May 31. (Sample Letter 5B)

> If you will <u>send me an order</u>--<u>just one</u>--in the next sixty days, <u>I can send you that catalog,</u> and I've had an order form printed with your name and customer number, just to make it easier for you. (Sample Letter 5C)

The following Guidelines offer some additional tips for writing sales letters.

──────────────────────── **GUIDELINES** ────────────────────────

Sales Letters

Some Caveats
1. Unless your price is your special offer—or, at least, very competitive—don't mention it in the early part of your letter.
2. Don't exaggerate. You are dependent upon your reader's confidence in your truthfulness.
3. Don't downgrade a competitor (openly). Your reader will find it unfair and off-putting.
4. Don't make your customer's response difficult. Offer a phone number. Enclose a coupon or a detachable blank. If you want the customer to come to your establishment, enclose a small map, especially if your address is difficult to find. If the action required is by nature complex, clearly list the steps to be taken.

And Remember
Address an individual human reader. Conjure up in your imagination a living member of your narrowed mailing list. Concentrate on that image until the person becomes real to you. Then compose your letter to that particular reader, following the recommended strategies.

SECTION B: *International Correspondence*

THE PROBLEM

In the 1990s the United States is fighting for its competitive edge. In many industries markets are global. American companies invest abroad. American and foreign corporations run joint ventures. Americans export. Americans import. Americans at all levels of the business hierarchy have to deal with foreign businesspeople. The chances that you will be asked to correspond with a counterpart in another country are very good indeed.

How to do it? How can you state your company's case to a foreign corporation and its people and not be at a disadvantage or put them at one? There are pitfalls to be aware of.

UNDERSTANDING YOUR READER'S WORLD
We *could* reasonably say, "Consider your reader in light of your purpose." But when you correspond internationally, you don't know your readers as well as you know your own countrymen and -women. And you don't know their system or their manners or the hundreds of ideas and concepts and courtesies and unspoken understandings that make up their world.

For instance: In Thailand during the last years of the Vietnam War, an American company installed some communications towers in the mountains along the Thai-Laotian border. The project's maintenance platforms looked down on the King's nearby summer quarters. Shortly afterward, the Americans were obliged to take the towers down at a considerable financial loss. They had discounted the intensity of the Thai veneration for their king; and they had disregarded the irrevocable rule: "No head shall be higher than the King's."

The American engineers had chosen the towers' position for technical reasons; the Thais had other considerations, more compelling to them, of which Americans were simply unaware.

UNDERSTANDING YOUR READER'S LANGUAGE

To make your international communication effective, we *could* reasonably say, "Empathize. Think how you would respond to the letter you mean to write." But although humankind is one people and human nature is essentially the same, people vary considerably in cultural values, social conventions, and the meaning of their symbols. And these are the very fabric of our written communication. There are differences in language usage that no translator, no matter how skillful, can overcome.

For example: General Motors' carefully worked out advertising campaign to introduce its Chevrolet Nova into the Mexican market had to be entirely revamped. The car itself had to be renamed to be sold there. No one had realized that the two syllables that signify "new" and "innovative" to Americans break into *no* and *va*. In Spanish they mean "it does not go." Not exactly the concept an automobile manufacturer would like associated with its product.

RESEARCH IS THE KEY

There are no easy answers. But we offer one cardinal principle:

Be sensitive, and look before you leap.

INFORMATION IS POWER

The more you know about the people you are addressing and their culture, the less hazardous your verbal or written journey abroad will be. Therefore, investigate *before* you communicate.

- Check the library. With the growing interdependency for all business, many books have been published dealing with business etiquette and practices in many cultures.
- Check with the nearest university. You may find a department or an expert on the country for which you need information.
- Check with your industry trade association.
- Check with other businesspeople who have dealt with the foreign culture or company you wish to address.
- Find a local national from that country who has some business savvy and can help you write what you have to write. Foreign nationals resident in the United States can be particularly helpful because they also understand something of U.S. culture.

A CAUTION. By all means check with all sources available to you. But exercise judgment in evaluating what you learn. The high school exchange student next door or Aunt Hester's friend who was a French major in 1946 might not have current information on foreign business-writing etiquette. *Don't guess. Research.*

- You might consult the U.S. Department of State or the U.S. Department of Commerce for published information they provide.
- For specific information on national protocol, you might consult embassies in Washington, D.C., or consulates throughout the country.
- You could also try the United Nations missions in New York.

Your city library will have directories of those useful names and telephone numbers. In many libraries this directory service is available to you by phone.

A FEW HELPFUL HINTS. The world has so many and such diverse cultures that any attempt to supply the information you need for international correspondence *in general* would be foolhardy. But the following hints will help you focus your own specific research.

A hint for Japanese correspondence. The Japanese language distinguishes between levels of formality much more precisely than English does. Business correspondence is conducted at the very highest of these levels. Therefore, even though your English cannot reproduce the exact nuances required, do your best to approximate a formal tone whenever you write to Japanese businesspeople. Specifically:

- Avoid contractions (write: *do not,* not *don't; cannot,* not *can't*).
- Use a formal salutation (write *Dear Sir:,* not *Dear Mr. Moto,*).
- Avoid personal references. For example, even if you knew your Japanese correspondent had just returned from a vacation, you would NOT write: "I hope you enjoyed your holiday." This would, of course, be a graceful, empathetic close to a business letter sent to an American.

A hint for German correspondence. Political, social, and linguistic differences also require that you be sensitive when you correspond with German concerns. Knowledge, however, can prevent embarrassment. For example:

- Labor policies in Germany are more restrictive on management than in the United States. Consequently, if your letter is to touch on such issues, research your ground carefully before writing.

- When you want to distinguish the former East and West German portions of this recently reunified country, use the terms the Germans are most comfortable with: *the New States* and *the Old States*.
- Courteous German usage requires greater use of polite social forms of address than is the American custom. You would address a German scientist with a PhD as *Herr Doctor Professor Klaus Mueller* (Mister Doctor Professor Klaus Mueller). The salutation for a letter in English generally follows the American form: *Dear Professor Mueller* or *Dear Herr Professor Mueller*. (In Germany, as in much of Europe, *Professor* is the more prestigious term.) Your salutation of a similarly named American would be simply *Dear Dr. Mueller*. For a German woman, whether married or single, the acceptable address is *Frau*: *Dear Frau Professor Schmidt* or *Dear Professor Schmidt*.
- Germany, like much of the rest of Europe, writes dates in the order of day, month, year: 3 November 1985. American practice reverses month and day: November 3, 1985.

  To avoid confusion, write out the month in full, instead of writing, say, 11/3. But remember the European custom when you are reading your correspondence.
- In writing numbers, Germans and Americans have different conventions. Germans use a period, not a comma, to separate thousands. For example: 15,000 (American style); 15.000 (German style). And, conversely, they use a comma rather than a period for a decimal point: 1.5 (American); 1,5 (German).

A hint for Chinese correspondence. The Chinese require elaborately phrased circumlocutions to make requests. The plain American style of simply asking a question briefly and straightforwardly can seem abrupt or even coarse to the Chinese. Negotiating is a particularly sensitive process. Chinese politeness dictates that deadlines and figures be kept vague. Confidence that the concealed specifics will be honorably carried out is a touchstone of goodwill. American directness and insistence on contractual spelling out of numbers and dates may seem to indicate a lack of trust.

A hint for East-European correspondence. The situation in Eastern Europe is in flux. Our suggestions fit the immediate circumstances, but you will almost certainly need to research and review to keep up with world events. Currently, the rule to remember when corresponding with East-European businesses is:

Never underestimate your reader's intelligence.

Never overestimate your reader's information.

And here are some specific applications for that rule:

- When you correspond with Eastern Europeans, remember that many of your correspondents will have had little experience with a market economy. You cannot even assume familiarity with such basic concepts as *stocks* and *bonds*. They are eager to learn; and it is essential for carrying out your mutual business that they do. Muster all your tact in including the information they will need. (See pages 85, 87 for some practical strategies.)
- Remember that nationality is a highly sensitive issue for the peoples of all the Eastern bloc countries.

  Address a Baltic correspondent in Latvia, Lithuania, or Estonia without reference to the "USSR." Your letter *will* arrive, and your envelope will not offend.

  Unless you are describing an inhabitant of the Republic of Russia, do not refer to a citizen from the Soviet bloc as a "Russian." Refer instead to "Georgians" or "Ukrainians" or whatever is the appropriate regional designation.

WRITING LETTERS ABROAD

The international business climate is extraordinarily complex. But if you research thoroughly for possible differences in culture and language and take care to make your writing reflect what you discover, you will be an effective global business communicator. And your firm will be the more prosperous for it.

LETTER WORKOUT

1. Although the following letter might be considered courteous and effective in an American setting, some Japanese might find it offensive. Revise the letter so that it would be acceptable.

```
Mr. Kazuo Ito
The Beikoku Corporation
Osaka, Japan

Dear Kaz:

I'm sorry to hear from our Eastern Division sales man-
ager that you've been a little under the weather with
a touch of stomach flu. Hope you're back at your desk
and feeling fine now.

We've certainly been walking a tightrope in this eco-
nomic turndown and hope we can adhere to the follow-
ing schedule for delivery and payments through the
next quarter:
```

Order Date	Our Delivery	Your Payment
June 7	July 8	July 24
August 20	September 10	September 30
September 4	October 1	October 20

That should do it, but if you've got questions, feel free to give us a call.

Once we're through with this project, I hope you'll have time to get away with your family for some well-deserved vacation.

Sincerely,

Chip

J. C. Forest

2. Revise the following letter so that it would be not only effective but also acceptable to a German reader.

Herr Dr. Hermann Willecke
Europa-Luft GmbH
Sophienstr. 5
2000 Hamburg 13
Federal Republic of Germany

Dear Herr Willecke:

By 4/3/92 we will need to have at least six of the units we have contracted for. Can you meet that schedule? It will be critical for us.

Have you checked it with your branch in East Germany? If you expect to run into trouble with your Workers' Committee, please let me know no later than 1/2/92. Because we have strict scheduling requirements, we might have to try to get what we need from a non-union supplier.

Many thanks for your help.

Yours,

Jerry Taylor

Jerry Taylor

AUTHENTIC BUSINESS PROBLEMS

1. Write an effective sales letter.
   a. Select a product or service that you understand well.
   b. Define a set of potential customers or clients for that product or service.
   c. Following the principles discussed in this chapter, compose a letter convincing your particular group of potential customers or clients to purchase your product or service.
2. Research a product with potential in a foreign market. (You may use the same product you chose for Problem 1 if you wish.) Then write a sales letter to a foreign distributor, convincing him or her of that potential.

   In addition to your usual courtesy and tact, be sure to keep cultural predilections in mind.

WRITING EFFECTIVE BUSINESS MEMOS

EXECUTIVE SUMMARY

In contrast with business letters, which are *external* communications, memos are *internal* communications. That is, they are the means of communicating *within* a business organization.

Memos Facilitate Orderly Business Procedure

Memos communicate recommendations or decisions, give assignments, set up meetings, record transactions, and chronicle actions taken. Effective memos are efficient. They:

- Orient the reader quickly and clearly.

- Report on actions, or give information succinctly.

- Set out required or recommended action in clear, precise terms.

- Indicate follow-up procedure, often including a time frame.

Memos Also Facilitate Organizational Process

Memo writing also leads the writer headlong into the political side of business. In between the lines memos give recognition, affirm rank or territory, and announce internal policies. They also communicate a variety of political or other subtle internal messages.

Clearly, to write an effective memo you should ground it in the basic axiom:

Consider your reader in light of your purpose.

Every memo you write must take into account:

- The hierarchical and political nature of the corporate culture or organizational context within which you write, especially comparative rank.

- The history, background, and political circumstances surrounding the project.

- The close, day-to-day working environment of your company and the need such proximity generates for tact and a businesslike tone.

I n Chapters 4 and 5 we discussed business letters, which are primarily *external* communications. Memos (short for *memoranda*) are even more complex and subtle business communications. They are used chiefly for *internal* communication.

WHAT IS A MEMO?

A memorandum can be defined in a number of ways:

- An informal record.
- A written reminder.
- An informal written note of a transaction or proposed instrument.
- An informal diplomatic communication.

True. A business memo is all that, but we would submit that it is a good deal more. In the hierarchical world of business, the memo is a highly versatile document. It facilitates:

- *Orderly business procedure.* Memos expedite the exchange of ideas. They can be part of the decision process, give orders or assignments, and set up meetings. They analyze gathered data and make recommendations.[1] They report on actions taken, and they record transactions. They provide an important "paper trail" of what goes on in a business. In short, memos help carry on the internal business of a company.
- *Organizational process.* As an adjunct to their avowed business purpose, some memos also give recognition, affirm rank or territory, and announce policy changes. They can also be used to protect the writer by providing a paper trail, a record of what was done when. And they communicate a limitless range of other political messages.

  Even the mechanics of memo writing have political implications. For example, *copy distribution* (that is, the list of those designated to receive copies of certain information) can signal status

---

1. The general information in this chapter applies to recommendation memos as well as the other memos discussed. But since recommendation memos have a special complexity, we will treat them in detail in Chapter 7. Writing them often also involves research, which we will discuss in Chapter 8.

and convey political information. In fact, memo copy procedure is one of the subtlest tools at the corporate business writer's disposal. (See pages 153–154.)

MEMO WRITING AS AN ORDERLY BUSINESS PROCEDURE

PURPOSE AND PRINCIPLES

Memos help the wheels of business turn smoothly. What precipitates a memo? Action. The need for it. The need to determine it, to suggest or recommend it. The need to report on it as it is going on. The need to describe or evaluate it after it has been taken.

Typically, in any job you hold you will be asked to take or assess action. You act or recommend an action and then follow up to see that the action has been satisfactorily completed. Memos facilitate the process. Through them you can make inquiry or gather or report information, you can put the information into action, and you can follow up.

To write an effective memo, use the axiom underlying all effective business writing:

Consider your reader in light of your purpose.

First apply the strategies derived from this axiom in earlier chapters:

- *The aim of business communication is to get something done.* Even informational memos report on action or potentially facilitate it. Most memos require action. For example, even a memo inviting guests to a business reception requires the action of an RSVP. Be sure you write your memos so that they can bring about action. Ask yourself: "What am I trying to get done?"
- *Time is money.* Every memo you write should carry a schedule for the action it recommends. In business jargon this is sometimes called a *time frame.* For example:

```
We expect to have an answer back from Accounting
by Wednesday, June 9. That report should enable
us to send you a plan for handling this budget
item next quarter by Friday, June 11.
```

- *Be brief. Be simple. Be clear. Be specific and precise.* Carefully determine what information you want your memo to ask for or to get across, and state it as clearly and as directly as possible. Be sure your information is accurate.

Other strategies that are more specific to memo writing may also be useful to you.

MEMO STYLE

ADOPT A CONVERSATIONAL TONE. Memos are in many ways like business letters, but they differ significantly in both tone and form. An informal memo, which is sent among colleagues, is more like a conversation—and a hurried conversation at that. The tone and diction you use in it are appropriately more informal than in a letter. You need have no hesitation about using contractions in a memo, for instance. And all "Dear so and so" salutations and "Sincerely yours" closes should be omitted.

Since brevity is essential, when you and your correspondent share a technical vocabulary, the shorthand of your field's technical jargon is appropriate. But even in a memo, avoid using the generalized jargon and pseudoimpressive vocabulary of gobbledygook.

RESTRAIN EMOTIONAL OVERTONES. Though both business letters and memos require a courteous and businesslike style, the tone of a memo is always cooler, less emotional. And in a memo courtesy is even more essential. Shrillness in a letter may be overlooked or in time forgotten. But a memo communicates between people who must see each other every day, and sharpness of tone builds. Moreover, because of copy procedure, a memo is a relatively public document, and memo-generated embarrassment is inevitably shared.

Try an experiment. Reread a complaint letter—say, Sample Letter 4E, from B. G. Girard, in Chapter 4—as if it were a memo addressed to a colleague of yours whose office is just down the hall. Here is the complaining paragraph from the Girard letter:

```
Since putting [your] two drums on line, we have been get-
ting nothing but rejected batches from our quality-con-
trol people, who have, in fact, recommended shutting
down the line on this product completely. According to
their test procedures, the two lines with these two
drums of product feeding into them have produced only
rejects.
```

As you see, what seems restrained and rational in a letter can sound carping and snide in a memo. If this complaint were made in a memo, the writer would have to tone down the phrases "nothing but rejected batches" and "only rejects" and substitute less jarring and more diplomatic ones. You need to use a greater degree of tact when you write a memo.

SAMPLE BUSINESS MEMOS

This chapter presents a wide assortment of sample business memos. Sample Memos 6A through 6F, grouped together on the following pages, are typical of those used regularly in business. Sample Memos and Memo Segments 6G through 6P, scattered throughout the rest of the chapter, demonstrate the use of memos to handle a variety of special or sensitive situations.

SAMPLE MEMO 6A
Charity Collection

TO: Jeremy Ticktin
FROM: Brittany Ackerman   *BA*
RE: United Charitable Appeals
DATE: May 18, 19—

As you know, I have been asked to round up the United Appeal contributions for our division. You have indicated your intention to contribute, but your initial check is one of the three still outstanding. I would very much appreciate your getting it to me by Thursday (either in Box 610 or at my office) so I can send off the whole batch by the end of the week. Thanks.

We appreciate your willingness to participate.

BA: jr

MEMO FORM

HEADING. Because memos are for internal communication, they dispense with the elaborate identification by name, title, and full address required on letters. All that is needed is a brief notation of the names of sender and addressee, the date, and often the sender's telephone extension. But memo headings also include a subject identification line. This "Re:" or "Concerning:" line acts like a headline and focuses the memo in a phrase. Its purpose is to expedite the reader's initial understanding and later to act as a prod to the memory. The more specific or the more meaningful the headline, the more useful it is.

STRUCTURE OF THE MESSAGE. A business letter begins with an empathetic statement, moves on to make its point, then ends with an empathetic statement. Memos of special sensitivity may also follow this form (see Sample Memos 6A and 6P). But a memo is action-oriented, and you need to get to its point as soon as possible. Therefore, the empathetic opening is ordinarily cut short. And usually the empathetic close is replaced by a time-signified request for a response or action (see the comparative chart, page 13, in Chapter 1). Consequently, to write an effective memo you should structure it in this way:

1. Begin with a brief statement orienting your reader to the background and purpose of your memo. For example:

SAMPLE MEMO 6B
Meeting
Announcement

TO: Marie Contreras
        Peter P. Eder
        Donald A. (Doc) Fell
        George G. Gander
      ✓John Horner, Jr.
        Marilyn Moffet
        Jeff S. Pratt
        Thomas H. Tucker
FROM: Brian Gallagher, Jr. *BHG*
RE: D'Angelo-Webb-Smilansky Project Meeting
DATE: September 6, 19—

I've checked, and Monday at 4:00 is OK with everyone for our initial meeting on the D'Angelo-Webb-Smilansky project. Let's meet in Room 203 in the South Wing.

BG: sj

Jack, please bring the material Smilansky and Smilansky sent you.

- As you know, I have been asked to round up the United Appeal contributions for our division. (Sample Memo 6A)

- To confirm our telephone conversation this morning... (Sample Memo 6C)

- As promised, I am returning the Zounds marketing plan draft with our comments. (Sample Memo 6D)

- Attached, as you requested, is a revised production schedule for the frozen-carrot-juice carton hangtags. (Sample Memo 6E)

2. Quickly set out the action you want to accomplish—the point of your memo.

- Follow your point up, where appropriate, with background, support, or other relevant information.
- Resist any tendency to editorialize. Let the facts speak for themselves.

SAMPLE MEMO 6C
Draft Transmittal/
Meeting
Announcement

```
TO:      Sarah Hardie [Assistant to the Marketing
         Manager]
FROM:    Hilary Katz [Assistant Director of   HK
         Packaging, Health Directions, Inc.]
RE:      Meeting Plan
DATE:    March 3, 19--

To confirm our telephone conversation this
morning, I am enclosing a draft of the marketing
plan for the new Zounds health drink.  As we
discussed, we will convene a meeting in Atlanta on
Thursday, April 5, of both your team and mine to
discuss the final plan.

It would be helpful if your review of the draft
could be back in my office by Friday, March 13, so
I can incorporate your comments and those from the
packaging firm in the final plan draft.

Many thanks for your help.

cc: Alexander Powell [Director of Manufacturing,
    Health Directions, Inc.]


HK: nt
```

- Present this supporting information in decreasing order of importance—with the most important point first. (This inverted pyramid structure is discussed in detail on pages 201–202.) Often you will find it useful to tag each supporting point with a bullet. (See Sample Memo D.)

3. Conclude your memo by describing the "next step," including dates where pertinent. For example:

   - I would very much appreciate your getting it to me by Thursday (either in Box 610 or at my office) so I can send off the whole batch by the end of the week. (Sample Memo 6A)

   - It would be helpful if your review of the draft could be back in my office by Friday, March 13, so I can incorporate your comments and those from the packaging firm in the final plan draft. (Sample Memo 6C)

SAMPLE MEMO 6D
Draft Evaluation/
Arrangements
Notification

```
  TO:  Hilary Katz
FROM:  Sarah Hardie   SH
  RE:  Marketing Plan
DATE:  March 11, 19—
```

As promised, I am returning the Zounds marketing plan draft with our comments. Comments from Fred, Anna, Althea, and Josh all focused on three points:

· The die-cut carrot on the package is critical to making our product package stand out from the competition's frozen-carrot-juice package. As you know, Whoosh, the competitive drink, has an eye-catching design that has proved very successful for them.

· We agree with you that pursuing endorsement by Bugs Bunny would give the entire campaign the wrong tone.

· Every effort should be made to have the campaign in full swing by September 1 at the latest.

For your information, we have managed to clear up everybody's schedule, and all members of the marketing team will be able to attend the Atlanta meeting. <u>By copy of this memo, I am asking all team members to confirm travel arrangements for March 31 with Angela [Secretary].</u>

If you have any questions, call any one of us.

cc: Fred Davis
    Alexander Powell
    Althea Lincoln
    Anna Carson
    Josh Unger

SH/bsn

• Unless I hear from you to the contrary, I will assume that your sign-off on the design--scheduled, as you will note, for March 21--is the final one and that all other approvals are in. (Sample Memo 6E)

SAY IT IN ONE PAGE. Ideally, your memo should be no longer than *one page.* The one-page form imposes a discipline that business considers valuable: it dispenses with the nonessential and concentrates on the action points.

SAMPLE MEMO 6E
Request to
Supervisor for
Approval of
Project

TO: John Allworthy   *PR*
FROM: Pamela Richardson
RE: Carrot-juice carton production schedule
DATE: March 12, 19--

Attached, as you requested, is a revised production schedule for the frozen-carrot-juice carton hangtags. As you know, once the color separations have been completed, on April 14, we will have made considerable cost investment in this design; so we must be sure that approvals are firm from all departments involved at least a week before the color separations are begun.

Unless I hear from you to the contrary, I will assume that your sign-off on the design--scheduled, as you will note, for March 21--is the final one and that all other approvals are in.

PR/bc

MEMO WRITING AS A POLITICAL ART

The strategies of memo construction that we have been discussing and illustrating are important. But they are not where you begin. You begin by thinking through not only *what* you will write, but *how* and to *whom*. In other words, you need to think of memo writing in terms of the psychology and politics of the corporate organization.

In letter writing, as Chapter 4 demonstrates, psychological concerns—and the empathetic strategies that derive from them—are crucial. In memo writing, these concerns are no less important, but political considerations are equally significant.

Politics is, very roughly, the art of wielding power or of exerting control to influence events. Related to the word *politics* is the word *politic,* the art of being, as a dictionary says, "shrewdly tactful," an art that is golden in business. Business organizations are inevitably political. Any business organization, large or small, is an organized political system with a hierarchical structure for governance. And within that structure is an informal, underlying power system. Take both systems into account in every memo you write.

SAMPLE MEMO 6F
*Meeting Report
(High-Tech
Industry)**

```
From:     PTVAX: :DNORMAN    DGN
To:       SSPC
Subject:  LMNOP789 DESIGN MEETING LOG
Date:     2/29/—

ATTENDEES: H. Clinker, J. Darcy, T. Jones, D. Norman, GOV
L617 (2 representatives)

REASON FOR MEETING: Discussion of Q Group's comments on
Theory of Operations

ITEMS RESOLVED:
   · GHT, RT, MNT tables are not critical, even though
     there should be some validity checks performed on them.
   · Our use of the Y group's nonexpansive method has been
     approved.

ITEMS TO BE RESOLVED:
   · Theory of Operations must expand on points listed in
     comments.  Its description of verification procedure
     needs to be clarified.
   · Our handling of the VB is critical.  We must take care
     of this and provide for a means of separating critical
     matter from noncritical.
   · We need to find a good calculation for protecting the
     GHT Table.
```

**FORMAL
POLITICAL
STRUCTURE:
THE
HIERARCHY**

Almost all business organizations are organized as hierarchies. For instance, in your job you have a supervisor (formerly called a boss), and so does your supervisor, and so does his supervisor, and so does her supervisor, and so on up to the CEO (the Chief Executive Officer) or the COO (the Chief Operating Officer). Don't miss the use of the term *officer*. The whole structure is very like a military organization. Even if your company has a President or a Chairman or a Director or a Partner, those titles generally carry some designation (like Chairman and CEO, or President and COO, or Partner-in-Charge) that indicates that somebody—some *one* body—is in command. That person has reporting to her or to him a kind of pyramid

---

*Note that the style of Sample Memo 6F, typical of communication in the high-tech industry, is slightly different from the style of the other memos. It is more terse and succinct, and its diction is marked by technical abbreviations and jargon. Its structure, however, is in fact conventional.

of other officers and directors or managers responsible for carrying out the work of the organization. The following organization chart is typical:

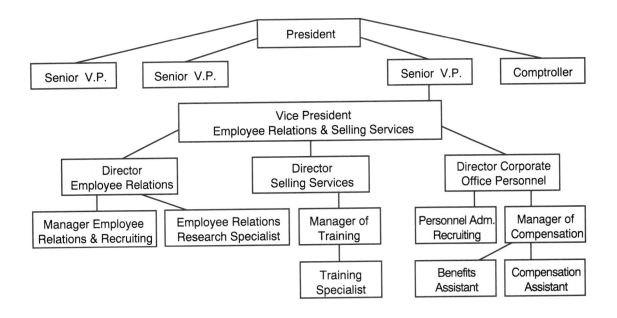

HIERARCHICAL GOVERNANCE. However forward-looking, most businesses are *not* democracies. It is true that employees now have more influence in the operation of a business than Bob Cratchit had with Scrooge. And many good business managers value employee contribution. But despite ongoing scholarly discussion of alternative styles of business leadership that operate more by collaboration and consensus than by hierarchical directive, most conventional businesses are still hierarchies.

Topic for Ethical Discussion

It's easy to see why business has chosen the militaristic, hierarchical model of governance. It's fast and efficient. A democracy is inefficient because it requires the hearing of many points of view. And it takes time and leadership skill to bring a body of equals to a consensus. Business goals and the competitive climate require fast, efficient action. Whether this method of organization is ultimately best for the company or the employees or for the entire economic system is a question worthy of debate. Perhaps you will want to consider it in class discussion (see page 166).

In this text, however, we are trying to make sure you manage to survive and thrive in business as it is presently governed. And that includes making sure you know how to communicate in a business hierarchy.

1. If you are now working or have worked in a sizable company, give the following information about your place of employment. Otherwise interview an acquaintance in business, and write:
   a. The name of the company.
   b. A brief description of the business and its sector (heavy or light manufacturing? service? high-tech? retailing? etc.).
   c. The name of its top officer.
   d. The title of its top officer.
2. What is your (or your acquaintance's) job title? How is the pyramid (or company or division or group or department) organized?
3. What is the title of the person you (or your acquaintance) report to?
4. What are the titles of those who report to you (or your acquaintance)?
5. Sketch an organization chart, like a segment of the illustrative chart on page 143, of your (or your acquaintance's) line of reporting.

CONSIDERING THE BUSINESS HIERARCHY IN MEMO WRITING. Hierarchy must be as much a part of your thinking and planning for a memo as the substantive recommendations you intend to make. Experience will ultimately be your best teacher in mastering the demands of hierarchy, but here are some strategies that will help with your communications:

Give due deference to rank. Both when you write and when you are considering projects you will recommend, begin to think politically. Consider the likely impact of your message on the person to whom it is addressed, on each individual who will receive a copy, and even on those who do *not* receive it (*not* receiving information also has political implications in a business hierarchy). Hierarchical implications even determine appropriate writing style. Compare, for example, Sample Memo Segments 6G and 6H.

SAMPLE MEMO SEGMENT 6G
Request to a Subordinate

```
...I will need your final report by the close of
business on Friday. Please be sure to get that to Jamie
even if I am not available.
```

SAMPLE MEMO SEGMENT 6H
Request from a Subordinate

```
...The final report from our group will have to be
completed by the close of business on Friday, so we
would need a final approval from you by Thursday noon in
order to leave time for any changes you might require. I
will call Jamie on Wednesday and see if you anticipate
any problems with the approval schedule.
    I would be glad to answer any questions you might
have.
```

Protect your protectors. The first ranking person you should think about is your own direct supervisor. It is an important part of your job to make that person look good—and competent and informed. This advice holds true even if your supervisor is incompetent, ill-informed, lazy, or stupid.

In many businesses, junior executives commonly draft memos that are then sent over their supervisor's—or even department head's—signature. The custom ensures that a ranking executive receives only communications whose recommendations have been reviewed and approved by experienced supervisors. Good managers will see to it that you receive credit for your efforts and ideas. Others may habitually rely upon your work without giving you specific credit. Nevertheless, it is usually to your advantage to comply cheerfully. On the one hand, this practice protects you, as a novice, from your own inexperience. On the other hand, organizational underground information systems operate efficiently. If you are the person at the bottom of the pyramid doing the good job, that will become known. Meanwhile, you show your maturity and your own organizational savvy by playing by the rules. And don't forget: in most cases, success for your supervisor can lead to a promotion that can also promote you.

No surprises. Remember that nothing you write or suggest should surprise your supervisor. Build in time for her or him to see what you have written before it makes its way up the hierarchy to its ultimate reader. A good supervisor may be able to offer comments for improvement. And nearly any supervisor will be grateful to see in advance something that may have to be defended in a meeting.

Don't embarrass. Embarrass nobody. That's right, we said nobody, nobody above you in rank and nobody you outrank. Business norms of courtesy and diplomacy decree that when you write you ascribe the best possible motive and performance to colleagues or the people in other departments or pyramids. For example, note the tactful approach to the inherently embarrassing situation discussed in Sample Memo 6I.

WRITING UP THE HIERARCHY

TO WHOM SHOULD YOU SEND A MEMO? Despite all the subtle ramifications, the purpose of memos, like that of letters, is to get something done or to report on what you have done. So whom should you send them to? Generally speaking, send to:

1. The person who asked you to get the task done.
2. Those who need to take some action or understand some information to further your purpose.
3. Those who need to know what you are doing and what you have said because your project touches on their area of responsibility.

The hierarchical organization of business does not allow you completely open channels of communication to everybody in those three

SAMPLE MEMO 6I
*Tactful Attention-
Calling*

TO: Brian Atchison
FROM: P. J. Farmington
RE: Advertising Problems
DATE: December 7, 19—

There may not be anything to all this, but I wanted
you to know about it just in case you want to act
on it.

We have had three customer complaints involving
Dan's stores in Utah. In all cases, the customers
took the time to find the headquarters number and
to make long-distance calls.

I would like to suggest that you give some consideration to counseling Dan about the advertised
"all sales final" pledge—that it probably shouldn't
include obviously defective merchandise, at least
not expensive items like cameras.

---

groups. These unwritten restrictions have evolved partly to save the
extremely expensive time of those at the top of the hierarchy, partly to
insure that decisions benefit from experience and are made on the most
efficient and appropriate level, and partly for the political and psychological reasons we have been discussing. Custom, experience, and your corporate culture may dictate specific exceptions, but, in general, you should
address your memos *only* to the following people:

- Your immediate supervisor.
- Those your supervisor suggests you address, with notice taken in
  the memo of that suggestion. (For example: "Frank has asked me to
  report to you the outcome of Monday's meeting.")
- Those just at or near your own level of hierarchy, in your own or
  other lines of reporting.
- Those under your immediate supervision.
- The person who requested your work or asked for information.

If you keep these guidelines in mind, you will save yourself and your
supervisor the sort of embarrassment that marred young Greene's career
in Chapter 1 (pages 9–13). You'll recall that, all unknowing, he sent an

unfortunate memo to a person of higher rank, in another reporting pyramid, and without his supervisor's knowledge.

WHAT SHOULD YOUR MEMO SAY? Like your letters, your memos must give the information needed to accomplish your purpose in writing, to get done what you want to get done. And your memos, like your letters, must be unvaryingly courteous and businesslike. But in every memo you write you also need to consider hierarchical implications.

Be careful not to seem to be issuing commands. When you address those above you in the pyramid, be tactful in phrasing requests. Avoid, for example, wording like the following, which *could* be interpreted as subtle insubordination:

```
                              MEMO

     TO:    Beryl Schmidt
            [Vice President, Plastics Division]
     FROM:  Chris Walters
            [Administrative Assistant, Plastics Division]
     RE:    Eastland Account
     DATE:  February 9, 19—

     Attached is this month's shipping plan.

     If you want the Eastland delivery to go out on the prom-
     ised schedule you will have to let me know by Friday.
     Also, tell me so I can inform Phillips if you are going
     to delay this project further. I will call you by Friday
     noon to remind you.
```

This memo is clear, but not tactful. Chris has managed to be abrupt and to seem directive to a vice president. Chris has even managed to suggest with inept language that the delay may be Schmidt's fault. Be more circumspect in writing your memos, as in Sample Memo 6J.

In the second memo Chris manages to get the project expedited without causing any possible offense.

Define terms tactfully. By tacit agreement, those above you or equal to you in the hierarchy (except perhaps those from a completely diverse department) are presumed to understand all that you understand. But, of course, they don't always. Therefore, when you are not sure that these colleagues share your knowledge, write your memo *as if they did.* But subtly define terminology with which they might not be familiar, and tactfully work in explanations of ideas that they might not understand. (See the example about markups on pages 85, 87.)

SAMPLE MEMO 6J
Tactful Request/
Decision Required

```
   TO:  Beryl Schmidt
 FROM:  Chris Walters  CW
   RE:  Eastland Account
 DATE:  February 9, 19—

Attached is this month's shipping plan.

An approval by Friday would enable us to make the
promised delivery schedule for Eastland.  We need
to let Phillips know by Tuesday, however, if there
is likely to be further delay.  I will call your
secretary by noon on Friday to check on your
decision.
```

Be formal and careful in your syntax and diction. You can write more colloquially and informally with those on your level and below you (see Sample Memo Segment 6G). But be warned that since memos are neither personal nor private, you should never write anything in one that you would regret *anyone* in your company reading.

━━━━━━━━━━━━━━━━━━━━━━━━━━ **GUIDELINES** ━━━━━━

Survival Techniques for the Novice Memo Writer

1. Until you are experienced, don't send any memo that your supervisor has not seen *before* its dispatch. That's only fair to your supervisor, and it's only good sense. Your supervisor can both help proof your work and make any necessary shifts in emphasis or changes in the tone required by a particular corporate culture.
2. Even after you have experience, give your supervisor the opportunity to approve—or at least to be informed about—your actions or recommendations *whenever the topic is potentially sensitive.* Bear in mind that your supervisor and your entire hierarchy are responsible for your actions.

   But, you might justifiably say, if I show them every memo, I won't be doing my job. I may be irritating them. They may decide that if they have to supervise everything I do, they don't need me.

   True enough—and that's good business thinking. But here we are talking specifically about potentially *sensitive* situations. A good technique for handling these without creating an administrative bottleneck is to send your supervisor his or her copy of the memo—with a note. The note could say something like this:

**SAMPLE
MEMO 6K**
Cover Note

```
TO: W.S.
FROM: A.H.
DATE: April 7, 19—
RE: Memo for C.B.

Attached is the recommendation I intend to make to
Charlie. He needs a decision from us by Wednesday,
so unless I hear from you to the contrary, I will
send this memo by the close of business Tuesday. I
am scheduled to be out of the office Monday morning
but will be in early Monday afternoon on if you have
questions.
```

   3. The higher in the hierarchy the source of a directive to you, the higher is the priority for the work, and the sooner the deadline for your memo.

**INFORMAL
POLITICAL
STRUCTURE:
REALPOLITIK**

Besides a formal hierarchy with its officially stated rules of procedure, every business has an informal political structure with its own power bases and rules, its own norms of courtesy and deportment. Such norms are rarely discussed, but they are clearly *understood*. Though every business has them, their form is particular to each organization. We cannot, therefore, specify what you will find in your own company. In general, however, there will be understandings of this sort:

- *Certain corporate customs.* "The way we do things here." For example: "Our company always sends letters, *never* memos to anyone at an operating division whose rank is higher than vice president."
- *Certain tacitly acknowledged centers of power.* "The way to get something done is to go to the President's secretary, who *really* runs this company."
- *Certain interactions and historical situations.* "The head of Accounting is feuding with the Vice President for Tax; see if anybody in Tax can get an expense check expedited without an act of the Chairman."
- *Certain understood policies.* "The memo that invites you to the company picnic calls it 'a voluntary recreational event for all employees,' but really means 'required occasion; be sure you show up.'"

And although no one will have time to set out all such implicit norms when you join a new company, your survival and advancement depend on your grasping the implications of the corporate culture as quickly as possible.

━━━━━━━━━━━━━━━━━━━━━━━━━━━━━ **GUIDELINES** ━━━━━━━━━━

More Survival Techniques for the Novice Memo Writer

1. Keep your ears open. Listen to the information on the grapevine. You don't have to engage in petty gossip in order to do so. Just listen. Pay attention to this informal information. File it in your mind. It will come in handy when you're thinking through what you want to write and to whom.

2. When you're new, find a comfortable, helpful, experienced co-worker to act as your mentor. But choose carefully. Ask confidentially and tactfully if you are unsure about a political situation. Your colleagues will probably be glad to be helpful; they will remember what it was like to be tiptoeing through the mine field.

PSYCHOLOGICAL CONSIDERATIONS

TERRITORIALITY: THE PSYCHOLOGY OF HIERARCHY

As we have seen, business is organized hierarchically, and the structure of every company can be outlined with each position graphed and labeled. But every label indicates a human being, a human being whose sense of self and sense of life's purpose is—often to a significant extent—bound up with that label. Since many businesspeople have their egos closely identified with position, they need to feel their position is important. People in business can be sensitive to anything that might be construed as a questioning of their importance. They are sensitive, for instance, to the suspicious implications of being skipped over in a distribution of informational copies or to possible innuendos if their department or function has been overlooked in a general consultation.

Furthermore, it is common for businesspeople to try to carve as large a niche for their position as they can, with as much power and prestige as possible. And our business system encourages, and is actually fueled by, the ambition that makes its participants eager to advance to the next position, the next level up.

Ethical Issue for Discussion See page 166

MANAGING MEMOS TO RESPECT YOUR COLLEAGUES' TERRITORY. When you write and send memos, be careful to acknowledge your colleagues' territory. Do not infringe on their boundaries, either horizontally (other departments or functions) or vertically (prerogatives or responsibilities of higher ranks). Where horizontal boundaries are blurred, tacitly acknowledge the people whose subject you are discussing and give due deference. Keep vertical boundaries clearly in mind and make requests only where authorization is clear.

Limit your recommendations to your own turf. Be sure you advise and recommend strictly on the basis of your own knowledge and responsibility and only on that part of the problem you have been asked to address. Do not, for instance, make a technical recommendation on a tax

---

Pepper Loses One

... Claude Pepper's [the late Congressman from Florida] colleagues gave him a standing ovation. Nonetheless, an unusual coalition of Democrats and Republicans sent Pepper's home-care bill down to a resounding 243-169 defeat.... The measure failed at least in part because Pepper antagonized two influential Democrats who head key House committees by bypassing them entirely and reporting the bill out of his own Rules Committee. That may seem a mere technicality, but nothing riles the ruling honchos faster than careless trespass on committee turf and House procedures.

From an editorial in *The Richmond News Leader* (15 June 1988). Reprinted by permission.

---

matter if you are in marketing. Do not make a political recommendation unless you are a member of the public affairs department. Do not offer technical widget-making advice if you are not a production supervisor or a widget engineer. The person who *is* in charge of the area on which you offer your advice will *not* be pleased.

If, for example, you, an engineer, have been asked to assess the possibility that asbestos, potentially harmful to workers, could be released by renovation in buildings owned by your company, that's all you need to cover in your memo. Do not attempt an extended discussion of the legal liability. Leave that to the legal department. Be sure to check your memo carefully for such inadvertent recommendations, because they have a way of creeping in.[2]

Send a copy. If, in a nontechnical way, you have to touch on the subject matter of someone else's department, send a copy of your memo to the person whose responsibility it is. This step is a necessary courtesy.

---

2. We understand that our advice here may seem unnecessarily restrictive to you. And so we urge you to discuss its implications. See Discussion Question 3, page 166.

Give credit. Acknowledge any help you have had in making your recommendation or formulating your strategy. You need not be long-winded or effusive, but do be sure that the contribution of the tax department or the data supplied by technical support people is acknowledged. It is the kind of courtesy that is both appreciated and returned. Sample Memo Segment 6L exemplifies one way of handling such matters.

**SAMPLE MEMO
SEGMENT 6L**
*Acknowledging
Sources, Help*

```
... Jim and Woody, in Insurance, kindly provided the
attached tables. They caution that these tables, when
reproduced, must carry the accompanying notes if they
are not to confuse the divisional managers. Both Jim and
Woody were particularly helpful in expediting this data
so that we could have the information available in time
for Tuesday's meeting.
```

Take care not to overstep your authority. Do not notify those who report to a given executive that they are to do something that only their supervisor should be directing them to do. Make sure that no one can even infer such an intention from your memo. Avoid, for example, this sort of gaffe:

```
FROM: Eric Milton [Public Relations Specialist]
TO:   Kitty O'Hara [A Manager in Human Resources]
RE:   Press Release
DATE: November 19, 19—

... Gerry would like the Human Resources managers to
send out their letters before the press bulletin is re-
leased on Monday.

cc: Delores Rodriguez [Director of Human Resources]
    Gerry Potter [Director of Public Relations]
```

This bad example suggests that an officer of one pyramid (Public Relations) is issuing an order to those who report to the officer in charge of another pyramid (Human Resources). A more tactful wording would be:

**SAMPLE MEMO
SEGMENT 6M**
*Communicating a
Request Across
Departments*

```
... If Delores approves this strategy, her directive to
the Human Resources managers would need to specify the
critical timing for the press announcement, which will
be released first thing Monday morning.
```

Eric's unedited memo would cause unnecessary resentment against him in the Human Resources division of his company. Furthermore, in sending a copy to his supervisor, Gerry, he implies her approval of the memo and could cause trouble for her too. Since implied encroachment of this kind happens more often than you might imagine, think carefully *before* you address your memo and designate the copies.

THE POLITICS OF COPYING

From the perspective of corporate territory, whom to send copies to is at least as important a decision as how to organize the the content of your memo.

THE PROCESS. *Copying* is the word businesspeople use for the practice of sending duplicate memos or letters to those whose names are listed (usually in the lower left corner) and marked with a *c:* or *cc:* (indicating "carbon copy" in preduplicator days). Copy procedure mirrors the hierarchical organization of business. Most businesses list those copied from the highest rank to the lowest. This works fine until you have to copy several department executives of equal rank. Companies solve this problem in various ways. For example, some alphabetize within a given category or rank, but some do not. Ask an experienced secretary to help you with the style for your company. Do not ignore such niceties, however. There is always a Wilmer Wolfgang, perpetually looking for something to be annoyed about, who would not appreciate being at the end of a distribution list. If you happened to list him below Harry Angel, whom he outranks by several steps, he might even have his secretary call your supervisor to point out the discrepancy. Very awkward and unpleasant for you.

THE POSSIBILITIES. Copy procedure truly is an art. Anybody can designate a memo *cc: John Q. Whombody.* But it takes real organizational skill to benefit from the full power of copy distribution. It also takes some sophistication to know what underlying message is being sent when you get a copy from someone.

■■■■■■■■■■■■■■■■■■■■■■■■■■■■■ **GUIDELINES** ■■■■■■■■■■■■■■■■

Uses of Copying

1. Copies keep the recipients informed and confirm understandings.

   - *A copy is a fast, courteous, and efficient way to follow up and report* in detail on what you have accomplished. When you get an assignment and write a memo or letter to handle it, you can simply copy your supervisor or the person who asked you to take care of the task.
   - *"FYI" forestalls action.* When you simply want to inform, and the recipient doesn't need to do anything, you write (or stamp) *FYI* ("for your information") or *Information Only* on the copy to indicate that no action is required or expected. Business is action-oriented, so when businesspeople receive a copy of something, they assume they should *do something* about it. If someone of higher rank copies

you on a memo, assume that something might be wanted of you and follow up to be sure—unless the FYI designation is on the memo.

- *A copy can inform people other than your memo's recipient.* When others need to know about the project you have in hand, notify them by sending a copy of the report you have sent to your supervisor.
- *Copies are a fast, effective way to keep all members of a team, committee, or task force informed.* You can also use copies to send a notice for, or distribute minutes of, a meeting of such a group (see Sample Memo 6D). Checking off a name on a multiple *TO:* listing is another technique for this purpose (see Sample Memo 6B).

2. Copies can be used to acknowledge help or service or to compliment or commend.

- *Copying provides a way to say "Fine job"*—a particularly welcome way as you will see when somebody does it for you. For example, in sending a memo-report to your supervisor or members of a task force, you might insert such a sentence as "Tiffany has contributed significantly to our analysis in this report" and then include Tiffany and Tiffany's supervisor among those copied. If Tiffany had been especially helpful, perhaps you would also copy her pyramid or department head. (For an example of this technique in practice, see Sample Memo 6L.)

3. Copies can also be used to nudge or tattle.

- *A copy is a discreet way to convey negative information.* Use copying, for instance, when someone is bottlenecking your project and you need to get the information to her boss and yours, but you don't exactly want to start World War III to do it. For example, you have been waiting for some days for Sally Norton to deliver important data. If you have tried *all* the regular channels and the situation is becoming truly difficult, you can say something like this in a memo to *your* supervisor:

SAMPLE MEMO SEGMENT 6N
Tactfully Surfacing a Problem

```
... As soon as we have the state figures from
Shannon Peters, we will be able to make a final
calculation for the full cost of the project.
Sally Norton has undertaken to have these to us
by next Friday at the latest.
```

Then, under the pretext of keeping everybody informed, you send a copy of the memo to Peters, Norton's supervisor, and to Ellamarie Small, Shannon's supervisor. That should crack those figures loose for you by Friday. If it doesn't, *then* you start World War III. But remember, a memo that declares war is a last-ditch measure only; use it with discretion.

IMPLICATIONS OF THE COPY LIST. The reason copying is such a politically complex procedure is that being included in—or excluded from—the copy list carries with it conventional implications well understood by people in business. Some of these implications are given below.

Copying your supervisor. When you copy your supervisor (and the other managers up your reporting line) on a memo you send to another department, you imply that they have approved the action described in the memo and the memo itself. By assumption, businesspeople are identified with the actions of their subordinates. This is the reasoning:

1. Everyone who is copied on a memo sees it and thus knows its contents.
2. If someone who is empowered to squelch your activity knows about it and has not done so, then that activity has met with approval.

Be sure that any copy distribution you are sending has your supervisor's approval.

Copying up the hierarchy. When you write a memo to a person above your supervisor in rank, you need to copy everyone between yourself and that person whose responsibilities would normally include your memo's subject. You do so in order to preserve the conventional prerogatives of rank. If you omit someone, all who receive the memo will wonder why—and so will that person.

MANAGING MEMOS TO PROTECT YOUR OWN TERRITORY. Businesspeople stake out territory, and we have suggested ways to help you deal with that psychological reality. But *you* are a businessperson too, with your own ambitions and your own vulnerabilities. Business savvy and effective memo writing can protect you too.

Cover your posterior. Everybody with experience in business knows very well what CYA means. It means cover your . . . a . . . hem, posterior. The first rule for "saving your bacon" is to save someone else's when you have the chance. Take care not to embarrass anyone—deliberately or inadvertently. And, in the case of minor missteps, make a point of not embarrassing the mildly guilty either. If you save somebody's bacon today, you are much more likely to have your own bacon saved when that's necessary. Given the vicissitudes of corporate politics, we can almost guarantee it will be necessary to have your own bacon saved one day.

Leave a paper trail. One of the most important uses of memos is to leave a paper trail—written evidence of the actions taken on a given project. Such a trail not only creates a record of historical and legal value, but can also protect you if the need arises. And since many business projects are complex or sensitive or have to be completed under stress, the need comes more often than you would think. Some specific ways you can make a paper trail work for you are described below.

<u>Filing</u>

If you have your own computer access, you have an electronic filing cabinet. All the communications you write on your word processor are automatically stored. You can make them easily accessible by providing a separate directory for every major client or project. Or you can divide your documents generically: customer complaint letters, sales letters, memos, etc. It is important that you devise a logical system so that you can locate each file when it is needed.

Many people find "window" or "desktop" software packages helpful for filing documents. These packages allow you to visualize your files and file structures, and to move, copy, and duplicate files by using only the mouse. Popular windowing packages for IBM PC's (personal computers) and PC clones include Microsoft Windows and GEM Desktop. If you use a Macintosh PC, you are already familiar with desktops, because the standard Macintosh "finder" is such a system.

Chronicle your work and file. Write dated progress reports as memos to your supervisor. For each major project keep a file, including copies of these memos and dated copies of all the written work you have generated for the project. This may sound like unnecessary extra work, especially if you're rushed. But often the person with a sheaf of corroborative memos in hand wins the day if there should later be a dispute.

Record oral agreements. After a meeting or a discussion, write down your understanding of what you agreed to do and send it as a memo to the person(s) involved. Such confirmation memos help avoid misunderstandings and are particularly useful when you are dealing in specific, detailed, or technical matters. A record can prevent problems that may arise because several people have genuinely understood the terms or situation in different ways (see Sample Memo 6C).

Confirm telephone conversations. In the Midterm ("Please Handle") Segment after this chapter we will discuss those times when the telephone is your best form of business communication. But though phone conversations are useful, they are ephemeral, and you are well advised to

SAMPLE MEMO 6O
Phone Confirmation

```
TO:   Jan Nelson
FROM: Meg Young   MY
RE:   Folders
DATE: March 14, 19--

This is to confirm my telephone order for 35 black
executive folders.  We need them no later than
noon on Monday, March 19, in order to prepare them
for the March 20 consolidation meeting.

Thanks.
```

follow up and confirm key calls with a written memo. For example, imagine your embarrassment if you ordered 35 black executive folders from the company supply department to be delivered the Monday before your department's planning meeting on Wednesday and the supply department sends you 25 pink ones on Wednesday—just in time for the meeting—alleging that that's what you said you wanted.

If you had confirmed that conversation with a memo (see Sample Memo 6O), you might experience a problem moment; but the pinkness wouldn't be your fault—and you'd be able to prove it.

PSYCHOLOGICAL MEMO WRITING

But, we hear you cry, what about empathy? Certainly. Everything in Chapter 4 is still valid. It *is* best to write as one human being to another. And with memos you do not have to imagine your correspondent. You usually are writing to a human being with whose characteristics and predilections you are, or can become, familiar. You can—and should—keep that person's face before you when you plan your memo and tailor your writing to him or her.

And when the memo you are writing requires a degree of sensitivity, even the formal empathetic opening and closing strategy still applies—though in memos the approach is often streamlined and sometimes short-cut (see Sample Memos 6C and 6P, pages 139, 162).

EMPATHY PLUS. But though the empathetic principle is just as useful in writing memos, the truth is that it is more difficult to apply. To write effectively, you still have to put yourself in the other person's shoes. But sometimes you may need to try out the shoes of a company vice president.

Since you have never yet been a company vice president, it may be harder for you to imagine how that feels. It is, however, important that you try.

Empathizing with upper management. If you can empathize with a person of higher rank and feel the magnitude of his or her responsibilities and the pressures that go with them, then you can understand how your projects appear to this person and act accordingly. For example, when you look at your pet project from the point of view of those responsible for the overall scheme, you may see that it is of less than major significance. Empathizing in this way may help your relations with those in charge. For it will keep you from flooding their desks with too-frequent progress reports and other intermittent memos on your favorite project.

On the other hand, higher executives *will* occasionally give you direct assignments, and some of these assignments may seem rather trifling. But before you put such an assignment aside to work on later, empathize. Understand that your chore may be a small but vital link in an enterprise of great significance to your company—or to someone crucial to your career. The old saw about a little neglect leading to great misfortune ("For want of a nail . . . the battle was lost") frequently applies in business. Thus this rule-of-thumb for setting your priorities: The higher the rank of the officer who suggests your assignment, the more urgent the need and the sooner the deadline.

Ethical
Issue for
Discussion

Does the underlying premise of this section, that you give due deference to rank, make you feel as though we are suggesting toadyism as a way of life? We don't really think so. For with the privileges of rank go responsibilities. Corporate executives are in charge of the whole business, and their work and decisions do determine whether the business succeeds or fails. Consequently, their performance may affect whether you and your colleagues will have something interesting and useful—and gainful—to do with your lives.

Empathizing with a person you don't like and don't trust. Sometimes, you may be writing memos to a person you have reason to think is quite different from you—a person you believe is ruthlessly ambitious or a person who rationalizes laziness by blaming others (sometimes you) or a person whose values you cannot share. We say, all the more reason for you to try to enter that person's mind imaginatively. Try to anticipate reactions so that you can forestall some and turn others to your advantage.

For example, you may have a friend in another department, otherwise well respected, against whom your supervisor has taken what seems to you an unreasoning dislike. All the empathy in the world may not put you any closer to understanding why. The antipathy may have nothing to do with business at all. It may be that they both once courted the same woman or hoped for the same promotion. It may be anything. But the kind of empathy that lets you imagine how you feel when you really dislike someone should keep you from bringing up your friend's name often in conversation with your supervisor and should certainly keep you from citing your friend as the source of your information or recommendations when you write memos to your supervisor.

Try the same sort of empathy when you compose memos to those you dislike or mistrust. You may not be able—or willing—to figure out what makes them tick. But you can identify with them at the most minimally human level. You know that what makes *you* angry will probably make them angry and what mollifies you will probably even mollify them. Thus, write to them with unfailing courtesy and keep the tone of your discourse with them cool and unemotional.

Few people in business—or elsewhere—are really vicious. Many in business, however, are ambitious. And the business atmosphere is often charged with aggression and tension. But the world of the memo—unlike that of the letter—is close-knit and daily. If the charged atmosphere explodes, the people in this world still have to work together the next day. The need to defuse this charged atmosphere and avoid internecine conflict accounts for these indispensable business communication conventions:

- Unremitting courtesy.
- Deference to rank.
- Bland, businesslike diction.
- Cool, tactful, unemotional expression.

The following Guidelines suggest overall strategies that should help keep your memos from causing you problems. We will then recommend some ways memos can help you out of difficult situations, should they arise.

━━━━━━━━━━━━━━━━━━━━━━━━ **GUIDELINES** ━━━━━━━━━━

Yet More Survival Techniques for the Novice Memo Writer

1. *Avoid the inflammatory.* There are idiosyncrasies to be reckoned with in any group of human beings working together. Add predictable human foibles, such as ego defensiveness, free-floating guilt, ambition, and impatience. Then add the fear generated by economic power wielded by less-than-expert managers. And you have a volatile mix that it is inadvisable to ignite by means of fiery rhetoric. Remember always to prefer the mild and the measured over the inflammatory.

2. *Avoid embarrassing.* Think through your memo so carefully before sending it that you are sure not to embarrass anybody inadvertently—either by implication or by awkwardness. If you embarrass any colleague or department, you will also embarrass your supervisor, your department head—and yourself. Such embarrassments can brand you as "not a team player"; incompetent; ill-intentioned; treacherous; at best, sloppy and unsophisticated. Don't take the chance. Take the extra time and trouble to examine your memos for

possible problems. Think about other people: in business this is the best advice you can practice in serving your own interests.

3. *Present each situation in the best possible light.* However bad any situation is, figure out how to present it with as much civility as possible. Remember, the underground information network will eventually show up the facts and bring you out all right. But no-body—*nobody*—will thank you for violating business norms of courtesy and diplomacy. Even when deserved, nastiness comes home to roost more quickly in business organizations than in any other kind of political situation. (For suggestions of subtle and positive ways to say the truth, see Sample Memos 6I and 6N, pages 146, 154.)

HOW TO DEFEND YOURSELF SHREWDLY. The time will inevitably come in your business career when you have to defend yourself because you've been blamed for something that wasn't your fault. You will have choices. You can keep quiet and accept the blame. You can write endless memos telling everybody—in painful detail—why you don't deserve the rap. You can wear out your supervisor and embarrass your department because you're so upset about the Situation (capital *S*). Or you can defend yourself professionally and shrewdly—this way:

- Write a *one-page* memo. Explain the situation, but be brief. Don't rehash. Don't belabor. State the facts—as briefly and succinctly and unemotionally as possible. Use the bullet outline.
- Find a compromise and offer it as quickly as you can—again briefly and succinctly, and in the most businesslike way. Don't plead; don't evade the issue; don't complain.
- Keep your tone cool. Leave out emotion, however justifiably aroused.

No matter how right you are, if you don't observe these rules you will look defensive or petty. If you seem to bluster or to whine, you will not be believed. Unfair though it may be, the whole situation will come to be associated in everybody's mind with you. So set the record straight; then forget it.

A sample situation. For several months, you have been working on the software for an important project. Because of the poor work of your counterpart in another department who is providing the hardware, the project has become snarled and delayed, and has run considerably over cost estimates. Clarence, the hardware engineer, has been behaving peculiarly. You could never locate him when you needed to get a decision, and he delayed all the parts of your project that you submitted to him. Now the project is overdue, and he has sent a memo to his boss (and copied your supervisor and *his* supervisor), "explaining" the snarl and the delay. Unfortunately, whether because of inept writing or deliberately, he has made the whole thing look like your fault—and it wasn't. You met your deadlines, and your part of the project was completed, to specifications, well ahead of the project deadline.

What should you do? Should you write to anybody? Yes. You need to set the record straight. You need to have your version of events supersede his version in the project's permanent file—and perhaps in your own personnel file.

First think of a plausible reason to write Clarence a memo: a reply to his suggestion, some action that he and you can take to bring the project to a conclusion. Then send it to or discuss it with your supervisor. She may want you to copy her supervisor and Clarence's supervisor as well. But leave the decision to her. She is responsible for the reputation of your department. Sample Memo 6P should do the trick.

Because this is an especially sensitive memo, you use the empathetic opening and close of the letter form. But unlike a letter—even one containing the same message—the memo leaves the explanation for later and begins with the proposed *action* and the compromise. Here is the place both to compromise and to make those demands you must insist on if the project is to be completed satisfactorily.

Note the restraint in the explanation. "Loss of a project coordinator" does not mention that the incompetent assistant Clarence hired had to be discharged—but everyone reading the memo will know this fact. The language is cool. You do not protest "I never missed a deadline," but still put the facts on record by insisting quietly that there were "no delays on the software side." The close is forward-looking and courteous, but the record will note that Clarence's attention has only been "recent."

You chose to send this memo to Clarence himself. You might have chosen to send it to your supervisor and copied Clarence. You would not, however, have sent it to Clarence's supervisor. That would smack of tattling, a strategy that can boomerang if you use it indiscriminately.

WHEN NOT TO WRITE A MEMO

As useful as the memo is, there are times when it is better to write no memo at all. Sometimes you do *not* want a paper trail. Use the phone or talk in person with your colleagues:

- When you have ideas you want to share but are not yet ready to express in a permanent way.
- When you need to heal a rift, undo a slight, or make an apology but do not want to record the conflict.
- In competitive or proprietary situations or whenever the issue is sensitive and you don't want the information to get around or to be quoted out of context to the embarrassment of the company.

HANDLING DISAGREEMENT. Sometimes when you find yourself in disagreement, it is better not to communicate that disagreement at all. This is one

time when putting yourself in another's shoes may fail you. If you have
just come from the academic world, where skillful intellectual jousting is
admired and rewarded, you may be tempted to write memos of disagree-

---

TO: Clarence Dawson
FROM: [you]
RE: The Telesecure Project
DATE: October 5, 19——

Thank you for your memo and for taking the time to set out your views on the
difficulties with the Telesecure Project. In spite of the problems this
project has occasioned, I now believe we need to take the following steps to
get the project back on a reasonable schedule:

· As agreed, the Engineering Change Order that you were to implement last
  Wednesday will be completed by the 12th.

· The test setup must be available for my use on the 14th.

· The results of the hardware performance evaluation should be submitted
  this week.

Given my understanding that the changes I requested on the 20th of September
would be difficult and might delay the project further, I agree that the
Engineering Change Request can be deferred and I will provide a temporary
software workaround.

To avoid a repetition of the difficulties this project has faced, we need to
review the departures from the company's customary development plan that
Telesecure has encountered.

These departures include:

1. the loss of a project coordinator early on
2. lack of an opportunity to discuss inconsistencies and poor fit between
   hard- and software components <u>before</u> they were incorporated into the
   masterplan
3. a sizable portion of idiosyncratic hardware design that demanded modification
4. lack of a timely submission of material despite no delays on the software
   side

I very much appreciate the attention you have recently been giving the
project. And I look forward to a smoother process as we move toward
production.

cc: [Your Supervisor]

SAMPLE MEMO 6P: *Setting the Record Straight*

Word-Processor Security

If you write or handle classified government documents or your company's proprietary papers, you will be given security procedures to protect them. But whether or not you handle such documents, from time to time you will be filing sensitive or confidential material. Perhaps you have written a frank letter of assessment at the request of the personnel department. Perhaps you have written some memos and letters to help your supervisor through an embarrassing situation. If you retain copies of such correspondence in your files, be sure that they are not accessible to those who ought not to see them.

If your PC is attached to a local network, the file-server should automatically provide security for the files you store in it. Otherwise, you could store such material on removable media such as floppy disks or Bernoulli cartridges. Or you could undertake more sophisticated measures by purchasing a PC security or file encryption system.

Whatever you decide to do, be sure to exercise caution here. You may recall that a national television news anchor came in for a great deal of embarrassment because of indiscreet comments stored in his word processor. Some informal documents contained his frank and less than flattering opinion of a colleague, a much beloved weather forecaster. Someone searched his private computer files, found the material, and publicized it. Not many of our own careers could stand such a brouhaha.

ment, expecting the sort of approval adroit argumentative papers brought you in college. But in most businesses such memos from a junior employee would be seriously misguided, as the following story demonstrates.

A Cautionary Tale

A member of upper management called a staff group together to discuss a new advertising campaign the company was about to embark upon. He described the principles on which the campaign was to be based, and, having given a few examples of how to reach the designated population, he asked the group for their suggestions. After the discussion, he warmly requested a continuation of the flow of ideas in writing. "We need your input," he said. "Be creative. Be frank. And let me hear from you."

Bud Nixon, who had been on the job almost a year, sat rather uncomfortably through the whole session. He questioned both the accuracy of the consumer research and the philosophy on which the new campaign was based. And when the executive warmly requested his "frank" opinion, he knew exactly what he would do. This was just like college. He would write a well-reasoned memo, carefully outlining his position, and even if he would have little effect upon already established policy, management would know what a valuable, thinking employee they had in him.

The executive who had called the meeting was sincere in his request for comments and ideas. He knew there was creativity in his staff beyond the advertising department and he wanted to tap that creativity for the grand new campaign. It did not occur to him that anyone would verbalize *disagreement* with the already accepted scheme. The morning Bud's memo arrived, the executive had discovered that his new customer service manager had not been handling complaints well, there had been a fracas "upstairs" on the vice-presidential level, and he had had an argument with his teenage son before leaving home. The executive called Bud in and gave him the worst chewing out of his young life.

Some memos should never be written. Think before you write.

HOW TO SUGGEST A GOOD IDEA

All right, you say, so I shouldn't rock the boat. But what if I get a genuinely good idea, an idea that would really be useful for the company? Surely I shouldn't keep that to myself? Of course not. But expressing that idea so as to help both the company and *you* is a delicate communication problem that will require subtlety.

THE DIFFICULTY. The whole process of offering an unsolicited idea is fraught with complications and pitfalls. Does that sound overly dramatic? Not so, in our experience. Eager beavers offering terrific ideas get into trouble in corporations far more often than not. If in your company ideas from junior executives are well and seriously received—and *credited* to their owners— your company is in a small minority. To say so is not to criticize corporations unduly. The truth is that you very well *may be* young and inexperienced. As a newcomer, you *are not* privy to which ideas have been tried, and tried, and tried again. You have no way of knowing that a given idea shouldn't be mentioned because it has already brought excess cost and/or disaster upon the very person to whom you propose to suggest it. Then, too, there is that ubiquitous time factor. Senior executives in your organization are busy carrying out their own job objectives and investigating and carrying out the objectives of *their* supervisors. Chances are they will be less than eager to spend their time and energy investigating and carrying out yours.

A METHOD. Having seriously considered the consequences, if you still feel your idea is worth a try, here is the most sensible approach:

- *Start with your supervisor.* Don't—repeat, don't—go around your supervisor. (If you find your supervisor unapproachable, then you will have to save your idea for a more propitious time.) If your supervisor is the cooperative sort, generous-spirited, and not threatened by the people she or he supervises, your first step is to try talking the idea over with him or her. You just might find a cordial reception for your idea.
- *If your supervisor is not the cooperative sort, make a paper trail.* In case your supervisor is given to taking credit for the ideas of those who report to him or her, you have to take another tack. In that case, make a paper trail by writing the idea in a memo and sending it to your supervisor. Include in the memo a request to discuss the idea.
- *If the idea is practical, plan your strategy.* Your discussion with your supervisor will determine the practicality of continuing with your idea. If there is good reason not to press the idea further up the hierarchy, your talk with your supervisor will prevent you from making a gaffe. And if the matter can prudently be advanced, your supervisor should be able to help plan a strategy for presenting the idea.
- *Write your memo.* That strategy will almost certainly involve describing your idea in a memo. It is unlikely that your supervisor will have time to write this memo. Moreover, it is to your advantage to come out of the meeting with an assignment to write up the idea yourself. That assignment should be your goal for the meeting.

THE MEMO. Chances are your supervisor will tell you to write a memo with his or her name on it, setting out the idea. The memo may be addressed to the supervisor's supervisor or to whomever your supervisor suggests. When you draft the memo, try this approach:

```
Lee Enthusiast has suggested a plan that I believe has
merit. The plan....
```

You, Lee J. Enthusiast, get your name in the memo and you get the credit when sales increase by 300 percent. If that happens, congratulations—to both you and your supervisor. In backing your idea in this way, your supervisor takes a risk. For if the idea is considered daft, it is your supervisor who has to take the rejection, a rejection far more direct for this experienced manager than it would be for you.

This procedure is far from guaranteed. But it is the only such method we can recommend. We wish you luck.

Ethical Issues for Serious Thought and Discussion

1. Should Americans of goodwill move toward democratizing business (page 143)? If you would like to go into this question in a more scholarly way, look up "Corporate Democracy" in the *Business Periodical Index, The New York Times Index,* or *The Social Science Index.*
2. Should you give due deference to rank even when you don't agree with the politics of those in charge or even if you feel some of them may not be worthy of their positions (pages 158–159)?
3. Are ambition and the territorial competition it breeds a good or bad thing for American business (pages 150–155)?
4. On page 150 we caution you about making suggestions outside of your area of immediate responsibility. Discuss the implications of this advice. Do you feel that good ideas might be lost in this way? That mediocrity might be perpetuated? Can you think of ways around the problem that would not be costly to you as the memo writer? See pages 164–165 and evaluate the related ideas suggested there.
5. Do you think it was fair for Bud Nixon (pages 163–164) to be severely reprimanded for taking the trouble to offer his frank opinion when it was asked for? Do you find the executive's actions in Bud's case hypocritical? What if Bud's views put him in serious moral conflict with the policy? What should he do?

AUTHENTIC BUSINESS PROBLEMS

1. As a trainee in the public relations section of your firm, you have been sent to a seminar on good professional techniques for public information. Your own training is not yet complete, but you learned many useful strategies at the seminar that you believe would help with problems you have observed in the company's secretarial staff.

   The secretaries answer the phones in an inappropriately casual way. They don't mean to be discourteous, but sometimes that is the way they sound. Sometimes messages are lost. Sometimes the messages are delivered so late as to cause the recipient to seem lax or discourteous about returning calls. Sometimes the messages are incomplete or the telephone numbers are inaccurately recorded.

   You very much want to write a memo to report on techniques (forms and checklists you brought back from the conference) that could improve the overall secretarial performance—and, incidentally, spruce up the performance of your section's secretaries, who have the most serious problem.

   You have a number of options open to you in writing this communication:

   • You could write to the head of your section—your own supervisor.

- You could write to the office manager, who is responsible for training the secretaries in all divisions.
- You could write to the office manager and copy your supervisor.
- You could write to your supervisor and copy the office manager.

Specify whom you have decided to write to and why.

You also have options as to the content:

- You could criticize the practices in your own section.
- You could simply report on the techniques you brought back from the conference.
- You could report on the techniques and then suggest a way to communicate them first to the secretaries in your section and then to the other secretaries.
- You have a number of brochures and teaching materials from the seminar. You could send these to your supervisor.
- You could send these materials to the office manager.

What strategy or strategies have you decided to adopt?

Think through this communication for the strategic problems it presents:

- Your position is one of a relatively new, entry-level management employee.
- The secretaries who must type your memo are also the people whose performance most needs to improve.
- The office has a very real problem in its need to present a professional and friendly image for the company.

Your Assignment. Write the necessary communication, worded tactfully. Your aim is to persuade the proper people to institute the necessary training and aids to improve performance. Remember your own performance will be judged on how effectively you are able to carry out this objective.

2. If you are faced with a similarly difficult situation in your own work:
   a. Write a memo to handle it, using the guidelines suggested here.
   b. Write an additional memo to your instructor, explaining the situation and why you approached it as you did.

FOCUS:
"Please Handle"

EXECUTIVE SUMMARY

In business, nobody organizes your assignments for you. Nobody specifies this letter or that memo. Business executives rarely tell you exactly what they want, how it should look, how long it should be, when it is wanted, what it should include. Rather, they say, "Please handle." And you are left to organize your own time, your resources, and the constraints the situation imposes. Your response must take account of political situations within your own organization, within whatever outside organizations you are required to deal with, and in the world at large.

How should you "handle" the assignment?

1. Familiarize yourself with the assignment.
2. Figure out what needs to be done.
3. Sort out time and situational constraints.
4. Establish a deadline.
5. Construct a workable timetable.
6. Make appointments.
7. Confer.
8. Reevaluate the project.
9. Write. Review. Revise.
10. Follow up.

PROBLEMS OF THE NEOPHYTE EXECUTIVE

For many years, teachers, professors, parents, camp counselors, and occasional others have been telling you what to do—in detail. "This is what I want. This is exactly how it should turn out. These are the steps you should take to produce it. Follow the attached guidelines, and ask if you don't understand. The final product should be turned in by _____ o'clock on _____."

In business, you *could* get an assignment like that. You could also win a state lottery, be struck by lightning, and be elected President by popular acclaim *before* you get an assignment like that. Business assignments almost never come to you in an organized, well-thought-out, tidy, or even rational state. That's because business is going to pay *you* to decide what the problem is, organize it, think through the solution, and take care of it. Be glad: that means you're needed.

Since the assignments you get will almost inevitably be sketchy, they will demand much of you—in judgment, in resourcefulness, and in fast, accurate performance. Almost invariably they will also demand writing skill. You will need to know not only how to compose letters and memos (see Chapters 4, 5, and 6), but also when to write them and what to put in them, and how to do it quickly. How to deal with this you're-on-your-own factor in business communication is what this chapter—indeed, this whole book—is about.

THE ASSIGNMENT

The most common kind of business assignment is verbal: "I need an analysis of our five top competitors by Wednesday noon." Or it's a scrawl on a document or a routing slip (sometimes called a "buck note") attached to a document or letter. The note says: "Please handle." Or "Please take care of this and copy me on what you do." Or "Please work with Ed on this and see if you can give me a recommendation by tomorrow morning. I have a meeting with Jameson at ten, and he will want to talk about what we should do."[1]

That last is a *detailed* assignment in business. Note that these directives do not suggest a course of action. Note that the directives do not specify how many pages (if any) of answers or recommendations are wanted or how the data should be organized. They drop into your lap what

---

1. Such vague directions are commonplace in the business world. But that does not make them an effective managerial technique. When it is your turn to make assignments, make them as clear and free from ambiguity as your time permits.

is readily available on the subject. They say "help," but they do not specify what kind of help they need. And even if the assignment is unusually clear-cut, you will have to make many decisions about how to select what you say and how to present your findings.

HOW TO "TAKE CARE OF THAT"

First, a caveat: It would be irresponsible of us to suggest to you that business problems are so simple or standard that you can handle them just by knowing how to write proper, formulaic communications. Business problems do not ordinarily lend themselves to tidy or ideal solutions. The people who have the information you need may or may not be cooperative. The organization's politics may or may not be conducive to the actions your solution involves. The ideal solution may be too expensive, or even too embarrassing, for a ranking executive or even the company as a whole. Or what you have to communicate may be only the least bad of a number of bad options.

Nevertheless, if you do not expect a perfect fit and if you understand that unforeseen difficulties may—and probably will—occur, you may find the following Guidelines helpful.

GUIDELINES

"Handling It"

Step 1. Read rapidly through the materials. Or study the notes you have taken if the assignment is given verbally. (Always have notepaper and pencil at hand.)

Step 2. Figure out what needs to be done and by whom. Identify the steps necessary to evaluate and resolve the problem. Make a list of the things that must be done. Make sure you know the answers to such questions as these:
- Who must write what to whom?
- Will the people you need to work with be available? When?
- What data do you need? Where will you find it? Whom will you need to consult?
- What time problems or supply bottlenecks are likely to arise? What can you do to forestall them or to work them out in the time available?

Step 3. Sort out the constraints under which you will have to work. These may include (but are not restricted to):
- Constraints on your time.
- Constraints on the accessibility of others whose help you need to get the job done.
- Constraints involving the person who requested your work.
- Constraints imposed by your commitment to other ongoing work.

- Lead time necessary to procure materials.

Step 4. Establish a deadline.

- If you have been assigned a deadline that is reasonable, base your timetable on it.
- If you have been assigned a deadline that seems impossible, inquire discreetly—either through your supervisor or through the secretary of the person who has set the deadline— whether it is a hard deadline driven by events or needs or whether it is arbitrary. (You will be astonished at how many deadlines are set arbitrarily.) Work out your timetable as close to the requested deadline as possible, and then present your case for the emended schedule to your supervisor. Your supervisor can be helpful in clearing away unnecessary or unreasonable obstacles, especially if the assignment has come to you direct, either from a department outside your chain of reporting or from somebody a rank or two above him or her.
- If the unreasonable deadline remains firm, however, adopt the slogan of the U.S. Army Air Force: "The difficult we do immediately. The impossible takes a little longer." In business such an attitude will net you a reputation for sheer brilliance, when all you have done is meet a tough deadline. It will also earn you a reputation for dedication.
- If you are not given a deadline, set up a tentative one for yourself and proceed to the timetable step. When scheduling is your own prerogative, make your completion deadlines as early as is reasonable. But remember, completing your work ahead of schedule is considered admirable; finishing even a little late is strongly disapproved—even if it is your *own* arbitrary deadline you miss.

Step 5. Construct a workable timetable (see pages 173–175).

Step 6. Make appointments to see or to talk by phone with those who can help you evaluate the problem and decide what is needed.

- If you need to have an extended telephone conversation with someone whose time is limited, call that person's secretary and make an appointment for the call. Explain your needs to the secretary. A good secretary is a pearl without price and can sometimes provide what you need without your even having to see the supervisor.
- Remember to make this set of inquiries *first,* because the people who are going to provide information for you may need to make calls or check or gather data themselves before they are able to help you.

Step 7. Keep the appointments. Meet or talk to your sources of information or of preliminary action.

Step 8. Having gathered your data, reevaluate the project. Think again:

- What is it I *really* want to accomplish?
- How can I best do it?

Step 9. Write the necessary communications, following the principles discussed in the earlier chapters of this text.

- Review
- Revise

Step 10. Follow up. In business, proper follow-up separates the women from the girls and the men from the boys—and may be the thing that saves your job or rescues your promotion. Ask yourself:
- What else needs to be written?
- What other actions need to be performed?
- Who else has to review the project?
- What other follow-up tasks should be performed?
- How can I expedite both the decision and the project?

CONSTRUCTING A TIMETABLE

The key step in the planning phase of any project is making a timetable. Because it is so significant, we need to discuss it in more detail. Some timetables may be as simple as several deadlines jotted on your desk calendar. Others may be the formal time and action calendars that will have to accompany your recommendations.

THE PROCESS: THINKING IT THROUGH. Ask yourself questions like the following:

- How much time will it take for me to collect the necessary data?
- How much time will I need to analyze it?
- Will I need to consult outside experts? (If so, factor in their schedules.)
- How much time will secretaries and clerical staff need to produce the final product(s)? When will the word-processing equipment be free? Do I need to reserve the time?
- How much revision is likely to be necessary? Do the people who may ask for the revisions understand the deadlines? Will the project be ready for review before the manager leaves for the annual trip to Uzbekistan? (Be sure your timetable reflects this sort of reality.)

Once you have arrived at answers to these tough questions, you are ready to construct your timetable.

THE PROCEDURE. The key to making a timetable is to start with your deadline and work backward from it, as the following Guidelines indicate.

GUIDELINES

Making a Timetable

- Note your final deadline on a calendar.
- Then back up to the present, filling in any firm or fixed dates that you know. No other single action is as useful, because this exercise tells you conclusively whether your deadline can be met. (For hints on handling truly nonmeetable deadlines, see page 172. But please be

sure that you have in fact run into a *truly* immovable object; never reject a set deadline on the first pass.)

- Using the information you have gathered in Steps 1 through 10, write down all dates and constraints in chronological order and fill them in on your calendar.
- Now study the calendar and observe any portions of the sequence that don't work. Think of ways you can make them work. Could Gerry possibly help you out and get you that data for the first draft on Monday instead of Thursday? Could the word processor be rescheduled to accommodate your problem?
- Check each date and make any needed adjustments to make the calendar workable.
- Build air into your schedule. Things always take longer than you anticipate. So wherever possible give yourself leeway for others to be late with interim deadlines. And leave time for illness, accidents, and miscellaneous snafus.

SAMPLE TIMETABLES. Sample A is the sort of timetable you might construct if you were asked to arrange an off-site meeting. José Esteban constructed this particular timetable when he was asked to set up a luncheon meeting for his company's Sales and Marketing Department and Public Relations Department to discuss a new product announcement.

```
-------------------------------------------------------
Sample Timetable A
-------------------------------------------------------
```

Meeting to Be Held	September 30
Memo to participants to find what audiovisual equipment they will require	August 1
Deadlines for reply to query	August 10
Reserve facility	August 15
Talk with caterer for lunch arrangements	August 15
Order audiovisual equipment	August 17
Materials submission deadline for both departments	September 21 (allowing time for duplicating)
Check on facility	September 24

```
Set up audiovisual equipment                    September 29
---------------------------------------------------------------
```

Sample B is a production timetable, scheduling budget requests. In the sample, Meg and Bri report to the writer. She reports to JH, who reports to CS. TC is the pyramid head, the senior executive in charge of the entire division.

```
-----------------------------------------------------------------
Sample Timetable B
-----------------------------------------------------------------
```

<u>Final departmental budgets due week of January 10</u>

```
Meeting with Meg and Bri                        October 15

Meet with CS and JH for final budget
items                                           October 20

First draft to CS                               October 30

Revisions                                       November 15

Final, all-department budget                    November 30
  meeting

Preparation of final spreadsheets              December 15

Final draft to TC—pyramid head                 December 28
  approval

Final revisions                                 January 4
-----------------------------------------------------------------
```

You will find an example of a complete time-and-action calendar in the appendix of the sample report in Chapter 9 (page 243).

AND NOW YOU ARE READY TO WRITE. Having organized your project, you are ready to follow the suggestions of Chapters 1 through 6 and to send the appropriate letters and memos. But before you commit yourself to writing, you might want to consider whether all the tasks in your project lend themselves to written communication.

WHEN WRITING IS NOT THE ANSWER

Even though this is a text on business writing, honesty compels us to say that there are plenty of times when writing is not the most appropriate form of communication. Sometimes the phone serves you better. And sometimes you should call *before* you write. A phone call:

- Is faster.
- Is more direct.
- Permits instant response.
- Does not leave a paper trail.

WHEN TO TELEPHONE. Because a call has those characteristics, you should use the phone when:

1. The time is so short that it does not allow a written exchange. (You may need to follow up with a confirming note or at least a memo for your file.)
2. The problem is simple and doesn't require documentation.
3. The problem is so complex you need a preliminary conversation to agree on guidelines.
4. The problem is too politically delicate to be written down. Or the situation is so sensitive legally that finding the precision of phrasing and diction necessary for a permanent record would demand more time than circumstances currently allow.

WHEN NOT TO TELEPHONE. On the other hand, though your telephone is near at hand and a call is always easier, there are times when you should resist the temptation to use the phone. Write when:

1. You need to have your ideas or your point of view clearly and thought-fully laid out for your correspondent *before* he or she has the opportunity to respond. A letter or memo gives your correspondent time to consider before responding.
2. You need a formal record of a request for data or assistance or another kind of transaction, either because you may have to cover yourself or because you want to show a supervisor how you have handled the problem.
3. The matter is so technical or detailed that all the people involved need to have the details or a checklist in front of them.
4. You have to inform a number of people. Even a simple notification becomes time-consuming if it involves many calls.

■ AUTHENTIC BUSINESS PROBLEMS ■

Questions Suitable for a Midterm Examination

1. *Working Out an Effective Strategy: "Take care of this"*
   "Take care of this" is what your supervisor, Mr. Claude Fidget, said to you. Here is the situation:
      You are assistant to the plant manager at United Widgets, Inc. You have orders to ship 15,000 yellow widgets to Big Gizmo, Inc., by March 15. The date is absolute. Big Gizmo must have the yellow

widgets by March 15th or the order will be canceled. Your production schedule is low this month, and the Gizmo order will improve it substantially.

You need 45,000 feet of 1/4" yellow plastic tape to assemble the widgets. You ordered the tape with plenty of lead time. The boxes were shipped and stored in your stockroom two weeks ago. Though your supplies inspector spot-checked the boxes at the time, you realize only now, when production has actually started, that some of the tape rolls being run down the line have turned out to be 1/2" blue.

The supplier, Tippy-Top Tape, Inc., of Brunswick, Maine, has apparently shipped only part of the order correctly, but your inspector checked the order in and okayed the packing slip and the invoice.

You have 10 days from the first taping operation to complete the widget order. Ordinarily, the tape supplier (who is small) works on special order only. And so he has to have a week to schedule you in, because he has other customers already scheduled. But you can't get the tape anywhere else.

This is not the first time (but the third) that Tippy-Top Tape has fouled up a crucial order. Still, old Mr. Tippy, who still runs the tape business himself, is inclined to be a bit testy. And he may give you a hard time because your inspector okayed the order. On the other hand, your firm does a substantial amount of business with him.

Mr. Fidget doesn't tell you how many pieces of correspondence (letters, memos, etc.) you have to produce. You're on your own. (And your performance evaluation comes up next Tuesday.)

Your Assignment
a. Think through the problem and plan your strategy.
b. Decide:
   (i) What letters (or memos) you have to write and to whom; what calls you need to make.
   (ii) What copies of what should be sent to whom.
c. Write the required correspondence.
d. In a brief memo to your instructor, explain your strategy. Then write a sentence or two of explanation for each piece of correspondence, telling why you feel it is necessary to write what you have written.

Use all the skills you have learned in the course thus far: Use tact, standard business courtesy, and good sense. Be clear, grammatical, neat, and precise. Be *effective*. (It's Mr. Fidget's favorite word.)

2. *Working Out an Effective Strategy: "You're on your own"*
For the past eight months, you, L. Novis, have been Assistant Manager for Corporate Sales for the Metropolitan Paradise hotel chain, headquartered in Philadelphia, with branches in Atlanta, Memphis, Los Angeles, Baltimore, Miami, Houston, and Jersey City. Your supervisor, Evalie Burden, Manager of Corporate Sales,

is away for five weeks on a tour of a number of Asian capitals. She hopes to wrap up some convention business for Asian travelers, because she has committed to a 12 percent sales increase as a personal job objective. A 15 percent increase would net both you and her a substantial bonus. Missing the objective could mean a meager—or no—raise for you both. So far, sales are not brisk. In her absence you have opened and must respond to the following complaint letter from Gerald Kniggle, Director of Internal Audit for the Honeyriver Corporation, headquartered in Atlanta.

Ms. Evalie Burden   September 25, 19—
Manager, Corporate Sales
Metropolitan Paradise Hotels
Philadelphia, Pennsylvania

Dear Ms. Burden:

Last Friday, the Honeyriver Accounting and Internal Audit Departments held their annual consolidation meeting at your Metro-Peach Paradise Hotel here in Atlanta. We have held the meeting there for more than twelve years. This year, however, the meeting room was untidy, and the air-conditioning was noisy (until it broke down). The coffee ran out by midmorning, and it took us until after lunch to get a fresh urn. Also, the Danish were stale, and the waitresses assigned to us were slovenly. Altogether, the facilities and service were inadequate.

Moreover, this Thursday my wife and I had dinner in the Peachy Room of your Atlanta hotel for our anniversary. We have always been great fans of Metro-Paradise dining rooms, as I told you, but our experience last week was dismaying. Not only had our reservations not been recorded, but my wife's entree had to be sent back because it was inedible. She had made the reservations more than a week in advance, but because there was a press of reservations that night, the only table left was right next to the kitchen, and we could scarcely talk for all the kitchen clatter. Her lobster was <u>not</u> fresh, and the maître d'hôtel was not helpful when we asked to have it replaced.

I write to inform you of these bad experiences because, as you and I discussed in our meeting last month, the Metro-Paradise in Jersey City is one of the hotels my auditor's professional association is considering for its annual meeting next March. As chairman of the annual meeting committee, I am not

disposed to recommend a Metro-Paradise if we can expect the service in Jersey City to be of a quality
comparable to that in Atlanta.

Since, however, your Jersey City facility would be
most conveniently located for our meeting, I would appreciate hearing from you by next Wednesday with some
reason why I should not change from my original plan
to recommend the Jersey Metro for the auditors' meeting.

Sincerely,

Gerald Kniggle

Before you can do anything about Kniggle's letter, you have to
know more about the situation, so you call John Snuteleigh, maître
d'hôtel at the Peach Room. He claims that Mrs. Kniggle is known
as a difficult patron. She forgets to make reservations, then pre-
tends to have done so to her husband, who always believes her. She
frequently sends food back. John, who had always before been understanding and had gone out of his way to placate the temperamental Mrs. Kniggle, was pressed and harassed that night and was
a bit frosty with her. You know that John Snuteleigh, who has been
with Metro-Paradise for 14 years, is a reliable maître d' and a valued employee. In fact, he has just been promoted and in April will
go to Jersey City to take over direction of the Jersey Room at that
hotel. He tells you he is tired of the Kniggles and has no intention
of making any sort of apologetic gesture this time.

To be fair to Mr. Kniggle, however, you are aware that the Atlanta Metro-Peach Paradise has had a high rate of turnover in its
management, and Metro-Paradise's usual high-service standards
have not always been adhered to there in recent months. The Jersey Metro-Paradise, on the other hand, is your newest hotel, the
flagship of your Northeastern Division. It has had the best of Metro-
Paradise's resources poured into it to make it competitive and is a
splendid facility, with only the company's first line of management
personnel.

Landing that auditors' association meeting would account for a
significant piece of your sales increase for next year. But Evalie
won't be back in time to handle this problem. You have at your disposal some authority and resources to act in her behalf.

Your Assignment
a. Write, call, do what's necessary. Take care of it.
b. In a brief memo to your instructor, explain your strategy. Then
   write a sentence or two of explanation for each piece of correspondence, telling why you feel it is necessary to write what you
   have written.

WRITING EFFECTIVE RECOMMENDATION MEMOS

EXECUTIVE SUMMARY

Like all memos, the recommendation memo should be brief, direct, and tactful. Other memos may be designed to report on *or* bring about action, but action is the *invariable* goal of the recommendation memo. Such memos always contain:

1. a statement of purpose,
2. recommendations, and
3. request for approval to implement the action.

Each part is usually supported by information or argument.

In writing recommendation memos you must gather appropriate data. Nevertheless, a simple recitation of the data in your memo is not sufficient, however neatly you tabulate it. Your job is to move from the data to information—inferences, conclusions, and suggestions. You should support and facilitate the decision making of your managers by presenting:

■ Clearly stated judgments and recommendations.

■ Support—in the form of clearly demonstrated data. Your data should reflect:

  • Careful and thorough gathering.

  • Judicious selection.

  • Sound inference.

  • Orderly presentation.

The entire process must take account of both the implications for your company and its goals for the project at hand.

THE NATURE OF A RECOMMENDATION MEMO

What is a recommendation memo? It is first of all a business memo. And thus everything we said about memos in Chapter 6 applies to a recommendation memo. To review, a memo is:

- An internal communication.
- Brief—ideally one page in length.
- Direct and clear in style.
- Businesslike in tone: informal, courteous, and tactful.

Its purpose: to report on or bring about action.

What distinguishes the recommendation memo—and its more complex form, the short report—is that its ultimate purpose is *invariably* to bring about action. Though some memos can be basically informative, the aim of the recommendation memo is always to recommend and support a specific line of action.

STRUCTURAL COMPONENTS OF A RECOMMENDATION MEMO

You will find a number of examples of effective recommendation memos in this chapter. The memos were written by businesspeople working in a variety of fields: insurance, computer technology, merchandising, heavy industry, retailing, and consumer-product manufacturing. The recommendations suggested by these writers are equally diverse: fax machine rental, a pilot bar-coding program, advertising budget allocations, ways of giving a laundry product more customer appeal, strategies to expedite an important meeting, and techniques for eliminating delivery-scheduling error. Despite their diversity, these examples are all typical of effective recommendation memos. So is the longer and more complex model in Chapter 9.

The sample memos may look more different than similar. Yet all such memos (and these examples do not by any means exhaust the possibilities) are actually composed of more or less the same elements. In fact, three key elements are *essential* for any recommendation memo:

1. Statement of purpose (and support).
2. Recommendation(s) (and support).
3. Request for approval to implement the action (and support).

To: Rick Hardwicke

From: Joyce Browne   **Ext** 4567

Re: A proposed solution to the problem of timely delivery of materials received on the fax machine

Date: May 16, 19—

At Jonathan's request, we have investigated the problem with timely delivery of materials received on the fax machine. Last week's snarl caused Makepeace to lose a sizable block of business. (The Alva contract alone was worth $25,000.) We believe the following steps, if implemented promptly, will avoid such a bottleneck in the future.

Recommendations

· <u>Lease a second fax machine, to be housed in the marketing office and designated primarily for marketing business.</u> Clearly, one fax machine can no longer handle our increased communications volume.

· <u>Hire one additional junior-level trainee to staff the communications room as backup for the two senior operators</u>. In recent months the number of duties each operator must perform has increased significantly. In addition to handling both outgoing and incoming communications, they now customarily serve as backup operators for the executive message center and cover phones when senior executive secretaries must be away from their desks.

Last Monday's situation, which required an unusually fast turnaround—and missed it— is occurring more often. As you will recall, Marianna and her department did not receive the Alva message until after lunch, missed the opportunity to rebid, and lost the contract. Marianna believes Makepeace would have been competitive for that business.

Costs

· Annual rental on a new fax machine	$ 0,000
Less 00% discount for two machines	$ 00
	$ 0,000
· Annual base salary for the new hire	$00,000
Estimated benefits cost	$ 0,000
	$00,000
TOTAL	$00,000

Rationale

· The additional cost would be more than offset by additional sales opportunities.

· Because of last quarter's consolidation of the communications functions, there is money in Budget 50A to cover the additional leasing contract. Marianna's department could pick up half the costs of the new hire from its salaries contingency budget. And we could contribute the remainder from this department's discretionary fund.

Implementation

John concurs with this strategy and believes we should expedite it. <u>Since Marianna currently has four critical bids out, may we have your approval before Friday to proceed with the leasing contract and authorization for one new hire?</u> A personnel search request form is attached for your signature if you agree.

I'll be in the office until Wednesday noon, should you have any questions, and Marianna will be available while I am away.

JB: jjr

SAMPLE RECOMMENDATION MEMO 7A: *Problem/Solution*

TO: Steve Wong
FROM: Barbara Lessing-Black *BL-B* Ext. 121
RE: FEASIBILITY OF BAR CODING IN SOUTHWEST DIVISIONAL OPERATIONS
           (CONFERENCE REPORT)
DATE: January 27, 19--

This summarizes information from the Retail Conference on Universal Bar
Coding that I attended in New York on January 23-24.   The Conference
brought together experts from general merchandise retailing, specialty
retailers, and food marketers to discuss the latest hardware and
applications for bar-coding technology.

GOALS OF THE TRIP
   o Investigate the advances in the uses of bar coding for possible
      application in a pilot program in our southwestern divisions.
   o Determine whether sufficient support is available from suppliers to
      make implementing a full system of bar coding possible.
   o Produce cost estimates for both a pilot and a full system, based on
      data available at the meeting.

BACKGROUND
Both Lettie Johnson and Hal Kendrick have asked the Systems Support
Department to investigate bar coding.   They would like to see a pilot
program in operation by fall, with an eye to rolling the program out to
all divisions by spring if results warrant.

KEY FINDINGS
1. Current technology in bar coding is sophisticated and would provide
   many advantages for inventory control and enhanced point-of-purchase
   efficiency.
2. However, presently installed cash registers must be reprogrammed,
   even if compatible with systems available, and that would require at
   least ____ weeks lead time, even for the simplest system.   There would
   also be cost associated with writing the necessary programs, install-
   ing them, and training floor personnel.
3. A number of major suppliers who attended the meeting claim to be able
   to have a system up and running inside of six weeks from contract
   signing.   Systems people from Microtek and Magnatron, however, both
   of whom have put programs into remote locations, say this amount of
   lead time is not adequate.   They advise that four to six additional
   weeks would be required to bring a system up to speed.

TENTATIVE RECOMMENDATIONS
   o Design and implement a pilot program in only one division to test
      technology.
   o Design a phased program of one, three, then all six southwestern
      divisions to take effect as results of the first pilot program can
      be evaluated.
   o Plan 10 to 12 weeks lead time for each installation.

IMPLEMENTATION
Lettie and Hal will meet on Monday to discuss setting up a task force to
study these findings further; and we will send you a report and further
recommendations on Tuesday.

SAMPLE RECOMMENDATION MEMO 7B: *Investigative Findings/Suggested Implementation*

FROM: PTVAX DNERNAN   *DGN*
TO: MBARNES, JMERRICK, HHINES, TKORBY
DATE: 14-May-19—
SUBJ: Microtek query list

From my perspective, there are three areas that we currently need to discuss with
Microtek to facilitate the development of a PPS2100 product for VX systems: ZBIT
protocol, hardware (ZBIT cable), and benchmark testing.

1) ZBIT PROTOCOL

Right now, we are defining PPS2100 ZBIT implementation by the following method:

   a) Start with the Version 1 ZBIT definition.
   b) Delete the ZBIT commands that are not to be supported initially.
   c) Add certain vendor-unique commands. These commands are listed in the spreadsheet
      table.
   d) If necessary, redefine remaining commands to support any vendor-specific nuances
      that we must handle.

We must ensure that the protocol resulting from following these steps—especially steps
(c) and (d)—supports VX satisfactorily. We need to stay up-to-date on the current
Microtek ZBIT specification.

There are four commands defined in the present Microtek specs that we cannot support:
Receive Diagnostic Results, Send Diagnostic, Write Buffer, and Read Buffer.

In addition, there are a number of other commands that we do not plan to support in our
first release. We should discuss the ramifications of this nonsupport.

It may be advantageous for Microtek to participate in a review of our final ZBIT subset
definition. In this case, we would need to know by what time our formal ZBIT subset
document must be completed.

2) HARDWARE/CABLING

Tom K., of course, would be the main source of questions in this area. To my knowledge,
Tom's query about cabling has never been answered. I think that the lines of
communication between Tom and Jim N. should be opened.

3) BENCHMARK TESTING

We will want to ask whether we can obtain the use of the VX9 system for testing our
product. I would still like a tour of Microtek's test setup. It also would be helpful
if we could obtain a list of the Microtek-supported ZBIT targets (along with
documentation).

We meet, as you know, with Microtek on Friday. If you have any additional suggestions,
let me hear from you by Thursday.

SAMPLE RECOMMENDATION MEMO 7C: *Suggestions for Technical Meeting Agenda*

Memos may also include other *optional* components (see Chapter 9, page 237). These three elements are indispensable, however. They appear in many different guises. But you will find them in some form in every effective recommendation memo and, of course, in each of the examples. Don't let your own memos leave your desk without them.

ELEMENT 1: STATEMENT OF PURPOSE

Why do you write a memo? What is its purpose? Your reader must know the answer right away or waste time trying to figure it out. You should, therefore, *begin every memo with some statement of purpose.*

DIRECT STATEMENT. Sometimes it is possible to orient your reader to your purpose with a statement that is both brief and direct. Note, for example, the statement that introduces Sample Memo 7C:

```
From my perspective, there are three areas that we cur-
rently need to discuss with Microtek to facilitate the
development of a PPS2100 product for VX systems: ZBIT
protocol, hardware (ZBIT cable), and benchmark testing.
```

This statement informs its reader in a straightforward way. Why has the writer sent the memo? To offer recommendations for a discussion with Microtek. What is its purpose? To facilitate development of a new product. Direct and to the point.

BACKGROUND INFORMATION. Though brevity is always preferable in business, the complexity of a situation may demand that you include background information in the purpose statement. *Often this information relates the memo's purpose to the objectives of the entire project.* The purpose of Sample Memo 7B, for instance, to report and make recommendations from an attended conference, would remain unclear unless the goals for the trip were also explained. The purpose statement of this memo, quoted below, extends to include sections for both project objectives (i.e., "Goals") and background:

```
This summarizes information from the Retail Conference
on Universal Bar Coding that I attended in New York on
January 23–24. The Conference brought together experts
from general merchandise retailing, specialty retailers,
and food marketers to discuss the latest hardware and ap-
plications for bar-coding technology.

Goals of the Trip
• Investigate the advances in the uses of bar coding for
  possible application in a pilot program in our southwestern
  divisions.
```

- Determine whether sufficient support is available from suppliers to make implementing a full system of bar coding possible.
- Produce cost estimates for both a pilot and a full system, based on data available at the meeting.

Background
Both Lettie Johnson and Hal Kendrick have asked the Systems Support Department to investigate bar coding. They would like to see a pilot program in operation by fall. We could then roll the program out to all divisions by spring if results warrant.

SUPPORTING INFORMATION. It is easy to understand why you need to support the recommendations in your recommendation memos. But sometimes you need to support the statement of purpose as well. Often the most pressing question is not What action should we take? but *Should we take action at all?* When this is the case, you should offer support to justify the memo's purpose in the opening statement. See, for example, the first paragraph of Sample Memo 7A. Here the writer both points out the purpose of the memo—to suggest a solution for a fax machine problem—and (in the portion we have underscored) clarifies and supports this purpose by explaining the problem itself:

> At Jonathan's request, we have investigated the problem with timely delivery of materials received on the fax machine. Last week's snarl caused Makepeace to lose a sizable block of business. (The Alva contract alone was worth $25,000.) We believe the following steps, if implemented promptly, will avoid such a bottleneck in the future.

THE PURPOSE OF THE STATEMENT OF PURPOSE. You thus need to vary your statements of purpose to meet the requirements of varying situations. But in any case, make the circumstances clear to the reader as quickly as possible.

Further, just as a good essay introduction points the reader toward the thesis, a good statement of purpose in a business memo points the reader toward the memo's recommendations—which are, after all, the memo's thesis. When you write your statement of purpose effectively, your recommendations, which usually follow immediately, will seem logical and inevitable.

**ELEMENT 2:
RECOMMENDATIONS**

The recommendations themselves are the heart of the recommendation memo. After you set up the purpose of the memo and propose the problem—perhaps explaining the project's objectives—offer the recommendations you have designed to solve the problem or further the objectives. And phrase these recommendations as active steps. Note how vigorously the writers of the sample memos phrase their recommendations.

SUPPORT. To be persuasive, all recommendations need support. But you can support your recommendations in a variety of ways and places in your memo.

- You can place the supporting material after the recommendations.
- You can embed the supporting material within the recommendations.
- You can do both.
- Occasionally, you might even offer the supporting material before detailing your recommendations.

Support can consist of arguments, statistics, cost tables, analyses, research findings, or a combination. Let's look at some examples.

Straightforward recommendations. Sometimes, you can make your recommendations in simple, one-line, action-pointed statements. This form is common in research-backed memos, such as Sample Memo 7B:

- Design and implement a pilot program in only <u>one</u> division to test technology.
- Design a phased program of one, three, then all six southwestern divisions to take effect as results of the first pilot program can be evaluated.
- Plan 10 to 12 weeks lead time for each installation.

Embedded recommendations. More often, however, recommendations carry with them their reason for being. These recommendations are mini-arguments, including both recommendation and rationale. Those in Sample Memo 7A are typical:

- <u>Lease a second fax machine, to be housed in the marketing office and designated primarily for marketing business.</u> Clearly, one fax machine can no longer handle our increased communications volume.
- <u>Hire one additional junior-level trainee to staff the communications room as backup for the two senior operators.</u> In recent months the number of duties each operator must perform has increased significantly. In addition to handling both outgoing and incoming communications, they now customarily serve as backup operators for the executive message center and cover phones when senior executive secretaries must be away from their desks.

Separate support. It is often effective to place additional support—especially facts and figures—in a separate section. You can make this separation even when supporting arguments are embedded in the recommendations. But when your recommendations stand alone, you will find such separate support essential.

The embedded support in Sample Memo 7A, for instance, is reinforced by an additional rationale:

```
Rationale
• The additional cost would be more than offset by the
  additional sales opportunity.
• Because of last quarter's consolidation of the communi-
  cations functions, there is money in Budget 50A to cover
  the additional leasing contract. Marianna's department
  could pick up half the costs of the new hire from its
  salaries contingency budget. And we could contribute the
  remainder from this department's discretionary fund.
```

It is reasonable that the separate support should follow the recommendations; and it almost always does.

Support for preceding recommendations. Occasionally, however, you will offer your support before making your recommendations. When you base your memo on research determinations—whether you glean the information from the laboratory, the library, a convention (as in Sample Memo 7B), or from a survey (as in Sample Memo 7D below), you will naturally support your recommendations with these findings. And "key findings" such as these are ordinarily listed *before* the recommendations. This format is logical, because it permits the reader to draw conclusions *from* research and is particularly appropriate to a scientific or semi-scientific methodology. Note the use of this order in Sample Memo 7D.

Despite such instances, however, you will usually find it most effective to *follow* your recommendations with supporting material or argument or to embed it within them.

Cost. Because cost-effectiveness is a primary criterion for business recommendations, *ordinarily include some assessment of cost as part of your supporting data.* When the cost reckoning is relatively uncomplicated, as in Sample Memo 7A, you can devote a brief subsection to it, and the whole memo will run no more than one page. But where the cost reckoning is complicated and extensive data must be shown, it is better to attach a page of detailed budget information and include a reference to it in the support section.

Pros and cons. You may have noticed that not all the "supporting" information included in the examples is completely supportive. For instance, the recommendations in Sample Memo 7E include negative material.

TO: Hal Finestein   *MC*
FROM: Mary Canby
RE: Laundry Light Survey
DATE: June 23, 19—

We have made an analysis of the results of Preliminary Marketing Survey V585, using the
XLLB light meter and the ASTA color scale, on the effects of basement lighting on
consumer color perception (taken from May 2 to June 15). The results help us achieve two
goals:

  · to understand the basis of varying consumer perceptions of laundry cleanliness
  · to profile the possible color shifts and fading caused by Product J.

KEY FINDINGS

1. Light sources in homes and laundry areas differ; therefore, consumers may literally
   see fabrics in a different light in the laundry—different from the way we see them in
   our lab as well. Incandescent, cool white fluorescent, north daylight, and standard
   fluorescent light produce markedly varied color perceptions of the same fabric.

2. The ASTA color scale is by far the most sensitive in quantifying perceptual changes in
   the colors of fabrics. Only this scale can:
   · compare data from different light sources
   · compare our data and that of the International Society of Textile Research
     Laboratories (ISTRL)
   · be accurate in the darker range

RECOMMENDATIONS

1. Follow up with a major survey to discover the specific laundry lighting used by most
   consumers. For Product J, the survey should concentrate on Midwestern working-class
   homes, its initial target customers.

2. Use the ASTA color scale to check Product J's effects on dark fabric under each of the
   various light sources.

3. Modify the formula for Product J so that it will keep the dark colors appearing most
   natural and least faded under the particular laundry light used in Midwestern
   working-class homes.

May we hear from you by Wednesday? Market Research has reserved time right now for
Product J and would be ready to begin solid plans for the proposed survey immediately if
you authorize it. Product J is slated for consumer testing at the first of the year and
is running slightly behind schedule. It would be a big help if we could get this color
problem cleared away quickly.

MC: kw

SAMPLE RECOMMENDATION MEMO 7D: *Survey-Based Recommendations*

TO: John Sealand [SVP, Marketing, Glotz's Department Stores,Inc]
FROM: Denise Jones [Director of Consumer Marketing]
RE: Budget, Fall Harvest Sale   *D.S.J.*
DATE: July 17, 19—

As you know, last year's Fall Harvest promotional event was not as well attended as we had hoped. Nor did the sales justify what we spent on its promotion. We would like to recommend a change in the amount of money being spent on the event this year, as well as a major change in the allocation of the dollars.

BACKGROUND
Last year's budget of $0,000,000 was allocated in this way:

Direct mail $000,000
Newspaper inserts $000,000
Broadcast effort $000,000

RECOMMENDATIONS
Allocate $1 million to this year's budget.

· 450 M for a newspaper insert (preprint). To be run in major city newspapers in our various markets on Sunday, October 17, 76 pages, 4 color, consisting of promotional merchandise from every department in the store, specific items to be cleared with the merchants involved and presentation in line with the fall nature of the promotion.

· $300M for direct mailing of some of the material from the newspaper insert.

· $250M for broadcast support of the print pieces.

ANALYSIS
1. The bulk of the money should be spent on the newspaper insert because, according to our latest marketing survey, this is currently the best way to reach our buying-oriented customers.

2. We can cut our normal budget for direct mail in half, since we now have a system that enables us to identify the most productive portion of our credit customer list. We should send only to the 30% that research shows are most likely to respond.

3. Using portions of the newspaper insert for the mailing will not only result in substantial printing savings, but will give the additional reinforcement advantage of repetition.

4. Further reinforcement should come from the broadcast component, which will be devoted solely to the support of the printed matter. It will alert customers when to look for the print pieces and where they can be found, and will provide reminders of the sale as it progresses.

5. The $1 million total represents a 20% decrease from last year's event. That could cause some apprehension on the part of the merchants that they are not receiving adequate support for this promotion.

   To speak to their concerns:
   · The united focus of this campaign plus the new direct mail system should result in maximum benefit from our resources.

   · But if we decide to increase the total allocation, we would recommend adding approximately $100M to the direct mail effort to catch the next most likely responders on the list and another $100M to the broadcast effort to support the print program more fully.

The numbers in this memo are only approximate. Different allocations could be made based on discussions with Jim and Martin, which we should have promptly.

If you could let me have your response by Tuesday, I would be able to set up the necessary meetings in time for the publication deadline.

SAMPLE RECOMMENDATION MEMO 7E: *Recommending from Among Diverse Options*

Since nearly any course of action has factors weighing both for and against it, it is not only fair but prudent and professional to mention the most important of these factors—what business refers to as "the downside risk." Most often you will explain why these factors do not call for a shift in recommendations. Occasionally, however, you will offer an alternative option. The recommendation in Sample Memo E, for instance, does both:

```
To speak to their concerns:
• The united focus of this campaign plus the new direct mail
  system should result in maximum benefit from our resources.

• But if we decide to increase the total allocation, we would
  recommend adding approximately $100M to the direct mail
  effort to catch the next most likely responders on the
  list and another $100M to the broadcast effort to support
  the print program more fully.
```

ELEMENT 3: REQUEST FOR APPROVAL TO IMPLEMENT

By definition, a recommendation memo recommends action—even if it recommends that *no* action be taken. And by business-writing custom, action on the memo is usually requested at the conclusion of the memo.[1] In fact, this request provides a conventional closing to the memo, furnishing both a necessary closure and an impetus to action.

The most effective requests for approval lay out the implementing steps requested so specifically that recipients will not have to spend time thinking about what is required of them. Sample Memo 7F offers a good example:

```
Action Required
Jim Hendrix concurs with this strategy and has directed
me to implement the program at once unless we hear to
the contrary from you by Friday. Along with your ap-
proval for the program, we would also need your specific
approval of the proposed transfers for Johnson and
Klizewski.
```

SPECIFY TIME. Furthermore, to be effective, the suggested action must carry *time designations*. The conclusion of Sample Memo 7C is typical. Note the combination of time and action:

---

1. Some business writers favor an alternative style, closely related to the report format. They put the action request first, sometimes even in the reference (Re:) line. For instance:
   Re: Request for your approval to change allocation of dollars spent on the Fall Harvest promotion.
   Or, as the memo's first sentence:
   This memo requires (or requests) your approval to proceed with changes in the budget amounts and allocations for this year's Fall Harvest promotion.

To: Paul Papagello *BF*
From: Brian Flaherty
Re: A program to eliminate schedule slippage in Southwestern
          operations

At Jim's request, we have analyzed delivery schedules for the last two
months in our Southwestern plants and have found slippage serious enough
to warrant an all-out effort to improve schedule adherence.. Word from
our sales office in Santa Fe is that another missed delivery to our
customers there could jeopardize those accounts.

Implementing the following recommendations would, I believe, bring all
plants up to speed within the month. This would also be a good time to
establish the high priority we have placed on schedule adherence in this
year's performance objectives for plant managers.

Recommendations
   o To monitor all schedules more closely, plant managers should
deliver an update of schedule status to the Director of Manufacturing
(DOM) by fax each Thursday by the close of business.

   o The DOM should review the lists and analyze the schedule adherence
problems.

   o Where a schedule is expected to be seriously off target, the DOM
should talk with the appropriate plant manager and ask for a plan of
action that will bring the schedule into compliance by the middle of the
following week.

   o When the DOM deems the problem to be serious or judges that the
delay in delivery would jeopardize a customer relationship, he may
dispatch a troubleshooter from the corporate office to assist the
regional operation.

   o A plant manager who has identified problems early in the
manufacturing schedule may also, at his or her discretion, request the
services of a corporate troubleshooter.

   o We would recommend that Joe Johnson and Jim Klizewski be relieved
of their present assignments and detailed to be called on as
troubleshooters for this region's operations. Both Johnson and Klizewski
know these particular processes well.

Action Required
Jim Hendrix concurs with this strategy and has directed me to implement
the program at once unless we hear to the contrary from you by Friday.
Along with your approval for the program, we would also need specific
approval of the proposed transfers for Johnson and Klizewski.

BF: sh

SAMPLE RECOMMENDATION MEMO 7F: *Problem/Complex Solution*

> We meet, as you know, with Microtek on Friday. If you
> have any additional suggestions, let me hear from you by
> Thursday.

HOW AND WHEN TO SUPPORT THE REQUEST. The comparable rank of writer and reader determines not only the tone you use, but also whether you need to include support for the request. Phrase the approval request section as a request or a polite directive—depending on the hierarchical relationship between you and the recipient.

When the recipients of your memo are of a rank lower or similar to your own, you can write a very simple implementation section. See, for example, the close of Sample Memo 7C. But when your rank is subordinate, you need to use a tactful tone and provide carefully considered support for your request.

Concurrence. One powerful kind of support is the concurrence of your supervisors or others of higher rank with related responsibilities. Concurrence is regularly used in the implementation section of memos (see, for instance, Sample Memo 7F).

Rationale. You might also include a rationale that supports and justifies the requested approval—as does, for example, this portion of Sample Memo 7A:

> John concurs with this strategy and believes we should
> expedite it. Since Marianna has four critical bids out
> currently, may we have your approval before Friday to
> proceed with the leasing contract and authorization for
> one new hire? A personnel search request form is at-
> tached for your signature if you agree.

Tentative action steps. The more specific you can be in your time request, the more effective your memo will be. Yet sometimes you have to send a report before a strategy is approved for implementation. Your time request then is necessarily tentative. For example, Barbara Lessing-Black, who had attended the bar-coding meeting in Sample Memo 7B, writes:

> Lettie and Hal will meet on Monday to discuss setting up
> a task force to study these findings further; and we will
> send you a report and further recommendations on Tuesday.

PREPARING TO WRITE YOUR RECOMMENDATION MEMO

FINDING THE NECESSARY DATA

You can't just sit down and write a recommendation memo. Before you can even begin to make a valid recommendation, you need to gather data relevant to the problem you are investigating. Then you will analyze the data[2] and base your recommendations on it.

---

2. For an explanation of this usage, see "Data" in the Painless Usage Guide (PUG).

- *Experiential data.* Sometimes such data is part of your experience. When this is the case, you need only search your memory and draw out what you require. Some people find that they can simply *analyze the problem in a systematic way* and bring up the needed solutions. Others find it useful to search their minds by *"free writing."* That is, they write down the problem and then, without any attempt at organized thought, write whatever occurs to them in a sort of stream-of-consciousness approach. Others make an *inventory of all relevant ideas:* they list pertinent concepts and, branching out, relate new ideas to those on the list. (See Chapter 3, Section A.)
- *Data from experts and experienced colleagues.* It is often helpful to consult with others who have had more experience with such problems. You can make use of the expertise of the man in the next office, the woman down the hall, or someone from the department most directly concerned. But they too are busy, so be considerate of their time. Ask tactfully: "Do you have a minute now to answer a question for me, or could we make an appointment to talk later?" And most would be happy to discuss your research problem with you.
- *Data from community sources.* Sometimes your search will take you into the community. Sometimes you can "shop" for needed data by contacting organizations whose business it is to sell the product or service you need to know about.
- *Data from printed and electronic sources.* Often you will need to rely upon more traditional sources available at a library or by phone.

Chapter 8 is devoted to a discussion of this sort of data search. However you locate your data, data is just the beginning. Raw data can do you no good until you convert it to information.

| **TURNING DATA INTO INFORMATION** | Data is not information. We aren't sure who said it, but it's a statement for the epoch. There is more data around these days—computerized, sorted, tabulated, and published—than anybody can deal with. Much of it is interesting. Much of it may apply to your problem and your task. In fact, we can almost guarantee that *too* much of it will apply in some way to what you are doing. |

But until you, or somebody else, organizes the data to fit a specific purpose, facts remain meaningless. There may be patterns or trends, but they will not become significant until somebody notices them. Even neatly tabulated into columns, numbers and facts imply no meaning until somebody infers meaning from them. If you can do that effectively, you will be on your way to steady advancement.

After you assemble for your current project as much data as is appropriate, ask yourself these questions:

- What do these facts or numbers imply for *my* company?
- What significance does that implication have for my company's goals?

- How can this data be used on this project to help my company
  — continue a favorable trend?
  — correct an unfavorable trend?

When you analyze the facts you have collected in this fashion, you turn them into information.

MAKING YOUR RECOMMENDATIONS

It is your job to provide information, but information is not the end of your job. When you have analyzed the information strictly in terms of *your* company and *its* situation at *this* time, your analysis must result in a recommended course of action.

THE COST-EFFECTIVENESS CRITERION. If you ask us what your principal criterion should be in deriving your recommendations, the simple answer is *cost-effectiveness.*

However, the cheapest choice is by no means *always* the most cost-effective. Rather, the cost-effective choice takes account of what you are trying to accomplish overall. It offers:

- The best that can be done
- For the least cost
- In the time you've got to do it in.

The cheapest contractor, for instance, may well be the slowest and would not be the most cost-effective on a project where speed is essential. The cheapest product may be less cost-effective than a more expensive model that will last longer or that will perform the needed task more efficiently.

Suppose, for example, you are on the committee to procure the additional fax machine recommended in Sample Memo 7A. You investigate and find that you have four options:

- **Option 1.** Rent, less expensive in the short run.
- **Option 2.** Buy a favorably priced product with a more expensive service contract and a shorter warranty than Option 3.
- **Option 3.** Buy a more expensive product but with a long warranty and a favorable service contract.
- **Option 4.** Rent at a higher rate than Option 1, but with an option to put some of your payments toward an eventual purchase.

To provide a valid recommendation, you would have to determine which option is most cost-effective.

Recommendations based upon cost-effectiveness often involve sorting out complex issues and weighing conflicting benefits. For example, suppose you want to increase sales in your retail shoe stores. You know you can do it by attracting more credit-card customers. But a credit-card promotion will take on some additional credit customers who will not pay or who will not pay promptly. Their presence on your credit-account roles will increase your costs to provide credit. Will the additional sales outweigh the additional costs? You will have to determine the answer in order to make the cost-effective recommendation.

MAKING FIRM RECOMMENDATIONS. Finally, as part of the process of turning your research information into recommendations, you must evaluate and choose the best options. Your manager is not interested in a series of objective, neutral options, presented without ranking. You must come to a decision and base your recommendations upon that decision. Or if your assignment is to investigate options, then you must rank them according to their desirability.

A major aim of a good recommendation memo is to set out options so clearly and persuasively that the executive who receives it will be able to make a rapid, clear-cut decision without wasted motion or time devoted to unraveling time-consuming details. *Your work is done when your supervisor can make a firm decision from the recommendations you have presented in your memo.*

SUPPORTING YOUR RECOMMENDATIONS

Your recommendations will be only as valid as the material you assemble to support them. Recommendations are, after all, the *thesis* of a recommendation memo (and of the short report). And just as you select the material for an academic paper that best supports your thesis, you should include the data—now information—that will best support your recommendations.

BASES FOR INCLUSION. Choose your supporting data carefully. Although supervisors want supporting evidence for your decision, they do not want niggling detail. They will be much more impressed with a succinct memo —one page if at all possible.

How can you judge how best to support your recommendations? Your data will be most useful to you if it conforms to the following criteria:

- *Specific significance.* The data should be specific. The more closely the data fits the situation and your company's interest in it, the more reliable it will be as a basis for judgment and the more useful for your memo or report. For example, to say that health-care costs for business have risen by more than 10 percent a year over the last decade is useful only as a way to help your company put its own 12 percent annual rise into perspective. Your commentary must make your supporting facts specifically significant. Even masses of figures will do your employer no good unless you can offer some analysis as to *why* the figures show what they show and *how* they relate to your company's own experience.

- *Accuracy.* Inquire into the nature and basis of the raw data you are examining, so that you can present your information accurately. For instance, are your figures based on a calendar or a fiscal year? Are they adjusted for seasonal factors or extraordinary items? Are they based on a sampling? Do they include data not usually included, or exclude data generally included in standard reporting? Are certain industry segments grouped in a way that skews the data?

  A certain skepticism is useful here. Not all purveyors of data are objective, and even government-provided figures may be oddly structured. Check.

- *Relevance.* Restrain any temptation to add a great deal of data just to show how much work you did. If you contacted 28 firms you need not describe each of these 28 experiences in detail. As one extremely busy executive says, "People don't read memos to find out how terrific the writer is."

  You, of course, want to communicate that your investigations have been thorough, but that can be done briefly and in a relevant way. See, for example, Susan's memo, page 205. She effectively lets her readers know about her thorough groundwork, but only in making a legitimate argument to reinforce her recommendation:

  <u>Of four suppliers consulted,</u> only Graphink will offer the option of warehousing without cost.

- *Consistency.* Examine your data for conflict. One of the most damaging things you can do to your memo's plausibility is to present diametrically opposed data in successive paragraphs. Examine your assertions to make sure they are not contradictory. All parts of your information must make sense when taken together to support your recommendations. Reread, and reread again, to make sure they do.

- *Thoroughness.* Anticipate questions and objections. Don't ever be content to send a memo that raises an important question in your mind without some attempt to answer that question. For if the question occurs to you, it will most certainly occur to a more experienced senior manager.

ORGANIZING YOUR MEMO

How should you organize a recommendation memo? You already understand the standard beginning, middle, and end structure of the three essential elements:

- Statement of purpose (and support).
- Recommendation(s) (and support).
- Request for approval to implement (and support).

Beyond these fundamentals, your structure will vary with the circumstances.

ORGANIZING PRINCIPLES

As you write your memo, most of your organizational decisions will come in selecting the best way to order supporting material. Pick the arrangement that presents your support to the reader as quickly, clearly, and convincingly as possible. Choose:

- Chronological order.
- Serial order.
- Divided order.
- Alternating order.
- Circumstantial order.
- Inverted pyramid.

CHRONOLOGICAL OR SERIAL ORDER. Most of the lists in our typical sample memos are chronologically arranged. That is, they are ordered in time, with first things first. Often there is no other meaningful way. For example, the list specifying the implementation of a technical definition in Sample Memo 7C:

```
1) ZBIT PROTOCOL
Right now, we are defining PPS2100 ZBIT implementation
by the following method:
    a) Start with the Version 1 ZBIT definition.
    b) Delete the ZBIT commands that are not to be sup-
       ported initially.
    c) Add certain vendor-unique commands. These commands
       are listed in the spreadsheet table.
    d) If necessary, redefine remaining commands to sup-
       port any vendor-specific nuances that we must
       handle.
```

Less obvious, perhaps, but a chronological arrangement nonetheless is the list of goals in Sample Memo 7B. These are listed in the order in which one could proceed:

```
Goals of the Trip

• Investigate the advances in the uses of bar coding for
  possible application in a pilot program in our southwestern
  divisions.
• Determine whether sufficient support is available from
  suppliers to make implementing a full system of bar coding
  possible.
```

- Produce cost estimates for both a pilot and a full system, based on data available at the meeting.

DIVIDED OR ALTERNATING ORDER. Your information often will lend itself to a comparative arrangement. You may wish to compare data, for instance, for two or more periods of time, two or more companies, two or more products. Despite the wide variety of possible subjects, there are only two basic comparative patterns: the divided and the alternating. The following outlines demonstrate how you might organize comparable material concerning two years:

<table>
<tr><td>

Divided Pattern

I. This year
   A. Point 1
   B. Point 2
   C. Point 3
II. Last year
   A. Point 1
   B. Point 2
   C. Point 3
</td><td>

Alternating Pattern

I. Point 1
   A. This year
   B. Last year
II. Point 2
   A. This year
   B. Last year
III. Point 3
   A. This year
   B. Last year
</td></tr>
</table>

The pattern you choose depends on your purpose. The writer of Sample Memo 7E, for example, uses the divided pattern to compare last year's budget with her current budgetary recommendations:

```
BACKGROUND
Last year's budget of $0,000,000 was allocated in this
way:

Direct mail                    $000,000
Newspaper inserts              $000,000
Broadcast effort               $000,000

RECOMMENDATIONS
Allocate $1 million to this year's budget.
```

- $450M for a newspaper insert (preprint). To be run in major city newspapers in our various markets on Sunday, October 17, 76 pages, 4 color, consisting of promotional merchandise from every department in the store, specific items to be cleared with the merchants involved and presentation in line with the fall nature of the promotion.

- $300M for direct mailing of some of the material from the newspaper insert.

- $250M for broadcast support of the print pieces.

On the other hand, if you were interested in comparing the cost, quality, and warranty of a number of products, you might decide to try an alternating pattern:

Cost
    Product A — $00,000
    Product B — $00,000
    Product C — $00,000

Quality
    Product A — Top of the line
    Product B — Conservative elegance
    Product C — Sporty

Warranty
    Product A — 3 months
    Product B — 2 years
    Product C — 18 months

Both comparative arrangements lend themselves well to setting out arguments for a recommended decision. We would urge caution, however, here. Unless your supervisor has specifically asked you to confine yourself to setting out the issues, you can assume that you are to come to a conclusion and make a solid recommendation yourself. Take care not to become too detailed in your support. Don't tell your correspondents more than they want to know.

CIRCUMSTANTIAL ORDER. Often circumstances suggest a natural progression. You can arrange your material in any sort of most-to-least or least-to-most order. For instance, in Sample Memo 7E, both last year's costs detailed in the "Background" and this year's costs listed in the "Recommendations" are ordered from most expensive to least expensive, though the ordering of the two lists differs.

INVERTED PYRAMID. When the support you need to organize does not fall into a natural progression, you should find the inverted pyramid a useful structure. This format, which presents information in decreasing order of importance, is a favorite in business because of its time-saving features. If readers are convinced by your first points, they need not take the time to complete the list. The "Key Findings" of Sample Memo 7D are organized in this way—as are the support items in the small bullet outline supporting Finding #2.

```
KEY FINDINGS
1. Light sources in homes and laundry areas differ;
   therefore, consumers may literally see fabrics in a
   different light in the laundry--different from the
   way we see them in our lab as well. Incandescent,
   cool white fluorescent, north daylight, and standard
   fluorescent light produce markedly varied color per-
   ceptions of the same fabric.
2. The ASTA color scale is by far the most sensitive in
   quantifying perceptual changes in the colors of fab-
   rics. Only this scale can:
   • compare data from different light sources
   • compare our data and that of the International So-
     ciety of Textile Research Laboratories (ISTRL)
   • be accurate in the darker range
```

FORMATTING

The most helpful ways to convey your message quickly, clearly, and convincingly are external to the message itself. Use the strategies discussed in Chapter 3 for indentations, white space, headings, and lists to give clarity to your message and impact to your recommendations. You might wish to review pages 67–73 at this time.

▬▬▬▬▬▬ GUIDELINES ▬▬▬

Writing a Recommendation Memo

- Think through the problem.
- Search out the relevant data.
- Turn the data into information by considering it in terms of the problem and your company's situation.
- Study the information and decide on your recommendations.
- Organize your memo so as best to support your recommendations. Consider how you will handle:
    Statement of purpose (and support).
    Recommendations (and support).
    Request for approval to implement (and support).
- Format your memo to highlight your recommendations and the other material you want to bring to your reader's particular attention.
- Edit your memo. Try to read it through your reader's eyes and revise accordingly.
- Proofread your memo.

WALKING THROUGH A TYPICAL MEMO-PRODUCING PROBLEM

We've analyzed the recommendation memo and considered how to write one. Now let's approach the task as you will in business. The following problem is real. Not long ago it was handed over to an entry-level manager, only six months on the job.

SCENARIO

Northeastern Indemnity is a large insurance company that operates offices all over the New England region. When John Neumann took over as Business Manager of the corporate office, he noticed that the largest item by far in the office-supply budget was imprinted stationery. The stationery is certainly an important component in the image the company presents, so the quality must remain high. But the costs looked out of line to John. He asked his administrative assistant, Susan Sterling, to look into the cost structure of this item. He asked her to find out how to reduce the costs.

Let's look carefully at this problem. It's a typical business assignment—similar to one you're likely to get.

THINKING THROUGH

What would you do first? We suspect you would take a little time and think the problem through. And that is exactly what Susan did. She listed the questions she needed answers for—and included steps she might take to find out:

- Why are the costs so high?
- Are we being charged too much? (Check with the supplier.)
- As a large buyer, shouldn't we be able to make a better deal?
- Shouldn't we be bidding this business? (Shop other suppliers.)
- Is there some problem on our part that might account for the discrepancy? (Study the order patterns.)

INVESTIGATING

Where would you begin? Would you call your supplier? That's what Susan did. She called Northeastern's account executive at Graphink, and here's what she asked:

"Can you help me analyze these costs? Our outlays for stationery last year were up by 28%. My supervisor considers that much too great an increase. What goes into the pricing of the items we buy? A cost breakout would be helpful. I would appreciate having it by, say, Friday. Is that possible for you? Then we could get together and discuss your findings."

What else would you do? Would you stop there and wait until after Friday's meeting? Susan didn't. She called three other suppliers of imprinted stationery and asked each of them to send a representative to call on her. When she told them what quantities of imprinted stationery her company uses, they were glad to come and talk to her.

Susan then spoke to the chief secretary in each of the company's branch offices and asked for the annual or semiannual stationery billings for that office. In most of these offices, she discovered that such billings were not available. When she asked why, she learned that there was a storage problem; and so each office ordered a small quantity of stationery from time to time as needed. No cost records were kept on these orders. In fact, the secretaries had no idea what their costs were.

PREPARING FOR THE MEETINGS

What would you do to prepare for the visits of the Graphink executive and the representatives of the other suppliers? Here is what Susan did:

- *She made an analysis of her own.* She figured out the total amount of the stationery and other imprinted materials used over a year and made a chart. (She did *not*, of course, enter any costs for these items. That information would be provided by the estimates when they arrived.
- *She prepared four identical packets of materials,* one for each of the three supplier reps and one for Graphink. In the packet she included a sample of each kind of stationery and other printed matter her company regularly used. She marked each sample with the quantity ordered in a year and mentioned the storage problem.
- *She also included in each pack a suggestion* that the representative propose ways of reducing the cost of the stationery without altering its quality.

Giving all of the suppliers identical information insures that the estimates offered will be figured on the same basis. Even so, Susan had to analyze the responses carefully to make sure she was comparing like costs, because each supplier assumes things the others do not. In one case, she had to call back and recheck.

DECIDING

What would you do once the estimates and information are in? Here is how Susan handled it:

- *She compared the four estimates.* The prices were similar, with Graphink's estimate just a bit higher than the others. But Graphink—in an effort to retain Northeastern's business—offered free warehousing, which would enable Northeastern to take advantage of Graphink's substantial price breaks for quantity ordering. Susan considered their bid preferable.
- *Then she went back to her other three suppliers.* Without telling them the specifics of Graphink's offer, she asked them if they could provide

warehousing and if they would consider price breaks for quantity ordering. The replies she received offered an array of options.

- *Susan analyzed all the bids and concluded* that Graphink's offer was, in fact, still the best on all counts.

THE MEMO

How would you write a memo recommending the cost-saving actions you had discovered? Susan wanted to recommend continuing with Graphink under new conditions, as well as a number of other cost-saving tips she had picked up from exchanges with the various suppliers. Here's what she wrote:

January 14, 19——

TO: JOHN NEUMANN
FROM: SUSAN STERLING
SUBJECT: STATIONERY COSTS

At your request, I have analyzed our rising costs for stationery and other printed materials and have defined some suggestions for lowering these costs.

KEY FINDINGS

1. Cost increases over the last year and a half did not result from supplier-generated price increases, but were incurred because we did not order our materials in quantities necessary to take advantage of available price breaks. (See attached cost analysis.)

2. We have not ordered to date in bulk because:
   · our storage space for paper items is severely limited
   · a pattern has developed of ordering supplies on the basis of immediate need

3. Graphink, our supplier, is willing to provide free storage space to enable us to take advantage of quantity ordering and bulk pricing.

RECOMMENDATIONS

· Continue our 15-year relationship with Graphink. Of four suppliers consulted, only Graphink will offer the option of warehousing without cost. In addition, our longstanding association with Graphink makes possible price breaks at a lower ordering level than other suppliers can provide.

· Order twice yearly in bulk and take advantage of the warehousing services. Based on last year's figures, bulk ordering should save us $0000 annually. (See attached figures.)

· Assign ordering responsibility for both the Boston and Hartford offices to a single contact here at headquarters. This strategy would avoid multiple ordering and insure that all orders are placed so as to take advantage of the price-break schedule.

· We could lower costs further by making minor design changes in the stationery:

   1. Change the letterhead imprint from raised to flat. This change would realize a cost saving of $0000 annually. In addition, the adjustment

```
                    would prevent possible damage to our new laser printer from melted
                    lettering.
                 2. Make minor modifications in the letterhead design. We can shorten
                    the blue bar so that it does not extend to the paper's edge and do
                    away with the necessity of printing and trimming oversized sheets.
                    Estimated annual savings for this change: $800.
                 3. Use preprinted labels instead of printed envelopes for larger mail.
                    This plan would reduce current envelope costs by $700 annually and
                    give us a flexibility of envelope size that we do not now enjoy.

                 Using last year's figures, savings from these measures would amount to
                 $0000—an amount double last year's cost increase and more than enough to
                 meet the budget guidelines you have set for the stationery item.

                 If you approve, I would like to notify Graphink by next week that
                 Northeastern can accept their offer.  Early scheduling of our bulk order
                 will ensure that there are no delays in filling it and will prevent any
                 shortages at our offices.
```

WHY SUSAN'S MEMO WORKS. Do you think Susan's memo is a good one? Since this is an actual situation and Susan Sterling (though that is not her name) is a real employee of a large company in the Boston area, we can tell you that it was a highly successful project. She received a commendation from her supervisor and from her supervisor's supervisor. The actual Susan Sterling is now considered a trainee to watch.

In what ways does Susan's memo itself succeed? In other words, how does it expedite her reader's decision? And how does it convey to her reader a sense of her careful, thorough work and her sound judgment? Here are some of the ways:

To expedite the decision:

- Susan made the physical memo as easy and fast to read as she possibly could. She organized it logically. She headed the sections. She indented and toplined the recommendations. Her recommendations are simply explained, and her arguments are brief.
- She spared Neumann unnecessary details, but provided background where appropriate to make her recommendations and support understandable.
- She asked only for approval. That is, she simplified as much as possible what he has to do to implement her recommendations.

To win approval:

- Susan's recommendations are well supported. Cost savings are indicated at each critical point.
- The simplicity and the clear arguments make it easy for Neumann to make a good decision.

- She sets out her request for approval in language which suggests that because the recommendations are well supported and comply with *his* guidelines for the budget, he will wish to approve.

To raise her credit:

- She needed to show Neumann that she had done a thorough job, but she did not want to burden him with all the data from all the suppliers. It was enough for him to know that she had consulted four different suppliers and that she had made an analysis of the information so that she could present him with a well-supported judgment.
- At the end she reminded him of the total amount that will be saved by her plan. And though she did not say it directly, it is clear that the savings are based on her good investigative work and sound recommendations.
- Furthermore, not only does her good job save the company money and enhance her reputation with her superior, but because she reports to him, Neumann also will get credit for the substantial saving.

DOUBLE-CHECKING YOUR MEMO

Check your memos at least twice *before* you send them off. Check once for writing and mechanics and once for political implications. When you are satisfied that your memo could offend on none of these points, then send it off, with a well-earned sense of satisfaction. The Double-Checklist Guidelines should be helpful to you.

---------- **GUIDELINES** ----------

Double-Checklist for Memos

Mechanics, Style, and Content
- Is the memo clear? If it is a recommendation, is my recommendation up front, clearly and precisely stated?
- Have I organized the memo logically so that someone less familiar than I am with the topic can understand the problem?
- Have I anticipated questions? A busy executive appreciates having questions anticipated and answered. What would I most want to know to be able to make a sound decision about this matter?
- Have I provided enough background to answer any questions that might arise? (On the other hand, have I provided too much background, or have I included background not completely relevant to the problem?)
- Is the memo complete? Does it include costs and times and schedules (where appropriate)?

- Does the memo include a follow-up statement? "I will call you on Monday to check on your decision." Or "When you have reviewed this material, please call me so that we can set up a meeting to work out a final plan."
- Is the memo accurate? Is all information correct? Have I checked and cross-checked and proofread all facts and numbers? (See page 230 for checking tips.)
- Is the information in the memo consistent? Do all the parts of the memo work with the other parts?
- Is the memo persuasive? Would *I* buy the ideas I am selling?
- Is the memo as succinct as it could be? Could anything be cut? Is the whole memo on one page? *(One page is best.)*
- Are the words simple, the sentences and paragraphs short, the language clear, with unfamiliar terms tactfully explained?
- Are the mechanics perfect? Have I checked for grammar, spelling, typos? *(Help is available in the PUG at the back of this text.)*

If your memo fails on any point, revise and correct it. Tip: *Allow time* in your memo's production schedule for this scrutiny, the inevitable rewrite, and for your secretary to process the final memo.

Political Checklist
- To whom am I sending this memo? Whom will I copy?
- Have I thought through the implications of what I am sending? Is there any potential embarrassment in anything I have said or any of the decisions I have made about copy distribution?
- Where I have made assertions, do I have the information and facts to back those up? And could I defend these assertions or recommendations and answer detailed questions if asked?
- Has my supervisor approved the thrust of this memo?
- If this memo makes recommendations, do they have any potential political fallout? If so, do I want to modify them in the light of the political situation? If I still want to stand by the recommendations, have I alerted my supervisor confidentially?
- Are the deadlines and promises I have made doable? (It is better to set out modest goals and exceed them than to set out impossible or well-nigh-impossible goals and miss them.)

━━━━━━━━━━ **AUTHENTIC BUSINESS PROBLEMS** ━━━━━━━━━━

1. Organize complex information for a recommendation memo or report.

Here is your scenario:

Your company has sent you to the annual meeting of the Institute of Food Technologists. They are considering initiating an irradiation process, and so you were particularly interested in a symposium entitled "Is Food Irradiation the Process of Tomorrow—and

Will It Always Be?" You attended the symposium and took the following notes. You need to:

- Study the notes.
- Decide on your recommendations based on the notes.
- Chunk them into appropriate categories for supporting your recommendations.

IFT Meeting (4/12/9—)

- Irradiation costs quoted by N. Teitch (U.S. Department of Commerce):
  5¢ per bushel for cereals, to kill insects
  1/4¢ per lb. to inhibit potato sprouting
  5¢ per lb. to extend shelf life of fish
- Svenholm (Perpick) claimed intensity of dose didn't affect the cost appreciably. The main cost was the handling of the food.
- Irradiation is now approved in several countries as a treatment for potatoes and/or onions to inhibit sprouting (10-15 K-rad dose).
- Approved in the Netherlands for extending the shelf life of asparagus and poultry (200-300 K-rad).
- Approved in the Netherlands for sterilization of hospital diets (2,500 K-rad).
- Approved in U.S. to inhibit potato sprouting and to kill insects, but has never been applied commercially because chemical treatments are effective.
- Irradiated foods were used in the Apollo program.
- None of the speakers seemed convinced that irradiation would play a major role in food processing in the immediate future in the U.S.
- R.L. Garner (International) thought application was more likely in developing countries where there was less competition from existing food processing plants.
- Garner predicted use in the U.S. by 1998.
- In the U.S. approval of new uses is handled by the Atomic Energy Commission (low dosage applications) and the Army (high energy applications).
- The Army has postponed its ham sterilization work because of the nitrosamine controversy; the beef project should be completed in 1998.
- A major barrier to use of irradiation in U.S. is its classification as a food additive rather than as a food process. Under this label, each application must be tested separately; cost: up to $5 million.
- Attempts are underway to have it reclassified as a process.

Harvester Staves Off Disaster by Pursuing Resourceful—and Risky—Ways to Get Cash

By Hal Lancaster
Staff Reporter of THE WALL STREET JOURNAL

CHICAGO — Before International Harvester Co. decided to unload its pension fund's more than $250 million stock portfolio in favor of bonds recently, its top executives agonized for six months. They consulted investments experts and actuaries. They studied equity returns since 1900.

The decision to plunge ahead is just one aspect—albeit a dramatic one—of the company's strategy to stave off disaster. Though it normally thinks mostly about trucks and farm machinery, International Harvester these days frets mostly about conserving and raising cash. Toward that end, the company will accept considerable risk, as long as that risk is deferred. But if Harvester survives, it might find that in salvaging the present, it has mortgaged its future, outside experts say.

Out of sheer desperation, Harvester is becoming downright resourceful in managing its new business. "We may have more willingness and guts to do things because we have a great interest in driving down costs," says James C. Cotting, the senior vice president for finance and planning who engineered the pension portfolio shift.

Nimble maneuvering is mandatory in this deep recession. The combination of high interest rates and slumping sales has forced a startling number of companies into, or close to, bankruptcy of late.

Many believe Harvester will join the bankruptcy list soon, although the company insists otherwise. To survive, it needs the continued forbearance of creditors and suppliers as well as a resurgent economy. Meanwhile the company must continue to find sources of cash for operations and debt repayment at a time when its major markets remain in the doldrums and a huge interest burden is draining its resources.

Ever-widening losses don't help, either. Harvester posted a $49.7 million loss in this fiscal year's first half, compared with the $175.5 million deficit a year ago. But Mr. Cotting points out that even though significant writeoffs have increased losses, they have also staunched cash leaks. Experts agree that for a company in Harvester's nearly terminal state, profits and losses, which include noncash items such as writeoffs and depreciation, become mostly meaningless. Cash flow is all that matters.

To create cash where there is none, Harvester has pursued the mundane, the arcane and the obvious. While it cut employment sharply, it also stopped ordering such small items as personal letterheads for stationery. Besides trimming salaries and winning union concessions, the company stopped leasing decorative plants.

The pension fund move probably was its boldest stroke, although other steps have provided larger savings. The bond portfolio, in an arrangement increasingly popular among corporations with large pension funds, locks in returns that financial sources estimate could run nearly double the fund's assumed interest rate of 7%. The strategy would save Harvester an estimated $50 million in annual pension contributions for its retired employees.

Overall, in fiscal 1982 Harvester estimates it will trim $770 million from its expenses. A $200 million inventory reduction will produce significant savings by lowering the financing costs that make holding inventory so expensive.

To achieve those savings, the company has reduced production schedules to the lowest range forecast to meet market demand. At the same time it has induced suppliers to deliver goods as close as possible to the time they would be used in production, thus reducing Harvester's carrying costs.

But will Harvester be caught short if demand picks up briskly? By shifting inventory among dealers as needed, Mr. Cotting says, some of that risk can be minimized. "But certainly we would accept some risk there," he adds. "When you don't have a lot of financial flexibility, you protect yourself on the down side."

Harvester also has moved to close down or sell cash-draining operations. A smaller, more efficient company, it reasons, can make money on fewer sales.

Its biggest money-raiser was the sale of its Solar turbines division to Caterpillar Tractor Co. for $505 million. But even that sale raises questions, because the division was a profitable unit with a bright future and its loss might reduce Harvester's competitiveness in the future.

"You want to be sure you don't sell off viable parts and get stuck with the losers," cautions Jerry Goldress, president of Grisanti, Galef, Goldress, Shiras & Osnos Inc., a corporate-rescue expert.

The same caveat might apply to Harvester's recent decision to sell its Victor Fluid Power subsidiary, which it had acquired just a year earlier. A spokesman said Harvester bought the company to capitalize on the booming business in hydraulic cylinders. Harvester still would like to be in that business, the spokesman says, but Victor didn't fit in with the current goal of shrinking to basics, primarily trucks and agricultural equipment.

On the other hand, Harvester has been stuck for some time with its biggest loser, the construction machinery division, which it wants to sell, but for a good price. If a high price can't be obtained, says Alexander Knofler, partner-in-charge of the Chicago-based accounting firm Seldman & Seldman Inc., "fire sale prices may be a viable alternative. Better some cash than an asset that is nonproducing. When a company finds itself in that position, it can't be too fussy."

Another concern is that Harvester will lag further behind healthy competitors in plant modernization and efficiency. That has long been a problem at Harvester, and the company, in an effort to catch up, has averaged a record $330 million of capital spending in each of the last three fiscal years. But in the first quarter of this fiscal year, Harvester could spend only $31 million, down from $90 million a year earlier.

The risk for troubled companies in survival planning, says Gary Silverman, a vice president of management consultants Booz Allen & Hamilton Inc., is that you "get down to the bare bones and then things loosen up and you don't have the resources to react and take advantage of market opportunities."

But besides avoiding the mistakes of desperation, Harvester must stay on good terms with those whose support is critical. Its union workers, for instance, are upset by the company's desire to seek manufactured parts from cheaper outside suppliers.

And some of its credit-union lenders are miffed (and apparently are considering litigation) over Harvester's decision to declare itself a dividend of all the earnings this year of International Harvester Credit Corp. Last year, the first time Harvester received a dividend from the finance unit, it got 60% of the subsidiary's $77.4 million profit.

"The company has invested and reinvested money in the credit company for a long time," says Mr. Cotting. "We ought to have the ability to realize money on our investment."

Some experts see the solution for Harvester and other troubled companies as relatively uncomplicated, although difficult to execute in the current climate. Companies must shrink to bring costs into line with lower market demand, must become more efficient and must turn unproductive assets into cash. They also must keep a tight rein on costs and pray for a recovery.

For Harvester, a crucial remaining task is to win further interest reductions from banks when it sits down in less than a year for its second debt-restructuring talks. The new plan will be presented to bankers by July.

The company is counting on its sheer size to persuade the banks to bend once again. "Not one of our constituencies benefits from Har-vester's leaving the scene," says Harvester's Mr. Cotting. "Our dealers and plants mean a lot to local economies. If we weren't so important in the marketplace, we'd disappear."

2. Carry out prepurchase research and write a recommendation memo.
   a. Write a two-sentence profile of a business, based (as closely as you choose) upon one you know well.
   b. Think of a product or a service that this company might be in need of. (For example, a word processor or a system of word processors; a tractor or a fleet of tractors; a display cabinet set; an exterminator or janitorial service; a copier machine.)
   c. With the first two steps accomplished, here is your situation: You have been assigned the task of discovering which product brand or type of service will best fit your company's needs.

   - Do the needed comparative research.
   - Decide which of the products or services you researched you will recommend. In making your cost-effective decision, do not forget about delivery, timing, servicing, warranties, and other such relevant issues.
   - Write an effective memo recommending the product or service you have selected.

3. Write a recommendation memo from an analysis of information.

   You are the beleaguered senior vice president for finance and planning of International Harvester, at a time when the company—then the nation's largest manufacturer of large farm machinery—was facing bankruptcy because of recessionary pressures. Using the data included in the accompanying article from *The Wall Street Journal,* write a memo to the International Harvester Board, recommending the three measures from those suggested that your financial team has decided are the best ways to keep the company afloat. Pretend that none of these measures has yet been adopted and that you have them among your options to recommend.

   Do *not* simply reproduce the article. Use the data carefully as you turn it into information and recommendations, and write it as a recommendation memo. Don't overlook explanations of the problems, but assume that your board will have some knowledge of the business and of financial strategies and will not need to have everything explained. On the other hand, be clear about what you recommend for the company and why.

RESEARCHING SHORT BUSINESS REPORTS

EXECUTIVE SUMMARY

The short business report is only a more complex form of the recommendation memo studied in Chapter 7. But it usually requires
more extensive research. This research is in many ways comparable to academic research. The time constraints of business, however, require modifying academic procedures somewhat. Business
research must use *specialized and timely resources* and more *rapid
means to record data.* Business research, therefore, relies more
heavily upon:

■ Oral data from industrial or trade experts.

■ Frequently updated references from your particular industry.

■ Government and private business-oriented research services.

■ Daily newspapers and weekly periodicals.

■ Electronic sources.

■ Almanacs, yearbooks, atlases, and biographical dictionaries.

Business researchers ordinarily do not have time to record data
on notecards. Instead they make "notecards" out of photocopied
pages. They:

■ Circle or highlight the relevant material, one idea to a page.

■ Summarize the highlighted passage in a brief label in the top
margin.

■ Key each page to a complete bibliographic list kept on the project by including the author's last name and page number on
each sheet.

Because you will be dealing with such current material in your
business research and because the stakes are so high, check
every bit of data upon which you base your recommendations at
least twice.

The short business report is only a more complex kind of recommendation memo, one that requires more extensive research. In Chapter 7, you saw that the memo form—brief, informal, and direct— is an effective way to convey research information and recommendations. Because it is more complex, the report, though brief, is likely to be somewhat longer than the memo. It may also include more optional components (see the chart on page 237). Headlines separate and distinguish major portions in both the memo and the report. But with the greater complexity of the business report, supporting material is more likely to be detached from the main body of the document. Still, the report has at its core the same essential components as the recommendation memo:

- Statement of purpose (and support).
- Recommendation(s) (and support).
- Request for approval to implement (and support). (The response request is ordinarily included in the transmittal memo.)

Since recommendation memos and reports differ more in degree than in kind, it is useful to consider them together. The process of writing is the same. To write a business report, follow the steps outlined for the memo in Chapter 7:

1. Find the necessary data (research).
2. Turn the data into information.
3. Make your recommendations.
4. Support your recommendations.
5. Organize and format your document.

We examined Steps 2–5 in some detail in Chapter 7. As we work with the more complex business report in this chapter, we'll concentrate on the first step, *the research process.*

BUSINESS REPORTS AND ACADEMIC RESEARCH PAPERS

From your college work you are familiar with the requirements of the academic research paper, and that experience will be useful to you as you write business reports.

SIMILARITIES AND DIFFERENCES

Both business and academic papers require research. To write either, you must analyze the research and draw from it a central point: the scholarly *thesis,* the business *recommendation.* You also must carefully document sources: overtly in the scholarly paper, covertly (that is, without expressing the documentation) in the business paper.

Nevertheless, the two kinds of writing differ in a number of critical particulars. The purpose of academic research is to add to the world's accumulated scholarly *knowledge.* The driving objective of the business report is *action,* and its purpose is to provide hard, factual information upon which to base decisions. This difference in goals accounts for the principal differences between academic and business reports:

- Business research must be *timely,* must be based on up-to-the-minute information.
- Business reports must be brief, the briefer the better.
- Many conventions of the scholarly paper are too cumbersome for the action orientation of most business reports.[1]
- Business reports are therefore modeled on recommendation memos.

RESEARCH TASKS

Both business research and scholarly research demand the same tasks:

- Focus in on your problem. Formulate your research questions.
- Find your sources.
- Gather and record your data.
- Check and recheck your information.
- Document your sources.[2]

We will discuss each task in detail.

FOCUS IN ON YOUR PROBLEM

CAREFULLY CONSIDER. Think your problem through in terms of research questions. Let us suppose, for example, that you work for a wonderfully solid but old-fashioned small-town bank. As newly hired assistant to the marketing vice president, you have been asked to research how to make the best promotional use of electronic banking innovations, such as ATMs (automated teller machines), direct deposit of payroll, automated bill payment, credit cards, and debit cards.

---

1. Longer, more scholarly papers *are* occasionally required in business for background on a subject for which action or policy are under consideration. The usual practice in such cases, however, is to hire academicians to write them.
2. This task is discussed in Chapter 9, pages 253–254.

REVIEW INFORMATION AT HAND. Formulate research questions that apply specifically to your company's situation. Focus in on your problem by starting close to home. In the banking example, you might ask yourself:

> What is our bank's experience with similar products? What do I know and what can I find out about the character of our clientele? What is the makeup of our customer base? Can I find any research available on a customer base that is similar to ours?

The last question expands your thinking a bit and permits you to make useful comparisons.

ELIMINATE THE IRRELEVANT. You can save valuable time by limiting questions to situations similar to yours. You might ask yourself:

> What can I find out about the uses of such products in banks of our size and location? What has been the experience of other banks like ours in using these products? What costs have they incurred? Losses? Increases in business? Profits? What banking regulations govern use of such instruments for financially secure banks like this one?

Having formulated these questions, you will not need to read or interview extensively on large banks, big-city banks, or financially troubled institutions. You have narrowed your research.

Whatever the assignment, begin your work with *specific* research questions in mind.

FIND YOUR SOURCES

WHY CARD CATALOGS WON'T SUFFICE. During your college career, you will have discovered the usefulness of your library's card catalog and its electronic counterpart. However, such catalogs have only limited value for business research. From a business point of view, by the time information makes its way into a library's permanent collection it is usually out-of-date or of only historical interest. In order to remain competitive, business must have the most current information available. And that information can change from day to day, sometimes from minute to minute. A lag in information could skew a business decision significantly.

Business thus tends to rely for its information on commercial and government sources that track data closely and update it on a frequent, regular basis.

USE SOURCES THAT UPDATE THEIR DATA REGULARLY AND FREQUENTLY. When you have a business problem to research, these are the first sources you should look to:

- **Industry scuttlebutt.** Word-of-mouth information gleaned by telephone and at meetings, seminars, or conventions can be the most timely and pertinent intelligence available. As with all oral expression, you have to weigh it with some skepticism and check it carefully. But it's a good way to begin.
- **Trade associations and industry-specific reporting services.** These resources are abundant. The American Society of Association Executives estimates that "there are 21,000 associations at the national level . . . and many times that number if you add international, state and local associations."[3] Most such groups provide a range of services to their members, as well as education and information to the public about their specific focuses of concern. To find out which association might help with your problem, consult *Gale's Encyclopedia of Associations.*
- **Standard industry sources.** As soon as you get your new job, find out the standard reporting services and references for your industry or area. If you are in accounting, for instance, you should familiarize yourself with *CCH (Commerce Clearing House) Federal Tax Service* and the *Prentice Hall Federal Tax Service.* If you are in advertising, you should know where to find and how to use *Standard Rate and Data Services* and other standard directories of rate and demographic data. If you are in public relations, you should join the local chapter of the Public Relations Society of America (PRSA), which will give you access to both local and national media directories and contacts. In addition, for useful standard lists of media resources, consult *Bacon's Publicity Checkers.*
- **Commercial services.** Market wire services and such exhaustive information services as the Washington-based Bureau of National Affairs (BNA), which covers all legislative and regulatory sessions, report daily activities of markets and government. In addition, a service called *Compact Disclosure* (available in some libraries) provides a computerized data base that includes corporate records of thousands of companies. Information available encompasses names of officers and directors, annual reports, and other financial reports required of publicly owned companies.
- **Business-oriented and business-supported research services.** One of the most prestigious of the business research services is The Conference Board—an organization that produces masses of economic and business reports and studies used extensively by journalists and other analysts. Through their wide corporate membership, The Conference Board has daily access to what is

---

3. *The New York Times* (3 Aug. 1988): 10.

happening in business; and their resident scholars, researchers, and publications can provide you with authoritative and reliable information.

Other such research institutions include the American Enterprise Institute (AEI), the Brookings Institution, the Heritage Foundation, and the Bureau of Economic Affairs. Check for their published materials.

- **Government-generated data.** Governments at all levels—local, municipal, state, and federal—churn out a wide variety of reports and data that your business may find useful. Some of these government reports are free; some require payment of a nominal charge. To find out what federal information is available, call the Government Printing Office [(208) 783-3238] for a catalog of available information and reports. For sources on state and local governments, call your statehouse or your state or local Chamber of Commerce.

  Or call the department or agency concerned with your inquiry and ask for the information it can provide. Such directories as the *Washington Monitor's Federal Yellow Book, Congressional Quarterly's Washington Information Directory,* and Carroll Publishing's *Federal Executive Directory,* which updates every two months, list names and titles of Federal Government officials and agency addresses and telephone numbers. Most Government agencies and departments have public information officers who are willing to help with business inquiries. They can't do your research for you, but they usually are glad to assist with advice and references as they can.

  Congressional committee staffers are among the most knowledgeable of experts in their respective subject areas. You can find them through the *Washington Monitor's Congressional Yellow Book* or the *Congressional Directory,* both of which list names and Washington office addresses of Congressional members and their staffs, as well as the committee staffers. Although the staffers should not be regarded as information services, most are willing to answer specific questions about current policy issues and legislative affairs in their areas.

  The Congressional representative in whose district your business operates will consider you and your company constituents and will be glad to help you or direct you to appropriate sources. Be sure, however, to organize and define your questions before you call.

USE DAILY SOURCES. Most business writing requires the kind of timely information that only daily sources such as newspapers and daily records can provide.

- **National newspapers.** No matter what you do, no matter what your field, you should have access to the two major papers with a national focus: *The New York Times* and *The Wall Street Journal*. *The New York Times* considers itself (and is widely considered) the newspaper of record. It pours massive financial resources into its wire services, coverage, reporting, and fact checking in order to maintain its reputation as *the* reliable source for coverage of daily events. *The Wall Street Journal* has a similar reputation for news of financial markets and business community interests. You will find both papers highly reliable sources. Check them against each other. Sometimes their coverage is supplementary. Either or both are a good place to begin a search.

  U.S.A. Today, with its early deadline and wide, though cursory, coverage of state news, can sometimes provide a starting point. You will, however, need to look elsewhere for depth of information.

- **Regional papers.** For national government issues, *The Washington Post* offers extensive coverage. And when your interest is regional, check the appropriate local paper. Indeed, a number of regional papers enjoy a national reputation. Among them: the *St. Louis Post-Dispatch, Cleveland Plain Dealer, Los Angeles Times, Chicago Tribune, Atlanta Journal and Constitution, Dallas Morning News, Miami Herald, Boston Globe,* and *Richmond News-Leader.*

- **Newspaper indexes.** *The New York Times, The Wall Street Journal, The Washington Post,* and *The London Times* have their own indexes, which are carried by most libraries. Other newspapers also have indexes, but these are less widely available. Articles in 200 newspapers are photocopied on microfiche and indexed by subject in *Newsbank,* a service available at most large public and university libraries.

- **Daily records.** Not all daily publication is in newspapers. The Bureau of National Affairs, for instance, covers most Congressional committee and subcommittee hearings and publishes a *Daily Report for Executives,* which summarizes Washington developments that concern business.

  The *Congressional Record* is also published daily. It is a verbatim (but edited) record of the daily floor proceedings in both the Senate and the House of Representatives. The *Federal Register* publishes daily all regulations proposed or promulgated by agencies of the federal government. Both the *Congressional Record* and the *Federal Register* are available at major libraries. But because they are sent by mail, you may find a time gap in their availability. Furthermore, both publications are cumbersome and somewhat difficult to use. If you can afford to wait, you will find the information they cover more readily available in the *Congressional Quarterly*

Weekly Report, which publishes weekly digests of what has happened in the national government, including Congress, the Supreme Court, and the White House. The *National Journal,* which also covers actions of both Congress and the bureaucracy, is known for concise issues analysis and behind-the-scenes political information.

USE PERIODICALS, MAGAZINES, AND JOURNALS. Industry-specific magazines and journals attempt to keep up with the latest trends. But all monthlies and quarterlies are necessarily a month or two behind, and even weeklies trail the immediate news by a few days. The interval provides time for evalu-

Help from Your Computer

<u>Electronic Sources</u>

If your company can afford a commercial wire service installed in-house, or an on-line service for your computer, you may have access to a number of electronically produced resources. Among those commonly used are:

NEXIS. A publications data base that stores items from major newspapers, magazines, periodicals, and wire services, including Reuters, AP, and UPI.

LEXIS. A law-reporting data base, which includes reports of judicial decisions and the text of statutes.

MEDIS. A medicine and medical-industry reporting service.

Dow Jones News Retrieval Service. This service includes both the Dow Jones wire (a daily ticker that keeps track of financial market information) and the Dow Jones news wire, which incorporates <u>The Wall Street Journal</u>, <u>Barron's</u>, and analysts' reports.

ation and assessment. Thus, if you should have the luxury of time or if the nature of your research does *not* require up-to-the-minute information, you will find periodicals useful.

But you may experience an overabundance of riches. We live in an "age of information," and anything anyone could possibly want to know has been published somewhere. The problem lies in locating it. Fortunately, most of what has been written down has also been indexed.

- **Printed periodical guides.** How can you find articles in current journals and magazines? They are listed in periodical guides and indexes. You will be especially interested in the periodical guides that index the journals in your particular specialty as well as those that index magazines covering business in general.

  If you need information from popular news weeklies such as *Time, Newsweek,* and *U.S. News and World Report,* you will find it listed by subject in *The Readers' Guide,* ordinarily located in a well-traveled part of the library. In the *Business Periodicals Index* (also available electronically), you will find indexed a wide selection of business magazines and journals from the general *Fortune, Forbes,* and *Business Week* to the more technical *Accountancy* and *American Banker.*

- **Specialized guides.** Furthermore, almost every field has its own index of pertinent literature; for example, the *Index to Federal Tax Articles* or the *Cumulative Index of the National Industrial Conference Board Publications.* Some of these indexes are remarkably complex. The Public Affairs Information Service (PAIS), for instance, offers four related publications: the *PAIS Bulletin,* self-defined as "a subject index to worldwide English language public policy literature," which includes a one-sentence abstract with each entry; a foreign language edition with abstracts in English; *PAIS International,* "an enhanced compilation" of the materials in the other two indexes, which is available both in print and electronically; and *PAIS Subject Headings,* which lists the indexed terms and provides a key to the other volumes. Because such indexes are specialized, they offer you a fuller coverage of a particular field of interest than the general guides, and they do not distract the researcher with extraneous material. On the other hand, because these indexes are less generally comprehensive, you may find a valuable article has been omitted.

- **Abstracting services.** Periodical indexes can be exceedingly useful. They are, however, limited to subject, title, and author and thus can lead you to an article that has little bearing on your research problem. At such times you may wish that you could see a brief summary or abstract of the article before you go to the trouble of locating it in its original publication. And in many cases you can.

Abstracts of many scholarly, professional, and government articles are indexed and collected in volumes by field or discipline. Among those that might interest you are *Managing and Marketing Abstracts, Economic Titles: Abstracts,* and *Personnel Management Abstracts.* Abstracts direct you to appropriate articles, and sometimes you can find the information you need in the abstract itself without having to check the original.

- **Electronic guides.** Both periodical guides and abstracting services are available electronically. *Infotrac,* for instance, is a general, easily accessible indexing service, which many libraries subscribe to. *Predicasts,* more specifically focused on business concerns, is available both in print and by computer, as is the *Business Periodicals Index.*

- **Computer searches.** Should you have trouble locating what you need, you can ask your librarian to conduct a computer search for you. Much material, otherwise difficult to discover, can be accessed by matching key words or topics stored in your library's computer system.

USE LIBRARY REFERENCE WORKS. When we emphasize the importance of up-to-the-minute resources, we do not mean to imply that you will never find traditional library references productive. These do provide many helpful tools. Among the most useful:

- **Almanacs and yearbooks.** Published annually, these reference books of miscellaneous information can often provide just the stray fact you need. *The World Almanac,* for instance, can tell you the incumbent representative from every Congressional district and the names and addresses of major corporations. *The Commodity Yearbook* provides an analysis of the trends, for example, in pork bellies. *The Municipal Year Book* is as its extended title suggests: *An Authoritative Resume of Activities and Statistical Data of American Cities.* If you need to know how many Chicago fires there were last year, for instance, here is the place to find out.

- **Statistical compilations.** There are also collections of numerical data similar to almanacs, but with a statistical emphasis. Among those you might find useful are the *American Statistics Index,* issued monthly by the Congressional Information Service, citing statistical information published by U.S. Government agencies during that time; and various publications of the U.S. Census Bureau, such as the annual *Statistical Abstract of the United States* and *County and City Data Book,* published every five years.

- **Atlases.** Primarily collections of maps, these references also offer a wide variety of geographic and demographic information. If you want the latest on retail sales distribution, for instance, or college populations, or military installations, try this year's *Rand McNally Commercial Atlas and Marketing Guide.* Or if you need topographic or demographic information, try the *National Geographic Atlas of the World* or *Goode's World Atlas.*

- **Manuals and handbooks.** For technical reference, often nothing is more useful than the manuals and handbooks that have been compiled in every field. Typical among these are *McGraw-Hill's National Electrical Code Handbook; Standard Handbook for Civil Engineers,* by Frederick Merritt; and *The Direct Marketing Handbook,* edited by Edward Nash. Check with your reference librarian or your professional technical association for information on handbooks in your field.

- **Biographical dictionaries.** These reference works will help you find *Who's Who in . . . Science, . . . Consulting, . . . Finance, . . . America*—practically any field, anywhere. Some of these dictionaries, it is true, are useful only for historical background; but most are updated frequently, some annually. And at least one is likely to contain the information you need on the person you are researching. Which dictionary? You can find out in *Biographical Dictionaries Master Index.* If you want to augment information from the dictionary entry, the *Biography Index* will lead you to biographical information in periodicals or books.

ASK YOUR LIBRARIAN. Even this scant outline of useful sources for your research must seem overwhelming. But it need not discourage you, for you will not be alone. Seek out a business librarian specially trained in these resources. Librarians as a species are knowledgeable professionals, eager to share their knowledge. If there are any exceptions, we have not met them. The more challenging the problem, the more they seem to enjoy the search. Don't hesitate to take your "Where can I find . . .?" questions to them.

A CAUTION. As you do your research, be aware that every article has a human author with human biases. Some publications have acknowledged positions that affect their point of view. And even authors who try to write objectively have personal views that color what they select for attention and what they write.

Fact, inference, opinion. To evaluate your sources, carefully distinguish between writing that relates fact, that which carries the author's inference, and that which only expresses the author's opinion. How can you know? Some articles are clearly designated as containing opinion: editorials in newspapers, columnists' essays in newspapers and magazines, and signed news articles. All of these contain a mixture of the three kinds of information. And, unfortunately, so do many news articles that ought to give straight facts.

How can you know whether you can rely on your source? All information—fact, inference, and opinion—is only as reliable as the person who writes it. You can judge reliability by the reputation of the publication and the individual writer. Or better yet—when it really matters—check out the writer's affiliations and publications in one of the biographical references suggested on page 223. But even here retain your skepticism.

How to separate factual writing from inference and opinion? Be watchful for biased wording, especially diction with an emotional charge. For example, a careful reader can spot what we believe is the author's pro–free-trade bias in a sidebar article of a popular newsmagazine. The mini-essay is headed: "A Close Call for Global Free Trade," a title that subtly assumes the pro–free-trade position. Its first sentence confirms this impression by describing protesting European farmers' behavior as "turning their sheep herds loose on highways and generally being a pain in the haunch." And its final sentence paraphrases unnamed "experts" who "warn" that "if the talks fail, a wave of protectionism will sweep the globe, hurting consumers and national economies alike."

Read thoughtfully. You cannot assume that any piece of writing is free from slant.

How to evaluate the facts? Even an overtly biased author can be reliable. But you need to understand and consider the bias. Take, for example, the following sentence from the article mentioned above:

> Insulted by the *paltry* European offer, U.S. representatives *openly* considered walking out—*imperiling* $1.5 trillion in commerce within all 15 of the GATT's trade areas. [Emphasis ours.]

Because the excerpt is from a usually reliable periodical, you can probably count on the accuracy of the figures. And if you discount the emotionally charged *paltry* and *imperiling*—but weigh in the implications of *openly*—it is probably also safe to assume that the delegates did contemplate leaving. Perhaps they were restrained by concern for the consequences, as the use of *imperiling* implies.

How much weight to attach to inferences and opinion? After you determine the facts, you will draw your inferences from them and come to your own conclusions. Of course, you will be influenced by the inferences and judgments of your sources, especially after you have determined that they are generally reliable. Nevertheless, be sure to consider carefully:

- The logic behind their inferences.
- The support they offer for their opinions.

Check the logic.   For example, writers in newspapers and popular newsmagazines frequently bring their subject close to their readers by beginning their articles with a case study, often an interview of a single individual. They then infer generalizations from this example. Some such inferences are valid, but some may not be. For instance, the introduction of a recent article describes Yang Huading, a Shanghai steelworker turned securities investor. The second paragraph begins: "Yang is living proof that 40 years of communism have not killed China's capitalist tendencies." Though based only on the single example, the inference is valid, since even one successful entrepreneur proves that capitalism in China is not completely dead. And the thesis becomes even more convincing as the authors accumulate statistical support.

In a similar article, however, another author's early inferences are less convincing. This article describes Jeff van Rooyen, a black South African accountant who predicts that "black business [in South Africa] will really take off." From this example, the author concludes that "many black South African businessmen are feeling bullish." And, without additional evidence, the article bases on that conclusion the unsupported premise that "President F. W. de Klerk's administration sees the emerging black middle class as a force for stability."

Be sure to analyze texts for their logical implications before making your judgment.

Evaluate the support. Before forming your own opinions, also consider what your sources use to support their points. If quotations are used, what are the qualifications of the speakers to comment on the particular issue? What are their vested interests in the subject? If statistics, how valid are the sources? What are the bases upon which comparisons are made? If the support is anecdotal, take that into account. And be especially wary of premises, like the one in the South African story, that are not supported at all.

─────────────────────────────── **GUIDELINES** ───────────────────────────────

Making Sure

Even when you use a highly sophisticated, generally reliable, and up-to-the-minute service, mistakes can be made; information can be misconstrued. Therefore, *check several sources* and *compare* them. Make sure that you:

- Do not report an inadvertent error because of a particular article's slant or a particular reporter's misunderstanding.
- Recount a balanced and objective view.
- Know your statistics are not skewed by a particular approach or analytical bias, or by an unusual basis for its numbers or facts (see Chapter 10, pages 279, 281).
- Check the publication or release date of every piece of information you use. (You can be tripped up by news accounts that are sketchy

about chronology, and nothing is more embarrassing than finding that more recent events you have overlooked would have changed your conclusions.)

<hr>

RESEARCH WORKOUT

1. Investigate the resources of some of the best-known reference tools by answering the following questions:
   a. What are the names and credentials of two men and one woman listed in *Who's Who in America* who might be suitable candidates for your company's board of directors?
   b. Cite the front page and the business page headlines in *The New York Times* on October 20, 19—— (your choice of year, but you might want to consider 1987). What were the front page and business page headlines in *The Wall Street Journal* that day?
   c. Did *Barron's, Forbes,* and *Fortune* report on any of these topics in their issues immediately following that date? Cite each relevant headline.
2. Where might you find answers to the following research questions? Do the research on *one* and give the answer.
   a. How did industry analysts react to the introduction of the latest IBM PC? Its latest clone? Or the latest Apple-Macintosh model? Its latest clone?
   b. What regulatory action has been taken on asbestos (or the workplace pollutant of your choice) in your state? In another state?
   c. Choose a publicly owned company. When did it last issue a stock or debt offering?
3. Any of the following organizations might someday be an important source of information for you. Research *at least two* of them that you are unfamiliar with. Define and record their function and objectives:

Federal Accounting Standards Board (FASB)

Securities and Exchange Commission

The Brookings Institution

Joint Economic Committee

American Association of Retired Persons

The Business Council

The Conference Board

American Enterprise Institute

The Heritage Foundation

Institute of International Economics

The New York Stock Exchange

NASDAQ

The American Stock Exchange

Bureau of Economic Affairs

National Association of Manufacturers

U.S. Chamber of Commerce

4. In doing your research you will often come across data derived from surveys or polls. To evaluate this data, you will need to exercise the caution we have discussed (see pages 223–225). How would you evaluate data derived from the following question used in a survey of public opinion on the free-trade/protectionist issue:

Would you be willing to pay $2.00 extra for a pair of shoes so that your neighbor up the street could keep his job?

GATHER AND RECORD THE DATA

Finding your sources is only a first step. You must record the material for later use. If you were doing scholarly research, you would copy down the significant passages on notecards, include the author's name and page number, and head the card with a brief summary of the copied quotation. (Before taking notes you would have written all relevant bibliographic information on a bibliography card.) The fact that this method is used by scholars in many disciplines all over the world attests to its effectiveness.

But most business projects are on tight time schedules, so tight that you usually will not be able to afford the luxury of proper scholarly note taking. Business researchers, therefore, have modified scholarly note-taking methods to accommodate these stringent time demands.

TAKE "NOTES." Modern technology has come to the aid of the hurried business researcher who can't take the time to copy by hand or even by typewriter. Use whatever help is available to you. If you are using electronic on-line sources, select the relevant material and collect it on printout sheets. If you are using microfilm, record appropriate data by photo printout. If you are using printed matter, photocopy relevant data. Be sure you also copy or record the name and page of your source.

Interview notes. If you are using any of these resources in conjunction with notes from telephone or personal interviews, take these notes on paper of comparable size.

- Label each page with a quick, identifying tag line to save reading time later.
- Date and number every page of your notes.
- Record the source of information from each interview, and do not neglect to note the telephone number.

MAKE YOUR "NOTES" WORK FOR YOU. These methods collect your data much more quickly and easily than note taking. *But* because the data thus collected is massive and undifferentiated, these methods leave unsolved the writing problems the notecard method is designed to handle. There are, however, efficient ways to solve them. The following Guidelines examine the problems individually.

━━━━━━━━━━━━━━━━━━━━ **GUIDELINES** ━━━━━━━━━━━━━━━━━━━━

Make Photocopies and Data as Useful as Notecards

- **Problem:**   Relevant material is mixed with nonrelevant on each sheet of notes.

Solution: Highlight the relevant material or circle it with a colored pen.

- **Problem:** The relevant material on a single sheet of notes may contain more than one distinct idea.

Solution: Photocopy a new sheet for each separate idea and high-light it individually. This duplication will also enable you to sort the sheets into files.

- **Problem:** Each time you work with a highlighted idea, you have to reread the whole passage.

Solution: Summarize the passage in a brief label in the top margin. (Never mind if this practice takes a bit of time. It will save time later when you organize your report.) When you review your notes, you will be able simply to scan the label instead of reading the entire passage. Furthermore, as you summarize, you can mentally process the ideas from the start and make it fit your purpose.

- **Problem:** Many of the sheets do not contain identifying features. You might not remember where your information came from.

Solution: Label each sheet with the last name of its author or an abbreviation of its source. Add page numbers where these are not visible, date or volume where relevant. The first time you use a source, record its bibliographic data in your permanent file for this project.

- **Problem:** You will waste time searching through the stack of pages you have collected.

Solution: Place all sheets containing material related to a single idea in a file folder labeled appropriately.

KEEP TRACK OF BIBLIOGRAPHY. Make it a habit to record bibliographic data for every printed or electronic source you use, for every person you interview, for every bit of information you receive by telephone. You may well need to reconsult a source to write your report. And you will need to keep a sound bibliographic record in case someone has a question about your data after your report is released.

Keep a bibliographic or resource list in each project's permanent file. It need not be beautifully typed. It just has to be legible and complete. Every time you come across material you think even *might* be useful to you, immediately record the following information (as appropriate):

- Author or source.
- Date.
- Title or headline.
- Publication.
- Publisher.

- Address and telephone number of interviewee(s).

Make sure each data sheet or photocopy is keyed to this list. Simply jot in an author or source's last name on each data page. Then check to see whether the page number and/or date appears on the photocopy page. If it does not, add it there too. Such basic notations are enough, because they refer you to the fuller information on the bibliography list in the project file.

Make use of your note files. Your note files can be helpful to you throughout your entire research project. And be sure to save them. You may need them later as well. Use your note files:

1. *As a basis for your thought.* The immediate purpose for your set of files is to serve as an "inventory of ideas" (see pages 8 and 60–62) from which you will define your recommendations and derive their support.
2. *As a means for organizing your report.* The separate file folders permit you to relate ideas to one another in a physical way. To organize, arrange your files in appropriate stacks. To test out the effectiveness of various organizational schemes, you simply rearrange the stacks.
3. *As a source for documentation.* These files are also the source of your documentation. Save them. They may prove invaluable to you one day. (See "Covert Documentation," page 253.)

PLAN YOUR REPORT

For a detailed discussion of the planning part of the process, see Chapter 7, pages 195–197. Here, however, is a quick review, with emphasis on using your research data.

TURN RELEVANT DATA INTO INFORMATION. As interesting as your researched data might be, it will only be useful to you after you turn it into information. Data becomes information, as we pointed out in Chapter 7, after you filter it through the screen of your particular company, situation, and project.

1. Sort your data files into stacks according to topic—especially as that topic relates to your project.
2. Review the material in the files and single out the relevant by asking yourself:

- What do these facts or numbers imply for *my* company? *Its* current situation?
- What significance does that implication have for the current project?
- How can this data be used on this project to help my company
  —continue a favorable trend?
  —correct an unfavorable trend?

By analyzing your data in this way, you turn it into information.

TENTATIVELY DECIDE ON YOUR RECOMMENDATIONS. Study the information you have gathered to reach your decision.

1. With the answers to the questions above in mind, separate out the files that contain relevant information and remove irrelevant data from these files.
2. Give serious thought to the information in the remaining files. See what options are available for your project.
3. Evaluate the options.

   - How well do the facts support these options?
   - What problems are likely to arise?
   - What steps can you take to overcome these problems?

4. From the answers to these questions, determine the course of action you think it best to recommend.

CHECK AND CHECK AGAIN

This section should bear a skull and crossbones or some other symbol to mark it as a life-and-death matter. Because it is.

You must base your tentative recommendations on the information you have gathered, and rightly so. Yet in business, as in journalism, there is no such thing as a "completely reliable source." Like a good reporter, you must remain skeptical. When it comes to the facts that support your recommendations, check *all* of them. Not some facts. Not most facts. *All* facts. Even if you got the information from your mother, who is one of the two world authorities on the subject, check with the other world authority—even if that is your father. Trust our bitter experience before you have your own: it's the fact you *don't* check that will bite you.

And need we add, when it comes to the report itself: do *not*, repeat *not*, make things up. When deadlines are bearing down on you and your secretary is sitting with fingers poised over the keyboard waiting for that last fact, you may well be tempted to include an educated guess. Don't. Don't even think about it. Write instead:

```
We expect to have final price data by 2 p.m. and will
let you know as soon as it arrives.
```

Should you go ahead with guessed data, imagine what could happen to your credibility, reputation—and even career—if your supervisor turns out to be the other world authority on the price structure of blue widgets?

MAKE YOUR RECOMMENDATIONS AND CONSIDER HOW YOU WILL SUPPORT THEM. Having checked the necessary facts and weighed them once again, decide on your recommended course of action. Then go through your files again to decide what support will be most effective. List your arguments. Now you are ready to organize the material for your report.

But that is a matter for Chapter 9.

GUIDELINES

Researching a Short Business Report

- Gather all the relevant data you can find. Organize, label, and file it by idea—always being careful to record the source.
- Turn the detailed data into information by analyzing it in terms of the specific problem. Assess how it is likely to affect your company in the current situation.
- Check and recheck all data upon which you base the information for your project.
- Draw your recommendations and conclusions from the information.
- Save your files for documentation use.

AUTHENTIC BUSINESS PROBLEMS

1. You have been assigned *one* of the following problems to research for your company. When you research, try to find a company in the trade literature or the news to serve as a model. This model will give you company statistics to work with—statistics such as size, sales, location, and number of employees.

    Select the problem that most nearly corresponds to your field of interest. (You will be writing a report on it following Chapter 9.)

    a. Marketing. Your company is about to bring out a new product, but your competition has already announced a competitive product. Choose any current consumer product that interests you to research as the "rival" product. Invent the facts for a comparable product from "your" company.

    Your Assignment. Research the market reception of the rival product.

    Research Tip: Begin by reading the business pages of any large daily paper or industry trade magazine for new product issues.

    (After Chapter 9, you will make recommendations for positioning your product in the market and for timing its announcement.)

    b. Personnel. Your company, a fast-food franchise chain, has been having a terrible time locating employees. The unemployment rate is very low in the region where your company has 13 hamburger restaurants. Because of the low unemployment rate, your company has to pay premium wages to get employees at all; and trained employees are frequently lured away by other food-service operations which have higher profit margins than your company and can pay more. Your company is not the only one having trouble finding employees, and your manager wants to know how other companies have approached the problem.

Your Assignment. Research the methods companies have recently used to attract entry-level employees in a workers' market.

Research Tip: Start with food and restaurant industry publications.

(After Chapter 9, you will write a report recommending a range of strategies to attract employers and reduce turnover, complete with recruiting costs to bring your work force up to support customer-service standards.)

c. **Marketing.** You are the newly hired assistant to the marketing vice president for a wonderfully solid but old-fashioned small-town bank. Nevertheless, your bank is interested in trying some of the new marketing techniques. (See the example on pages 215–216 for more detailed information.)

Your Assignment. You have been asked to research how to make the best promotional use of electronic banking innovations, such products as ATMs (automated teller machines), direct deposit of payroll, automated bill payment, credit cards, and debit* cards.

Research Tip: The American Bankers' Association puts out a wide number of publications; or you might want to begin with the *Business Periodicals Index* or one of the electronic search services like InfoTrak.

(After Chapter 9, you will write a report recommending which of these products your company should promote, how they should promote them, and on what schedule.)

d. **General Business Problem.** Because of the economic slowdown, your company's labor costs must be reduced. Decisions about such things are typically made by teams or committees of managers. Your supervisor sits on such a committee. She has been asked to come up with a fair plan to cut 20% of the work force. The cuts are to be made primarily by eliminating job functions.

Your Assignment. You are to do the necessary research for your supervisor. You will want to consider fair severance packages, what reductions might come normally by job attrition, how to deal with rumors and the effect they might have on present employee morale and thus productivity, and how to preserve those

---

*A debit card looks like an ordinary credit card but works like an electronic check. When it is used for a purchase, the bank charges a debit (deduction) against the consumer's bank account just as if the transaction were being paid by check.

people who are outstanding workers and whom the company does *not* want to lose.

Research Tip: To begin your research and see how other companies have handled reductions in force, you might want to check into the publications of the American Society of Personnel Administrators, the National Association of Manufacturers (NAM), the U.S. Chamber of Commerce, or the Bureau of National Affairs personnel reports.

(After Chapter 9, you will draft the report for your supervisor to present to the committee, recommending how to evaluate job functions, how to implement cuts at the departmental level, what personnel problems might be encountered and giving costs and a time plan.)

  e. **A current research problem you have been assigned.** If you choose this assignment, check out the details with your instructor.

2. Research your problem in at least three sources. List these sources and evaluate them. Would you turn to this source again for help with a similar problem? Why or why not?

3. Record data relevant to your problem in the ways suggested on page 227.

4. Take your notes according to current business practice (see pages 227–228). On each photocopied page, highlight the appropriate passage. Add a brief summary of its contents. Include name of author or source; where relevant, add page, date, volume. File by idea, not by source. (Save these files for the report.)

5. Judging just by the data you have assembled here, what are your tentative recommendations?

6. You reached those recommendations by relying on some specific information. Cite that information and record its source.

7. Check the information in another source. Cite the source. Does your second source confirm the information exactly? If not, what is the discrepancy? Cross-check the information yet again. If it checks out this time, you are probably safe in relying on it.

8. Having completed your research, think ahead to your report. At this stage in your thinking, list briefly:
   • Your research problem and the purpose of your forthcoming report.
   • Your solution to the problem and major recommendations.
   • The primary supports for your recommendations.
   • Tentative strategy for carrying out your recommendations.

WRITING SHORT
BUSINESS REPORTS

EXECUTIVE SUMMARY

The short business report has the same essential components as the recommendation memo studied in Chapter 7:

- Statement of purpose (and support).

- Recommendation(s) (and support).

- Request for approval to implement (and support)—here embodied in a transmittal memo.

But since a recommendation *report* is usually a good bit longer than a recommendation *memo,* it requires some differences in formatting.

Because of its greater length, a business report is much more likely to include preliminary matter, such as a title page, an executive summary or abstract, and a table of contents. And since the support material is more detailed, a business report is more likely to conclude with a variety of supporting or explanatory appendixes. The most obvious addition is the transmittal memo, which contains an approval request and its support. A transmittal memo always accompanies a business report but is not necessary for a memo.

In both kinds of documents, however, clearly stated recommendations for action are central. And in both cases, these recommendations must be supported effectively and persuasively.

WRITING YOUR RESEARCHED REPORT

You have completed your research. You have thought it through and have decided what you want to recommend and what material will support your recommendations most persuasively. Now you are ready to assemble and write your report. How do you put a short business report together? See Chapter 7 on recommendation memos, especially pages 186–194.

Even though you do more complicated research to collect data and turn it into information for a report, you do not have to create a new form of writing. The formatting principles for recommendation memos also apply to short business reports.

When you have more complex information to put into your report, you are more likely to include appendixes. To make clear the more complex information that supports your recommendations, you might find it effective also to illustrate with charts and graphs such as those we will discuss in Chapter 10.

But making your report more physically elaborate does not change the basic principles, which remain those of the recommendation memo. The sidebar on page 237 is a list of the *essential* and *optional* parts of a recommendation memo and a report.

A MODEL SHORT BUSINESS REPORT

The sample report reproduced on pages 238–246 was written by Ann Severn, a pseudonym for a public affairs junior executive with the central office of a national jewelry chain. She researched, planned, and wrote the report for her supervisor's signature. We have included it in its entirety for your information.[1]

ANALYSIS. Let's analyze the example report in terms of its formatting strategies.

Notice first that the report has a number of parts, and that within the parts it is heavily subdivided by headings. Because it is a complex business policy plan and because it is slated for top executive readers, its author needed to make it quickly accessible. The signposting permits readers to go at once to those parts which interest them most. [*Text discussion continues on page 247.*]

---

1. Note that this business report is a *major* strategy plan. Its length is not typical. Keep your own reports much shorter: 4–5 pages should usually suffice. Brevity will only improve them in the eyes of your management.

The Components of Recommendation Memos and Reports

[ESSENTIAL ELEMENTS ARE LISTED IN CAPITALS]
TRANSMITTAL MEMO [essential for reports; absent in memos]
Preliminary Material

- Title page [needed only for a formal report]
- Table of contents [for a formal report only]
- Executive summary *or* abstract [rarely both]

STATEMENT OF PURPOSE (and SUPPORT)

SUPPORT {
Concurrence ("at Blank's suggestion") ("at your request")
Background
Description of problem
Graphic illustrations (tables, graphs, charts)
 [See Chapter 10.]

RECOMMENDATIONS (and SUPPORT)

SUPPORT {
Facts/data/information
Analysis
- Explanation of requirements of problem
- Impact of recommendations on problem
Key findings [precedes the recommendations in research memos]
Pros and cons
Graphic illustrations (tables, graphs, charts)
 [See Chapter 10.]
Concurrence ("Blank agrees with . . .")
Program for implementation
Means to measure progress

REQUEST FOR APPROVAL TO IMPLEMENT (and SUPPORT) [Reports: in TRANSMITTAL MEMO]

SUPPORT {
Time component
Concurrence ("Blank believes we should have this underway by . . .")

End Matter [minimal in memos]

- Appendixes to support recommendations

    Time-and-action calendar
    Exhibits (blueprints, sketches, samples, etc.)
    Supplementary background or resource material
    Graphic illustrations (tables, graphs, charts)
     [See Chapter 10.]

- Lists of resources (included only in a long report) [Always saved in project file in case of requests for documentation]

[Transmittal Memo]

TO: John Thames [President and CEO, Glitz Jewelers, Inc.]

FROM: Valerie Strickland
         [Director of External Affairs, Glitz Jewelers, Inc.]

RE: Credit Legislation Strategy, 1986-1987

Attached is the strategy developed for management of the credit rate issue at both the federal and state levels.

Please note that the time and action component is built into the plan, Attachment B. Unless we hear from you to the contrary, we will implement the plan on that schedule and will keep you posted on developments in the states as that seems warranted.

If you have any questions, comments, or additional concerns, please let me know.

cc: Mr. James M. Fitzgerald [Chief Financial Officer, Glitz]
    Ms. Andrea MacMillan [Corporate Counsel, Glitz]
    Mr. Michael W. Nightingale [Manager, Corporate Credit Services, Glitz]

EXECUTIVE SUMMARY

At the request of senior management, an interdepartmental Glitz task force assessed:

· the likelihood that federal and state legislative bodies will enact consumer credit rate ceilings in 199___;
· the cost risk to Glitz posed by such legislation.

The Task Force concluded that state legislation, which can arise unexpectedly and move swiftly, is the most likely threat.

· Legislative action is possible in ____ Glitz-operating states, with projected cost exposure on the order of $_____ million.

The Task Force has developed and recommends a plan to minimize exposure. The Action Plan includes:

· Education Programs Develop a packet of basic materials, including a CEO letter to enlist support from operations managers; customer inquiry letters; briefing papers to educate internal spokespersons and inform legislative contacts; media contingency statements and Q's & A's for use with legislators, customers, and news media; a Glitz position statement on finance charges to be used as a basis for all operations communications; and graphic presentations to illustrate the company's position on the issue.
· State Legislative Programs Operations will designate "lead" contacts to coordinate the monitoring of state issues and legislative contact programs. An internal team, coordinated by the Task Force, will deploy trained operations personnel as contacts with legislatures and media.
· Crisis Avoidance and Crisis Intervention Programs When potentially harmful federal or state legislation is impending, the Task Force will coordinate a response that gathers intelligence; assesses the financial and operational impact; assesses the political situation; identifies allies and opponents; and recommends strategies. The intervention program will employ trained operations representatives to contact appropriate legislative committees, offer testimony, and carry out a program of information for customers and media.

The Task Force will report periodically to the Chairman and will submit status reports on federal and state legislation quarterly to Glitz senior management.

Credit Legislation Action Plan
November 22, 1985

PROJECT DESCRIPTION

The purpose of this plan is to set objectives and outline a course of action that will limit negative effects of federal and state credit legislation on Glitz' Jewelry Chain. Attachment A (Chart) shows the current status of rates and requirements of present law, and indicates expected legislative or regulatory action in states where Glitz operates.

OBJECTIVES

The objectives of Glitz' credit legislation action plan are:

· To persuade key members of the present Congress that it would be counterproductive both for the consumer and for business to approve federal legislation that would regulate finance charge rates on retail credit.

· To avoid state legislation that would lower finance charge ceilings in states with ceilings already in place at acceptable levels, and to prevent the imposition of variable rates, which would be both costly and difficult for Glitz' credit operations to administer.

· To generate consumer and legislator understanding of retail credit pricing and cost structures in states with unrealistically low finance charge ceilings—so that, when prime and discount rates begin to rise, state legislatures can understand the need to take action to raise or abolish ceilings.

STATUS OF FINANCE CHARGE RATES

Of the states where Glitz operations offer credit, _____ currently have no finance charge ceiling; _____ have legislated ceilings set below 21%; _____ have ceilings at 21% or higher; and _____ have a finance charge ceiling with rates at or below 21%, depending on either the balance or a preestablished index. Currently, the average credit rate across all Glitz operations is 21%.

LEGISLATION PROPOSED/ANTICIPATED

Because lowering finance charge ceilings is a popular consumer issue, legislative action can surface unexpectedly and move swiftly. Glitz' challenge is:

· To educate consumers and legislators so they understand how retail credit structures work before legislation is introduced;
· To be poised to act decisively and quickly when and where credit becomes an issue.

Proposed legislation currently pending in the U.S. House of Representatives includes bills that would cap finance charge rates on credit cards at a specified number of points above the prevailing discount rate (currently _____%). Hearings on these bills have been conducted by the Consumer Affairs Subcommittee of the House Banking Committee. To date, the proposals have attracted little interest and appear unlikely to reach the floor of either house of Congress.

On the state level, however, the prospect of tightened finance charge regulations poses a potential problem in some states where Glitz stores operate. Glitz staff and various state retail organizations report that action to impose or lower finance charge rate ceilings is likely in at least _____ Glitz states during 1989.

Total Glitz-Operating States with:	Current Number:	Number of States in Which Action Expected
No ceiling		
Ceiling below 21%		
Ceiling at 21%		
Ceiling at/below 21%		
TOTAL		

THE RISK

For Glitz' principal operating states, taken together, it is estimated that losses as a result of the imposition of unrealistically low credit rates could be on the order of $ _____ million. This estimate assumes the provisions of currently proposed federal legislation (which sets a rate of five points above a _____% discount rate), applied to Glitz' 1988 credit operations results. Most state legislation anticipated ties a ceiling to some such index or mandates an unrealistically low flat rate without reference to credit market forces. Give a higher likelihood of legislation at the state level, it is necessary for Glitz to concentrate its resources and activities toward monitoring legislation in its principal operating states.

Potential for credit operations losses in eight key states is as follows:

    California
    Florida
    *Georgia
    Massachusetts
    New Jersey
    New York
    Ohio
    *Tennessee

*Denotes greatest danger of action in current legislative sessions.

STRATEGIES

Objectives of the credit legislation action plan will be attained by these strategies:

· Continue to educate legislators and legislative staffs, consumers, and the media, as necessary, on the economic and social impact of low finance charge ceilings on retail credit.

· Monitor closely federal and state legislative arenas for developments and potential developments.

· React promptly to any legislative action that could adversely affect Glitz' finance charge income.

· Direct, coordinate, and monitor federal and state credit activities at the corporate level, with operations support and implementation. This is imperative to ensure consistent, ongoing, and clear direction, as well as effective and measurable follow-through.

· Assign specific responsibilities to regional operations staff to coordinate Glitz efforts with those of other groups working on this problem—state and national trade associations and state banking and commercial credit groups.

ACTION PLAN

The following actions will be implemented. Timetables and responsibilities are outlined on the action matrix. See Attachment B.

Education Programs

Develop packet of basic materials to include the following:

1. Letter to regional operations managers from John Thames that informs them of the credit-related actions being taken and solicits their support and participation. This letter is necessary to show concern and commitment from top management. See Attachment C.

2. Model response letter to customer inquiries and complaints about high finance charges. This will insure that all Glitz operations offer the same response to customers and will relieve regional managers of the burden of preparing such materials. See Attachment D.

3. Executive summary on the credit ceiling issue for briefing internal spokespersons, contacts, and coordinators. See Attachment E.

4. List of potential questions and suggested answers for use in communicating with legislators, customers, and the news media. As you know, there is widespread misunderstanding of how our credit operations are structured and what price the consumer actually pays for credit. These questions and answers are designed to assist regional managers to address some of the misconceptions. See Attachment F.

5. A Glitz position statement on finance charges to be used as a foundation for all communications. See Attachment G.

6. A Glitz finance charge fact sheet to supplement and support the position statement. See Attachment H.

7. Several graphic presentations that can be used to demonstrate the company's position on the issue. These can include bar charts, flow charts, and other graphics that show the composition of retail credit, and how it differs from bank credit. (These will be developed on an as-needed basis and as the character of the debates becomes clear.)

State Legislative Programs

1. Designate a regional operations finance or credit executive to be the "lead contact" in each of the targeted states identified as crucial.

6. Develop and maintain a file of news media reports (from national, regional, and local media) on the credit issue for use in analyzing trends and as resource materials.

Crisis Avoidance Program

When action on an issue is likely or impending, at either the federal or state level, a Glitz support team and communications effort will be mobilized. The Glitz crisis management support will be drawn from the Credit, Law, and External Affairs functions. Components of the effort will include these activities:

1. Visit key representatives or their staffs in districts where Glitz operates.

2. Follow up visits with letters and telegrams, as necessary.

3. Meet with editorial boards of major newspapers to present retail information.

4. Follow up editorial board meetings with additional informa- tional materials, as warranted.

5. Meet with employees to request support if the issue develops rapidly.

6. If and when the issue should become active, contact custom- ers through bill inserts and ask them to write to their Congressional members.

7. Conduct a press conference, if necessary, to present the retail viewpoint—preferably under the auspices of retailing or credit industry organizations.

8. Offer testimony before appropriate committees, including distribution of testimony to the news media.

9. Disseminate previously developed graphics to the media to support other materials and visually demonstrate key points.

10. Report progress of the particular bills to headquarters and regional operations managers on a day-to-day or week-by-week basis, as appropriate.

Crisis Intervention Program

When it is clear that harmful legislative action is imminent, a crisis management support team will be mobilized. The team will

2. After the key state coordinators are in place, identify regional "leads" in the other states where Glitz offers proprietary credit.

3. Establish a relationship between those lead contacts, the Credit Legislation Task Force, and regional operations External Affairs contacts, through which regional repre- sentatives' activities can be directed, coordinated, and supported.

4. Train and brief regional leads; provide background materials.

5. Establish and continue working relationships with other organizational allies in order to coordinate strategies and educational efforts most effectively.

6. Identify and train regional executives who can be called upon to testify as necessary, when specific legislation emerges and is debated.

7. Acquaint state legislators with our credit operations through a series of on-site/in-store meetings and briefing sessions.

8. Brief regional media relations contacts on the issue and provide them with materials and information that will enable them to respond appropriately and effectively to questions on retail credit.

9. Design an internal team approach that will allow each state lead to draw upon the resources of other Glitz operations.

Federal Legislative Programs

1. Develop a list of members of committees which would debate credit legislation in the House and Senate, cross-referenced by Glitz constituency districts, so that if letters need to be written or contacts made, the list will be ready for use.

2. Identify from the list those key leaders to be targeted for educational efforts.

3. Meet with committee staffs to present positions.

4. Brief headquarters public relations staff to handle media questions from a national perspective.

5. Coordinate and integrate Glitz positions and actions with the appropriate trade associations.

include members of the Credit Legislation Task Force designated by
the Task Force Chair. As part of its action, the team will:

Gather Intelligence

- Activate existing regional external affairs staff resources to
  gather political information and assess likelihood of bill.
- Confer with the executive officer of the state retailing
  association.
- Coordinate with Glitz' Washington representatives and with
  national industry and interindustry trade groups as appropriate.
- Contact other major credit grantors concerned to establish
  their positions and to coordinate action.
- Coordinate with regional operations crisis team designees.
- Submit a report to the Senior Vice President for Finance within
  the most expeditious time frame possible.

The report will:

- assess the financial and operational impact of proposed
  legislation on Glitz' operations;
- assess the political situation (status of legislation,
  relative strength of legislation's sponsors and supporters,
  legislative timetable, etc.);
- identify allies and opponents and estimate the strength and
  political effectiveness of each;
- recommend strategies and estimate resources needed.

Coordination

The Task Force Chair will coordinate all elements of the crisis
intervention plan:

- with crisis management support team;
- with senior management;
- with industry groups;
- with regional operations team members;
- with other concerned groups, as appropriate.

Reporting

The Task Force Chair will report daily to you and to the vice
president in charge of credit operations, as required, the progress
of the effort. The Chair will also prepare a final report on the
outcome of the crisis intervention at the conclusion of the effort.

Evaluation and Quarterly Reporting

I will submit a report on the status of federal and state legislation
quarterly to Glitz senior management. Also included will be progress
toward objectives and on action items. The reports will be
distributed on the first Friday of each fiscal quarter.

ATTACHMENT B

CREDIT ACTION CALENDAR - PAGE 1

ACTIVITY	RESPONSIBILITY	STATUS	DEADLINE	COMMENTS
1. Draft of JT letter Attachment C	AS, VS	Draft complete	Apprvd and mailed 1/10	Establish issue urgency
2. Customer response letter Attachment D	AS, VS, MN	Draft complete	Final due 1/15	Used to make coordinated response to inquiries at all stores
3. Executive summary briefing Attachment E	AS, VS, JMF	Draft complete	Final approval by 1/15	Use for internal background
4. Develop Q & A Attachment F	AS, VS, AM	Draft complete	Final approval by 1/15	Use for internal background
5. Develop position Attachment G	AS, VS, AM	Draft complete	Final approval by 1/15	Use for internal background
6. Develop fact sheet Attachment H	AS, VS	Draft complete	Final approval by 1/15	Use for internal background
7. Write contingency Op-ed column	AS	First draft final	1/20 1/31	Hold for use in crisis
8. Develop graphic devices (charts, graphs, etc.)	AS, BR	To be assigned	Final, 2/15	For distribution to news media
9. Designate lead contacts in key states	AS, VS	To be assigned	Final approval by 2/15	Implement strategies

ATTACHMENT A

DRAFT 11/15

State	Current Maximum	Glitz Div.	Glitz Rates	Lgsltv. Session	Lgsltn Actn. Expctd.
CA	19.2%	I,J,M	19.2%	1/6-8/31	Governor has asked for report, with recs for permanent solution
FL	18%	L,O	18.0%	4/8-6/6	No take-down legislation in
GA	22%	G,Y	18.0%	1/13-3/1	Bill to reduce rate pending
MA	18%	X,M	18%	1/1-12/31	Legislature passed banking bill last year allowing variable rates; no new bills in
NJ	None	X,K	19.8%	1/14-12/31	Bill to cap rate expected
NY	None	X,K,M	19.8%	1/8-12/31	Situation here regarded as serious
OH	25%	G,H	21.6%	1/6-12/31	No bills in; none expected
TN	21%	G,Y	21%	1/1-5/1	House majority leader has asked for study; report expected 2/1

ATTACHMENT C

DRAFT

Letter from John Thames to regional operations managers

Dear _____ :

As long-term interest rates have declined, we have seen a corresponding increase in proposed legislation to impose new, lower ceilings on retail credit rates.

For Glitz, this could pose considerable cost. One bill now pending could reduce rates to a level below Glitz' cost to provide credit to its customers. The total cost to the company could be in excess of $ _____ million annually.

While we do not expect to see federal legislation this year, serious activity is expected in a number of the states where we offer credit. If all the legislation and regulation proposed in those states were passed, the cost could rise to $ _____ million for Glitz.

Because this is a serious issue with heavy stakes, I have appointed a task force to prepare the company to act decisively in the event a challenge arises at either the state or the federal level.

Valerie Strickland, of our corporate public affairs staff, will head this task force; and she will be assisted by representatives from the credit, accounting, and external affairs departments, as well as by representatives from regional operations.

We need your help and support in several ways:

· Please appoint someone from your own operations to work with the task force and coordinate the corporate activities with your own.
· We will provide materials and instruction to any members of your staff that you designate so that you can prepare to handle this issue in your own areas. Please arrange to make use of these materials and resources.
· If a crisis arises, such as threatened action on a damaging bill or regulatory proposal, a corporate crisis team will be available to help you with the effort.

I hope you will do everything you can to secure the cooperation of your operation's managers. Please impress upon them the bottom-line damage that could be inflicted if unreasonable legislation or regulation should be passed.

We will keep you informed as the program develops. Feel free to give Valerie Strickland a call if you have further questions. If you have comments or concerns, feel free to call and talk with me or any other member of the team.

Sincerely,

John Thames
President and CEO

ATTACHMENT D

DRAFT

Model Customer Response Letter

Dear _____ :

Thank you for your letter of _____ (date) _____ about Glitz' policy on finance charge rates.

We appreciate having you as a Glitz customer, and we look forward to continuing to serve as your family's jeweler in the future.

Glitz is committed to providing credit terms for its customers that allow us to offer you the convenience that you have become accustomed to over the years. While we are aware that some nonretail credit card issuers offer rates that may look lower than ours, it is hard to make cost comparisons for a number of reasons. For example, many credit plans charge an annual fee that could add several additional points to the expressed annual percentage rate.

There are also other differences between your Glitz account and other kinds of credit. Our costs are different because of many billing conveniences that our customers have come to rely upon but that they do not always understand add to our cost to provide credit. Even so, if you examine the service and convenience of your Glitz account and compare it with other plans, you will find, I believe, that the cost for credit charged by Glitz is a nominal one.

Remember:

· If your account is paid in full each month, there is no finance charge.
· We do not charge an annual fee for your Glitz account; you pay only the annual percentage rate applied to your average daily balance.
· As a Glitz credit customer, you continue to receive advance notice of special sales, promotions, and events. These special services for our credit customers are in addition to the convenience of our credit plan.

We appreciate your taking the time to write to us. We look forward to continuing our pleasant relationship with you and your family and to providing remembrances for your loved ones with our fine jewelry and gifts.

Sincerely,

Glitz Regional Operations Manager

ATTACHMENT F

DRAFT

Potential Questions and Suggested Answers:
Credit Rate Ceilings

1. Where does your store operate?

   In addition to _____ stores in (state), Glitz operates in _____ other states, including _____.

2. What do you charge your customers for credit?

   We charge an annual percentage rate (APR) of _____, computed on the basis of _____.

3. How does that compare with the rate ceiling in this state?

   This state currently has no rate ceiling.

   Or: The state ceiling is _____. Our APR is _____%.

4. If the legislature does not set a ceiling, won't rates become unreasonably high?

   Experience shows that that simply has not happened. Competition seems to keep finance charge rates at a fair level in relation to the market. In states where credit is deregulated, rates have not skyrocketed. And in adjacent states where one has a cap and the other has no ceiling, the same rate is charged in the deregulated state as in the regulated state.

   The danger is that limits on rates, which remove competition from the cost equation, result in the loss of control which competition provides. Money is a product like any other; its price will fluctuate in a free market as the market's competition decrees.

5. What would happen if a low ceiling were to be set? You wouldn't really let that determine whether or not to provide credit to help your customers finance purchases and increase your sales, would you?

   Realistically, credit would always be available for those customers who are the best credit risks. But for those whose credit backgrounds made them a higher credit risk, the credit might no longer be available. Those higher risks include people who need credit the most—the young just buying their wedding jewelry, for instance, or buying their silver flatware, which we also sell. And for the customers of other items on credit—in, say, department stores, big-ticket necessities like appliances or emergency purchases on credit might no longer be available. Credit ceilings would not only affect businesses like ours but would certainly affect department store and other retail customers as well.

6. If this state sets a higher credit rate ceiling, won't your customers in this state be subsidizing your credit customers in other states with lower rates?

   Theoretically that could occur; but studies made by several universities show that in both Washington state and in Arkansas, where credit rates have been legislatively set at very low levels, consumers have sought credit in neighboring states with higher credit rates because the credit there is more widely available to them.

ATTACHMENT E

DRAFT

Executive Summary/Credit Rate Issue

The following arguments can be used to oppose regulatory or legislative imposition of unrealistically low credit rates.

Deregulation

Deregulation of credit rate ceilings is favored because:

- The marketplace causes rates to settle at the lowest level consistent with widespread credit availability.
- Cash customers should not have to subsidize credit customers; rates that permit the credit grantor to recover costs insure that equity.
- Credit is a commodity like any other; if it becomes scarce, its price will rise. The result of that would be that those most in need of credit might be priced out of the market.

Support Realistic Rate Ceilings

The position we support is deregulation. If that is not achievable politically in your state, the fallback position should be to support rate ceilings that will be sufficiently high to cover realistic costs of credit operation.

- Furthermore, studies show that realistically high ceilings do not cause the rates charged to be pushed by grantors all the way to the ceiling. Competition among credit grantors provides a moderating effect.
- In states where credit rates are not realistic in terms of the costs to provide credit, credit availability has been shown to be adversely affected.

Oppose Unrealistically Low Rate Ceilings

Low rate ceilings may seem like a good idea for the consumer, but, in fact, they are not.

If creditors cannot recover their costs or if they lose money on their credit operations, they have no choice but to take drastic measures to bring their costs under control. Experience with unrealistically low rates shows that:

- when creditors are pressed by increased costs, they are forced to restrict credit availability—which can make credit less available to those in lower income groups;
- merchandise prices increase—for both cash and credit buyers.

Studies of states where credit rates have been unrealistically low also show that such restrictions have a devastating effect on the volume of business transacted in the state—by retailers, wholesalers, manufacturers, and others in the distribution chain. Thus, rate restrictions can affect both the rate of consumption and the tax base dependent upon it.

ATTACHMENT G

DRAFT

Glitz Position Statement

Glitz Jewelers, Inc., opposes credit rate ceilings imposed by states or the federal government because:

· We believe that free credit markets will set rates at the lowest levels consistent with continued and widespread credit availability.

· Free credit markets also ensure the most equitable treatment of both credit and cash customers.

Glitz opposes variable credit rates because they are difficult to administer and result in increased cost to the credit grantor—cost which causes related rises in the cost of credit or restricts credit availability to the most credit-worthy customers. Glitz also believes that a credit customer should be able to understand the credit rate at which a purchase is made and not have to be concerned with the uncertainty of rate fluctuations over the life of the credit agreement.

Glitz also opposes efforts to tie credit rates to the cost of money indexes. The cost of money is only one component of the cost structure a credit grantor incurs to provide credit to the consumer, and these other costs are not always under the control of the credit grantor.

ATTACHMENT H

DRAFT

Fact Sheet

· If credit costs cannot be fully recovered, the availability of credit to consumers will be affected, particularly for marginal credit risks and young persons just entering the credit market and trying to establish credit.

· Experience has shown that realistically high credit rate ceilings—or complete deregulation—do not result in inflated consumer credit rates. In one state where the credit rate ceiling is 25%, credit rates have stayed around 21% because of brisk competition. Only in states where ceiling rates are unrealistically <u>low</u> do the actual rates settle at the maximum permissible rate.

· Low rate ceilings have a negative effect on consumers, business, and governments.

· Under unrealistically low rates, credit grantors may have little choice but to keep rates at the ceiling and restrict credit to only the best credit risks in order to insure recovery of their costs.

· Restricted credit availability falls hardest on high-risk, low-income consumers—often the consumers who most need credit.

· Price increases to subsidize credit operations that are not paying their way are clearly an unfair effect for cash customers.

· Low rate ceilings can cause credit to dry up throughout a state and reduce the volume of business transacted, with resulting effects on the entire distribution chain and state or local economies that depend upon the taxes generated by such business.

· Retailers like Glitz do not make excessive profits on their credit-granting operations. Glitz offers credit as a convenience to its customers and as a marketing tool. The company's cost to provide such credit is not directly related to the cost of money—as many critics claim. Glitz incurs other costs in its administration of credit—including items like bad debts, postage, computer support services, rent, depreciation of equipment, and payroll. These costs, which account for a substantial part of the cost of Glitz' credit operations, continue to rise steadily and are not subject to fluctuations in the cost of money.

Notice next that, although portions of the report are designated by a variety of titles, they can all be comprehended under the three essential elements we discussed in Chapter 7:

- Statement of purpose (and support).
- Recommendation(s) (and support).
- Request for approval to implement (and support).

Don't be put off by unfamiliar headings. "Project Description," for instance, is only "statement of purpose" under a different guise. And when you read the (unheaded) transmittal memo carefully, you will discover a clear example of an "approval request."

In fact, there are few formatting differences (besides length) between the typical recommendation memos in Chapter 7 and this typical report. However:

1. The report has more optional supporting elements.
2. In the report some of these elements are separated from the central report and put into addenda.
3. The report's approval request is included in its transmittal memo.

Let's examine the essential and optional elements listed in the chart on page 237 more closely.

ESSENTIAL ELEMENTS

STATEMENT OF PURPOSE (AND SUPPORT)

Begin a business report just as you would a recommendation memo: state the purpose and explain briefly the problem it addresses. In our sample report, Ann Severn sets out the purpose in the sections labeled "Project Description" and "Objectives." She supports this statement of purpose and explains why a Credit Legislation Action Plan is needed:

- By discussing current problems in the sections headed "Status of Finance Charge Rates"; "Legislation Proposed/Anticipated"; and "The Risk."
- By providing two illustrative charts within those sections.
- By referring to an attachment—A, which presents background by detailing the current situation.

RECOMMENDATIONS (AND SUPPORT)

As in a recommendation memo, the recommendations for solving the specified problem are at the heart of a business report. In our sample report, Ann Severn first sets out the general strategies she recommends. Then she suggests an "Action Plan" and notes specific ways of approaching the problem. She divides this plan into programs that deal with education, state legislatures, the federal legislature, crisis avoidance, and crisis intervention.

She specifies each of these programs in brief action steps and heads each step with an active verb. Note, for example, the items listed under "Federal Legislative Programs." They begin: "Develop," "Identify," "Meet," "Brief," "Coordinate and integrate," and "Develop and maintain."

PERSUASIVE SUPPORT

Sometimes recommendations need explanation or argument to be convincing. Most of the action steps in Severn's report justify themselves. But now and then she includes supporting material with the steps. She does so, for example, in the first item of "Federal Legislative Programs":

1. Develop a list of members of committees which would debate credit legislation in the House and Senate, cross-referenced by Glitz constituency districts, <u>so that if letters need to be written or contacts made, the list will be ready for use.</u> [Support indicated by underscoring.]

Such occasional bits of rationale are all that Severn found necessary to support her recommendations persuasively. She might have attached to the appendix such items as copies of articles, summaries of interviews, and photocopies of laws and regulations. But since her action steps make their own arguments, she wisely kept her report lean.

IMPLEMENTING SUPPORT. Another way to support your recommendations is to show how what you recommend can be done. Most effective reports include such direction. Severn's recommended action steps include plans to accomplish them. In addition, she provides further implementing support in other parts of the report. She adds both a section within the central report ("Coordination") and an attachment (B, a detailed "time-and-action calendar"). Precise timetables to carry out the recommendations are especially useful. Severn's attachments demonstrate that her plan is practical and can be expedited. The busy executives who accepted the plan and put it into action were grateful for the careful groundwork. And we heartily recommend this kind of thorough procedure.

APPROVAL REQUEST: TRANSMITTAL MEMO

The most visible difference in the structures of recommendation memos and short business reports is in the location of the third essential element, the approval request. In both forms you request a response to trigger action and implement your strategy. In a recommendation memo your request for a response brings the memo to a graceful close (see Chapter 7, pages 192–194). In a business report, you ordinarily make the request in a transmittal memo that you attach to the beginning of the report.

TRANSMITTAL MEMOS. Business writers use transmittal memos to orient their readers to the attached material as well as to request approval. In the sample, Severn states the report's aim. Then she alerts the reader that the action steps are both an integral part of the main report and are included in an attached time-and-action calendar. Finally, she offers the manager a negative approval option.

Negative approval option. Sometimes, where you expect approval for your memo, as Severn clearly does, you can phrase your request so that approval can be indicated by no response at all. For example, she writes:

```
Unless we hear from you to the contrary, we will imple-
ment the plan . . . and keep you posted. . . .
```

The negative option phrasing permits action without further expenditure of an executive's time. The technique (see also pages 140, 148–149 in Chapter 6) assures that action on the plan need not be held up if the reader is too busy to give the proposal a thorough reading. It also implies that the writer is handling the situation efficiently and decisively—though not neglecting hierarchical precedence in decision making. Nevertheless, use the negative approval option only with caution. Some managers prefer a simple request for approval. Your choice should depend on the psychology of the manager addressed and the norms of your particular corporate culture. Where the technique is accepted, however, it is understood as a proper, action-oriented procedure from a competent and self-assured subordinate.

OPTIONAL ELEMENTS

When you add optional parts, the rule is "be brief, be simple":

> **Add the parts and information (and *only* those parts and information) that will answer your reader's questions and facilitate your reader's decision.**

PRELIMINARY MATERIAL

TITLE PAGE. If a report is long, or must (for political reasons or otherwise) list those who contributed, a title page is useful. It sets out the title and makes quick work of the formalities. The sample report did not require a title page. Had it required one, its title page would have included information like the following:

```
                    Glitz Jewelers, Inc.
                 Credit Legislative Strategy
                        1990-1991

          Members of the
          Task Force:
          Jeremy England
          Michael Nightingale
          Ann Severn
          Valerie Strickland
```

TABLE OF CONTENTS. A table of contents can help your reader locate information rapidly in a long report or in one with a large number of appendixes.
It is, however, rarely needed in a short report. It is useful only when the
report has so many components that it is difficult to move through it
rapidly and efficiently. Had Ann Severn thought a table of contents necessary for her report, it would have looked something like this, with the
actual page numbers replacing the zeros typed here:

```
          [Transmittal Memo: attached to top of report]
```

CONTENTS

```
Attachment D: Draft Customer Response Letter            0
Attachment E: Draft Executive Summary                   0
Attachment F: Draft Q's and A's                         0
Attachment G: Draft Position Statement                  0
Attachment H: Draft Fact Sheet                          0
```

EXECUTIVE SUMMARY OR ABSTRACT. Both abstracts and executive summaries sum up the reports they precede *briefly*—usually in less than a page. The aim of both is to permit a busy executive to understand the gist of a report quickly.

Executive summaries and abstracts are similar in essence, but differ in format. The abstract, used chiefly with technical papers, is a *précis*—a summary in a paragraph. The executive summary is formatted like other business communications, with heads, bullet outlines, and the other devices that facilitate reading. The major topic areas of the report are highlighted. Because it is easier to read, we recommend that you choose the executive summary over the abstract wherever corporate custom permits the choice.

The executive summary can be of real importance. *It is sometimes the only part of the report the executive gets to read.* He or she must, therefore, be able to rely on its being complete in its presentation of the concept and accurate in tone and information. Review the following tips for writing an executive summary:

- Skim your completed report to refresh your memory.
- Summarize the purpose and the recommendations, that is, the problem and your proposed solutions.
- Back them up with a listing of the important headings.
- Telescope the supporting material under each head, eliminating all nonessential detail.
- Keep technical language and particulars to a minimum, because summaries often have a wider audience than the reports they cover.
- Do not add information not contained in the report.

For examples of executive summaries, see the second page of the sample report and those that precede every chapter of this text.

Please be good enough to put your conclusions and recommendations on one sheet of paper in the very beginning of your report so I can even consider reading it.

—Winston Churchill

OPTIONAL ELEMENTS

The specific requirements of a particular business report or recommendation memo determine both what optional elements are needed to support the three essential elements and their placement. As we demonstrated in Chapter 7, you can intermingle support with statements of purpose or the recommendations. Or you can state them separately. When optional support items are lengthy or otherwise distract from the straightforward flow of the report, remove them from the central report and include them instead in appendixes. Effective writers, like Severn, make reference to each item of appended support at the relevant point.

END MATTER

APPENDIXES. To support a report and make its text clear, you might append such *exhibits* as contracts, photographs, maps, and floor plans. *Graphic* exhibits (tables, graphs, charts, and other graphic illustrations too lengthy to insert) also make effective appendixes (see Chapter 10). Often a graphic can press points home much more dramatically than a paragraph. A picture sometimes really is "worth a thousand words." A chart can organize a welter of confusing information—especially numbers—so that their relationships are clear or trends apparent. See, for instance, Attachment A, the geographic legislative chart, in the sample report.

You might also want to consider appending a *time-and-action calendar* to offer implementing support. Attachment B of the sample report is such an example. Other kinds of implementation support in common use are *sample letters, position papers,* and *press releases,* represented in the sample report by Attachments C through H. Send these documents along with your report to show what you have in mind—to suggest a tone and demonstrate projected use. The reader doesn't have to call or ask for further details. He or she can approve or disapprove the plan, confident of having looked at all its parts. Further, because such documents go along with the report, there need be no delay after acceptance while they are prepared. Including them makes for a complete job, which expedites both the decision and its implementation.

RAW DATA AND SOURCE MATERIAL. Occasionally it is a good idea to append some of the raw data or source material upon which the report's recommendations are based. Sometimes the data is so complex and so interesting that a summary or analysis cannot do it full justice. And some managers like to have access to sources so as to be able to check the data personally.

But, as a rule, a manager does *not* want details. Most managers would rather trust that all bases have been touched without having to spend time reviewing all the materials the writer has already reviewed. They would rather be able to rely on the information and recommendations in a report. The sample report's appendix does not include any such material.

COVERT DOCUMENTATION

Footnotes, endnotes, and parenthetical notation are so closely identified with scholarly research writing that they are almost part of its definition. Yet, despite the similarities noted, business research writing *looks* as though it is almost completely devoid of documentation. That's because its documentation is rarely expressed in the report or memo.

Documentation is, nevertheless, equally essential in business. Every piece of information in a recommendation memo or report is subject to question. Where did you find this out? Who said that? Where did this come from? How accurate is the source upon which we are about to base a decision which may have an impact on the profitability or the reputation of the company? How much can our correspondents or clients rely upon this information? Can *we* rely upon it enough to minimize exposure to litigation?

What we are describing only seems like a paradox. Although business memos and reports use little open documentation,[2] effective business writing is *always* backed by ample covert documentation.

You may wish to review Chapter 8, pages 228–229, where you will find the process businesspeople use to keep the bibliographic record necessary for effective covert documentation. And this documentation is *essential*.

IN-TEXT DOCUMENTATION
In business writing, you will have less occasion than in scholarly writing to quote a source directly. But should you have occasion to do so, remember to:

1. *Identify your source in the text.* For example:

       According to P. H. Smith from XYZ Corporation:

2. *Surround the quotation with quotation marks if it is short.* For example:

       "Interest rates are sure to rise."

3. *Block-quote if the quotation is long.* That is, make a new line and indent the entire quotation if it will run more than a line. For example:

       In an article on American associations, The New York
       Times cited a list of them almost comic in its variety:

---

2. An important exception is tabular financial data. See page 281.

```
Associations represent industries, trades, profes-
sions, interests, philosophies or enthusiasms. There
is, for example, the Possum Growers and Breeders Asso-
ciation, the National Paint, Varnish, and Lacquer As-
sociation, the American Association of Sex Educators,
Counselors, and Therapists, the American Baseball
Fans Association and the Confederate Memorial Associa-
tion. (August 3, 1988, p. 10)
```

4. *Add any necessary documentary information* not included in your text itself in parentheses following the quotation—as we do in *The New York Times* quotation above.

A FINAL WORD

It's all over but the writing. As you work through the thinking and the writing processes that will create a recommendation report, you may find the following Guidelines useful.

GUIDELINES

Writing a Short Business Report

After you have finished your research (by following the process outlined in Chapter 8):

- Begin your report by setting out its purpose. Explain the situation that has generated it.
- Detail your recommendations. Explain the strategy that inspired them and offer a plan of action to carry them out.
- Add relevant support material.
- Reference your documentation if references are required, following the procedure suggested on pages 253–254.
- Finally, write a transmittal memo that includes a request for approval to implement the action.

When you have finished writing, complete your covert documentation (see page 253). Save your note files and make your bibliography as suggested. But remember: Don't send this material with your report.

AUTHENTIC BUSINESS PROBLEMS

1. Write a short business report or recommendation memo based on the data you gathered and checked in the earlier exercises (pages 231–233). Remember to make your covert documentation sheet, and (just this time, because for you this is an academic assignment) turn it in with your report.

Perhaps you can support your recommendations more persuasively by some graphic presentation of your material (see Chapter 10).

2. Draft a policy statement for consideration at your company's management meeting next month, when one of the mandated employee benefits issues is expected to be brought up. Choose one issue from those currently under discussion, such as *child care, parental leave, minimum levels of health insurance, worker right-to-know laws,* or *worker hazards from operation of video display terminals.*

Research the way other businesses in your chosen industry respond to the issue. And, as many businesses do, base your recommendations on their response.

ILLUSTRATING RECOMMENDATION MEMOS AND REPORTS

EXECUTIVE SUMMARY

You can make your business communications more persuasive and effective if you support your points with graphics. Graphics help to clarify and amplify your message. And they are particularly useful in highlighting relationships.

Business graphics include:

- **Graphs**

    Line.
    Bar.
    Circle (pie chart).
    Pictograph.

- **Charts**

    Flowcharts.
    Organization charts.

- **Tables**

    Tabulated numerical data.
    Tabulated verbal data.

You can construct professional-looking graphics manually if you follow a few key tips. Or you can use computer graphics programs to produce sophisticated graphics on your personal computer. Whichever method you use, your graphic devices should be accurate and present your data without distortion.

GRAPHICS: PURPOSE AND METHOD

One picture is worth a thousand words. True enough. Most people understand better when they're shown as well as told. Like written arguments, graphics support your assertions or recommendations. And they explain quickly to make your point as tellingly as possible.

Graphics give you dramatic ways to present your facts and figures. Graphics also permit you to highlight, reinforce, or support your verbal arguments or descriptions. You can use graphics to track and present such information as employee productivity, product results, cost increases, changes in sales and profits, and hundreds of other kinds of data business is concerned with.

Consider using graphics when:

- Your topic is complex and difficult to explain.
- You are dealing with complicated quantitative relationships.
- You need to focus on a particular aspect of your data or you need to focus attention on a particular point of view.
- Your reader will understand your point better or more quickly if you clarify, amplify, or support it visually.

Your purpose in using graphics is to clarify and support your point.

CLARIFYING YOUR POINT. Make clarity your major goal in presenting your graphics.

- Be sure that each graphic is clear-cut and amply spaced, with no distracting clutter.
- Include an easily comprehended key if the meaning is not completely self-evident.
- Whenever necessary, also include a scale of relative distances.
- Letter from left to right; avoid lettering vertically.

The graphic, of course, should speak for itself. But for greater clarity—and to be sure your reader approaches it from your perspective—describe it and interpret it within your text. If you incorporate a graphic within the text of your report, try to discuss the point it supports *before* it appears. In any case, place it as close as possible to the describing text. Give each graphic a brief, but identifying, title and a number—"Figure 4," for in-

Graphic Excellence

In his authoritative and scholarly book on graphics, *The Visual Display of Quantitative Information,* * Professor Edward R. Tufte defines excellent graphics by the following criteria. He writes:

> Excellence in statistical graphics consists of complex ideas communicated with clarity, precision, and efficiency. Graphical displays should
>
> - show the data
> - induce the viewer to think about the substance rather than about methodology, graphic design, technology . . . or something else
> - avoid distorting what the data have to say
> - present many numbers in a small space
> - make large data sets coherent
> - encourage the eye to compare different pieces of data . . .
> - be closely integrated with the statistical and verbal descriptions of a data set.
>
> Graphics *reveal* data.

*(Cheshire, Conn.: Graphics Press, 1983), 13.

stance. (*Figure* is the conventional designation for all kinds of visuals except tables. Tables are usually designated *table.*) In the text of your report, refer to your graphics by title and number.

Do not distract by including too many graphics. The effect of a single visual support can be striking. But the effect of each individual graphic is diminished when the reader perceives it as part of a group or one among many. Therefore, choose your graphic effects carefully. Decide which of your points most need this sort of support, which can best profit from it.

SUPPORTING YOUR POINT. What graphics do best is to point up relationship and correlation. They show how parts relate to each other and how they relate to the whole. They are particularly useful for conveying numerical relationships. Use graphics for support whenever understanding such relationships would make your point more persuasive. The graphics most useful for business application are graphs, charts, and tables.

- *Graphs* show relationships of variables plotted within a geometrically shaped enclosure or along two or more axes. (An axis is a reference line in a system from which coordinating relationships can be measured.)

- *Charts* lay out and show relationships usually in a spatial, chronological, sequential, or hierarchical fashion.
- *Tables* arrange data in columns and rows to show their relationship.

It is important to choose the graphic form that most effectively depicts *your* data.

GRAPHS

Graphs fall roughly into four categories: *line, bar, circle,* and *pictorial.* Choose the one whose particular strengths best fit your purpose. Figure 10.1 lets you compare various graphings of essentially the same data. (In graphs 10.1F and 10.1G the periods of time have been telescoped.)

SINGLE LINE GRAPHS

Line graphs depict trends over continuous intervals—usually over an unbroken period of time. They use two intersecting scales: a horizontal and a vertical. Typically the horizontal scale represents the passing of time, while amounts or levels of a related variable are graphed on the vertical axis. The single line graphs in Figure 10.2 exemplify effective uses of this form.

DESIGNING A LINE GRAPH.   When you want to make a point about trends—rising, falling, or steady—support it with a line graph.

First, draw two lines intersecting perpendicularly. Then mark off the horizontal axis into divisions of the time of interest to your discussion. Figure 10.2A measures in years, 10.2B in days, and 10.2C in 30-second intervals. Mark the relevant quantities on the vertical scale. Then plot the line of the graph by marking the relevant intersections. For instance, 10.2A's graphmaker marked the intersection of 1970 and 7% of the population, 1971 and 8%, 1972 and 10%, and so on.

ACCURACY IN RECORDING TIME INTERVALS.   Note that line graphs record measurements only at the stated intervals. The lines drawn between these points are approximations. For example, the reader has no way of knowing from Figure 10.2A whether the growth in cable viewers occurred steadily throughout 1980 as the graph seems to indicate or whether sales remained steady for most of the year and only took off in the final quarter. The closer together the points measured, the more nearly accurate are the lines. Compare, for example, the yearly approximations in this graph with the minute-by-minute assessment in Figure 10.2C.

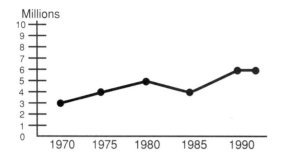

10.1A. Single line graph.

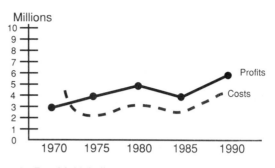

10.1B. Multiple line graph.

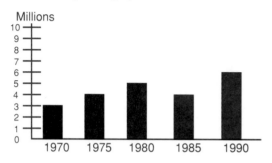

10.1C. Single bar graph.

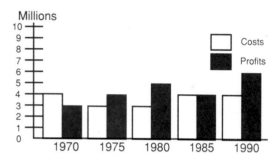

10.1D. Multiple bar graph.

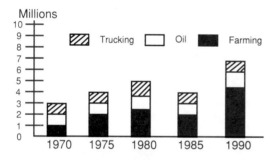

10.1E. Segmented bar graph.

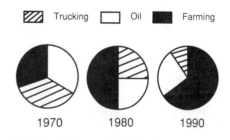

10.1F. Circle graphs (pie charts).

10.1G. Pictograph.

FIGURE 10.1: *A Comparison of Graphing Techniques Depicting Profits of Amalgamated Inc.*

10.2A. The Assault on the Networks
Percentage of U.S. homes served by cable

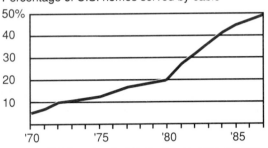

"Percentage of U.S. Homes Served by Cable," from *National Journal*, January 2, 1988. Copyright © 1988 by National Journal Inc. All rights reserved. Reprinted by permission.

10.2B. A Look at Navistar International

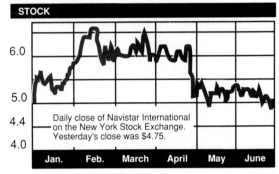

Daily close of Navistar International on the New York Stock Exchange. Yesterday's close was $4.75.

"A Look at Navistar International" from *The New York Times*, July 6, 1989. Copyright © 1989 by the New York Times Company. Reprinted by permission.

10.2C. The Dow: Minute by Minute
Position of the Dow Jones industrial average at 30-second intervals yesterday

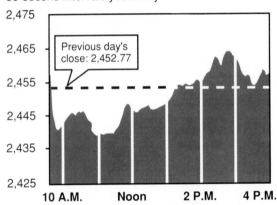

Previous day's close: 2,452.77

"The Dow: Minute by Minute" from *The New York Times*, July 6, 1989. Copyright © 1989 by the New York Times Company. Reprinted by permission.

10.2A. This graph records the percentage of American homes with cable television each year over a 17-year period. It supports the idea of rapid continuous growth in cable television subscription and, because there has been no falling off, it would seem to argue for even more rapid growth in the future.

10.2B. This graph records the daily price of a single stock over a six-month period. It shows that although there was a significant increase in February, March, and April, by June the price had returned to January levels and the final trend was downward.

10.2C. This graph gives a close-up of a day's trading as reflected in a minute-by-minute recording of the Dow Jones average, with the previous day's close clearly indicated. On this day there was a falling off in the morning, a rise well above the previous close in mid-afternoon, followed by a slight decline, which set the final figure at some 4 points gain for the day. Although in its minute-by-minute recording, this is primarily a line graph, the area between the line and the base has been shaded and divided into hourly segments, giving the figure some of the characteristics of a bar graph.

FIGURE 10.2: *Single Line Graphs*

MULTIPLE LINE GRAPHS

Multiple line graphs operate the same way as single line graphs, but they permit you to compare additional variables. See Figure 10.3, for instance.

SINGLE BAR GRAPHS

Bar graphs use bars of varying lengths, either horizontally or vertically, to show comparative relationships. Each bar indicates a quantity. A bar graph shows at a glance which has more, which has less; which has most, which has least (see Figure 10.4). A glance at Figure 10.4A tells us that IBM has sold the most computers. One look at 10.4C shows that *Ghost* was 1990's most popular movie.

Bar graphs can also show trends. When they are used in this way they are similar to line graphs. Look, for example, at Figure 10.1, where the bar graph in 10.1C is based on the same information as that in 10.1A. If you drew declining bars from the points on the line graph in 10.1A, you would have 10.1C. Which do you think conveys the information more effectively?

BAR GRAPHS EMPHASIZE RELATIONSHIP. Though bar graphs may not show trends as dramatically as line graphs, they can point up relationships between individual entities that line graphs cannot accommodate. Use bar graphs when you want to focus on the relationship among separate entities.

MULTIPLE BAR GRAPHS

Multiple bar graphs offer additional layers of comparison in the same way multiple line graphs do. They add one or more contrasting bars for each point of intersection. See Figures 10.1B and 10.1D.

The most common form of multiple bar graph is made multiple by the addition of a time dimension. You can compare entities (the income of "Big Money Law Firms," for instance, as in Figure 10.5C) and add bars representing different times to each set to show trends for each entity. Figure 10.5B offers another such instance.

Multiple bar graphs, however, are not limited to this format but are open to a variety of such comparisons. In Figure 10.5A, for instance, the gross income and the revised income of each entity are recorded.

SEGMENTED BAR GRAPHS

Segmented bar graphs give you an opportunity to add one more set of data to a bar graph. For instance, Figure 10.1E adds an analysis of the profit source to the comparison of annual profits displayed in 10.1C.

Segmented bar graphs are especially effective when each bar represents a whole, or 100%. Then each segment becomes a quickly understood visual percentage. For example, even a quick glance at Figure 10.6C confirms that women are notably overrepresented in clerical positions and underrepresented in managerial positions of the trial court discussed.

Segmented bar graphs can handle additional variables of complex material. By the same token, however, they can complicate an issue. Use them when your material demands a complex treatment. Avoid them when

10.3A. The Party of Prosperity

Which party, the Republican or Democratic, do you think will do the better job of keeping the country prosperous? (Gallup Organization Inc., through January 1987)

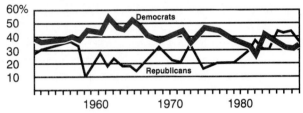

"The Party of Prosperity?" from *National Journal,* November 14, 1987. Copyright © 1987 by National Journal Inc. All rights reserved. Reprinted by permission.

10.3C. Venture and the Competition

Number of advertising pages each year of magazines aimed at small business. Because of heavy discounting in the industry, the number of ad pages may not accurately reflect revenues.

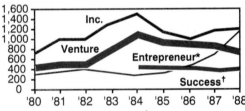

*Data from Entrepreneur Magazine. †Data prior to 1984 not available.

"Venture and the Competition" from *The New York Times,* June 18, 1988. Copyright © 1988 by the New York Times Company. Reprinted by permission.

10.3B. The Environment: A Higher Priority

Do you agree or disagree with the following statement: Protecting the environment is so important that requirements and standards cannot be too high, and continuing environmental improvements must be made regardless of cost.

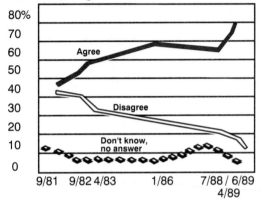

"The Environment: A Higher Priority" from *The New York Times,* July 2, 1989. Copyright © 1989 by the New York Times Company. Reprinted by permission.

10.3A.   This graph records the result of a yearly survey of voters. It shows the contrasting percentage of those questioned who identified Democratic or Republican policy with prosperity. The Democrats were clearly ahead until 1974, when the trends suddenly reversed. In 1980 the trends reversed again and, except for another reversal for the Democrats in 1982, the Republicans have continued to have more voter confidence. On the other hand, those polled have not, for the most part, shown particular confidence in either party. Only in 1961 and 1964 has any party (here the Democrats) gained the confidence of more than 50% of the public.

10.3B.   This graph, which combines and thus compares three line graphs, also records the results garnered from a survey question asked over a period of time. Here the question sorts out those who put a high priority on environmental concerns from those who did not and those who had no answer.

This graph would effectively support an argument for a company coming out with an environmentally helpful product, sales campaign, and sponsorship, because it shows a steady growth in environmental commitment throughout the eighties with a substantial upturn at the end of the decade to include almost 80% of those asked. One might also use such a graph to support an argument against a course of action that might appear environmentally destructive.

10.3C.   This graph, which combines and thus compares four line graphs, shows the number of advertising pages in magazines in the small-business market over an eight-year period. It seems to demonstrate the success of *Entrepreneur,* which has recently managed to catch up with *Inc.,* the longtime market leader. But the graphmaker cautions readers to weigh into their interpretation the fact that "ad pages may not accurately reflect revenues" and that *Entrepreneur* itself provided its data.

FIGURE 10.3: *Multiple Line Graphs*

10.4A. February PC Sales

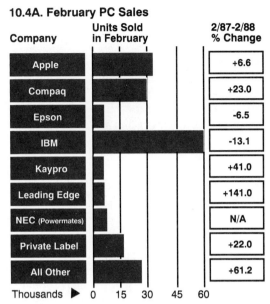

Company	Units Sold in February	2/87-2/88 % Change
Apple		+6.6
Compaq		+23.0
Epson		-6.5
IBM		-13.1
Kaypro		+41.0
Leading Edge		+141.0
NEC (Powermates)		N/A
Private Label		+22.0
All Other		+61.2

Thousands ▶ 0   15   30   45   60

"February PC Sales" from *Infoworld*, May 2, 1988. Copyright © 1988 by Popular Computing, Inc. Reprinted by permission.

10.4B. Dow Jones 30 Industrials

Daily highs, with closes at arrow tip

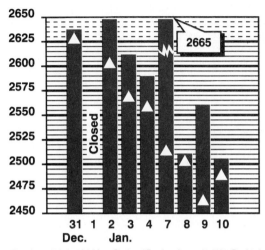

"Dow Jones 30 Industrials" from *Cincinnati Enquirer*, January 11, 1991. Reprinted by permission of the Associated Press.

10.4C. Hot Flicks

Top-grossing films that opened in 1990 (as of Jan. 1, 1991)

1 "Ghost" *OPENED 7/13/90**

$206.1 million

2 "Pretty Woman" *OPENED 3/23/90*

$178.4 million

3 "Home Alone" *OPENED 11/16/90**

$152.7 million

4 "Teenage Mutant Ninja Turtles" *OPENED 3/30/90*

$133.0 million

5 "The Hunt for Red October" *OPENED 3/2/90*

$120.7 million

*Still being tracked.

"Hot Flicks: Top-grossing Films That Opened in 1990." Reprinted by permission of the Associated Press.

10.4A. This horizontal bar graph compares a month's sales for computer companies. The panel on the right shows, for each company, how this February compared to the year before.

10.4B. This vertical bar graph gives 10 days of Dow Jones averages at a glance. It not only shows the daily highs, but also notes (with the white triangles) the figures at the close of each day.

10.4C. The bar graph can also be used to render statistics in an artistic or witty fashion. Graph bars of sprocketed film are an appropriate vehicle for displaying motion picture information, especially in the less conservative arts market.

FIGURE 10.4: *Single Bar Graphs*

quick clarity is a more important aim. The examples in Figure 10.6 show some effective uses.

CIRCLE GRAPHS (OR PIE CHARTS)

Use circle graphs (also called pie charts) when you want to highlight the relationships among the parts of some entity and the whole. A circle is a good way to show simple percentages. It is often used in budgets, for instance, to show how much of the total pie each expenditure represents. Compare Figures 10.1E and 10.1F to see how bar graphs and circle graphs handle much the same information.

Note the following hints for constructing circle graphs.

- Be accurate in dividing the circle into percentages. Remember that 100% of a circle is 360 degrees. Each percentage point, therefore, equals 3.6 degrees.

10.5A. Income vs. Real Income

Median household income in 1986 and a revised income subtracting taxes and adding capital gains, employer-provided health insurance, and government payments like Social Security, Medicare, Medicaid, food stamps and housing subsidies. A median figure has an equal number of people above and below it.

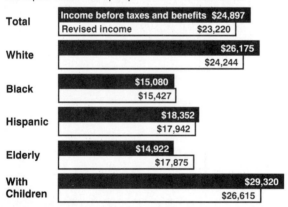

Total	Income before taxes and benefits **$24,897** / Revised income $23,220
White	$26,175 / $24,244
Black	$15,080 / $15,427
Hispanic	$18,352 / $17,942
Elderly	$14,922 / $17,875
With Children	$29,320 / $26,615

10.5A. This graph compares median income of American households designated by race, age, and the presence of children. It shows that most groups have less money after taxes are subtracted and Government or private subsidies are included, but that black families benefit to a small extent and the elderly fairly substantially.

10.5B. This graph compares the percentage of women graduates in the various disciplines in 1976 and again in

10.5B. On the Forefront
Percentage of female graduates

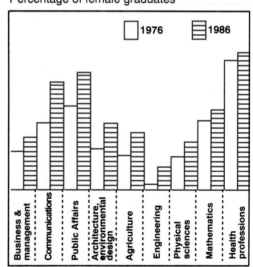

1986. A problem with a percentage graph like this is that it can be used to support contradictory contentions. One could argue, as the author does, that over the decade women have increased in no field as much as they have in engineering, where they show an 85% increase. And yet one could argue just as plausibly from the same figures that even by 1986 there was a smaller percentage of women in engineering than in any other field.

FIGURE 10.5: *Multiple Bar Graphs*

- Specify the percentage value for each wedge.
- Label horizontally for easy reading.
- Try to keep the number of wedges under five or six. Beyond that, the graph looks cluttered.

10.5C. Big Money Law Firms
Ranked by gross revenues. Also shown is net income (●). Both are in millions of dollars. ☐ 1988 ■ 1987

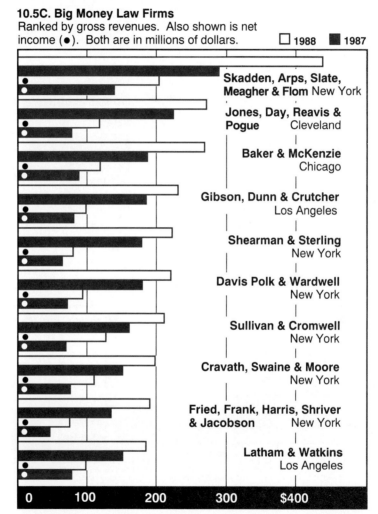

"Big Money Law Firms" from *The New York Times*, July 6, 1989. Copyright © by the New York Times Company. Reprinted by permission.

10.5C. This graph shows which law firms are most prosperous. It also demonstrates graphically (pun intended) that some law firms make a great deal of money and that this amount increased remarkably between 1987 and 1988.

FIGURE 10.5 *(continued)*

10.6A. More Mail, Different Mix

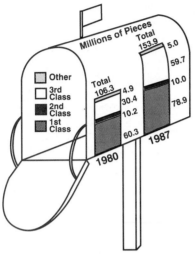

"More Mail, Different Mix" from *National Journal*, June 4, 1988. Copyright © 1988 by National Journal Inc. All rights reserved. Reprinted by permission.

10.6B. Three Elections, Shifting Choices

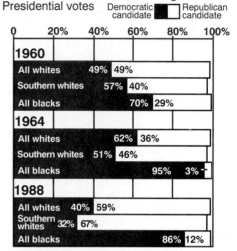

Figures for 1960 and 1964 are based on post-election polls by the Gallup Organization made available by the Roper Center for Public Opinion Research. 1988 figures are based on a New York Times/CBS News Poll of voters leaving voting places on Election Day.

"Three Elections, Shifting Choices" from *The New York Times*, July 2, 1989. Copyright © 1989 by the New York Times Company. Reprinted by permission.

10.6C. Trial Court Employees
Percentage of men and women in five of the largest job categories of the trial court.

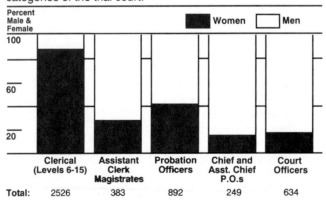

10.6A. This pictorial segmented bar graph compares the percentages of first-, second-, and third-class mail in 1980 and 1987. It shows a substantial increase in mail during this period and demonstrates that the increase came in first- and third-class mail. This imaginative rendition of a postal analysis graph on the side of a mailbox might be an effective visual to accompany a speech.

10.6B. This horizontally segmented bar graph compares the political choices of Southern white voters, white voters in general, and black voters in the Presidential elections of 1960, 1964, and 1988. It points up the defection of what used to be the "solid" Southern white Democratic vote to the Republican party in 1988 and the strength of the black Democratic commitment.

10.6C. Each bar of this vertically segmented bar graph represents a set of jobs; each segment within the bar, the percentage of males and females holding these jobs. The graph effectively supports the point that women have been vocationally subordinated in the particular work environment analyzed.

FIGURE 10.6: *Segmented Bar Graphs*

- To make your graph as clear as possible, consider following the traditional conventions (now often disregarded, as our examples show):

—Begin first wedge at 12:00 o'clock.
—Proceed clockwise from largest percentage to smallest.
—Start with your lightest coloring and end with your darkest.

Figure 10.7 contains examples of effective circle graphs.

PICTOGRAPHS

Pictographs are bar graphs with the bars constructed of replicated pictorial symbols. Each symbol stands for a quantity or a unit of value. For instance, Figure 10.1E shows, by a striped bar segment, the $325 million that the company's farming activities contributed to its 1990 profits. And Figure 10.1G shows the same $325 million by three and a quarter replicated miniature barns.

The advantage of pictographs is that if the visual symbols are eye-catching or witty, they can help dramatize a presentation and make it memorable. It is important, however, to make the symbols self-explanatory. Figure 10.8 exemplifies the variety of effective pictographs.

CHARTS

A chart is an ordered arrangement of informational elements, organized so that their relationships can be immediately comprehended. Although there are a wide variety of charts, two of the most useful in business are the *flowchart* and the *organization chart*.

FLOWCHARTS

A flowchart shows the sequence of actions involved in accomplishing a task. You'll find it a useful map when you want to simplify an activity, such as a manufacturing process, that is particularly complex or requires analysis in order to communicate it. Use a flowchart as a visual aid so that you can keep your written descriptions brief.

Flowcharts are by nature complicated. Thus, label each step carefully. If you choose to use the conventional flowchart symbols, consult *USA Standard Flowchart Symbols and Their Usage in Information Processing,* Publication X3.5 from the American National Standards Institute. Figure 10.9 is an example of an effective flowchart.

ORGANIZATION CHARTS

Organization charts are often called "tree charts," because their relationships branch from a single stem. Indeed, the most familiar kind of organization chart is the "family tree" that plots genealogy. In business, however, organization charts are ordinarily used to sketch out the hierarchical structure of a company's personnel. Figure 10.10 reproduces the organization chart exemplified in Chapter 6.

10.7A. International Book Rights

Percentage of total print rights sold for "Fade the Heat," by country. Sales of foreign book rights are becoming increasingly valuable for authors as well as publishers. In some cases, foreign rights account for more than half the total rights sales. Indeed, about 79 percent of the print-rights sales for "Fade the Heat" were made overseas.

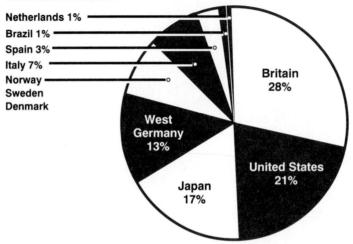

Netherlands 1%
Brazil 1%
Spain 3%
Italy 7%
Norway
Sweden
Denmark

Britain 28%
West Germany 13%
United States 21%
Japan 17%

"International Book Rights" in *The New York Times,* February 26, 1990. Copyright © 1990 by the New York Times Company. Reprinted by permission of the New York Times Company and Virginia Barber Literary Agency, Inc.

10.7B. Where They Live

Regional distribution of farm population: 1950 and 1986 (in percent)

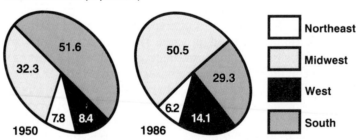

□ Northeast
▨ Midwest
■ West
▨ South

1950: 51.6, 32.3, 7.8, 8.4
1986: 50.5, 29.3, 6.2, 14.1

"Where They Live" from *National Journal,* January 9, 1988. Copyright © 1988 by National Journal, Inc. All rights reserved. Reprinted by permission.

10.7A. This circle graph shows how book sales are divided among countries. It demonstrates the growing importance of foreign print-rights sales.

10.7B. Here two pie graphs compare the location of the U.S. farm population in 1950 and 1986. Multiple circle graphs like these are similar to segmented bar graphs.

FIGURE 10.7: *Circle Graphs (or Pie Charts)*

10.7C. Pepsico's Business Worldwide

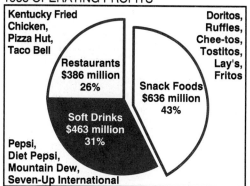

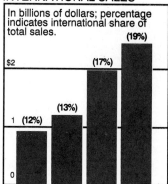

10.7C. In this double graphic, a circle graph shows the sources of Pepsico's 1988 profits, and a two-dimensional bar graph demonstrates the progressively greater share accounted for by international sales.

FIGURE 10.7 *(continued)*

GRAPHICS WORKOUT

Review the following data and choose the graphic form that would present the facts most effectively. List your reasons for choosing that form, and clarify those reasons with a quick sketch. *You need not construct the graphic.*

1. Japanese investment in U.S. real estate:

1985	1.86 billion
1986	7.53 billion
1987	12.77 billion
1988	16.54 billion

2. The value of the U.S. dollar in Japanese yen during the first half of 1989:

January	125–130 yen
February	130–125–128 yen
March	128–132 yen
April	132–125–135 yen
May	135–141 yen
June	142–148–137–146 yen
July	145–138–143–140 yen

3. Amount of garbage thrown away by the average American family:

In one week	6.73 bags (87.5 gallons)
In one month	29 bags (379 gallons)
In one year	350 bags (4,550 gallons)

4. Country of origin for applicants seeking permanent residence in the U.S. through the provisions of the 1986 immigration amnesty act:

69.0%	Mexico
6.1%	El Salvador
4.9%	Haiti
2.0%	Guatemala
18.0%	Others

10.8A. Bringing Up Baby
Children who live with both parents

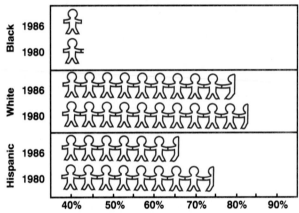

10.8B. Briefer Hospital Stays
Average length of stay (in days)

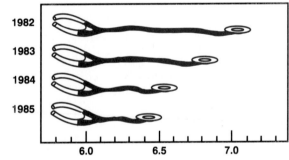

10.8A. This pictograph symbolizes with a paper cutout each 5% of children living with both parents. Because the symbol is appealing, representational, and accurate, it effectively conveys the graph's tragic implications.

10.8B. This pictograph measures the average length of hospital stays by the length of the stethoscopes. It demonstrates the progressive shortening of stays from 1982 to 1985.

FIGURE 10.8: *Pictographs*

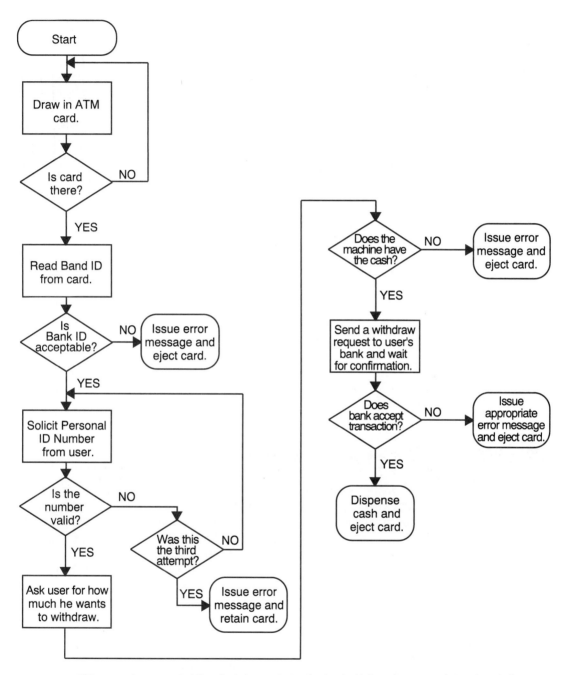

This computer-generated flowchart demonstrates the fund-withdrawal process of an automated teller machine. It uses standard flowchart symbolism: start and termination boxes are oval; process boxes are rectangular; and decision boxes are diamond-shaped.

FIGURE 10.9: *Flowchart*

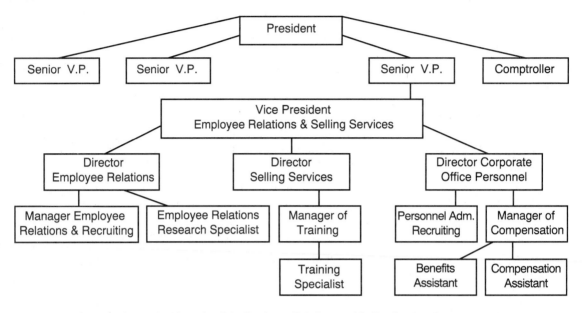

This chart shows the hierarchy of the Employee Relations and Selling Services Department of a large corporation. It shows how its head, a senior vice president, fits into the overall organization of the company and it details the reporting chain of the salaried personnel serving under the vice president.

FIGURE 10.10: *Organization Chart*

TABLES

Like graphs, tables are organized on two axes. A series of vertical columns is intersected by horizontal rows. The left-hand column organizes the data in the rows into categories. The row at the top of the table organizes the numerical data or other information in the columns.

Use tables when you want to present exact numerical data and are less concerned with showing trends. Tables permit you to organize and quote many numbers in a limited space. Give your tables plenty of margin room. It is particularly important for tables to be uncluttered. And when you construct related tables, be sure you label them consistently.

Although most tables are numerical (as in Figure 10.11A), they can also be constructed of words (as in Figure 10.11B) or of symbols.

DESIGNING TABLES

Even though your purpose in providing a table is primarily informational, you can construct it so as to direct your reader's eye to what you want to show. Space your rows and columns to reflect what you want to emphasize.

Items that you want compared should be placed close together and surrounded by spacious margins. Note Figure 10.12A. Here the eye reads down the columns comparing economic indexes in the various countries and groupings. But in Figure 10.12B, which contains some of the same material, the horizontal spacing makes us read across the rows. Our interest here, by contrast, is directed to the much more recent performance compared with the 10-year growth rate. Note also how the spacing between years in 10.12A guides the eye and the thought.

FIGURE 10.11

Tables

Sweetening the Pot

How have the guardians of the nation's coastline fared at the hands of the guardians of the nation's purse? Despite the Coast Guard's vociferous complaints, its fiscal pot has consistently been sweetened by Congress. From fiscal 1981–88, in fact, Congress has given the Coast Guard almost $1.2 billion more than requested, the biggest increases being funneled into acquisition and construction.

	Requested	Enacted	Defense Dollars
1981	$2,050.6	$2,034.5	——
1982	2,074.5	2,525.5	$300.0
1983	2,303.2	2,455.2	——
1984	2,549.5	2,799.5	300.0
1985	2,591.3	2,592.4	——
1986	2,555.9	2,661.9	350.0
1987	2,609.8	2,930.1	335.0
1988	2,737.8	2,661.5	128.0
1989	2,976.1	——	——

"Sweetening the Pot" from the *National Journal*, June 18, 1988. Copyright © 1988 by National Journal Inc. All rights reserved. Reprinted by permission.

10.11A. This simple, easy-to-read table supports its attached article and records the discrepancy between the amount of money requested yearly by the Coast Guard from 1981 through 1989 and the money it received.

Recommendation for Product Adoption

	Large Company	Medium Company	Small Company
Product A	Yes	Yes	No
Product B	Yes	No	No
Product C	No	Yes	Yes

10.11B. This table is modeled on a much more complex one which uses symbols to recommend (or not recommend) a number of computer systems to a variety of businesses.

INDEXES, WORLDWIDE AND BY REGION, 1986-87

		10 Countries		9 Countries excl. U.S.		North America (2)		Europe (4)		Pacific Region (4)	
			Indexes, 1980 = 100								
		Perf.	Lead.	Perf.	Lead.	Perf.	Lead.	Perf.	Lead.	Perf.	Lead.
July	86	114	118	115	115	113	121	108	113	125	119
Aug.	86	114	118	115	115	113	121	108	113	125	120
Sept.	86	115	119	115	116	114	122	108	113	127	122
Oct.	86	115	120	116	117	114	122	108	113	127	124
Nov.	86	115	120	116	118	114	121	109	114	127	126
Dec.	86	116	121	116	119	115	123	109	114	128	128
Jan.	87	116	122	117	120	114	124	109	115	129	131
Feb.	87	116	124	117	121	116	127	109	115	129	132
Mar.	87	116	125	117	123	116	128	109	116	129	137
Apr.	87	117	127	118	126	116	129	110	116	129	142
May	87	117	128	118	127	116	128	110	116	129	146
June	87	117	131	118	130	116	131	111	117	131	153
July	87	118	132	119	132	117	131	111	118	132	157
Aug.	87	118	134	119	134	118	132	111	118	132	163
Sept.	87	119	134	120	134	118	132	112	118	134	163
Oct.	87	120	133	121	134	119	132	112	118	134	161
Nov.	87	120	132	122	132	119	131	113	117	135	158
Dec.	87	121	132	122	132	120	131	113	117	136	159
Jan.	88	121	133	123	133	120	131	114	117	137	161
Feb.	88	122	133	123	133	120	132	113	118	139	160

10.12A.   This table organizes the information vertically, directing the eye down the columns.

Summary Of Growth Rates, Ten Industrial Countries

	Ten-year Growth Rate	Indexes of Economic Performance Growth Rates*			Leading Business Cycle Indexes Growth Rates*			Current Reading on the Cycle
	1976-86	6 mos. ago	3 mos. ago	Latest month	6 mos. ago	3 mos. ago	Latest month	
		annual rates, percent						
North America (2)	3	4	5	5	9	4	2	Expansion continuing
Europe (4)	2	4	5	4	4	1	1	Expansion continuing, leaders weak
Pacific Region (4)	4	5	7	9	42	17	9	Expansion continuing
United States	3	4	5	5	8	3	2	Expansion continuing
Canada	3	6	7	5	5	6	3	Expansion continuing
West Germany	2	3	4	3	6	1	1	Expansion continuing, leaders weak
France	2	5	5	5	7	2	3	Expansion continuing
United Kingdom	2	6	6	5	5	1	0	Expansion continuing, leaders weak
Italy	2	1	4	7	−1	−1	−2	Expansion continuing, leaders weak
Japan	4	4	7	9	50	19	10	Expansion continuing, leaders strong

* Ratio of current month's index to average index over the preceding 12 months, expressed as a compound annual rate.

"Indexes, Worldwide and by Region, 1986–87" and "Summary of Growth Rates, Ten Industrial Countries" from *International Economic Scoreboard*, May 1988. Reprinted by permission of The Conference Board, Inc., New York, New York.

10.12B.   Use of white space in this table guides the eye horizontally, across the rows.

FIGURE 10.12:   *Tables with Special Points of Emphasis*

PRODUCING GRAPHICS

To create effective graphics, notice the professional graphics that appear in newspapers, magazines, and business reports. Study those that have features you admire and include in your own graphics any features that meet your needs. By all means use a computer if one with graphic capabilities and appropriate software is available to you. But if not, you can still produce professional-looking graphics working by hand.

CREATING GRAPHICS MANUALLY

Experienced communicators have developed techniques that can help you give your manually produced graphics a professional look. You may also find a number of commercial products useful. The following Guidelines can help you produce effective graphics to support and enhance your reports.

◼◼◼◼◼◼◼◼◼◼◼◼◼◼◼ **GUIDELINES** ◼◼◼◼◼

Tips for Professional-looking Graphics

1. *Be precise in your draftsmanship.* If there is one thing that makes a product look professional, it is copy that is precisely laid out and pasted down, with all lines squared and all graphic symbols in a straight and precise pattern. To achieve this effect:

   - Measure and position everything you lay down so that it fits precisely where you want it to go.
   - Draw guidelines, and use a *T-square* or a *straightedge and triangle* to keep your type and the other parts of your copy both straight and square.

2. *Make sure your lettering is uniform in size and style.*

   - *Transfer letters.* To make headlines without the expense of having them set by a typesetter, you could use transfer letters. These come in sheets and in many different type styles. Transfer them by "burnishing," or rubbing the type down with a wooden stick or any dull, stylus-like tool.
   - *Lettering guides.* Or you might try lettering guides, stencils, or templates that you draw around with a fine pencil and then ink in.
   - *Calligraphy markers.* If your own printing is neat and clear, you might try making your letters by hand. Calligraphy markers can help you achieve the kind of variable lines and gradations in calligraphic width you need.
   - *Headline machines* are still in use in some companies. These machines enable you to set headlines photographically. They produce a strip of film lettering that you can paste into position.

3. *Duplicate symbols to achieve a uniform appearance.* To construct a pictorial graph, find or draw the symbols you select and use a photocopying machine to make as many copies as you wish. Many cur-

rent copiers will also adjust the size of your symbol to fit your graph.

4. *Texture transfers.* If you want to add texture, color, or tone to your work, try using one of the commercially available sheets of patterns or color. There are screens of stippling dots, cross-hatching, and many other patterns available on film or acetate sheets that can be "burnished" onto your work. One widely distributed brand is called Zipatone.

5. *Work on a flat, smooth surface.*

   - A drawing board will provide a firm, smooth work surface and a straightedge against which you can place a T-square. You can anchor your work by taping its corners to the board with masking tape or drawing pins. But be sure to square up the edges of your worksheet before you tape or pin it down so that your work and its placement will be square and true.
   - *A light table,* a sheet of glass with a light under it, enables you to place a grid sheet under your work to use as a guideline.

6. *Prepare spotless material.* The photocopying machine may be your greatest secret ally. When your text is properly treated, the copier will overlook any errors and pick up only the reproduceable parts. The result will be clean, presentable work.

   - Correct any mistakes with *white correction fluid.* Your corrections will NOT show up on the photocopy.
   - *Light blue pencils* produce markings that will not photograph. Use them to draw guidelines or mark instructions on artwork.
   - Use *cloudy transparent tape* or rubber cement to affix cuttings to your work. Unlike staples or some other mucilage, cloudy tape is not picked up by the photocopier. Rubber cement permits you to move a cutting into precise position after you have laid it down.

CREATING GRAPHICS ON A COMPUTER

Almost all professional graphics are now computer-generated. They are cleaner and more precise than graphics most of us can make by hand. And they are faster. Often much faster.

For constructing graphs and charts, two kinds of computer software can be useful: business graphics packages and line art (or Draw) packages. For producing tables, spreadsheet programs are also helpful.

USING BUSINESS GRAPHICS PACKAGES. Business graphics packages can directly convert numeric data into graphs and charts. These packages can automatically produce the lines, bars, and other geometric shapes you need for effective graphics. Some also have "canned" figures such as people, houses, and other often-used symbols that you can incorporate into your pictorial graphics.

Many of the sample graphics in this text were produced by business graphics software.

USING LINE ART PACKAGES. With line art packages you measure and draw the actual lines, bars, and pie wedges, but your work is aided by the software. These packages give you freedom to introduce into the charts images that business graphics packages cannot provide.

You can also combine the benefits of both kinds of software. Some business graphics packages can present their output in a format that can be subsequently processed by the line art packages. That is, you can create your graph or chart automatically by feeding your data into a business graphics setup. And then you can embellish your graphic by making use of line art capabilities. Such graphics are attention-getters. When they display their information with imagination or wit, they can be highly effective.

Figures 10.6A, 10.8B, and 10.13 illustrate graphics produced by line art packages or combined with business graphics software.

USING SPREADSHEET SOFTWARE. Business graphics and line art packages can help you design graphs and charts. For tables, you may want to use the grid formatting capabilities of a spreadsheet program. A spreadsheet facilitates the entry of tabular data. It provides you with many options for tabular output, and it automatically performs calculations. The tables in Figure 10.12 were probably produced in this manner. Some word-processing programs also have capabilities for presenting columnar data.

Computer software is advancing rapidly, and already provides graphic capabilities beyond this chapter's suggestions. Investigate to find the applications you need.

ETHICAL PERSUASION

Your purpose in using graphs, charts, tables, and other graphic effects is frankly persuasive. The better a graphic helps you make your point, the more effective it is.

But though your graphics should support your point as convincingly as possible, guard against constructing them to create a false impression.

1. Be absolutely certain of the accuracy of your statistics.
2. Be sure that you do not distort your data visually.

   - Make certain, for example, that the segment of a circle graph labeled 25% actually occupies a quarter of the circle's area—no more and no less.
   - Construct your graphics so that the distance between points accurately reflects their relative values and the length of the lines and the size of the bars are true to the fact.
   - Fulfill your reader's visual expectations. For instance, if you start a scale at regular intervals, your reader should be able to expect this

10.13A. Shaking the Money Trees in New York

☐ Financial   ▨ Legal   ▩ Real Estate   ■ Other

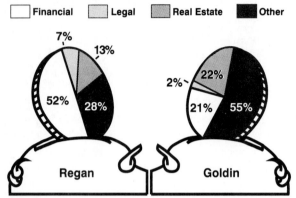

10.13B. Peer Group
International infant mortality ratings, 1985

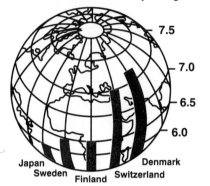

10.13C. Taking the Plunge
Men and women who have never married

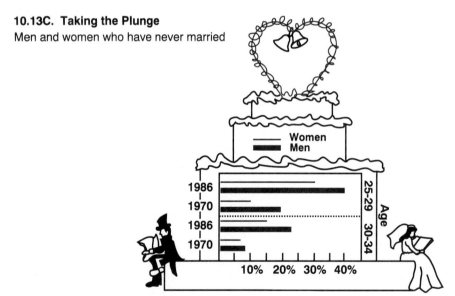

10.13A.   These circle graphs are presented as coins to show the large percentage of donations to two New York politicians that came from interests doing business with the state. To emphasize the point, the coins are shown sliding into piggy banks. Pigs are a doubly appropriate symbol, both in the banking usage and because of their connotation of avarice.

10.13B.   This three-dimensional globe background, with the curving, almost clutching, black bars of the graph,

strikingly presents the information about international infant mortality rates.

10.13C.   This graphic presents a wedding cake with the miniature bride and groom no longer decorating the summit but separated at the base, their backs determinedly to one another. An imaginatively appropriate way of showing data on the single life.

FIGURE 10.13: *Graphics Produced by Line Art Packages*

regularity to continue consistently throughout. A suddenly compressed interval will visually exaggerate the trend depicted.

- Make all quantities comparable. Be especially careful to adjust money figures for inflation.
- Make sure that all comparable visuals are adapted to the same scale. If, for example, you are showing price of oil by size of barrel, be sure the symbol increases in size precisely proportionately to the increase in price.
- And do not make a sales trend, for example, look much more impressively steep on a vertical axis by compressing the time period on the horizontal axis. Resist such temptations.

3. Label clearly and in detail to counter ambiguity and inadvertent distortion. Be sure to make clear the basis for your figures.
4. Use footnotes or other documentation. Since statistics are only as reliable as their sources, substantiate the validity of your statistics.

Graphs, tables, and charts are *the* notable exception to the general rule of thumb we discussed in Chapters 8 and 9—the rule that says business doesn't want to take the time to deal with footnotes. Footnotes are used extensively, for instance, in presenting accounting information in such financial instruments as annual reports, quarterly reports, and other financial disclosure documents that must be absolutely accurate.

5. Use notes also to clarify points of information and to specify particulars that may not be clear from the graphic approximations of the data.

Statistics, as we know, can lie; but they shouldn't. Be careful not to let your statistics make false implications. Far too much is at stake in the decisions that will be based on them.

Never slant your statistics. But do verbalize in your report the point they are intended to make so that the reader will understand the statistics from your point of view.

GUIDELINES

Tips for Working with Graphics

1. Be sure to refer to your graphic when you discuss the point in the text it is meant to support.
2. Place your graphic as near as possible to the reference in the text.
3. If you use a desktop publishing program, anchor a frame for your graphic to the point where you reference it. The program will automatically place your illustration where it belongs and will cause the text to flow around it.
4. If you are in doubt about how to make your graphic most visually effective, study other graphics. And model your own after graphics that have solved a similar communications problem successfully.

AUTHENTIC BUSINESS PROBLEMS

1. Present in graphic form at least one set of data that you used to support your recommendations in the report for Chapter 9. Choose the form or forms that convey your point most convincingly.

2. Select any set of authentic business data from a major daily newspaper business page, and construct two visual aids to present the data. Experiment with more than two if you wish, and when you have finished, choose the one that best makes your point. Keep in mind:

   • What do you want to say with this graph, chart, or table?
   • Does the form you have chosen make the point in the most effective or dramatic way?
   • Does the form you have chosen depict the situation the data describes in an accurate way? Are you certain you have not permitted any inadvertent distortions?

   Be sure to turn in with your graphics a copy of the article you use for your data.

FOCUS:
Individual Business Problems

In working your way through this book, you have acquired information to help you complete most kinds of writing tasks you are likely to be assigned in your first years in business. This Project Segment is designed to give you practice.

The assignments in this Segment are authentic. The names are changed, of course, but every problem is one that has been assigned by a working executive. The problems cover a variety of departments and business sectors. Some of them are from big businesses, some from midsize enterprises, and some from small companies. You will be able to select assignments that are right for you.

As you work, keep in mind the cardinal rules for business communication:

- The purpose of a business communication is to lead to a decision and action. Make the best judgment you can for your company's welfare.
- Keep in mind the constraints of time, cost, and operational feasibility.
- Don't neglect details. Be sure that you have investigated every possible difficulty, and make sure that your communication answers all questions your managers may raise.
- Be brief. Be clear. Be accurate.
- Keep your documentation orderly in your files. You may have to refer to it again, or you may be asked to back up what you say. (For our current academic setting only, hand in your documentation with your assignment.)
- If your topic could conceivably have implications for liability exposure or you risk giving away proprietary information, be absolutely precise in your language. Consider the possibilities of your memo as legal evidence. Be careful about what you say. If in doubt about a statement, leave it out. Just be ready to answer if your manager asks. (For our current academic setting only, add a brief explanatory memo concerning material you decide to omit, should your problem have potential legal exposure.)

CASE STUDY ONE: FINANCE

At Large Corporation, Inc., you are a junior financial analyst, a member of a small but highly qualified analytical staff at corporate headquarters. You report to the Assistant Treasurer of the company, who in turn reports to the Treasurer. This assignment was given to you verbally by the Treasurer himself this morning. The Treasurer is a good manager, so he has already discussed the project with your immediate supervisor. But since he likes to take part personally in the training of his junior managers, he called you in to discuss the assignment.

This is what he told you: "I want you to do a comparative analysis of our top five competitors for the past five fiscal years." He asked you to include information about:

- Sales and percentage increases (year to year).
- Net income and year-to-year percentage increases (or decreases).
- Net income as a percentage of sales.
- Itemized cash flow and year-to-date percentage increases (or decreases).
- Capital expenditures.
- Return on equity.

A hint: The Treasurer didn't tell you, but we will: All this information should be available from the annual reports of the companies you choose. Select an industry and obtain five annual reports from competitors in the same industry. Be sure the data presented is *comparable*—that is, for the same fiscal year, computed on the same basis, etc. Take special note of accounting changes and changes in capital structure (e.g., issuance/repurchase of shares). After you have assembled the data, you will have to decide:

- How to present the information.
- How to summarize your findings so the information is immediately useful to your managers.

If you need some technical help with this assignment, you might check it with your professor of finance or accounting.

CASE STUDY TWO: PUBLIC RELATIONS

You are working as an assistant to the Director of Public Relations of City Symphony, a large metropolitan symphony orchestra. The PR director has come down with the flu and you are handling her job in her absence. She is available to you by telephone, but she is so hoarse that you can hardly understand what she says, and besides she feels so terrible you are reluctant to disturb her.

But you have a crisis that will require you to send out some urgent communications. Today is Thursday, and City Symphony plays concerts on both Friday and Saturday nights. This week's soloist, Josh Newly, is a singer of international reputation who trained in your city's conservatory.

He is extremely popular, and tickets for the concerts have been selling briskly. Newly is, however, also temperamental and opportunistic. And although he was engaged last year to sing this concert, he got a last-minute offer from a prestigious European orchestra and accepted it. His manager neglected to notify you until your orchestra's publicity had already gone out.

Things might be worse, however. By luck the City Symphony's management has been able to secure the services of another fine singer, Drew Sterling, whose reputation is perfectly respectable but who is less well known than Newly.

Because of a series of well-reviewed but poorly attended contemporary concerts earlier this year, the orchestra needs these concerts to be a success. With your supervisor so ill, your contribution to the box-office success or failure will be important.

You need to organize publicity for the replacement singer, and you have to do it fast. You need to write a press release announcing that Drew Sterling will replace Josh Newly as the baritone soloist for both concerts. You can't tell the truth about why Newly won't be coming, so you will have to come up with a tactful phrase. The idea is to play up Sterling so that those who were coming to see Newly will still buy tickets and those who already have their tickets won't be irate and return them.

Sterling, who is a nice guy, has agreed to be available for interviews on Friday morning to help you promote the concert. You may need to write some communications to get him onto a local arts talk show. Or you might try to get him into the afternoon paper's feature music column. Its writer, Russell Witherspoon, is usually amenable. Above all, you need to alert Althea Glueck, the critic for the morning paper, and provide her with some background on your substitute singer.

Write the communications, including a report to the orchestra's director of marketing, to explain why the Director of Public Relations is not handling this herself and to let him know the arrangements. It would be nice if you could also copy the orchestra manager and the music director (the conductor) to let them know what is happening.

Remember: The more specific and prestigious the credentials you can come up with for Drew Sterling, the more likely you are to keep the concert engagement from becoming a disaster.

A hint: To find samples of the kind of specific data that appears in press releases of performing artists, check *The New York Times, Variety,* or your own newspaper.

CASE STUDY THREE: SALES (REAL ESTATE)

You work for John Franklyn, a midsize real-estate firm, with its central office in a city of about 450,000 inhabitants. It operates some 20 suburban offices in a commercially close-knit tristate area. Your firm handles commercial, industrial, and investment real estate, but has in recent years specialized in residential. It has a relocation department that has lately enjoyed some success with its corporate programs for executives relocating in the city.

Corpco, a large, publicly held corporation based in the Northeast, has just been acquired by a local company, and its headquarters have been moved to your city. This move will cause an influx of top-level executives who will require housing. Your supervisor has asked that you survey the current listings and prepare a list of houses suitable for showing to these prospective clients. You will need to consider:

- Price range.
- Area/location.
- School districts.
- Size of houses (based on number of bedrooms as well as square feet).
- Other features (size and placement of garage, swimming pool, patio, fireplaces, etc.).

Before you write your memo, you may need to set up a profile of the probable clients, as well as some criteria for judging the listings. You will almost certainly need to use charts and categories of information to present the data effectively. In formulating your recommendations, don't forget that your object is to maximize sales for your company, John Franklyn.

In addition to the recommendation memo, consider drafting a letter to Annette Lanski in personnel at Corpco to describe your firm's relocation program and sell Corpco on working with your company. Once you have amassed the data for your recommendation memo, you will have considerable specific information to offer as sales ammunition.

> *A hint:* Use your local real-estate listings for sample data. Select a firm from local newspaper real-estate ads (or a local real-estate office) to be the model for John Franklyn. Categorize appropriate houses according to those listed with your company and those listed with other firms, where Franklyn's agents would not realize the maximum commission. Part of the strategy you recommend might well be based on your analysis of which areas the relocating executives are likely to prefer and how many of John Franklyn's current listings are in those areas.

CASE STUDY FOUR: ACCOUNTING

At Massive Enterprises, Inc., you have signed on in the Controller's Office for your first job. You are a cost accountant, reporting to the Chief Cost Accountant.

Massive is a large corporation with multiple divisions. Your supervisor wants you to prepare a Cost Trend Analysis (five-year trend analysis) in which you:

- Analyze costs by division.
- Analyze cost of sales and expenses as a percentage of sales.
- Compile data.
- Prepare graphs comparing divisions by major cost elements.
- Write a commentary presenting your findings.

A hint: In choosing a company to be the model for Massive, be sure to select one that reports its operating results *by company division* in its annual report. Also be sure that all data presented have been computed on the same basis.

CASE STUDY FIVE: BANKING

You are a communications specialist at Fourth Federal Bank. Your bank has made heavy loans to Megovia, a third-world country with overwhelming economic problems. Megovia had only begun to recover from last year's drought and famine when, with the encouragement of internal revolutionary forces, it was attacked by its well-armed neighbor to the southeast. At present, it cannot begin to pay off its debt or even to keep up with its debt-service payments. Fourth Federal has had to set aside a significant fund to cover anticipated losses. The bank managers still hope for a miracle, but the funds set aside will mean that Fourth Federal's profits for this year will be seriously affected.

Your supervisor, Jamala Jefferson, has asked you to draft a communication for the signature of H. W. Humphreys, the company's chairman. This communication will be published in the annual report, explaining what has happened, why the set-aside action was deemed necessary, and when your shareholders may again expect earnings and dividends.

A hint: Research *The New York Times* and *The Wall Street Journal* for articles about just such a problem, which occurred for a number of large banks in 1987. Use these articles to derive mock data to accomplish your assignment.

CASE STUDY SIX: COMPUTER FIELD

You are the Assistant Manager of Operations at Schocker Electronics, Inc., of Philadelphia, a manufacturer of integrated circuits. Your company has just acquired Bleep Systems in Sunnyvale, California. This acquisition naturally requires a coast-to-coast link between your operation and theirs. The Philadelphia Operations Department work has been done on 10 PC clones connected by a Novell Ethernet network; the new company has been using 7 Macintoshes connected by Apple-Talk.

Your job is to propose several connectivity options between the two installations and to present cost and functionality trade-offs. Your supervisor, Martin Smilay, the Manager of Operations, has asked for a recommendation memo for transmission to Patricia O'Malley, Manager of Bleep's Operation Department.

Hints:

- Look in publications such as *Byte* and *PC Week* for information. See the ads especially.
- Connections can be made between a PC clone and a Macintosh— with or without modems—or with gateways between the two networks.
- Coast-to-coast communications can be performed with such options as leased lines, public switched packet network, and microwave links.
- The functionality trade-off of the combined network should be measured in terms of ease of communicating and special tools provided (such as electronic mail and remote printing).

SPECIAL TYPES OF EFFECTIVE BUSINESS WRITING

WRITING EFFECTIVELY TO PLAN YOUR CAREER

EXECUTIVE SUMMARY

The basic business writing rule is:

Consider your reader in light of your purpose.

When your purpose is to get a job, considering your readers takes on special importance—because your readers are prospective employers who will also be considering *you*.

- They will examine everything you write for what it says or implies about you.

- They will want to find out in what ways—or whether—you can be useful to them.

Find out what you want to do through careful assessment. But to convince employers that you are the one to invite for an interview, focus your job-hunting communications on what you can do for them. Your job-search business writing will include three types of communication: letters of application, résumés, and letters of thanks.

Use a word processor and other electronic aids to produce your job-hunting materials, but make every application a *specific* response to the employer's requirements.

The most important business-writing task you may ever perform is to write the letters and résumé that will land you interviews that, in turn, lead to a job. Throughout this book we offer one basic rule:

Consider your reader in light of your purpose.

Important in all business writing, this principle is crucial here. If the communications you write in your job search are to be successful, you need to imagine the employers' point of view and look at your application material through their eyes. Why? Because application letters and résumés will be judged by their readers strictly in terms of their own circumstances and needs.

THINK BUSINESS

This viewpoint may not be easy for you to acquire. After all, *you* are naturally the focus of your own concern. And ever since the days of "What do *you* want to be when you grow up?" you have been thinking about what career would be best for *you*. Even now your thoughts are—and should be—occupied with making vocational choices. You must consider where you would like to live, what sort of work you would like to do, with what size company, and what sort of workplace atmosphere would be most comfortable for you. (See the Personal Workout for some suggestions on thinking through these issues.)

ASK NOT WHAT THE COMPANY CAN DO FOR YOU . . . Such questions are important as you make your decisions about where to apply for work and what job to accept. But they must not dominate your application letter. The executives of the company you apply to—the company you hope will spend a substantial sum of money on your training and on your salary—are more interested in what you can do for *them*. It is not that they have no interest in you. But that interest is almost entirely concentrated on whether and how you will be able to enhance *their* operations.

The focus of your letter and résumé must be on what *you* can do for *them*.

**YOU WILL BE
KNOWN
THROUGH
YOUR WRITTEN
WORDS**

Though the company's interest in you has a single focus, that interest is real. Prospective employers will examine everything you send for clues about how well you would answer their needs, how well you would fit their organization and their style.

Your résumés and cover letters, probably more than any other writing you will ever do, will be read for exactly what they say—and imply—about you.

The businesses you apply to will incur some cost to consider your application. Even preliminary interviews take up expensive executive time. Thus, the businesspeople to whom you write need to find out as much about you as they can before they suggest an interview. And they have little to go on: just your cover letter, your résumé, perhaps a phone call, perhaps a note of thanks.

They will examine these for clues to the qualities that are important to them. For instance, does your written communication reflect self-confidence? Or is there an overconfident or condescending tone that suggests arrogance or foolhardiness? Even what you don't say can radiate meaning. Prospective employers will assume that you would naturally want to put your best foot forward in application letters. If there is a conspicuous blank in your work record, for example, they may wonder. For the same reason, your mention of what your readers would consider trivial might also make them suspicious about major points omitted. Almost nothing else you ever write will be given such close and personal scrutiny. You can, however, make this scrutiny work to your advantage.

■■■■■■■ **PERSONAL WORKOUT** ■■■■■■■

Find Out What You Really Want to Do

Some of us find our career goals early. When we racked up that first success in Junior Achievement, we decided to be an entrepreneur one day and have never wavered. But some of us, less lucky, find ourselves graduating from college and still uncertain. Perhaps you are one of these. You've chosen business. But business offers such a wide variety of opportunities that you still lack direction. What should you do? Work the following exercises. Fortunately, the exercises that help you determine what you *really* want to do will also help you present yourself to the prospective employer you have chosen.

Exercise 1. Assess Your Accomplishments

- Make a list of your accomplishments. Include both those related to your work experiences and those related to nonprofessional projects that have given you satisfaction in achievement.

- Divide your work pages vertically and write at least 25 of your accomplishments in the left column. Describe them as specifically as you can, using active verbs (such as those listed on pages 303–304). See the left column below.

Exercise 2. Inventory Your Skills

- Translate your *accomplishments* in the left column to a *skills list* in the right column, as shown below.

Sample Skills List

Accomplishments	Skills Used
1. Managed and produced the university's annual Folk Music Festival. Event received national news coverage, earned $000,000 for student activity fund. Attendance broke all previous records.	Leadership Problem solving Budget managing Communicating: written, verbal Organizing Scheduling Trouble shooting Negotiating contracts
2. Organized and implemented moving of Chem. Library to new facility. Helped set up new procedures and arrangements.	Organizing Managing Problem solving
3. . . .	. . .

Exercise 3. Assess Your Skills

When you have finished your chart, count the number of times each skill appears, and rank the top 10 on a separate page. Now ask yourself this question: Are the skills at the top of the list the ones I have most enjoyed using? What you're looking for here is the secret shiver, or the sense of pride that tells you what delights you.

- If the skills you most enjoy are *not* those at the top of that list, then make a new ranking for your "enjoyment" list. If the lists are not similar, rethink some of your vocational choices. To do that thoroughly, we recommend that you begin with the extensive self-assessing exercises in Richard N. Bolles's frequently updated *What Color Is Your Parachute?**
- If the skills that have most delighted you *are* at the top of the list, you automatically know something important about the kind of work you would like to do: it should use as many of these skills as possible.

---

*(Berkeley, Calif.: Ten Speed Press).

Exercise 4. Match Yourself with an Available Job

Investigate what jobs or fields match your experience, skills, and preference lists most closely in these ways:

- Take advantage of the career center on your campus. Read the printed information available there and in libraries, as well as that accessible in computer data bases. As you read, make a list of names, addresses, and telephone numbers of people whom you can write or call to get more specific information. Leave at least five empty lines after each entry so you can make a clear follow-up record.
- Make a similar list of the names, addresses, and telephone numbers of friends and acquaintances who might be able to help or advise you in your search. If you consider really carefully, this list will be longer than you think. Then contact the people on your list. (Perhaps offer to take them to lunch.) Ask them what they know about the fields or companies you are interested in. Then ask them whom they know who might also be helpful, and expand your list.

This process is like pulling the end of a string. People like to be helpful. They remember how it felt to be starting out. You will find that one contact leads to another—and another—and eventually to the goal or information you are seeking.

WRITING A LETTER OF APPLICATION: YOUR MOST IMPORTANT SALES LETTER

Your letter of application is a prospective employer's first perception of you. Together with your résumé, it often becomes the means of comparing you with other candidates and the evidence from which the company will decide whether to offer you an interview. It can be tremendously important to your job search.

PERSONALIZE

Tailor your letter to the specific character and needs of the business to which you apply. Immersed in their own urgent concerns, those who read your materials will not make allowances if your letter includes inapplicable statements that suggest it was meant to be sent to the industry at large. They are likely to think that you are not seriously interested in *their* company.

Personalizing takes research. And making each letter individual will also take a little time. But surely it's worth spending an extra hour or two to research a company you might commit years of your life to. After you discover what the company is like, modify your letter to correspond to this knowledge.

SELLING YOURSELF

An application letter is a sales letter, but you are selling a most important commodity—yourself. Look back at the discussion of sales letters in Chapter 5, Section A. In brief, these are the principles discussed there:

- Catch the reader's attention.
- Create a desire for the product (in this case, your services) by convincing the reader of its usefulness.
- Cause the reader to take action.

These principles will also help you write an effective letter of application. They are embodied in the opening, body, and closing of the letter in the following Guidelines.

GUIDELINES

A Model Letter of Application

Although no model or form can respond to all situations, the following is general enough to be widely applicable and conservative enough to be safe. (Specific examples of application letters appear on pages 306–310.)

```
                                        Your Street Address
                                        City, State ZIP
                                        Date

Mr./Ms./Dr. Full Name
Title and/or Department
Name of Company
Street Address
City, State ZIP

Dear Ms./Mr./Dr. Lastname:
```

[The opening] Write one brief paragraph in which you awaken the prospective employer's interest, explain why you write, and summarize the following information: (1) the name and position of the person who suggested you write and/or the advertisement or notice to which your letter responds; (2) the job for which you apply; and (3) the qualifications that make you a particularly desirable candidate for it.

[The body] Sell yourself here as just the person the employer needs for the position. You may wish to organize this section into paragraphs that point out first your previous occupational (job or volunteer) experience, and then the preparatory training and schooling that make you suitable for the job. If you have had little employment experience, reverse the order. Focus on the relevant facts of your résumé in light of the job's specifications.

If you can cite no comparable job experience, emphasize other pertinent aspects of your experience. For example, in applying for a sales position, you might mention the valuable opportunity to meet the public you found in working as a library assistant. You can even make extracurricular achievement relevant. For instance, you can show that you are a leader by citing election to class or club office, that you are competitive by referring to athletic team membership.

[The closing] Where action is proposed. The idea here is to elicit an offer for an interview or, at least, to keep the door open for further contact. Try to make it possible to follow up yourself if you can. To keep the ball in your own court, you might write, for instance, "I would welcome an opportunity to discuss the position further with you and will call your office next week to see if you would be able to schedule an appointment."

Yours sincerely,   [or alternatively]   Very truly yours,
[Signature]   [Signature]
First M. Lastname   First M. Lastname

Let's consider each sales strategy individually.

CATCH THE READER'S ATTENTION: THE OPENING. Just as in sales letters, use your letter's introduction to interest readers. Orient them and attract them to your product—that is, to you.

Name your contact. Your best opening is to mention a familiar name. Cynics sometimes say "It's not *what* you know that counts; it's *who*." And there may actually be something to this. After all, in a world of strangers and the unknown, a familiar name gives a sense of safety and plausibility. Write, for instance:

- John Smith suggested I write to you. He is familiar with my sales performance, because I worked in his department at _____ [another company].

- My friend Mary Brown tells me you recently mentioned an opening in your financial department. I believe she plans to call you to discuss the possibility of my applying.

- Alice Johnson of MNOP Consolidated suggested I contact you about a position in public relations with your company.

- James Gruen suggested that my education in Marketing at State University and my extensive co-op and summer experience in retailing might be of interest to you and your company.

After you have caught your reader's attention with a familiar name, follow up with a summary of your qualifications phrased so as to show how you fit the job. The James Gruen sample, above, illustrates this point. This summary should become the thesis of your letter. Expand it and support it to show that you are worthy of an interview with the company.

Responding to an advertisement.   If you are writing in reply to an advertisement, mention it at the start. You might begin, for instance:

- Your advertisement for a marketing specialist in the July 8th edition of the <u>Cincinnati Enquirer</u> is of interest to me.

- I am writing in response to your advertisement for a trainee in circulation in the July edition of <u>Editor and Publisher</u>.

- The list of vacancies that you posted at the June conference of _____ Trade Association caught my attention. I am particularly interested in the position of _____.

When you reply to an advertisement, respond directly in the introduction, and then cast your entire letter in terms of the ad. One Midwestern outplacement firm[1] advises: "Tailor your response to meet their need by using as much of the ad language as possible." Note how Mark Cunningham handles the situation in his letter on page 308.

Opening without a contact.   We discourage you from mass mailings of your résumé because that strategy so rarely works. Nevertheless, if you have researched the company carefully and can address yourself to specific, identified needs, you might find an unsolicited letter a useful first contact. Research the vocational possibilities in the geographic location where you would like to settle and identify companies where your particular skills might be needed. Then find out more about these companies through further research—including the name of an appropriate person to address. Finally, write a letter *to that person.*

This letter—where you have no contact—is more difficult, but if you have done your research well, you can discover a way to catch this reader's

---

1. Schonberg and Associates, Cincinnati.

attention too. Here are some sample openings you might modify to fit your circumstances and those of the company you have investigated:

- State University has just provided me with a sound education in marketing. And with my extensive co-op and summer experience in retailing, I feel I could make a strong contribution to Amalgamated Department Stores. I would like the opportunity to make that contribution.

- Although Consolidated may not need a marketing specialist with my capabilities at this moment, with your continuing growth in this area, it seems reasonable that you will soon.

See also Eric Soderstrom's letter on page 309.

CONVINCE THE READER: THE LETTER BODY. Your aim is to get an interview. In the body of your letter, link the facts of your experience to the needs of the

---

Writing Application Letters on Your Word Processor

Though your application letters should be tailored to fit each position, there is no need to reinvent the wheel each time you write one. Store your letters on a computer disk. For each new situation, call up a letter and modify it appropriately.

If your computer has merge-mail capability (see pages 118–120), you might apply it to your job search—especially if you are searching in diverse areas. If you were job hunter Mark Cunningham, for example (see pages 307, 308), you could make two lists of variations on your base letter. One list of fill-ins would make the letter appropriate for a position in social services and the other for a position in management. For an application letter, most of your fill-ins would be more than simple words or phrases. You could fashion entire paragraphs to be filled in or to replace any given paragraph of your stock letter.

We suggest that you use the available technology to make the difficult task easier and therefore more effective. But in a document as important as a letter of application, be sure to re-edit your final version carefully and tailor it to the particular situation. And if your printer produces only dot-matrix copy, do not use it for your final letter.

company or the position. Support every assertion with specific details from your experience. Always tell the truth. But don't be afraid to be imaginative and creative as you make the fit.

Best foot forward.   Start where you shine. If you have had successful experience in the field, begin the body of your letter with a discussion of this experience, because it is what employers look for most. Even if this experience was as an intern or summer employee, it is still direct experience and valuable.

The best approach is to show how your earlier work experience relates precisely to the job you are applying for. Don't just tell: show and explain. Back up each assertion with specific, relevant details. Note, for example, how this student makes even manual labor in a dairy an asset for an entry-level position in marketing:

```
My summer work at Bossy Dairy--though largely manual la-
bor--gave me a valuable opportunity to observe and help
implement a number of marketing strategies. I believe I
now have a good sense of what will and will not work in
the marketing of a consumer staple like milk. Further,
while at the dairy, I developed several strategies that
my former group there is considering for next spring's
promotions.
```

When you lack direct experience.   If you lack direct vocational experience but are a good scholar (and within a year or two of your schooling), begin by discussing your education. Show how what you learned has prepared you to serve the business to which you apply. If you have studied at an institution or under professors well known in your field, name it or them and shine in reflected glory. If you have been an outstanding student and have received awards or commendation—especially in your field—let your correspondents know.

If you do not have direct experience but have had other business experience, make that work for you. For example, if your only business experience is two years as a restaurant busperson and server, make this job demonstrate your reliability or sense of responsibility. There is scarcely a job—full or part-time, paid or volunteer—that doesn't offer something you can put to use in your chosen field and at your chosen company. Discuss that something in your application letter. Note how Mark Cunningham makes his not completely relevant experience work for him in his letters on pages 307–308.

Extracurricular achievements.   Should you mention nonacademic, nonprofessional activities in your letter? There is some risk, and we advise you to go easy here. If you overemphasize extracurricular accomplishments, you might call attention to a lack of achievement in more relevant areas. Furthermore, in some quarters a certain stigma of immaturity attaches to those who cling too tightly to the rah-rah of their college days.

On the other hand, without a doubt, some firms *are* interested in extracurricular achievements. They want to make sure you are well rounded. Or they believe leadership is leadership wherever it occurs and that achievement in one area promises achievement in others.

So how should you handle your extracurricular achievements? You should certainly not begin the central portion of your letter with them. Even slightly related work experiences should take precedence. But if you were an editor of the paper, the president of the senior class, the captain of a team or an outstanding varsity athlete, an officer of the student legislature, or a student participant on a faculty committee, that's worth talking about. If you have had a one-man or one-woman art show or soloed with the college orchestra or starred in or directed a number of plays, these are significant achievements and, at least for your first postcollege job, may be mentioned to your advantage.

But make your extracurricular achievements relevant to the position you are applying for. You might say, for example:

- I have gained management skills from my responsibilities as class president. In this position, I directed....

- I have learned about leadership from my position in the Student Assembly. I succeeded in managing an innovative reform through that assembly. Though unpopular at the start, the new system has resulted in significant improvements in student health services.

- From my football experience (three years as varsity defense tight end, captain of the freshman team) I learned how to work as a team member striving for the conference championship. I believe I learned how to compete successfully, and that knowledge should be transferable to work in a company such as yours.

And see how Lisa Lowell uses her college-paper experience to her advantage in her letter on page 306.

Phrasing your support. Whatever achievements you choose to support your assertion that you are the answer to the prospective employer's needs, phrase them dynamically. Rely on active verbs. Note the use of verbs in the sample letters (pages 306–310) and résumés (pages 323–326). Here is the sort of verb we have in mind:

directed	implemented	expanded
maintained	developed	coordinated

determined	managed	designed
completed	set up	projected
initiated	chaired	improved
tested	wrote	planned
evaluated	trained	budgeted
negotiated	performed	presented
researched	evaluated	controlled

Think back over what you have actually done in your work experiences—paid, volunteer, extracurricular—in terms of these verbs and others like them. You may discover that your accomplishments are more impressive than you had thought. Use such verbs and you will be able to convey that impression effectively.

CAUSE THE READER TO TAKE ACTION: THE CLOSING. In an application letter, the action you want the reader to take is to invite you for an interview. As you close your letter, attempt *closure* in the sales sense by tactfully suggesting an interview. Write something like:

```
I would appreciate an opportunity to discuss these mat-
ters further with you. I will call your secretary next
week and, if you agree, will try to schedule an appoint-
ment at your convenience.
```

Try to leave the opportunity open for a move on *your* part. The last example leaves the ball in your court, and you in a far better position than had you written: "If you would like to see me, please call me at. . . ."

If you are writing to a concern some distance away and are willing to make the trip at your own expense, the following sort of close might get you the interview:

```
I plan to be in your area the week of the ...[3-4 weeks
distant] and would appreciate the opportunity to meet
with you if you could schedule an appointment at that
time. I will telephone your secretary next week to see
if we can make arrangements.
```

If you can't afford the trip and company recruiters cover your part of the country, you might write:

```
If a company representative will be in my area soon, I
would appreciate an appointment at that time.
```

What Makes a Letter of Application Succeed?

To find out, Professor Steven Schreiner of the University of Missouri–St. Louis studied the letters of 20 applicants for a job.* Ten applicants were immediately rejected and 10 were invited for interviews. There were significant differences between the letters of the two groups. Among them:

- Most of the rejected letters had mechanical errors.
- The lack of "specific details distinguish[ed] rejected letters" from those whose writers were accepted for interviews. Rejected writers more often wrote in "general" terms, and "they failed to support their statements with pertinent details."
- On the other hand, "writers of rejected letters tended to say too much, to include irrelevant details . . . and to elaborate needlessly on items on the vita."
- "Successful letter writers pay more attention than unsuccessful to effective use of the active voice. . . . [The] active voice and sentences in which the writer is the agent performing any work described establish a candidate's enthusiasm and capacity to work."

---

*Schreiner presented the results of his research in 1988 at the Conference on College Composition and Communication in St. Louis.

SAMPLE APPLICATION LETTERS

The selection on the following pages includes sample letters to known contacts, letters in response to ads, and "cold" letters to researched companies. These letters were written by the students whose résumés appear on pages 323–326. Notice how they turn the qualities and experiences listed on the résumés into qualifications for the positions applied for. (None of the names are real, however.)

INSIDER TIPS AND WARNINGS

These suggestions and examples should help you write a good application letter. But here are a few hints that can spell the difference between adequate and effective:

1. *Address the company's needs—not your own.* Businesses do not necessarily lack compassion, but nobody hires for charitable reasons. Mentioning your need will only make potential employers uncomfortable.

   Never write: "I will do anything—I really need a job."
   Don't begin: "I am looking for a job . . ." or
   "I will graduate on May 17, 19——."

3404 Highfall Avenue
East Contrast, New Hampshire 00000

May 21, 19—

Mr. John H. F. Cooper
Talbot, Cooper, and Lytrall
Attorneys at Law [a public affairs law firm][2]
343 East Grosvenor Square
Boston, Massachusetts 00000

Dear Mr. Cooper:

Professor J. Manley Smith has suggested that your firm might find my research and writing skills applicable to an entry-level position in public affairs research. I believe he has already written to you on my behalf.

As you will see from my enclosed résumé, I have worked with Professor Smith on his recently published voter survey and am familiar with a method that I understand your firm has already put to use. Over the six-month period during which the study was designed and administered, I was fortunate to participate as Professor Smith's assistant in every phase of the work. I now know how to design the survey instrument, how to administer it, and how to tabulate and evaluate it. As Professor Smith may have told you, the first draft of the report, which I compiled, was changed very little in the final document.

In addition to my experience with the survey, I have had considerable experience in researching articles for the college newspaper, and I have for years assisted my father with the record-keeping and evaluation of planting and grafting operations on my family's fruit farm.

My dual major in business communications and political science would, I believe, be well suited to the kind of work undertaken by a public affairs law firm; and I am eager to apply my research and writing skills in the field of public affairs.

If you agree that my experience and career interests would be useful to you, I would very much appreciate an opportunity to discuss the matter with you further. I expect to be in the Boston area next month, attending a meeting as Professor Smith's representative, and could easily schedule an appointment during the week of June 15 if you would find that convenient. I can be reached at the Political Science office, (000) 555-1234, during business hours, or at one of the two dormitory numbers listed on my résumé after business hours or in the evening. I look forward to hearing from you.

Sincerely,

Lisa H. Lowell

Lisa H. Lowell

SAMPLE APPLICATION LETTER A: *With a Contact and with Relevant, Though Unpaid, Experience*

---

2. Public affairs law is a designation applied to the activities of law firms that represent clients in the legislative process. Such firms often employ researchers, analysts, and others who are not lawyers.

1234 State Street
Wabash, Ohio 00000

April 8, 19—

Mr. George Custis
Manager of Manufacturing and Sales
Midwest Tool, Steel Gear and Pinion Company
147 East Markham Drive
Manheim, Indiana 00000

Dear Mr. Custis:

John Fleming suggested that I write to you about an entry-level management opening in your sales operations. He tells me that you mentioned your interest in hiring several trainees at your last lunch with him.

My studies have prepared me for such a position. The general business major listed on the enclosed résumé does not show that I took a number of courses over and above those required in manufacturing and sales. But I come very close to having minors in each of these areas.

Those courses and my experience working at the Utica, Ohio, rural electric company in the summer constitute a wider view of industry than might be readily apparent. At Licking Rural Electric, John Fleming, to whom my work-crew foreman reported, spent many hours with me at the end of many work days helping me to understand the overall operation of the utility and its place in the economy. Whenever the opportunity presented itself, he arranged for me to observe business routines not strictly associated with my duties there. Additionally, my counseling experience and social administration at Wabash College gave me excellent opportunities to acquire skills in managing and motivating people.

I believe that this experience would not be wasted in a training position in a sales operation, and I am eager to begin applying what I have learned to a real business situation.

John is familiar with my work and has indicated that he would be glad to discuss my qualifications with you. With your permission, I will ask him to call you sometime next week.

And I will follow up with your secretary the week after that to see if you would find it useful to schedule an interview. I very much hope to hear from you.

Sincerely,

Mark Cunningham

Mark Cunningham

SAMPLE APPLICATION LETTER B: *With a Contact but Little Relevant Experience*

1234 State Street
Wabash, Ohio 00000

May 14, 19—

Box 351
Chicago Tribune
000 Michigan Avenue
Chicago, Illinois 00000

Dear Sir or Madam,

Your advertisement in the May 13 edition of the Chicago Tribune for a human resources trainee is of interest to me for several reasons. I believe my education is applicable. The general business major I am just completing as a June graduate at Wabash College emphasized human resources issues. And I completed enough courses in psychology to constitute a minor and almost a dual major.

Your ad specified both "academic and experiential credentials." In addition to extensive course work in human resource management, the experiences of my college jobs have been geared to personnel management as well. Two years in residence hall management and one as the chairman of the Residence Halls Council gave me experience in a wide variety of human resource issues, including management of hall security personnel and responsibility for dormitory social events.

Additionally, in my summer jobs I supervised a work crew often under emergency conditions. I am particularly proud that my last crew—all men older than I am—chose me to be their spokesman when they wanted to raise an issue of workplace safety with the management of the public utility we worked for. We resolved that issue in a satisfactory way for both management and the employees, and I gained valuable insights into the art of negotiation.

I believe that I would be able to apply the skills I have acquired to a position in benefits management, and I hope that you will find the enclosed résumé of interest. I will be available for an interview after the 17th.

I hope to hear from you.

Sincerely,

Mark Cunningham

Mark Cunningham

SAMPLE APPLICATION LETTER C: *"Cold" Letter in Response to an Advertisement, with Semirelevant Experience*

Sander Center, Box 1022
Metropolis University
Metropolis, PA 00000

March 23, 19—

Ms. Julia McCorkill
Director of Import Services
Associated Importing Corporation [an international program developer]
00 E. 46th Street
New York, NY 00000

Dear Ms. McCorkill:

I am writing to you to propose an exchange. I would value an opportunity to widen my horizons and learn about large-scale importing. In return, I feel that I could offer unusual experience and a close practical knowledge of the import-export business.

Three years ago, when I was 19, I founded my own importing and exporting business. Soderstrom Imports grossed $_____ last year, and we expect to nearly double that by the end of this year.

To run my own company, I used financing skills acquired in a 1987 internship with Bank Nederland in Amsterdam and language skills in Dutch and Swedish acquired from my Dutch mother and Swedish father.

I will certainly continue to run Soderstrom Imports, but for two years I have been training my younger brother to take that over as soon as he finishes college so that I can learn more about larger-scale trading. My own research and my knowledge of the field tell me that there is no more professional or successful organization than AIC; and I have for some time been interested in the new Caribbean Basin trade programs I know your company is now developing.

I enjoy the import-export business very much and believe that, with my newly acquired facility in Spanish, I could bring a wide assortment of skills and experience to program expansion. For instance, during a recent trip to Costa Rica I found an exciting new source of textiles manufacturing that could, I believe, be developed into a successful domestics line with only minimal design modifications.

I would very much appreciate an opportunity to talk with you about some of my own program development ideas and would like to discuss as well whether the skills I have to offer might fit into your organization.

With your permission, I will call your office next week to see if a meeting might be possible when I go through New York on my way to Sweden for the spring buying trip. I will have a two-day stay in New York in early May and should be able to schedule an appointment at any time for your convenience.

I hope we will be able to meet.

Sincerely,

Eric M. Soderstrom

Eric M. Soderstrom

SAMPLE APPLICATION LETTER D: *"Cold" Letter, Without a Contact but With Considerable Paid Experience*

1541 Blue Ridge Drive
Roanoke, VA 00000-0000
June 12, 19—

Mr. John Henry Colossal
Colossal Consulting Corporation
456 Engineering Way
Homewood, IL 00000-0000

Dear Mr. Colossal:

Jim Conrad thought you might be a good person for me to contact as I pursue career objectives in systems engineering. I have worked in my present job at COMPSYS for six years, with steadily increasing responsibilities, and Jim thought you might find my particular combination of systems and manufacturing experience of interest.

I believe that I am ready to assume a more senior position and am directing my investigations toward established consultants who would find my hands-on knowledge of manufacturing systems with close tolerance requirements helpful.

I have worked on a wide range of assignments, including systems design and implementation and operator training. My assignments have included systems in industries that I know Colossal serves as well.

I enclose a résumé and would welcome an opportunity to meet with you and discuss my qualifications. Certainly I would appreciate any suggestions or direction you might be able to offer.

I will call next week to see if we can arrange a meeting. In the meantime, although my travel schedule is heavy, you can reach me with a message at my office number during office hours or at home on weekends.

I hope to hear from you.

Sincerely,

John H. Kohler
John H. Kohler

JHK/bn
enclosure

SAMPLE APPLICATION LETTER E: *From an Experienced Applicant with a Contact*

Until you interest prospective employers in you because of something you can do for them, they really do not care when you graduate or what your plans are.

After you have interested them, however, you can turn your graduation date to an advantage to the company by writing: "I would be ready to start work after the 20th."

2. *There is no need to mention your drawbacks.* A negative approach suggests *not* modesty but a lack of confidence—or maybe even inability.

Remember: Prospective employers may not believe everything good you say about yourself. But they will *not* doubt the bad.

3. *Watch out for negative implications.* For example, if you mention that you made the Dean's List in your sophomore year, your readers might wonder about the years you don't mention. Or if you emphasize your high school achievements or your favorite hobbies, they might wonder why you have not included more recent or more pertinent accomplishments.

4. *Don't mention salary until the interview.*

5. *Don't convolute your sentences with passives to avoid using "I"; but also don't start every sentence with "I."*

6. *Don't forget to follow up your letter.* Always give yourself the last word, the last contact.

7. *Make your letter brief, tidy, and correct.* Some companies make it a practice to throw out all applications that are sloppy or have errors. Others have a rule not to read more than one page.

▬▬▬▬ JOB APPLICATION WORKOUT ▬▬▬▬

The following examples are excerpted from three letters sent by college seniors. These letters did *not* win approval. Explain why in each case.

1. Opening: "Next Sunday, June 10, I will be graduated from Saints Peter and Paul College, having spent the last four years acquiring an education here. I will then be ready to join the labor force."

2. Body: "I haven't any really marketable skills, but I am badly in need of money and I will work very hard at whatever you want me to do."

3. Closing: "And whether or not you choose to accept me, I sincerely wish Procter & Gamble great success in all your future endeavors."

WRITING MARKETABLE RÉSUMÉS

Include a résumé with your letter of application. If your letter interests your correspondent, he or she will want to know more about you in order to make a decision about an interview and will be glad to have the specifics at hand. Moreover, résumés sometimes are passed around in a company to see if people in other departments might have an interest in a candidate.

Résumés also often have uses beyond enclosure with your letter of application. You may want to leave one with your intermediary contacts. Take one to every interview. And, where appropriate, enclose one in your letters of thanks.

MARKETING YOURSELF

Résumés sum you up. In advertising parlance, they "package" your qualities and experience to make you as attractive as possible to potential employers. The key to writing effective résumés is to turn your skills and experiences—whatever they are—into marketable assets. The sample résumés on pages 323–326 demonstrate this process for a variety of entry-level applicants—those who have had job experience relevant to the career they want to pursue, those with job experience unrelated to the chosen career, and those with no job experience at all. There is also a résumé model for experienced applicants seeking to advance their careers.

HOW FAR SHOULD YOU PERSONALIZE? Résumés highlight that portion of your life, character, and experience which would interest a potential employer. A particular potential employer? Ideally, yes. But though you should certainly tailor every application letter individually, business considers duplicated résumés acceptable. In fact, you will find it useful to have on hand a supply of carefully—perhaps professionally—prepared résumés. If you are looking at jobs in more than one field (for example, accounting and business education or agribusiness and county agency work), write a specific résumé for each.

SHOULD YOU DO MASS MAILING? We strongly discourage wholesale distribution of résumés. Mass mailings are rarely successful. One important study shows that, on average, companies reject 245 résumés for every one that gains an interview. The specific figures range from those firms that eliminate 35 out of every 36 to those in a highly competitive market that have actually rejected 1187 out of every 1188.[3] You would be wiser, therefore, to concentrate your efforts on the number of businesses you can approach in an individualized way.

---

3. A study by Deutsch, Shea, and Evans, cited by Bolles in *What Color Is Your Parachute?* (1978), p. 35. Admittedly, this study is an old one. However, as Bolles points out in the 1988 edition, "after studying the[se] depressing findings, no one has thought it useful to repeat that study since that time" (fn., p. 14).

RÉSUMÉ FORMAT	There are almost as many formats for résumés as there are job applicants. And there are almost as many preferred formats as there are hiring employers. So what should you do?

WHEN IN DOUBT, BE CONSERVATIVE. One aim of your résumé is to make you stand out in a crowd, so you may be tempted to make a distinctive creation. But, paradoxically, you are likely to be picked out of the crowd because some employer believes that you will fit right in. And if your résumé is too distinctive—say, printed on pink paper; say, illustrated with symbols; say, interspersed with inspirational quotations—very few employers would feel that you would fit right in with their companies.

No advice suits all situations. Advertising, entertainment, and other creative industries *may* be—although they are *not always*—looking for signs of originality and ingenuity. But business, in general, is inherently conservative. And even creative businesses often have conservative clients. So unless you have specific and overriding reasons for deciding otherwise, use:

- White, cream, or the palest beige paper.
- Standard print fonts.
- Standard paper size (8½ x 11).
- No illustrations or decorative embellishments.

You really cannot go wrong making a conservative, tasteful choice.

MAKE YOUR RÉSUMÉ CLEAR AND QUICKLY READABLE. All the conventions of the résumé are aimed at making it clear and quickly readable. We advise you to follow these conventions. Your résumé should:

- Be one page in length (two at the most if you are widely and variously experienced).
- Set off well-defined chunks of data with plenty of white space and generous margins.
- List, rather than paragraph.
- Categorize under headings.
- Use phrases rather than sentences.
- Avoid personal pronouns whenever possible. (Hint: try drafting sentences and then eliminating the *I*'s.)

SELECT RÉSUMÉ ELEMENTS CAREFULLY	The box on page 314 lists the elements traditionally included in résumés. For some elements the order is optional; it depends on how you can best put your best foot forward. Other elements are optional altogether—again dependent upon making the best possible impression. And some we have

---

Elements of a Résumé: Suggested Order

1	Name, address(es), telephone number(s)
2 (or 3)	Work experience
	Military experience
	Summer experience
	Volunteer work
3 (or 2)	Education
	Honors and awards
4	Publications
5	Professional participation and membership
6	Languages, computer languages, licenses, special skills
7	References

Questionable
    Introductory objective, summary
    Interests and activities (after 6, where included)
    Personal data (before 7, where included)

---

strong reservations about including at all, except in unusual circumstances.

NAME, ADDRESS(ES), TELEPHONE NUMBER(S). Arrange this vital information so that it is both clear and attractively spaced. Make it easy for a prospective employer to reach you. Give phone numbers where you can be reached or messages can be taken for you both day and evening. If you are living at a temporary address (at college, for instance), be sure to include also a permanent address where mail will always reach you.

WORK EXPERIENCE. Where to place Work Experience? Should you begin by describing it, or should you detail your education first? The résumé item most relevant to prospective employers is your work experience. Logic would then indicate placing Work Experience first to save readers time and effort by providing the information they need for a decision as quickly as possible.

But you are not aiming at just *any* decision; the decision you want is a favorable one. And what if you still have had very little work experience but have achieved an enviable record in your studies? By all means, then, begin with Education—certainly for the first year or two after completing your schooling.

The chronological approach. The traditional method of organizing Work Experience is in reverse chronological order. List from the *most recent* item *to least recent*. Each of the following formats follows a chronological structure:

Chronologically Listed by Position

Work Experience

Residence Hall Counselor
1990-91 Resident Director   Wabash College, Wabash, OH
1989-90 Resident Adviser   Wabash College, Wabash, OH

Tree Trimmer
Summers 1989, 1990   Licking Rural Electric, Utica, OH

Clerk-Salesman
Summer 1988   Corvair Auto Parts, Heath, OH

Attendant
Summer 1987   SOHIO Service Station, Wabash, OH
Summer 1986   Velvet Ice Cream Parlor, Utica, OH
Summer 1985   Ye Olde Mill Swimming, Utica, OH
Summer 1984   Harris Dairy Farm, Licking Co., OH

Chronologically Listed by Employer

Work Experience

Wabash College, Wabash, OH
  1990-91 Resident Director, Boise Hall
  1989-90 Resident Adviser, 3rd Floor, College Hall

Licking Rural Electric, Utica, OH
  Summers 1980, 1990   Tree Trimmer

Corvair Auto Parts, Heath, OH
  Summer 1988   Clerk-Salesman

Chronologically Listed

Work Experience

1990-91   Wabash College,
           Wabash, OH   Resident Director

1989-90   Wabash College,
           Wabash, OH   Resident Adviser

```
Summers 1989, 1990  Licking Rural
                    Electric, Utica, OH   Tree Trimmer

Summer 1988         Corvair Auto Parts,
                    Heath, OH             Clerk-Salesman
```

When you use the chronological approach in any of its forms (including the combined form, pages 317–318), be sure to include:

- Any military experience you may have had.
- Internships.
- Volunteer work, if relevant or major.

And don't leave gaps in the chronology if you can help it. Some employers regard such gaps suspiciously.

The skills-based approach.   In recent years the skills-based (some call it functional) résumé has become popular. This method introduces a new category—Areas of Experience or Skills and Qualifications—and details the major tasks you have accomplished or the skills you have developed. Only then and only briefly does it chronicle your Employment or your Work Experience. For example:

```
                Skills and Qualifications


Personnel and Management Skills
• Kept careful records for 25 freshmen.
• Counseled students informally; referred problems to ap-
  propriate resources.
• Chaired Residence Halls Council.
• Advised and helped train assistant tree trimmer.

Administrative Skills
• Assisted administrator for a dormitory of 200 students.
• Administered the Thursday-night movie and the Invite-
  the-Faculty-to-Dinner programs. The latter program won
  an all-campus award.

Sales Skills
• Worked as summer clerk in an auto-parts store.
• Received special commendation from several longtime
  customers.
• Was offered permanent employment.

Merchandising Skills
• Trimmed windows and created counter displays for an
  auto-parts store.
```

Teamwork and Leadership Skills
* Played three years on the Wabash College baseball team.
* Worked as member of tree-trimming team.
* In second summer as tree trimmer supervised an assistant.
* Elected assistant team leader.

Work Experience

1990-91	Wabash College, Wabash, OH	Resident Director
1989-90	Wabash College, Wabash, OH	Resident Adviser
Summers 1989, 1990	Licking Rural Electric, Utica, OH	Tree Trimmer
Summer 1988	Corvair Auto Parts, Heath, OH	Clerk-Salesman

Evaluation of the approaches. Chronological formats are brief, to-the-point, and safely conservative. You may find them useful, though a bit stark, even if you have had a good bit of work experience. But if you have not yet had many jobs, this method can leave your résumé looking blank. And unless you list at least *some* of the major duties for each job, this approach can be misleading. It may not do justice to the extent of your responsibilities or skills.

The skills-based approach also presents problems. Unintegrated, it can be puzzling to the reader, who tries—sometimes in vain—to match "managed $60,000 budget" with the appropriate work experience in a later category. Moreover, the floating items of Skills and Qualifications, unless scrupulously businesslike and concrete, can appear frivolous, empty, or aggrandized. To the skeptical businessperson the whole section can look like filler. We recommend a mixed approach.

Mixed chronological–skills-based approach. You can present your experience in the most advantageous way by combining the two methods. To use this approach, add skills information as a job description under each item. For example:

Work Experience

1989-present	Wabash College, Wabash, OH Administrator, Counselor

<u>1990-91 Resident Director, Boise Hall, a dormitory for 200 students</u>
- Student administrator of the Residence Hall.
- Administered the Thursday-night movie and the Invite-the-Faculty-to-Dinner programs. The latter program won an all-campus award.
- Chaired Residence Halls Council.

<u>1989-90 Resident Adviser, 3rd Floor West Corridor, College Hall</u>
- Counseled students informally; referred problems to appropriate resources.
- Kept careful records for 25 freshmen.

<u>Summers 1989, 1990</u>   Licking Rural Electric, Utica, OH
                        Tree Trimmer

- Worked as member of tree-trimming team.
- In second summer helped train assistant tree trimmer.
- Supervised an assistant tree trimmer.

<u>Summer 1988</u>   Corvair Auto Parts, Heath, OH
                    Clerk-Salesman

- Worked as salesclerk.
- Trimmed windows and created counter displays.
- Received special commendation from several long-time customers.
- Was offered permanent employment.

Use active verbs. To make the most effective presentation of your accomplishments, rely on active verbs. For suggestions, note the verbs used in the examples above and in the sample résumés. And check the list again on pages 303–304.

EDUCATION. List your post–high school educational institutions, the years attended, and the degrees awarded. Begin with the most current and work backwards. You would want to put your list in directly chronological order only if your first years or your undergraduate training were at a particularly prestigious school.

Do not include high school data if you have been away from college more than a year. And do not include it even initially unless you attended an especially renowned public or private preparatory school.

Be specific about your major: BA in what? And include your minors as well. If your cumulative average or your vocational major is B or better, note it on the résumé.

```
Education
1986-90          BA         Wabash College, Wabash, OH
June 1990                       General Business
                                Minor: Psychology
                                GPA 3.3
```

If you did not graduate, your entry would simply be:

```
1986-88             Wabash College, Wabash, OH
```

Honors and awards. List your college honors and awards with their dates as a subhead under Education. Start with the most prestigious, whatever the date. For example, even if you made Phi Beta Kappa your junior year, record it first (and let its date speak for itself). Identify and define all local awards. The Green Key, for instance, is the most prestigious scholarly honor awarded by a small Midwestern college, but its name has little significance off campus. When you list such awards, add an explanatory tag line.

We would advise caution in the honors category. If you made the Dean's List four or five semesters, mention it, of course. But recording "Dean's List, first quarter sophomore year" raises needless doubts about your academic proficiency during the other years. Do not list high school prizes or scholarships unless they have national significance.

PUBLICATIONS. Be sure to list any nationally circulated publications. It's not just in the academic world that publication is appreciated. A recent graduate in computer science cited on his résumé a short story of his published by a national journal. Nothing on his résumé was mentioned more often during his interviews—except perhaps his minor in Russian language and literature.

Writing published in the college newspaper or literary magazine is less notable but may still be worth listing, especially if you have achieved recognition for your work. Be sure to mention the recognition as well.

PROFESSIONAL PARTICIPATION AND MEMBERSHIP. If you have presented papers or participated in presentations at professional meetings, note the occasions, dates, and titles of presentations on your résumé. Such activity speaks well for you. Even attendance at such meetings is worth mentioning if you attended by invitation or at the suggestion of your professor.

Membership in professional organizations is worth recording if you serve on a committee or hold an office—or if you need to fill out your résumé page. The fact of your membership alone shows professional interest. But if you have a full résumé, don't water it down with a lengthy list of memberships.

LANGUAGES, COMPUTER LANGUAGES, LICENSES, SPECIAL SKILLS. Include any such skills you may have. You never really know what will strike the prospective employer as relevant. Furthermore, sometimes the mention of these skills suggests employment possibilities to your correspondent or your interviewer that have never occurred to you.

REFERENCES. If your recommendations are on file with your school's Career Service, say so under this head; and give your references' full names and titles.

But if you are not involved with such a service, it is better to write: "References available upon request." *Do not include the names, addresses, and telephone numbers of your references on your résumé.* Giving written or oral recommendations is a favor. You do not want to impose on your references too often. And you will want to remain in control of the requests.

Include at least one professor on the résumé you use immediately after graduation. After you have been out of college for a while, most of your citations should be business references—unless one of your professors is a recognized authority in your own or a related field.

OPTIONAL RÉSUMÉ ELEMENTS

INTRODUCTORY OBJECTIVE OR SUMMARY. Though some vocational guides recommend that you begin a résumé with a sentence that expresses your vocational objective and a paragraph that summarizes your qualifications, we have yet to meet a business executive who required these elements or who even found their inclusion especially desirable.

Not only do these elements take up valuable space—remember, you are aiming at a one-page résumé—but they are difficult to phrase so as not to create a negative impression.

A statement of objectives. Even a well-phrased statement of objectives such as: "An entry-level position in Human Resources Management" can restrict your application possibilities. Stating your career objectives might make it difficult for the employer to consider you for another position your qualifications might suggest.

Moreover, too many statements of objectives are not phrased effectively. Sometimes the wording makes an applicant sound immature. For example:

```
Objective
An entry-level appointment in Human Resources leading to
a managerial position of growth and responsibility and
eventually to a position of corporate leadership.
```

There is something naive and touching about applicants who share their dreams in this way, but the blunt truth is that few potential employers are much interested in eventual career goals. They want to know how you can help them today. And naivete is not a quality much valued in business. Other statements of objectives attempt a crude sort of flattery, which when applied to a major company has an almost gauche ring:

```
Objective
An entry-level position in Human Resources with a com-
pany of recognized growth and potential.
```

Not every job-search authority agrees with us here, but we recommend that you not ordinarily include a statement of objectives in your résumé. One possible exception: If you are changing careers or your experience is not *apparently* relevant to the position or field for which you are applying, a statement of objective might be useful.

A summary of qualifications. Like a statement of objectives, an introductory summary, which is meant to sum up your best features in a nutshell, takes up valuable space and *can* do you more harm than good. On the other hand, under certain circumstances you could put such a summary to good use. If you have special qualifications, such a summary calls attention to them. It can show at the start why you are singularly fitted for the position and thus can make your résumé stand out from the rest. You might well choose to add a summary of qualifications to your résumé, for instance, if you have won a national award in your field or have had years of specialized experience.

Even if you are just beginning, there may be circumstances in your life that warrant using the summary. Let's suppose, for example, that you were raised as a participating member of a farm family, that your father became partly incapacitated in your junior year of high school and gradually put the management of the farm into your hands. You commuted to college to get your degree, while still managing the farm. The summary you might write in applying for a position in agribusiness could put you on an inside track for the job:

```
Farm manager with a BS in Agriculture and six years of
experience as acting manager (since owner's disability
in 1985) of 500-acre corn and hog farm. During this time
profits rose from $_____ to $_____ .
```

Or perhaps you are one of the several undergraduates each year who has published an article in a scholarly journal in your field or, more likely, whose name, as a valued researcher, has been included among the authors. Or perhaps you were the recipient of a nationally recognized fellowship—a Fulbright or a Woodrow Wilson—to study your specialty abroad. Such distinctions should bring you favorable notice with employers and are worthy of including in an introductory summary.

The summaries that business executives object to, and sometimes even smile over, are those that have little substance and rely on adjective-dominated phrases, such as *skilled manager, proficient organizer, able salesperson.*

Here is a rule of thumb you can follow: Introduce your résumé with a summary only if you can mention at least two *unusually* advantageous qualifications. (See page 326 for an example of an effective summary used in the résumé of an experienced applicant.)

INTERESTS AND ACTIVITIES. If you add sections to your résumé for interests and activities or personal data, they should be at the end, just before References. But should you include them? Business executives are divided on this subject. Some regard any such references as unbusinesslike and tend to suspect you of using them to fill out your résumé. Yet others regard them as evidence of a well-rounded personality.

If you have personal knowledge of the person you are addressing, you can make a judgment on that basis. But if you don't, we suggest that you not dilute a strong résumé with what some could consider frivolity. We would, however, make an occasional exception for the sort of real achievement listed on page 303. National or Olympic competition, for instance, is nearly always of interest to an employer because it shows perseverance. Thus, if yours is an exceptional talent for which you have received significant recognition—whether it is football, bridge, acting, chess, or playing the banjo—you might mention it, and the recognition you have received, in this category.

PERSONAL DATA. Birth date, height, weight, health, race, religion, national origin, marital status—all used to be standard information on résumés. Now there are laws that protect you from having to provide such information, and their gratuitous disclosure suggests that you aren't conversant with current practice. We suggest omitting this final category altogether.

SAMPLE RÉSUMÉS

The students represented by Sample Résumés A through D have varying amounts of relevant work experience. But they all highlight their experience and their other qualifications to fit the needs of their prospective employers. Letters of application based upon these résumés appear on pages 306–310.

Lisa H. Lowell
3404 Highfall Avenue
East Contrast, New Hampshire 00000
(000) 555-8672 (Evenings)   (000) 555-6754 (Days)

Education BS	Henry Duane College, Duane Center, Vermont Major: Business Communications Dual Major: Political Science	
Skills Writing and Research	Faculty Research Assistant, Government and Public Affairs Department, Henry Duane College	1987-89

Skills
Writing and
Research

Faculty Research Assistant, Government and Public Affairs
Department, Henry Duane College   1987-89

  · Assisted Prof. J. Manley Smith in a voter research study:
    designed questions for voter survey; administered
    questionnaires; tabulated and evaluated data.
  · Wrote initial draft for Prof. Smith's report.

State Legislative Associate-Researcher (Internship)   1986-87

  · Researched and analyzed proposed bills for state legislature.
  · Maintained bill memos for Transportation Committee.
  · Collected and evaluated materials for a forthcoming bill
    dealing with transportation of hazardous materials.

Features Editor, The Duane Banner (College paper)   1986-89

  · Researched, wrote, and edited articles for weekly publication.
  · Assigned and created story assignments for own staff and
    other Banner staff.
  · Assisted with layout and photography.

Publications

"Are There Steroids on Campus?" Duane Banner, November 3, 1988.
Honorable Mention: Society for Professional Journalists' Mark of
Excellence Contest (Division 1).

(Credited) J. Manley Smith et al. "Current Trends in College
Voting." Political Science Journal, 18 (1989): 103-112.

Leadership
and Admin-
istration

Dormitory President, Spanish House   1987-89
  · Planned social events for House.
  · Served as liaison to faculty and student government.

Secretary, Spanish House   1986-87
  · Kept records of House and Executive Council meetings.
  · Wrote monthly Banner column on House activities.

Treasurer, Freshman floor, Simon R. Falls Hall   1985-86

Receptionist, Admissions Office, Henry Duane College 1985-86

Operations and production assistant, Lowell family fruit
  farm.   Summers 1986-89

References

Professor J. Manley Smith
State Representative Charles L. Bradshaw
Dr. Laura L. Higgins, Dean of Students
Professor Marilyn R. Schmidlapp, Banner advisor

Available on request from Vocational Placement Office
                    Henry Duane College
                    Duane Center, Vermont 00000

SAMPLE RÉSUMÉ A: *No Paid Experience*

```
                          BIOGRAPHICAL SUMMARY


Personal Data

Name:          Mark Cunningham

Address:       1234 State Street          5678 Maples Road
               Wabash, OH 45000          Friendly Corners, OH 45000
               [Before June 1990]        [After June 1990]

Telephone      (000) 555-0000            (000) 555-0000


Education

1986-90        Wabash College, Wabash, Ohio          BA, June 1990
               Major: General Business
               Minor: Psychology                     GPA 3.3


Work Experience
1989-present    Wabash College, Wabash, OH. Administrator, Counselor

    1990-91 Resident Director, Boise Hall, dormitory for 200 students
      · Student administrator of the Residence Hall.
      · Administered the Thursday-night movie and the Invite-the-Faculty-
        to-Dinner programs. The latter program won an all-campus award.
      · Chaired Residence Halls Council.

    1989-90 Resident Advisor, 3rd Floor West Corridor, College Hall
      · Counseled students informally; referred problems to appropriate
        resources.
      · Kept careful records for 25 freshmen.

    Summers 1989-90 Licking Rural Electric, Utica, OH. Tree Trimmer
      · Worked as member of tree-trimming team.
      · In second summer helped train assistant tree trimmer.
      · Supervised an assistant tree trimmer.



References.  Available on request from: Wabash College Placement Center
                                 Wabash, OH 42000
```

SAMPLE RÉSUMÉ B: *Little Relevant Paid Experience*

Eric M. Soderstrom

Present Address   Permanent Address
Sander Center, Box 1022   5244 Joss Place
Metropolis University   Byrnie, PA 00000
Metropolis, PA 00000   (000) 000-0000
(000) 000-0000

EDUCATION: BA   Metropolis University   June 1989
            Major: Marketing
            Minor: Computer Science
            GPA: 3.76/4.0

            Languages: Dutch, Swedish, and Spanish
            Honors: Phi Beta Kappa   1989

WORK
EXPERIENCE: Owner and founder, Soderstrom Imports, Inc.,
            a Dutch-based partnership which imports and
            exports products among Sweden, the
            Netherlands, and the United States.   Summers 1986-

            Intern, Bank Nederland, Amsterdam. Paid
            internship. Performed various duties
            connected with product import and export.
            Extensive work with letters of credit.   June-Aug. 1987

            Computer Lab Assistant. Assisted students
            in the use of programs and equipment.
            Maintained and scheduled equipment.   Sept.-Dec. 1988

INTERESTS: 35 mm photography, foreign travel, soccer and
            skiing, tournament chess. Runner-up: Pennsyl-
            vania Junior Chess Championship, 1984.

REFERENCES: Available upon request through Metropolis
            University Career Development Center, Metropolis,
            PA 00000

SAMPLE RÉSUMÉ C: *Some Relevant Paid Experience*

John H. Kohler
1541 Blueridge Drive
Roanoke, Virginia 00000

Office: 703/321-7000   Residence: 703/523-7768

SUMMARY: Seven years' experience in data processing. Responsibility has
             progressed from programmer/analyst to systems analyst/project leader.

Hardware	Languages	Software
IBM 360-30/50	COBOL	IBM DOS/DOS-VS
IBM 370-130/	AUTOCODER	IBM OS/MVS/TSO/SPF
135/135	TIS	
IBM 3081/3083	MANTIS	TOTAL Data Base

EXPERIENCE
1985 to   COMPSYS, Inc., Roanoke, Virginia
Present   (Systems consulting firm)

                 Systems Analyst
                 Member of team responsible for systems consultation and development
                 for four of company's major clients, including two government
                 contractors.

                 National Information Agency, Crystal City, Virginia
                 · Assessed the on-line requirements and transaction volumes
                   required to operate financial systems under development to
                   ensure that the systems were designed to handle required work
                   volume.
                 · Provided support in requested areas of design and development for
                   agency's overall systems.

                 Maryland Biotech Research (Division of Biosystems International),
                 White Flint, Maryland
                 · Designed and installed an on-line control system using specially
                   developed software to interface with the parent company's data base
                   for U.S. subsidiary of a large international corporation.

                 General Pharmaceuticals, Champaign, Illinois (A subsidiary
                 of ABC Chemicals U.S.A.)
                 · Defined and installed a computer-to-computer order entry system to
                   help reduce personnel costs. Anticipated savings of $100,000 in
                   first three years of operation.
                 · Converted existing financial control system to accommodate
                   increased volume and complexity.
                 · Consulted with in-house training personnel to retrain existing work
                   force in new systems and interfaces.

1984-1985   TYRO Corporation, Philadelphia, Pennsylvania
                 Programmer/Systems Analyst
                 · Provided programming and design support for installation of
                   programs to control ordering, inventory and production.
                 · Conducted training workshops for systems users in financial and
                   manufacturing functions.

EDUCATION
1984   Miami College, Cambridge, Indiana
                 BS in Business (with honors)

SAMPLE RÉSUMÉ D: *Experienced Applicant for a Technical Midmanagement Position*

WRITING THANK-YOU'S AND OTHER COURTEOUS LETTERS

**OR DOING
WELL BY
DOING GOOD**

There is no way we can overemphasize the importance of personal courtesy when you are job hunting. Human thoughtfulness can make all the difference between attaining the sort of job you really want and not getting one at all. Therefore, we offer an unalterable rule:

Never let the sun set on an unthanked kindness.

Send a note or letter *immediately* to every person who has done you a favor, who has helped you in any way, or who has expressed interest in you during your search. If you can't get it out immediately, at least don't let a whole business week go by.

PEOPLE TO BE THANKED. Who, precisely, are the people you need to thank? Here's a list:

1. *References: Those who agree to write letters of recommendation for you.* Don't wait to hear that they have written for you. Thank them the day they consent to your request. Sample Thank-You A is an example of the sort of letter you might send.

March 14, 19—

Jacob L. Jones
General Manager
Corvair Auto Parts
Heath, Ohio

Dear Mr. Jones:

Thank you for agreeing to be a reference for me. I very much
appreciate your willingness to write on my behalf.

Sincerely,

SAMPLE THANK-YOU A: *To Reference*

July 24, 19—

Mr. Ira P. Goldstein
Vice President Acme Distribution Services, Inc.
333 North Industrial Park Court
East Lansing, Missouri 00000

Dear Mr. Goldstein,

Thank you for suggesting that I contact Amalgamated Industries. Your advice
and insights into the structure of that organization have been extremely
helpful. I have talked with their director of personnel and have secured an
interview for next Friday, which I am looking forward to with great interest.

I would not have thought of that myself and am grateful for your imaginative
suggestions. Thank you for all your help. I will let you know how the
interview turns out.

Very truly yours,

Joel R. Davies

Joel R. Davies

SAMPLE THANK-YOU B: *To Primary Contact*

2. *Contacts: Those whom you call on for advice and assistance.* Take your acquaintance to lunch or meet him or her where suggested. Explain your situation and ask for ideas on where to look for appropriate work and for the names of others who may be able to advise you further. People like to help others get started—especially if there are no strings attached. Asking advice is an effective, nonpressuring approach to take even if you secretly hope this acquaintance might be able to provide a job more directly. As soon as you return home, write a thank-you letter along the lines of Sample Thank-You B.

   If your acquaintance has referred you to a secondary contact, write a thank-you note to keep your primary contact informed. It might go something like Sample Thank-You C.

3. *Secondary contacts: Those to whom your primary contacts referred you.* After your acquaintance has suggested a person who might be helpful to you, you can call him or her or write a letter such as Sample Thank-You D (see page 330).

Your thank-you letter to a secondary contact is similar to one you would write to your first contact after a meeting—and, also, should be sent immediately. Sample Thank-You E (page 331) is an example.

4. *Interviewers: The person or people who interviewed you.* Your thank-you after an interview offers the opportunity not only to express your appreciation but also to respond to the interview. We so often say, "If only I had thought to say that then." This letter gives you that chance. It provides an occasion to show how your skills would be useful to the project or problem your interviewer discussed. And if your interviewer was not particularly skilled in bringing out your professional qualifications and ideas, this letter allows you to make up for that lack. Sample Thank-You F (page 332) should give you some ideas.

5. *Those who turn you down.* Even if you are ultimately rejected, it is a good idea to close the interchange on a friendly note (see Sample Thank-You G, page 333). After all, this company found you worth

---

May 4, 19—

Ms. M. E. Lincolnshire
Manager
United Printing Technologies Corp.
555 Kiersarge Street
Chicago, Illinois 00000

Dear Ms. Lincolnshire:

Thank you so much for introducing me to Jean Kidd at Deauville Corporation. We are scheduled to have lunch together when she returns from Chicago next week; and from our preliminary telephone conversation, I expect to find her a source of much information.

I very much appreciate your help. I have not yet reached Jim Ford, your other suggestion; but I will keep trying and let you know how the project turns out.

Cordially,

Marcia M. Fricke

Marcia M. Fricke

SAMPLE THANK-YOU C: *To Primary Contact*

June 21, 19—

Mr. David Martin Ford
Director of Corporate Training
Eli L. Hobson, Inc.
66541 Northern Raceway Blvd.
Indianapolis, Indiana 00000

Dear Mr. Ford:

Martha Lincolnshire tells me that you are the person most likely to know
about the current state of the art in corporate training. She suggested that
you might be willing to chat with me briefly about what kinds of
opportunities might be available as I begin my career information search.

I would greatly appreciate any advice you can give me and will call your
secretary to see if you might spare me a few minutes next week.

Yours truly,

Marcia M. Fricke

Marcia M. Fricke

SAMPLE THANK-YOU D: *To Secondary Contact*

considering seriously. And a thank-you at this time permits you a final
positive impression. Some day your paths may cross again, and a
favorable remembrance could serve you well.

6. *Those whom you must reject.* You cannot hold more than one full-time
job at once. But you can leave more than one employer wishing you were
with her or his firm. And as for later on—you never know what the
future holds. Your rejection letter should also be a thank-you note. Try
phrasing it something like Sample Thank-You H (page 334).

A PERSONAL NOTE. In showing you that courtesy and human consideration
can work to your advantage, we do not wish to be misunderstood. Their
use in this way is accepted in business as a helpful practice. But they ought
not be thought of as only a means to promote advancement. If you treat
every person with courtesy and consideration—whether or not that person
is in a position to "do you some good"—you will be operating by the
principles of human decency that should underlie the ethical conduct of
any business.

June 30, 19—

Ms. Jean Kidd
Operating Vice President, Human Resources
The Deauville Corporation
441 Science Plaza
Winston-Salem, North Carolina 00000

Dear Ms. Kidd:

Thank you for agreeing to meet with me last Monday to talk about ideas for my job search. Martha Lincolnshire promised me that you would have wonderful suggestions, and indeed I found that true.

I particularly appreciated your offer to introduce me to your own personnel manager and would very much like to follow up on that when I return from my vacation in early July. I will call you then to set up an appointment.

Meanwhile, I am proceeding with the suggestions you made for my résumé. I look forward to seeing you again sometime this summer. Good luck with the Teller project; I know that will be a great success.

Sincerely,

Marcia M. Fricke

Marcia M. Fricke

SAMPLE THANK-YOU E: *To Secondary Contact After Meeting*

AUTHENTIC BUSINESS PROBLEMS

1. Write a résumé for your own use, following the principles outlined here.
2. Research a prospective employer in your chosen field. Answer the following questions about this company:
   a. What does the company produce? Or is it in the service sector? Where does it operate? How old is it?
   b. Is it a conglomerate? Is it diversified? Is it privately or publicly held? Does it engage in government contracting?
   c. What is the current state of the sector (service, manufacturing, heavy industry, high-tech) to which the company belongs?
   d. What has been the company's performance over the last five years? What are the factors that might affect its future—techno-

Mr. Jonathan Brubow   April 21, 19—
Managing Partner
Hartshorn Marketing
123 Hall Street
San Francisco, California 00000

Dear Mr. Brubow:

I very much enjoyed meeting with you and touring the offices of Hartshorn
Marketing. As we discussed, I want to find a job that will permit me to build
on what I learned from my summer marketing internships and become more
familiar with marketing consumer products.

Although we did not have a chance to discuss the experience I had last summer
working with consumer surveys, I believe that experience would be tailor-made
for the kind of survey your A Group expects to undertake for Millikind next
summer. I enjoyed meeting Jennifer Pound and Andrea Biggs and thought their
project outlines were exciting and just the sort of thing I would like to
work on.

In any case, I was extremely grateful to have an inside look at an agency like
Hartshorn and thank you for both the interview and the morning's program. I
expect to be back on the coast at the end of the month and would be pleased to
hear from you if you believe that my experience could be of use to your agency.

Sincerely,

Natalie MacPherson

Natalie MacPherson

SAMPLE THANK-YOU F: *To Interviewer*

logical, competitive, economic, legal? (Are there any major liability suits pending, for instance?) How mature is the industry and how up-to-date is its technology compared with its world market competitors?

e. How many people does the company employ? What is its reputation as an employer? What is its benefits structure? How does it deploy its work force? Does it, for example, lay employees off on a seasonal basis? What does the information I have gathered imply for the career path of an entry-level person like me?

f. What is the company's record of corporate citizenship—responsible stewardship of the environment, compliance with work-place

June 17,19—

Mr. Francis X. Kowalski
Chief Financial Officer
Kowalski Securities, Inc.
312 Wall Street
New York, New York   00000

Dear Mr. Kowalski:

Thank you for letting me know the outcome of your search for a junior
financial analyst. I am sorry that I was not the candidate chosen, but I
feel pleased and flattered to have made the short list.

Certainly I am grateful for the time and attention you gave to the interview
and the evaluation of my credentials. That was a most thorough process, and
I enjoyed meeting all the members of your team.

I would be pleased to have my résumé remain on file for consideration if
another position should open up in the near future; and, as you have so
kindly suggested, I will keep in touch.

Sincerely,

Dale Cartwright

Dale Cartwright

SAMPLE THANK-YOU G: *When You're Rejected*

safety regulations, charitable contributions, cultural program
underwriting?

3. Research a department in this company that you might wish to
   work for. Answer as many of these questions as you can about it:
   a. What exactly does this department do? Is its role line or staff
      (strictly advisory)?
   b. What is the name of the person who hires for the kind of job you
      are interested in? Who is the department head?
   c. What can you find out about these people? What is important to
      them? What are their managerial philosophies, background,
      aims, objectives for the department?
   d. What is the reporting structure within this department? To
      whom in the corporate hierarchy does the department report?
      How does it interface with other departments? What is the

August 14, 19—

Ms. Deanna Wu
Managing Director
Plumtree Corporation
Coronation Way
Vancouver, British Columbia 0000

Dear Ms. Wu:

Thank you so much for your letter and the handsome job offer. Certainly, you have made it difficult to make a decision. I must, however, reluctantly decline in favor of an offer from Amalgamated Industries. Your offer and the job configuration you suggest were certainly tempting, but the Amalgamated opportunity will permit me to move at once into an area that is much closer to my training and eventual career goals.

I am grateful to you and to everybody at Plumtree Corporation for the time and careful attention you devoted to interviewing me and evaluating my qualifications. You make me sorry that I cannot accept two full-time jobs at once.

I do hope that you will be successful soon in finding someone for that exciting position, and I thank you for leaving me feeling that I have made a number of friends at Plumtree.

Very truly yours,

Joel R. Davies

Joel R. Davies

SAMPLE THANK-YOU H: *When You Reject an Offer*

    managerial reputation of the department head? What is her or his managerial style?

  e. What is the probable future for the department's top managers? Are they known to be slated for bigger and better things within the company? Are they known to be at odds with senior managers currently in the ascendancy?

  f. How does senior management (CEO, president, pertinent senior vice presidents) view the department? (You don't want to sign on to a department the CEO regards as frivolous or expendable.)

Hint: Besides researching Problems 2 and 3 in the library, talk to people who work for the company if you can. Do not ask direct questions about the matters in Problem 3c–f, but listen carefully. You often can find out what you need to know. Pay particular attention to gripes and jokes. They often will tell a great deal.

4. Write a letter of application to this department or company, following the principles outlined in this chapter.

WRITING EFFECTIVE BUSINESS PROPOSALS

EXECUTIVE SUMMARY

Business proposals are, in essence, sales letters with documentation—often lengthy and complex documentation. They serve two basic purposes: bids for business and requests for funding or financing.

Proposals are distinguished first by a fundamental structure that includes:

- A sales letter.

- Specifics on what is proposed: plan, schedule, budget.

- Documentation that demonstrates the writer's qualifications for carrying out the proposed plan.

Proposals are also distinguished by the straightforward way their writers **"consider the reader in light of their purpose."**

The *purpose* of all proposals is to have the reader accept the proposed plan. *Considering* a proposal's *readers* means to understand and speak to their particular specifications.

In some situations clients provide detailed specifications. In others, the proposal writer has to research to discover the client's sometimes covert—but always real—agenda.

To write a proposal, write a sales letter and then fill in the blanks—either of a proposal form supplied by the client or one you construct yourself from what you know of the client's needs or specifications. In either case, describe your proposed activity in terms that will make its approval or funding compelling.

The business proposal is a hybrid form. Like a sales letter, it sells a proposed activity or service. Like a recommendation report, it frequently requires researched data to support its arguments. Once you know how to write a sales letter and a recommendation report, you have mastered the techniques to write a proposal. You need only put the two forms together.

DEFINITION

A business proposal is a business communication in which you, as writer, propose to the recipient a course of action. Such proposals have two major purposes:

- *Bids* (for business). A bid may be as simple as a bid to paint a house or as complex as a proposal to provide design services for a major architectural project, or auditing or accounting services for a business over a long term.
- *Requests* (generally either for support or financing of a project or for approval to proceed with a course of action). A request may propose funding of a single project or of a long-term operational action.

There is a fundamental difference between a bid and a request. A bid responds to an expressed client need and follows criteria specified by the client. In a request, the need is yours: you propose a course of action.

Nevertheless, all proposals—whether bids or requests, whether simple or complex—have an underlying similarity. They propose what you wish to do and make a case to convince the reader that your proposal is worthy of approval.

In order to make your case compelling, you must understand the reader's specifications—stated or unstated—for approving the proposed course of action. In fact, proposals differ from other forms of business writing chiefly in the straightforward way their writers **"consider the reader in light of their purpose."**

The *purpose* of all proposals is to have the reader accept the proposed plan. In proposals, *considering readers* means to understand and speak to their particular specifications. Psychological empathy and political intuition are only sometimes needed. In some situations clients provide you with specifications, often detailed specifications. In others you will have to do a little research, but the client's requirements are usually concrete. In proposal writing, your job is to persuade that your concern can fill the requirements.

STRUCTURE

A proposal is ordinarily formal in structure. In fact, the Government, large clients, and many charitable foundations often specify a required format. In such cases, your job is to fill in the specified "blanks" as persuasively as possible. When a specific format is not provided, it is a good idea to locate specifications for a similar proposal and derive your format from it.

Whether you write a complex proposal of 20 to 200 pages or a simple bid of only 2 or 3, your business proposal should have this three-part structure:

1. *A sales letter* to show why it is to the reader's advantage to buy your services or back your activity.
2. *Specific information* about the activity you propose or the service you intend to provide, ordinarily including:
   - *A plan*—breaking down and explaining what you propose to do.
   - *A schedule*—detailing when and in what sequence you propose to do it.
   - *A budget*—specifying how much your plan will cost, item by item.
3. *Documentation* to demonstrate that your firm is particularly qualified for the proposed job—including, for instance:
   - A list of previous experience.
   - Biographies of your firm's principals (partners or professionals likely to be assigned to the proposed project).
   - A statement that offers a client listing—but only "upon request." It is not a good idea to send out lists of your clients as a matter of course.

As the examples in this chapter illustrate, proposals come in a wide variety of sizes and patterns. But this three-part structure is common to all.

WRITING BIDS

Perhaps the most familiar type of proposal is the bid. Bids are usually solicited by clients in need of specific services. The effectiveness of your bid is directly dependent upon how precisely you address the client's specific requirements. Therefore, before you write a bid, investigate the prospective client's problem thoroughly. Decide:

- How your firm can best solve the problem.
- How much compensation you will need to cover your costs and make an appropriate profit.
- How long the job will take.

Having made a careful evaluation, write the proposal.

WHEN YOUR BID PROPOSAL IS SIMPLE

If your bid is a simple one, you may choose to outline your plan of action, schedule, and budget within your cover letter (see Sample Proposal A).

ANALYSIS. Within a single letter Pygmante has supplied a plan, budget, and schedule. He has also documented the quality of his work by providing an opportunity for the client to check it for herself. The bid is especially persuasive because of Pygmante's capable tone. He demonstrates his competence in his assured handling of his client's specifications. And in protecting himself by warning of a possible overrun in the back study and by covering his out-of-pocket costs, he demonstrates his competence still further.

WHEN YOUR BID PROPOSAL IS MORE COMPLEX

A simple bid may require nothing more than a letter. But bids that offer complex plans for products or many-faceted services over long periods of time can be relatively complex (see Sample Proposal B).

GOVERNMENT PROPOSALS. More complex proposals are not necessarily more difficult to compose. Many institutions requiring such proposals specify exactly what information must be included. Government proposals, for example, are generally explicit about what questions must be answered, what data supplied, and in what form. Such specifications are helpful guides for collecting the necessary information. On the other hand, they can also complicate the project and make it more time-consuming. For instance, the specifications alone for some U.S. Government proposals can run several hundred pages.

Sample Proposal C is an introductory summary attached to a typical Government specifications form. Note that even this complicated proposal request is simply an expansion of the universal format: plan, schedule, budget, documentation.

When you are given specifications of this sort, you know precisely how to structure your proposal. With such explicit instructions, all you have to do is fill in the blanks honestly—though you must do that in a way that puts your company in the best possible light. For this kind of proposal:

- Write your answers as specified.
- Check carefully for tone.
- Proof for errors.
- Compose a transmittal letter.

Harold L. Pygmante
True Blue Painting Contractors, Inc.
13 Chrome Avenue
Albany, NY 00000-0000
Tel.: 000 000-0000 ■ Fax: 000 000-0000

February 13, 19--

Mrs. Henry P. Stith
875 Robinsway Drive
Hyde Park
Albany, New York 00000

Dear Mrs. Stith:

We are pleased to offer you our estimate to paint your third-floor rooms.
Total cost for painting all three rooms, two coats, if you supply paint
and materials, would be $785. If we supply the paint, the total would
be $834.40.

These prices include:

o Master bedroom: walls, all woodwork and detached book shelving in Splats
   Premium #101 Ivory white latex (walls) and oil enamel (woodwork)

o Back study: walls, woodwork and small built-in cupboard in Splats Premium
   #103 Sand white latex (walls) and oil enamel (woodwork and cupboard)

o Middle room: walls and baseboarding only in Splats Super #103 Warm grey
   (walls) with #108 Grecian Ivory oil enamel (baseboarding)

All surfaces would be washed, sanded, and prime-coated. As we discussed,
the back study walls require considerable spackling and sanding, and if we
should run into extensive problems with the plaster, surface preparation
might entail some additional cost. We would, of course, notify you and give
you an estimate for such charges before we proceed.

If you decide to accept our bid, we could begin work sometime the week of
April 20 and should be able to finish in no more than three days.

We need three days to schedule your job into our weekly roster, so we would
need to know by April 17 at the latest if you wanted us to begin that week.
Should you wish to furnish the paint, please call me at your earliest
convenience so that I can give you a list of the materials and quantities
needed. We generally ask that customers make a 20% cash deposit if they do
not furnish paint.

We do careful work. Should you like to see samples of it, you might look at
1101 Lois Drive and 4234 Red Bud in your neighborhood where we have recently
done the exterior painting. We will gladly supply interior-painting
references on request.

We appreciate the opportunity to bid and look forward to hearing from you.
·Please feel free to call me anytime during business hours if you have
further questions.

Sincerely,

Harold L. Pygmante

Harold L. Pygmante
True Blue Painting Contractors, Inc.

SAMPLE PROPOSAL A: *A Simple Bid*

August 20, 19—

Mr. Arthur Leavinswood
Leavinswood and Trot, Ltd.
Toronto, Ontario
Canada

Dear Mr. Leavinswood:

I am pleased to offer the attached bid to produce your firm's history, <u>Revolution in Specialty Metals</u>.

As you requested, I have included the cost of supplying the typesetting as well as the camera-copy preparation, printing, and binding. Because we do not have typesetting capabilities, we have to go out of house for that service. We customarily make a 10% surcharge for handling the typesetting, and that charge is itemized on page 2 of the bid and included in the overall price.

We have estimated on the basis of specifications supplied by Mr. Trot of your firm:

· 1000 copies of a hardbound, 8 1/2 x 11 (oversized format) trim size, 240 pages; Papyrustone 70# stock, Papyrustone coverstock, coated 85#; Smyth-sewn and -bound linen-covered boards, gold stamping on cover.

· 28 black-and-white halftone photos to be supplied by you and to be ganged in one signature, plus 13 black-and-white halftones to be printed in sepia tone and run randomly throughout the text.

· Type specifications: Baskerville 11/13 text; Baskerville bold heads on a measure of 25 characters. Acknowledgments in 8/10.

You will note that the bid includes a production schedule. According to Mr. Trot, you want to have books in house by November 24 so they can be prepared for a holiday mailing to shareholders. The schedule allows for scheduling the binding the week of November 20—which is a firm date, because the bindery cannot easily adjust its own schedule for so short a run as 1000 copies. Strictly speaking, it would be possible to get the binding done if we lost that scheduled time at our usual bindery, but the cost would go up very considerably.

The other date to be noted is the date (September 26) by which we would have to have approved copy in hand to send to the typesetter. All other deadlines are, of course, dependent on that initial one.

To give you some idea of how <u>R.I.S.M.</u> might look, I am sending you under separate cover a copy of a similar book we did for Amalgamated Industries last year.

If you decide to accept our bid, please call me before September 5 if possible, and I will stop by at your convenience to collect the signed agreement and to answer any questions you might have about the process.

We hope to hear from you soon.

Sincerely,

Lawrence Slesick

Lawrence Slesick

SAMPLE PROPOSAL B: *Moderately Complex Bid*

Budget

Typesetting
Approximately 128 pages of text, set according to designer's specifications:
Baskerville 11/13 text, c & lc; heads in 14/16 Baskerville bold; acknowledgments
8/10 c & lc. $000
Two sets of proofs: galleys and page proofs.

Layout and Dummy
Supplied by designer (See Copy Preparation below).

Copy Preparation
Pasteup, according to layout and dummy provided by book's designer.
Shoot and strip negatives, including 41 halftones.
Provide one set of negative proofs.
Make plates.

Presswork and Printing $000
Makeready and press preparation.
Offset, two color (black and sepia), 128 pages, 8 signatures, uncoated stock;
all glossy halftones ganged one signature.

Cover
8 1/2 x 11 natural linen on boards, gold stamping.

Binding
1000 copies Smyth-sewn, 7 signatures 60# uncoated stock, 1 signature glossy
halftones, trim size 8 1/2 x 11. $000
                                                                  $00,000

Schedule

Approved copy	September 26
Galley proofs	October 10
Page proofs	November 2
Boards approved	November 9
Negatives and plates	November 12
Printing	November 15
Binding	November 20
Books in house	November 24

SAMPLE PROPOSAL B: *Moderately Complex Bid (continued)*

SOLICITATION, OFFER AND AWARD	1. THIS CONTRACT IS A RATED ORDER UNDER DPAS (15 CFR 350)		RATING	PAGE OF

2. CONTRACT NO.	3. SOLICITATION NO.	4. TYPE OF SOLICITATION ☐ SEALED BID (IFB) ☐ NEGOTIATED (RFP)	5. DATE ISSUED	6. REQUISITION/PURCHA NO.

7. ISSUED BY	CODE	8. ADDRESS OFFER TO (If other than Item 7)

NOTE: In sealed bid solicitations "offer" and "offeror" mean "bid" and "bidder".

SOLICITATION

9. Sealed offers in original and _____ copies for furnishing the supplies or services in the Schedule will be received at the place specified in Item 8,

handcarried, in the depository located in _____ until _____ local time _____
(Hour)   (Date)

CAUTION — LATE Submissions, Modifications, and Withdrawals: See Section L, Provision No. 52.214-7 or 52.215-10. All offers are subject to all terms and conditions contained in this solicitation.

10. FOR INFORMATION CALL:	A. NAME	B. TELEPHONE NO. (Include area code) (NO COLLECT CALLS)

11. TABLE OF CONTENTS

(✓)	SEC.	DESCRIPTION	PAGE(S)	(✓)	SEC.	DESCRIPTION	PAGE(S)
		PART I — THE SCHEDULE				**PART II — CONTRACT CLAUSES**	
	A	SOLICITATION/CONTRACT FORM			I	CONTRACT CLAUSES	
	B	SUPPLIES OR SERVICES AND PRICES/COSTS				**PART III — LIST OF DOCUMENTS, EXHIBITS AND OTHER ATTACH.**	
	C	DESCRIPTION/SPECS./WORK STATEMENT			J	LIST OF ATTACHMENTS	
	D	PACKAGING AND MARKING				**PART IV — REPRESENTATIONS AND INSTRUCTIONS**	
	E	INSPECTION AND ACCEPTANCE			K	REPRESENTATIONS, CERTIFICATIONS AND OTHER STATEMENTS OF OFFERORS	
	F	DELIVERIES OR PERFORMANCE					
	G	CONTRACT ADMINISTRATION DATA			L	INSTRS., CONDS., AND NOTICES TO OFFERORS	
	H	SPECIAL CONTRACT REQUIREMENTS			M	EVALUATION FACTORS FOR AWARD	

OFFER (Must be fully completed by offeror)

NOTE: Item 12 does not apply if the solicitation includes the provisions at 52.214-16, Minimum Bid Acceptance Period.

12. In compliance with the above, the undersigned agrees, if this offer is accepted within _____ calendar days (60 calendar days unless a different period is inserted by the offeror) from the date for receipt of offers specified above, to furnish any or all items upon which prices are offered at the price set opposite each item, delivered at the designated point(s), within the time specified in the schedule.

13. DISCOUNT FOR PROMPT PAYMENT (See Section I, Clause No. 52-232-8)	10 CALENDAR DAYS	20 CALENDAR DAYS	30 CALENDAR DAYS	CALENDAR DAYS
	%	%	%	%

14. ACKNOWLEDGMENT OF AMENDMENTS (The offeror acknowledges receipt of amendments to the SOLICITATION for offerors and related documents numbered and dated:	AMENDMENT NO.	DATE	AMENDMENT NO.	DATE

15A. NAME AND ADDRESS OF OFFEROR	CODE	FACILITY	16. NAME AND TITLE OF PERSON AUTHORIZED TO SIGN OFFER (Type or print)

15B. TELEPHONE NO. (Include area code)	15C. CHECK IF REMITTANCE ADDRESS IS DIFFERENT FROM ABOVE - ENTER SUCH ADDRESS IN SCHEDULE ☐	17. SIGNATURE	18. OFFER DATE

AWARD (To be completed by Government)

19. ACCEPTED AS TO ITEMS NUMBERED	20. AMOUNT	21. ACCOUNTING AND APPROPRIATION

22. AUTHORITY FOR USING OTHER THAN FULL AND OPEN COMPETITION: ☐ 10 U.S.C. 2304(c)( ) ☐ 41 U.S.C. 253(c)( )	23. SUBMIT INVOICES TO ADDRESS SHOWN IN (4 copies unless otherwise specified)	ITEM

24. ADMINISTERED BY (If other than Item 7)	CODE	25. PAYMENT WILL BE MADE BY	CODE

26. NAME OF CONTRACTING OFFICER (Type or print)	27. UNITED STATES OF AMERICA (Signature of Contracting Officer)	28. AWARD DATE

IMPORTANT — Award will be made on this Form, or on Standard Form 26, or by other authorized official written notice.

SAMPLE PROPOSAL C: *Specification Form (Introductory Summary)*

A practical tip: Photocopy the proposal form and draft your answer on the copy. When you have completed the form to your satisfaction, have the original typed.

TRANSMITTAL LETTER. In this special kind of sales letter, first set out the particulars of the circumstances under which you are submitting the proposal. Sketch the plan briefly but persuasively, in summary fashion. Then say thank you for the opportunity to submit the proposal.

WHEN NO FORMAT IS PROVIDED

Sometimes circumstances require a complex proposal, but your client has provided no specific format. In such cases, invent your own form. Do not, however, think that you must, as businesspeople are fond of saying, reinvent the wheel. In fact, your proposal should look very much like a proposal tailored to supplied specifications.

WHAT TO INCLUDE. The precise form you use is quite simply an exercise in common sense: Use the form best suited to answer a reviewer's probable questions as quickly and persuasively as possible. You might, for example, include:

- How you evaluate the prospective client's problem and on what you base your assessment.
- What products or services you propose to provide.
- How much of the products or services are needed and why they would suit the client's needs.
- How a service would be carried out; how a product would be delivered.
- When the services would be carried out or/and the products delivered (a timetable or schedule for carrying out the plan).
- A schedule of fees.
- Who will provide the service or produce the product. If your business is a consultancy, for instance, include bios or short narrative résumés to show your staff's qualifications and capabilities.
- Your firm's experience in handling such matters for other clients.
- A list of your firm's clients. (But be careful here. Don't provide a list without permission from your clients or a go-ahead from one of your company's senior officers. You can always offer a confidential list or a verbal listing upon request.)
- An explanation of your firm's history (if it is distinguished) or of its founding (if interesting or pertinent).
- A discussion of your firm's resources (if pertinent). (For example, an accounting firm might want to discuss the tax information services to which it subscribes to reassure a prospective client that its advice will be up-to-date.)
- Any other piece of data, graphic or narrative, that would support your recommendation of your firm's services.

- A short table of contents (to make the whole proposal as easy to read and refer to as possible).
- An executive summary to accompany the proposal if your plan is especially long and complex.

WRITING REQUEST PROPOSALS

DISCOVERING THE REQUIREMENTS

The other purpose that proposals serve, besides bidding for business, is to request funding. Bids differ from request proposals chiefly because their recipients specify their requirements openly. Sometimes it takes some well-aimed questions to find out, but the nature of the services or products they need is straightforward and readily available. To write an effective bid, you persuade clients that you can fulfill their requirements well and at a competitive price.

The specifications of funding institutions, however, may not be as readily available. Yet to write an effective request proposal, you need to be just as precise in addressing the requirements. How to find out?

- *Research.* Call to see if your institution publishes its guidelines. Find out what proposals have been funded. If you can, also find out which have not. Search for a pattern.
- *Request an interview.* Funding institutions are eager for good proposals for their own self-interest. Ordinarily, they will be glad to tell you what they mean by *good.* Usually, they will even offer advice on your particular plans. An interview is a good idea even when a proposal form is supplied. The form may be too general. Remember the institution has an agenda—even if it is not immediately clear.

WRITING LOAN OR FINANCING PROPOSALS

Most businesses must at one time or another prepare a financing proposal to submit to a bank. What form should a loan proposal take? If you consult your accountant or your banker, you will probably hear that most financing proposals contain certain standard items. And when you look at a standard listing, such as the one included below, you will discover categories that are logical to figure out. Remember the principle to consider your reader in light of your purpose? Think what information you would need if *you* were the loan officer receiving your application.

WHAT YOUR FINANCING PROPOSAL SHOULD INCLUDE. Introduce your proposal with a cover or transmittal letter. In it say what is attached and ask for the loan or line of credit. Follow the letter with the following:

- Your company's name, address, telephone number.
- Owner's name, address, telephone number.
- Description of the business.
    Products or services.
    Plant, facilities.
    Personnel.
- History of the company.
    Position in the industry.
    Growth and development.
- Market
    Description of the market.
    Marketing plans (including target market and pricing policies).
    Major customers (current).
    Suppliers.
- Owner experience.
- Company's goals.
    Near term.
    Long term.
- Current balance sheet.
- Current income statement.
- Projected end-of-year income statement.
- Projected end-of-next-year income statement.
- Cash flow projection to end of this year (including debt service for the loan being proposed).
- Assumptions used to produce projections.
- Credit references (including present creditors, CPAs, and other financial institutions).
- Professional references (attorneys, other persons of some standing within the community where you are applying for the loan).
- Owner's personal financial statement (including owner's net worth).

As a businessperson, you can readily understand why each item is necessary. And if you provide such a complete disclosure to your banker, your proposal will say at once that you know how to do things professionally.

WRITING GRANT PROPOSALS

If you work for a nonprofit institution, you will almost certainly be involved in grant proposal requests. "Grantsmanship" has become a highly desirable skill. Prospective employees who have this skill are eagerly sought.

> ### Computer Boilerplate
>
> Boilerplate is standardized, formulaic (sometimes called "canned") text that can be used over and over again, in many different documents. And proposals are one of the best uses for boilerplate. Although of course you should always tailor each proposal to its specific situation and be careful not to overuse canned text, such general material is useful because it's fast. It's fast because it speeds composition and it's fast because it has already been approved. For instance, if you have to write many proposals, you might write (and have approved) standard paragraphs that describe your company or its personnel or a specific kind of service that you offer in much the same form everywhere. Store these paragraphs in your computer, and trot them out whenever you need them. You can modify them as needed or just plug them in in specified locations. Saves time. Saves mistakes. But a caution: Whenever you use such standard language, proofread your entire document carefully to be sure that the boilerplate integrates sensibly with new material, because it's easy to produce howlers.

Except for the lack of a profit motive, grant request proposals scarcely differ from other financing proposals. The suggestions and caveats we offer on page 346 apply to grants as well.

FORM AND STYLE: SOME FINAL HINTS

How long should your proposal be? *Long enough to do the job.*

How short should your proposal be? *As brief as possible.* No matter what your proposal is about or how it is written, it should *look perfect.* Not nearly perfect. Perfect. In this situation, double your usual efforts to make your submission attractive and error-free. In a proposal that solicits business, one grammar or typing error, one misspelling, one smudge, one page omitted by a careless secretary could make your company look inadequate to handle the business you are competing for. In a financing or project-support proposal, an arithmetical or substantive error could call all your calculations and projections into question.

Proofread. Then proofread again.

■■■■■■■■■ AUTHENTIC BUSINESS PROBLEMS ■■■■■■■■

1. Select a business you know well. (You may disguise the name if you choose.) Think of a situation where this business would have cause to offer a bid or request funding. Investigate enough to make your facts authentic.
2. Compose a proposal to request funds from a genuine institution or to offer a bid to an actual client. (Again you may choose to disguise the name.)
3. Write your instructor a memo that describes the company and the situation and justifies the effectiveness of your proposal under these circumstances.

COMMUNICATING EFFECTIVELY IN PRINT: CREATING BROCHURES

EXECUTIVE SUMMARY

Business uses brochures to communicate information and to sell products or services. Like most business publications, a brochure must be designed to produce *results.* You may be asked to create one. If you are, you need to know how to:

■ Schedule the production of the brochure.

■ Create a concept—either by free-writing copy to assemble your ideas or by analyzing the project's purpose.

■ Write effective copy.

■ Manage the in-house approval process.

■ Buy design, type, and production services intelligently.

The time will almost certainly come in your career when you are asked to produce a brochure. If you are asked to "handle" the creation of a brochure, there are a number of ways to do it. These range from handing the whole job over to your corporate public relations department or a competent outside advertising agency to managing the entire job (concept, writing, editing, layout, and production) yourself. There also are many variations in between. You might write the copy but farm out the design and production. Or you might have the copy given to you and then edit it and produce the concept. Whatever assignment befalls you, however, understanding some fundamentals about brochures and their production will help you to do a good job.

WHAT MAKES AN EFFECTIVE BROCHURE?

A brochure is a publication designed both visually and verbally to communicate information or sell a product or service. Brochures vary considerably in size, style, concept, and cost to produce. But what they all have in common is the need to communicate a message—whether sales or information—in the most direct, effective, dramatic, and memorable way possible.

If the brochure is informational, the information has to be clear and easy to follow, with supporting illustrations that help bring about communication. If the brochure is to sell or promote, the message must be effective and bring about some *action*—sell the product or service or increase sales. Even if the brochure is informational, its effect should be measurable—and produce results. It might, for instance, lead to improved customer satisfaction in using a product, to increased safety in an industrial facility, or to better understanding of a product or service or employee benefit. And this understanding can contribute, for example, to additional sales or decreased worker compensation costs or improved employee satisfaction.

RESULTS

Specifications for an effective brochure, such as these, necessarily focus on purpose; and *a brochure should always be designed (concept, text, and format) with its end result in mind.* In the heat of choosing beautiful paper, elegant type, and dramatic photographs, illustrations, or formats, it's easy to be distracted and begin to concentrate only on producing an attractive publication. But results are what count. The only thing about a brochure that really matters finally is that you communicate what you mean to communicate.

HOW TO PRODUCE A BROCHURE

To produce a brochure, you need to focus your attention on four major matters:

- Time.
- Copy.
- Concept.
- The production process.

Let's consider each of them in turn (with the exception of production, which is beyond the scope of this text).

TIME

In producing a brochure, you must *first* consider time. That statement may sound strange in a text on business *writing*. Shouldn't you write a brochure's copy or formulate its concept first? Isn't there time to worry about such matters as scheduling after that? No, and no. Even the simplest printed product takes a good while to produce. And that time is invariably longer than you—and those who requested the brochure—imagine.

SCHEDULING.   So you begin by scheduling the date on which you want to have the brochure in-house, ready for distribution. Then you back up through all the steps in the process and arrive at a *copy deadline*—the date on which you want to have the copy or text of your brochure finished. Then construct your schedule (see the sidebar).

Constructing a schedule.   Nothing is more sobering than formulating a schedule. You will see at once whether or not the deadline suggested by your supervisor is doable. When absolutely necessary, most publication production schedules *can* be rushed; but such rushing comes usually at an extremely high price. If you have a time problem, you will want to check with the person who assigned you the brochure to see whether the budget can tolerate extra costs or if the deadline itself can be adjusted. You may find the following sample schedule helpful.

```
                        Brochure Schedule

                                            Deadline
        Publications in-house, ready
        for distribution.                   May 5

        Print and bind.                     April 24-May 5
        Final approval of press proof or
        proofs from negatives.              April 21

        Camera copy to printer.             April 14

        Pasteup, final reading, and approval
        of photocopied boards.              April 10-14
```

Steps in the Process of Producing a Brochure

Schedule time for these steps:

1. *Make and gain approval of a schedule.* Go over your schedule carefully with your supervisor or the person who assigned the brochure. Or send the schedule out to all who will have to contribute either facts or copy or who will participate in the approval process. In your accompanying memo, ask for comments and ask for agreement on the copy and approval deadlines, noting that these must be met in order to keep publication costs under control.

2. *Create the copy and concept.* See pages 355–361. And don't forget to allow time for research, if necessary, and for rewriting—at least two additional drafts.

3. *Secure approval on an early draft.* Be sure to build in enough time for all who will be affected by your publication to see the copy and offer suggestions at an early stage.

4. *Get professional advice or bids.* Show your draft to a designer and discuss what you want the brochure to do and how it might do it most effectively. Discuss all aspects, both the words and the pictures. Be sure to allow time in the schedule for presentation of the concept to others who must approve it and for such changes as they might choose to make.

5. *Acquire photographs or other illustrations.* To support your brochure's message, you may need to find illustrations or have photographs taken and processed or drawings prepared. If so, you must build in time for this process. (To make your brochure look professional, be sure all illustrations are clear, with sharp definition and good contrast between dark and light tones.)

6. *Copyedit.* Prepare the final copy from which the typesetter will set the type and copyedit it carefully. Correcting errors in type can be expensive.

7. *Have your designer "spec" (pronounced "speck," short for "specify") the type.* In addition to specifying the size of the type, the designer will "fit" the copy properly to the page, specify the width of the text lines and margins, the spacing, and the use of display type for heads or emphasis. He or she also decides how the copy is to be indented and how the blocks of copy are to be positioned. Even if you have managed without a designer thus far, these decisions are extremely tricky and *require* a professional eye.

8. *Proof.* Read the proofs carefully against the original for errors and have your designer read it too for deviations from design specs. Mark your corrections in the margins of the proofs. But save and do not mark the original, rough, copyedited material. You will need a pristine copy should there be a dispute.

   You will also need to proof the camera copy, the final proof from which the printing plate or plates will be made. Should any corrections still be needed at this stage, *do not mark them directly on the proof.* Instead write them carefully on the tissue overlay.

9. *Oversee the printing and binding.*

10. *Make arrangements for distribution.*

Final proofs returned to you from
typesetter, with repros (reproduction-
quality proofs) to be pasted into
position for the camera copy. (Step
may not be needed if your computer
typesetting system permits you to go
directly to pages.)   April 7

2d proof (read and corrected) back
to typesetter.   March 23

Final approvals (copy and concept).   March 6

Copy (first draft).   February 27

Meet with designer (concept).   February 23

Brochure assigned.   February 20

This would be a comfortable schedule for a not-very-complicated, not-very-large publication with no full-color art, no complicated art to prepare or photos to shoot, no die-cut (shaped) pages or exotic paper stock. The dates allow for intervening weekends, vacations, and travel schedules of executives who have to approve copy or design, and for other unforeseeable problems.

LIFE AFTER SCHEDULING: CONCEPT AND COPY. Once you have the schedule in hand, you can start working on concept and copy. *Concept,* when applied to brochures, is an inclusive term. It refers to the set of ideas by which a brochure's purpose is to be imaginatively achieved. A brochure's concept is to a large degree visual—that is, it ordinarily involves the size and shape of the brochure and the general design of the pages. But although brochure concepts do not ordinarily include the exact wording, they often have verbal components. For example, a whole concept might be based on the specific words of a striking headline. Or if a concept suggests just a few words per page, chances are some of these words will be part of that concept. *Copy* means the text of the brochure, the specific words through which the purpose is achieved.

Whether you start thinking about concept first or about copy depends to some extent on the purpose of the brochure you've been assigned and a great deal on your own thinking processes and experience. If you usually compose by free-writing (see pages 8 and 62–63), then you should find free-writing the copy a good way to develop your brochure's concept. If, on the other hand, you are a lister, a structuralist (see pages 8 and 60–62), you will probably find it more effective for most projects first to decide upon the overall concept and then fill it in with written copy.

Let's look at both approaches and see how they apply to typical brochure assignments.

**COPY:
WRITING COPY
TO DEVELOP A
CONCEPT**

THE ASSIGNMENT. Put yourself in Mark K.'s shoes. Mark has been working on a team assigned to market a new alarm clock produced by his company. He has been asked to create a brochure to accompany the product. The brochure is necessary because the consumer doesn't really understand how to make full use of the clock; and some of its best features—the characteristics that should be giving it its competitive edge—are going unnoticed.

Mark's problem: To create a small brochure for the clock, to be attached to its box, with product descriptions that will serve both as an incentive to the consumer to buy the clock and as directions for the buyer using the clock.

PRELIMINARY JOTTINGS. Because he likes to approach a problem through free-writing, Mark decided to write down exactly what he wanted to communicate—just for his own use. First he addressed the product's special features. Without any special attempt at concentration, he typed:

> The snooze alarm feature on our dreamland model clocks is the best in the market--but people don't know about it. It's not highlighted on the current brochure and the directions for it there are fuzzy--Brawn's survey said 56% of our customers don't even use the snooze--and some even say the clock's too expensive--but that alarm is unique! The 1st time it sounds: you hear a gentle chiming melody--the 2nd time: a slightly louder repeating chime--the 3rd time: an intermittent buzz--the 4th time: a <u>loud</u> continuous buzz...
>
> It would be great if we could just highlight the snooze feature and explain how to use it--that would justify our price being slightly higher than the competing model--and that model's been gaining on our share of the moderately priced market.

WRITING PRELIMINARY COPY. To use free-writing as an effective composing tool, you write with almost total freedom initially. Then you study what you have written, derive ideas from it, and write again with greater focus. You can apply the same process in developing copy for brochures.

Just making quick notes of what he needed to do in the alarm clock example had the effect of determining and almost organizing Mark's material for him. He studied his first notes and underlined:

<u>highlight the snooze feature and explain how to use it</u>

That was it. He could get the job done by writing copy that would simultaneously explain the feature and offer directions for how to operate it. He reread his free-writing and found the clue to that copy:

```
The 1st time it sounds: you hear a gentle chiming
melody--the 2nd time: a slightly louder repeating
chime--the 3rd time: an intermittent buzz--the 4th
time: a loud continuous buzz.
```

In this patch, he found both the structure and the point of view he needed for the brochure.

A brochure's copy is likely to undergo many revisions before it is set in type and printed. And so realizing that the very earliest stage can be as tentative as one wishes, Mark composed the preliminary copy draft much as he would try a second free-writing:

```
1. The first time you hear your alarm, you will hear
   reveille played in chimes. Just press the red snooze
   bar (it's large and sturdy, so you can just press
   anywhere on the top and front of the clock to acti-
   vate it), and go back to sleep for another ten min-
   utes.
2. The next time the alarm sounds, you will hear the
   chimes again, but this time they will chime on the
   same tone. All right, press the snooze bar again, and
   go back to sleep for another ten minutes.
3. The third time the alarm sounds, you will hear a
   pleasant but insistent beeping sound, rhythmic and
   pulsing. If you really want to continue sleeping,
   press the snooze bar yet again, and you can go
   back to sleep, but this time for only five
   minutes.
4. When the alarm sounds for the fourth time, you will
   hear an insistent and unbroken buzzing sound. This
   time the snooze bar won't turn the alarm off. You
   must reach around to the back of the clock, locate
   the alarm interruption button, and move this to the
   left to its off position.
5. Frankly, the final buzzer is not a particularly pleas-
   ant sound, and finding the alarm interruption button
   is a bit of a nuisance: most of our customers have to
   heave themselves up on an elbow and open at least one
   eye to be able to do it. But you see, that's just
   part of our strategy. You've asked us to get you up
   in the nicest way possible; and that's what the Dream-
   land Alarm Clock does. We can't help it that you have
   to get up; but we can make it all as gentle as possi-
   ble.
6. We hope you enjoy your Dreamland Alarm Clock.
```

DEVELOPING A CONCEPT FROM COPY. Getting this far with the copy may give you some ideas for a concept. It did Mark. Here are some of his ideas for this brochure's concept:

- So that the copy might serve as directions and also for promotional purposes, it could be published in the form of a small booklet that could be attached by a cord to the clock package.
- Each of the points could be illustrated with a cartoon of a sleepy figure progressing through the four-stage alarm sequence. At the same time the pictures could illustrate the various positions of the snooze bar and maybe (somehow) the different alarm sounds themselves.
- The six-step copy suggests an eight-page booklet with six small pages and back and front covers.

The mock-up Mark developed from this concept is shown in Figure 13.1.

CONCEPT: CREATING A CONCEPT TO INVENT COPY

Starting with free-writing worked well for Mark—and it may for you. It is a technique well worth trying. On the other hand, free-writing is not for everyone. You just might have a structuralist mind, the sort of mind that is more comfortable working from the whole to the parts. In that case, you should begin with the concept instead of the copy. Furthermore, some assignments lend themselves better to analysis than to free-writing. Let's examine this approach.

THE ASSIGNMENT. Jill S. works in the personnel department of a large corporation. She was given the unenviable job of announcing an increase in health insurance costs to the company's 50,000 employees. Neither the increase nor the new and complex claims procedures were likely to be popular. Jill's job was to make clear the necessity for the increase and point out the benefits of the new procedure. She was asked to create a small booklet to communicate the news of the rate increase, set out the new coverage guidelines, and detail the new claims procedure.

SCHEDULING. As Jill worked out a schedule, she realized that, in addition to the usual difficulties in constructing brochures, the projected brochure might also run into legal difficulties. She would have to provide time for extra copy reading. For she would need to make sure that her language was strictly accurate. She must not, through careless language, seem to offer more than the health care contracts did in fact supply or inadvertently mislead any employee. She would also have to build in time for the copy to be vetted by the corporate counsel, the insurance carrier, and the benefits department. Furthermore, because she would be working with such a complex, technical subject, she also needed to schedule time for talking to benefits people with experience and expertise.

FIGURE 13.1: *Alarm-Clock Brochure Mock-up*

ARRIVING AT A CONCEPT. Since Jill's assignment was (1) "to communicate the news of the rate increase, (2) to set out the new coverage guidelines, and (3) to detail the new claims procedure," you probably think, as she did at first, that the brochure ought to have three separate parts. Nevertheless, that is not the structure that careful analysis led her to.

Analyzing. Jill began by asking herself the fundamental question: What end result do we want? And she answered: We want the employees to understand the situation fully. We want them to know that the company has negotiated hard to keep both its costs and their costs down, but that these costs were, in the end, determined by the market. We also want the employees to understand the complexities of their new health contract and how to deal with them.

As soon as Jill had made this analysis, it became clear to her that she was dealing with two kinds of information—the first, a one-time notice that the cost for health insurance had increased and why; the second, how-to information to be referred to over the lifetime of the contract period.

Since we are dealing with two kinds of information, she reasoned, perhaps we should have two separate communications. Why not put the information about the one-time cost increase into a letter, which we could then attach to a more permanent benefits information booklet or pamphlet? Jill checked this plan out with her supervisor, and found her agreeable to it.

Jill still had a brochure to construct, however. But now she had a better grasp of the project and was, therefore, much closer to the brochure concept she was aiming for.

CRITERIA. What sort of criteria could Jill set up for herself that would make the brochure achieve the results she had in mind? Since the brochure would have to be used by a large number of people over a long period, she decided that it should be in a form that would be easily accessible for answering questions. And from a practical point of view, it should also be comfortable to use, easy to file, and hard to lose. In setting up these criteria, she knew that they would affect not only the brochure's copy, but also its design and layout—indeed, the total concept of the piece.

Easily accessible information. In order to make the information easily accessible, Jill decided to structure the brochure into the two informational parts it seemed most naturally to fall into. She labeled them "Coverage Guidelines" and "Claims Procedures." And that decision took care of the first organizational division for her copy.

She had especially wanted the brochure to be easily accessible to answer questions. And so she thought: Wouldn't it be a good idea to think of the questions the employees would most want to ask and present the information in terms of these questions and their answers? She decided to proceed in this way, thus setting up much of the structure within the two divisions of her brochure. She also decided to use some discretionary time she had built into her schedule to do a limited sampling of employees to see what their actual questions were.

Comfortable to use. The brochure shouldn't be too small, and the type should be large and easy to read. It should be simply organized, with plenty of headings to direct the reader to the particular section needed. With an accessible index too. Black type on white paper is the clearest and most comfortable to read. Jill decided to forget about reversing white type on a black background or using that red type on beige paper which made her friend Sara's last brochure so attractive. She hoped hers would be nice-looking too, but she knew that it was more important for her informational brochure to be quickly and easily read.

Easy to file. Jill reasoned that if we want recipients to keep a brochure, it should be easy to file. Most people file their employee benefits information with their household and financial records. The size easiest to file, then, should be the standard letter size—$8^{1}/_{2} \times 11$. Any larger, and it wouldn't fit in a standard file. Half the size ($5^{1}/_{2} \times 8^{1}/_{2}$) would work and is a perfectly comfortable format; but it would also be thicker and might be too bulky for a file. Jill discounted any nonstandard in-between size, because it would not be as economical to produce, and decided on the $8^{1}/_{2} \times 11$.

Hard to lose. Size, shape, and color make an object distinctive and therefore hard to lose. Jill had already ruled out an unusual size or shape in making her filing decisions. But color was another matter. She decided on a brightly colored cover with a bold graphics design.

After this thorough analysis, Jill had a good grasp of the concept for the health insurance brochure and was ready to write the copy.

THE TRADITIONAL SIX-PANEL BROCHURE

Sometimes a brochure assignment comes with its concept already partly in place. You might be asked to fashion the concept to fit a single-fold, four-panel brochure with a pocket. Or, more likely, you would be required to use the traditional two-fold, six-panel brochure, an especially useful and popular format (see Figure 13.2).

For example, you might be asked to write a simple brochure with a returnable coupon, which for budgetary reasons must be limited to a single page and mailed in a business envelope. In this case, you would have to start out trying to think up ideas to fill five of the conventional six front and back panels (the sixth is needed for the return coupon) of a traditional double-fold $8^{1}/_{2} \times 11$ sheet.

WHERE TO GET IDEAS

Whether you have the services of a designer at your disposal or you are on your own, you want the product to look clean and professional in concept and design. Because you want to do an outstanding job, you also want your product to look original or arresting. But a cautionary note.

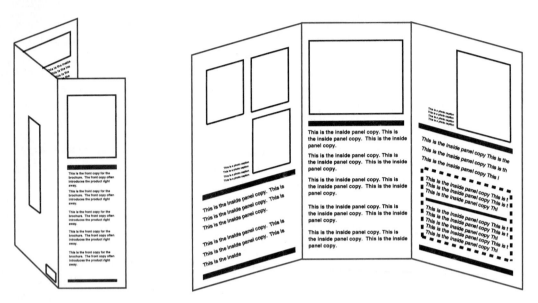

FIGURE 13.2:   *Traditional Six-Panel Brochure*

David Ogilvy, who founded one of the world's most successful advertising agencies (Ogilvy and Mather), says:

> Until you've got a better answer, you *copy*. . . . I never cease to be struck by the consistency of consumer reactions to different kinds of headline, illustration, layout and copy—year after year, country after country.[1]

If Ogilvy is right—and he makes a most persuasive case—you have a free, built-in way to be successful by modeling your brochure on other brochures that have proven themselves to be attractive and effective.

Get hold of some good examples. They're everywhere you look. And as with any other field, the more examples you examine, the more the good quality will stand out from the merely mediocre and the bad. If you look at enough brochures, you can model yours on the ones you value. Free. A brochure itself may be copyrighted; but nobody will mind if you approximate one you admire on a different subject. After all, imitation really is the sincerest form of flattery. However, be careful not to plagiarize. That is, you may approximate a concept, but you may not use exact text or design or any logo or design element that is proprietary or the original work of a graphics designer.

For ideas on writing sales copy, you might reread Chapter 5 on sales letters; for ideas on graphic support, see Chapter 10. And if you're a

---

1. *Ogilvy on Advertising* (New York: Vintage Books, 1983): 70.

beginner, or even if you have been at it for a while, you probably cannot do better than to read "Wanted: A Renaissance in Print Advertising," Chapter 7 in Ogilvy's book. That chapter is full of invaluable consumer research, copywriting, layout, and design techniques derived from Ogilvy's experience on what communicates and what sells. In the following Guidelines, we have assembled a selection of Ogilvy's tips[2] that you might find helpful in constructing sales brochures.

━━━━━━━━━━━━━━━━━━━━━━━━━ **GUIDELINES** ━━━━━━━━━

Ogilvy's Tips

Layout

- Readers look first at the illustration, then at the headline, then at the copy. So put these elements in that order [to] follow the normal order of scanning, which is from top to bottom. (p. 88)
- Help the reader into your paragraphs with arrowheads, bullets, asterisks and margin marks. (p. 99)

Headlines

- The headlines which work best are those which promise the reader a benefit. (p. 71)
- Headlines which contain *news* are sure-fire. The news can be the announcement of a new product, an improvement in an old product or a new way to use an old product. . . . If you are lucky enough to have news to tell, don't bury it in your body copy, which nine out of ten people will not read. State it loud and clear in your headline. (p. 71)

Copy

- When people read your copy, they are *alone*. Pretend you are writing each of them a letter on behalf of your client. One human being to another, second person *singular*. (p. 80)
- Copy should be written in the language people use in everyday conversation. . . . (p. 81) It pays to write short sentences and short paragraphs, and to avoid using difficult words. (p. 80)
- Always try to include the *price* of your products. When the price of the product is left out, people have a way of turning the page. (p. 83)
- If you have a lot of unrelated facts to recite, don't use cumbersome connectives, simply *number* them. . . . (p. 99)

Illustrations

- The *subject* of your illustration is all important. If you don't have a remarkable *idea* for it, not even a great photographer can save you. (p. 76)

---

2. From *Ogilvy on Advertising* by David Ogilvy. Text copyright © 1983 by David Ogilvy. Reprinted by permission of Crown Publishers, Inc.

- More people read the captions under illustrations than read the body copy, so never use an illustration without putting a caption under it. (p. 89)
- The kind of photographs which work hardest are those which arouse the reader's curiosity. He glances at the photograph and says to himself, "What goes on here?" Then he reads your copy to find out. (p. 76)

Typography

- The eye is a creature of habit. People are accustomed to reading books, magazines and newspapers in *lower case*. (p. 96)
- People are accustomed to reading newspapers which are set about 40 characters wide. . . . (p. 96) [Set your copy in several columns no wider than] 35 to 40 characters. . . . (p. 90)
- The more outlandish the typeface, the harder it is to read. The drama belongs in what you say, not in the typeface. (p. 96)
- Set . . . copy in *serif* type [the sort that has fine-line extensions finishing the strokes at the tops or bottoms of letters. The main text of this book is in a serifed type]. (p. 90)
- Set . . . the main text of the type . . . black on white. . . . (p. 90) When [Ogilvy] suggested that [a charity using white-on-black advertisements] test black type on a white background, they raised twice as much money. (p. 101)
- Set key paragraphs in bold face or italics. (p. 99)

■■■■■■■■■■ AUTHENTIC BUSINESS PROBLEM ■■■■■■■■■■

Write copy for an advertising brochure based on the information below. Stress the benefits of the product for the customer. Create marketable trade names for the different features. Decide on the best order for presenting the features.

Your copy should contain 300–500 words and include:

1. A headline of five to seven words, all in capital letters.
2. Five paragraphs of copy, each with 50–100 words.
3. A subhead of two to five words above each paragraph.

Client: Drake Skate Company

- Produces roller skates chosen by champions.
- Accurate machining to closest tolerance.
- Founded in 1930, continuous operation, family-owned.
- Designs and manufactures roller skates and skate parts.

Product: New Drake Figure Skate

- New steel plate—stainless spring steel, thinner, more flexible, more sensitive.
- All-new design specifically for figure skaters—feels like an ice blade; precision adjustment and control; excellent response and action for champion skaters or amateurs.

- New precision adjusting mechanism—uses single skate tool; requires only one hand to change tension; mechanism clicks each time it is turned an eighth of an inch; procedure requires between one and three seconds.
- New roller bearing—rolls farther, glides smoother; space-age technology; only on Drake skates.

Note: This assignment, a favorite of Professor William Guthrie, Wilmington College, was actually given to a copywriter just starting to work for an advertising agency. Only the names have been changed.

WRITING EFFECTIVELY TO ORGANIZE MEETINGS

EXECUTIVE SUMMARY

Business executives average 23 hours a week attending or preparing for meetings. Thus organizing meetings to use time productively is a money issue.

Organizing any meeting, large or small, is a job with a heavy communications component. If you have to handle a meeting:

- Invite and schedule with attention to the meeting's objectives and due deference to rank.

- Structure and write an agenda to achieve the meeting's purpose.

- Organize and confirm in writing arrangements for facilities and services.

- Prepare materials or coordinate their preparation.

- After the meeting, follow up, with summaries, minutes, or action plans. Don't forget thank-you notes.

Who hasn't called a business number only to hear, "I'm sorry, she's in a meeting. May I have her call you?"

Everybody in business complains about meetings, but not much can be done about them, because *everybody* goes to them. Like them or not, in one form or another, they're necessary. People in business have to meet to do the work they must do—as teams, as departments, as staff, as work groups, as part of a professional system.

Yet despite their importance, the organization of meetings—of all kinds, formal and informal—is a task frequently given to entry- and mid-level managers. You may very well receive such an assignment early in your career. This chapter aims to help you with this assignment, which is a job with a heavy communications component.

THE BUSINESS MEETING

According to Peter Drucker, the dean of business management experts, businesspeople meet because:

- People holding different jobs have to cooperate to get a specific task done.
- The knowledge and experience needed in a specific situation are not available in one head, but have to be pieced together out of the knowledge and experience of several people.[1]

ITS IMPORTANCE

Business executives spend a surprising proportion of their time attending meetings. In an average week they spend 17 hours in meetings and another 6 hours preparing for them, according to a study reported in *The New York Times* of May 31, 1988. Ronald E. Gerevas, president of Heidrick & Struggles, a management recruiting firm, points out that:

> Because top executives typically work 61 hours a week, the meetings— and thinking about them—account for almost 38 percent of their time.

In a world where time is money, business meetings thus have extraordinary significance.

---

1. *The Effective Executive* (New York: Harper & Row, 1967).

"*Sorry! We are no longer involved in produc-tion, sales and service. Now, all we do is ATTEND MEETINGS!*"

From *Berry's World.* Reprinted by permission of NEA, Inc.

ITS IMPORTANCE TO YOU

When you are the organizer, meetings can have more than ordinary significance to your career. When it's up to you to organize the meeting and see to the attendant communications, you have a chance to make the most effective use of executive time. This contribution to the efficiency and effectiveness of your department and your company is a highly visible one. If you do a good job, somebody will notice. The information in the rest of this chapter is designed to help you do that good job.

ORGANIZING A BUSINESS MEETING

```
To:     Stan Clements,
        Jim Sharp,
        Henry Coleman,
        Joan Henreid.
From:   Brad Holtzman
```

```
Re:      Contributions Budget Meeting
Date:    November 4, 19__

This memo is to confirm our plans to meet Wednesday,
November 9, at 2 o'clock in the 3rd floor conference
room. We'll probably be finished by 3:30.

I've attached the agenda.
```

Brad's organizing memo couldn't be simpler. And yet some complex thinking and a good bit of work lie behind it—as they do behind any meeting-planning memo. Let's look at it more closely.

To organize an effective meeting you have to arrange for, and write communications appropriate to, the three essential components of the process:

- Attendance and scheduling.
- The agenda.
- Materials and facilities.

You may not be the one who decides on the schedule. You may not control the agenda. You may not be the one to select a room or a place. You may not have to produce the materials. But if you organize the meeting, see to it that each part is attended to *before* the meeting. That *is* your responsibility. So make yourself a checklist of "things to do" and take care of every single item.

ATTENDANCE AND SCHEDULING

Before you can send out meeting notices, you will need to decide on the participants, arrange a time, and reserve a place.

INVITE THE PARTICIPANTS. Include as few people as possible in your meeting. The more people, the longer it takes to get something accomplished. And the more people, the more complex the relationships within the group and, therefore, the harder it will be to achieve a consensus. The 3M Management Team[2] suggests a number of research-based rules of thumb, classified according to a meeting's purpose; they appear in the following Guidelines.

---

2. Stephen P. Birkeland, David J. Cooper, Marshall Hatfield, Virginia Johnson, Frank E. Poole, and Joseph M. Ramos, the members of 3M Corporation's Meeting Management Team, meeting management experts with a variety of corporate experience and authors of *How to Run Better Business Meetings: A Reference Guide for Managers* (New York: McGraw-Hill, 1987), a most useful text in this field. The Guidelines are adapted from page 34. This material and other material from the 3M guide used in this chapter are reprinted by permission of McGraw-Hill, Inc.

━━━━━━━━━━━━━━━━━━━━━━━━━━━━ **GUIDELINES** ━━━━━━━━━━━━━━

Optimum Number of Meeting Participants

• Decision-making and problemsolving meetings:	5 persons or fewer.
• Problem-identification meetings:	10 persons or fewer.
• Committee meetings:	Maximum effective number is 7 (beyond 7, the work slows markedly).
• Training meetings:	15 persons or fewer, especially if there is a hands-on phase.
• Seminars:	Fewer than 15 participants for optimum effectiveness.
• Informational meetings:	Under 30 to maintain personal contact.
• Presentations:	Unlimited—everyone who needs to know.

The politics of inclusion.   Determine what your meeting's purpose is. And include only those people who really need to be there. Be sure, on the other hand, that all those who are necessary to the meeting's purpose are invited. For instance, all departments that will need the information should be represented. So should all groups who are likely to be affected by decisions taken. And in the case of decision-making meetings, try to be sure that those included have authority to make a necessary decision. Except in very small meetings, whenever the matter under discussion will be controversial you should include those who hold the opposing opinion. Make sure, however, that those representing competing views are of equal status.

As a matter of fact, for all kinds of discussion meetings, you need to be mindful of status when choosing the participants. If you want a frank, freewheeling, or creative discussion, you should make sure the participants are more or less equal in rank. If you need both a supervisor and a subordinate for a meeting, you should expect the subordinate to provide information within his or her own expertise, but to participate only minimally beyond that.

ARRANGE A TIME. You will need to fit the meeting time into the schedules of all those who will attend. Generally, telephone calls work best for preliminary organizing—for arriving at a date and time—because the telephone lends itself well to negotiation of an agreeable time. When the meeting arrangements are final, write the appropriate informational memos and reminders.

Unless you already have a directive ("Joan Henreid wants to meet with everybody in her department next Monday at ten"), don't start your organizing phone calls with a firm date in mind. Because business calendars are complex, and because they have a tendency to change, a firm date at the outset will only make the negotiation more difficult.

The politics of scheduling. Start by discovering what time is best for the highest-ranked person who will attend the meeting. That schedule is certain to be the most complicated and his or her time the most limited. This procedure has, in addition, two other advantages:

- It is a courtesy that defers to rank.
- Either it will tell you which dates you have to work with, or the executive will tell you that she or he really doesn't have to be there—and that knowledge will give you more leeway in scheduling the meeting.

Procedures vary with the particular corporate culture, but ordinarily when you call to discuss a meeting time, talk first with the executive's secretary. He or she keeps the calendar and often knows more about what time the executive has free than the executive does.

When you call, say, the secretary of Stan Clements, one of your company's vice presidents, you might say something like this:

"Joan talked with Stan yesterday about meeting to review the contributions budget. We need to find a time before the end of the week, and I think we'll need a full hour. Could we block out some times, and then I'll get back to you with a confirmation?"

Then you call the person of the next-highest rank:

"Joan and Stan Clements want a meeting to review the contributions budget. She wants you to be there to talk about new requests, and we need to set a time, about an hour, before the end of the week. Both Joan and Stan could work it in either Tuesday morning or Wednesday afternoon. Could you make it either of these times?"

As you can see, the process requires tactful negotiation and a series of telephone calls.

The psychology of scheduling. What is the best time for meetings?[3] Clearly, when the participants will be at their best. Some bad times

---

3. Some of the material on pages 372 and 373, including the research results reported here, is adapted from the 3M guide *How to Run Better Business Meetings,* pages 36–37. See note 2.

are early Monday morning, late Friday afternoon, or the final minutes before closing time on any day. Another time to avoid, if you can, is that hour after lunch when almost everyone becomes sleepy.

How long should the ideal meeting be? Just as long as it takes to fulfill its purpose—and not a minute longer. There are limits to human productivity. Research psychologists have given us some insight into these limits. Adults think and work at their best in spans just under an hour. An hour and a half is the outer limit of their productive maximum—even when a group is fresh. In two hours their productivity has declined to a low ebb. If your purpose requires more than an hour or an hour and a half, divide the meeting and schedule a 15-minute break between sessions.

Two rather long sessions are fine in the morning. But shorter sessions are more effective in the afternoon. And don't forget to allow some free time to fill that sleepy period after lunch. You might also consider scheduling time for participants to call their offices or pick up messages and return calls.

RESERVE A PLACE. Where should the meeting be held? The meeting should take place in a room that is neither too large nor too small for the number of participants and the planned activities. A room that is too small not only restricts movement and often becomes warm and stuffy, but can also be psychologically distressing. Tensions build when participants feel their necessary space, their psychological comfort zone, intruded upon. And good discussion does not flourish in such an atmosphere.

When the room is too large, on the other hand, participants can feel overwhelmed by the size. Research shows that some experience an inhibiting self-consciousness akin to stage fright in a large, empty room. Unless you can screen off the extra space, discussion might be curtailed here as well.

When you find an appropriate room for your meeting, telephone to make sure it is available for your date and time, and reserve it. Follow up your call with a confirmation memo. (For a discussion of confirmation memos, see Chapter 6, pages 156–157.)

Write the arrangement memos. Once the schedule is set, let everybody know. Most people appreciate a confirming memo, if there is time to get it to its destination. Remember to include in your confirmation memo:

- The purpose of the meeting.
- The time of the meeting, including how long you expect it to take.
- The place of the meeting.
- Any materials the participants will need to bring along.
- Your telephone extension, or your secretary's, to make it easy for participants to call with questions.

Ordinarily attach an agenda to your memo. (See the sample confirming memo on page 370.)

MAKE SURE WITH FINAL CALLS. If the meeting is an important one, it is also a good idea to have your secretary call the morning of the meeting to check politely on attendance. These reminder calls can go from secretary to secretary, and most executives appreciate them. Such calls are particularly useful if a person vital to the meeting has had one of the sudden changes of schedule that are common in business. If the dropout is the ranking person, find out from the secretary if she or he would suggest going ahead with the meeting anyway. If so, notify the person who requested the meeting, because the person's absence could require a restructuring.

THE AGENDA

If you are new to business management, you will probably chair few important meetings. Chances are good, however, that you will be asked not only to organize such meetings but to write agendas for them. Writing an agenda is an exceedingly responsible assignment, since the agenda determines a meeting's success, and the one who controls the agenda controls the meeting.

FEATURES OF AN EFFECTIVE AGENDA. Because of the agenda's importance, distribute it, if possible, in advance of a meeting to give the participants time to prepare. It is also helpful to include with the agenda the list of meeting participants and a reminder of time and place.

A well-conceived agenda insures that the meeting will proceed in an orderly fashion, that the intended topics will be covered, and that participants will have a sense that something has been accomplished. An effective agenda:

- Embodies clearly defined discussion goals divided into doable segments.
- Is organized in a logical order.
- Concentrates on a small number of related topics.
- Sets up discussion topics in specific rather than generalized form to keep the discussion on track. (For example, discussion on "pricing product X" might be divided into: "price of competitive products," "marketable features of product X compared to competing products," "cost considerations of product X," and "cost-related marketing strategies.")
- Is optimistic and encouraging, and suggests opportunity. (It should *not* contain items such as "Another chance to muddle through Difficulty Z again.") Even if the meeting has been called to discuss a serious problem, the agenda should suggest the truth that the meeting offers an opportunity to find a solution.

- Ends with some time for the Chair to sum up what has been done so that participants can depart with a sense of accomplishment.

THE HIDDEN AGENDA. The expressed goal of a meeting's agenda is usually to create open discussion where ideas can be engendered or opinions vented and a decision reached. But frequently there is a hidden agenda as well. The meeting's sponsor has a preference for a specific decision or favors a particular point that the decision should include. If you are writing the agenda for the sponsor, you will want to order the items so as best to promote that point of view. What strategies can you adopt to do that? Your strategies must be based on an analysis of the situation in terms of the personalities, predilections, and rank of the people involved. Let's consider an authentic situation.

Authentic business situation. Your supervisor, Joan Henreid, who has called a meeting to consider Amalgamated's charitable contributions budget, has a pet cause (the Central Girl Scout Council) that was not included in last year's budget. *Problem:* The aims of the Central Girl Scout Council are a little outside the policy guidelines for this corporation's giving. Everybody knows that the guidelines are rubber and can be both bent and stretched. But the budget is tight this year, and to include the Girl Scout Council, this work group will have to agree to refuse funding something that was in last year's budget.

Who will attend the meeting? People from all the departments traditionally involved in this decision have been invited. Most of them are fairly agreeable people who have no particular ax to grind on the charity issue. Jim Sharp, the company's treasurer and a trustee of the company's charitable foundation which will fund the giving, however, may be difficult. He can be recalcitrant about departing from the guidelines unless he is convinced that the project requesting funding has merit and is not just the pet of a particular executive. Stan Clements, the vice president to whom Joan Henreid reports, will make the final decision; but he is disposed to honor the consensus of this meeting.

How can you structure the agenda to favor your project? Specifically, how can you give the Girl Scout Council the best chance to be included? You—and, in this case, your supervisor—need first to decide exactly what you want the configuration of that budget to be when you come out of the meeting. Well ahead of time you and she should meet, go over the entire budget, and determine which cuts could most painlessly be made to make room for the Girl Scout Council project. Only then can you structure the discussion to give your objective the best possible chance.

Having decided which projects you believe could be cut, you could either lump them together under one agenda item and plan to make the case for cutting them all at once, or you could group them at the agenda's end, when everybody is eager to be finished and might be expected to deal with them as expeditiously as possible.

What about the rest of the agenda? As with other business communications, put the most important projects first. You may want to consider, in fact, putting the Girl Scout Council project first of all. You could add an explanatory note that since this item would be a departure from the usual policy and might set precedent for the handling of the entire budget, it should be taken up first. This stratagem gives you plenty of time to make a good case for the project as you discuss the process. And don't forget to allow sufficient time to discuss Jim Sharp's particular issue, fixed multi-year funding.

Your agenda for the meeting might look something like this:

```
                        AGENDA
Contributions Budget Meeting
October 14, 19—
Conference Room, 2 p.m.

1. Budget process review               Joan Henreid
2. Policy guidelines                   Stan Clements
3. New requests: The Greater Midvale
   Girl Scout Council (discussion of
   this project with policy guidelines) Joan Henreid
4. Fixed multiyear funding commitments  Jim Sharp
5. Review and discussion of requests
   for continued project funding       Henry Coleman
6. Task Force assignments              Stan Clements
7. Summary and scheduling of Spring
   Review Meeting                      Joan Henreid
```

You will find an example of a more complex agenda on pages 392–394.

If the agenda-crafting process looks to you shockingly manipulative, think of it as good sales technique. You are making the most effective presentation of your case that you can. In this instance, you control the agenda.

━━━━━━━━━━━━━━━━━━━━━━━━━━━━━ **GUIDELINES** ━━━━

Creating Agendas

There are four major steps in preparing an effective agenda, according to the 3M Meeting Management Team:[4]

1. Determine the ultimate goal of the meeting.
2. Determine the intermediate steps needed to reach that goal.

---

4. Adapted from the 3M guide, page 59. See note 2.

3. Analyze the probable positions and attitudes of the people who will attend.
4. Consider possible barriers to the goal and develop the agenda so as best to circumvent them.

MATERIALS AND FACILITIES

When you're in charge of arranging a meeting, your aim is to make sure that the meeting runs smoothly—that is, that the mechanics of the meeting are so well oiled that nothing slows down the effective conduct of its business.

PREPARE THE NEEDED PAPERS. For those meetings—and they are probably the majority—where discussion is focused on ideas that are not altogether familiar to all participants, the papers laying out these ideas are crucial. It is your job as meeting arranger to see that all such materials are:

- Legible, clean, professionally presented—in folders if they are confidential or if there are a number of loose pieces.
- Available in sufficient numbers.
- Organized properly with respect to the meeting's agenda.
- Labeled clearly. Put the agenda item number at the top, if necessary, but make it easy for the participants to find what they need to consider.
- Ready on time.

GET THE MATERIALS READY ON TIME. Begin to prepare the materials as soon as the meeting has been scheduled, and make yourself a production schedule. Take into account who and what facilities will be needed to produce the materials. If you start with a time when you want them to be ready—say, the afternoon before the day of the meeting—then you can back up from there and establish deadlines for each phase of the production process.

You want to be sure you know such practical matters as when the necessary information or data will be available and how long it will take a clerk to make and collate the copies, assemble all the exhibits, and prepare folders. It's a good idea to have a contingency plan for every conceivable emergency. (What if the secretary on whom you depend comes down with the flu? What if the copier breaks? What if the computer is "down"?) There is a good deal of truth in Murphy's Law: Anything that can go wrong will go wrong. Be prepared.

If it's your meeting, it is your responsibility to get the materials ready on time—even when others supply them. First, find out what materials those who are planning to attend the meeting think will be necessary. Then ask those who are supplying these materials to deliver them a day ahead of the meeting. This way you can see that they are distributed on time.

READY THE MEETING ROOM. Planning ahead is essential, but last-minute details can make a real difference in the success of a meeting. Make a list and check it off just before meeting time.

You are ready for the meeting when you have checked to be sure that:

- The room has been reserved for the day and time required.
- Note pads, pencils, etc., are available.
- Coffee or other refreshments have been arranged.
- There are enough chairs and place cards, if required.
- Equipment for the expected presentation is in place and in working order (overhead and slide projectors, sound equipment—amplifiers, microphones, speakers). Are projector lenses clean? Do all needed electric outlets work?
- The room's telephones are cut off to avoid interruption; arrangements are in place for messages to be taken for the meeting participants.
- Agendas are prepared and placed.
- Reference materials and handouts are in place.
- If needed, chalk and erasers, flip charts, mounted paper pads, flashlights, pointers, and water and glasses are in place.
- Spare lamps, fuses, and replacement equipment are available; lighting controls are located and work.[5]

Though these details have little glamour, they can be truly significant. Once a Fortune 500 company's board and all of its officers grew so impatient waiting for a replacement for a broken multimedia projector that they simply abandoned a highly important meeting. After that, the career of that meeting's manager took a downward swing.

AFTER THE MEETING: FOLLOWING UP

The best meetings end with a strong summary from the Chair. Such a summary recounts the meeting, pulls the diverse parts together into a unity, relates decisions, reaffirms assignments, and, in short, resolves doubts as to what really was decided. A summary gives participants a chance to feel they have accomplished something.

A *written* summary (sometimes in a specialized form, as minutes) should achieve the same purposes. Besides presenting the meeting in a way that all can agree is accurate, effective summaries condense and unify the action taken and focus in on the most important accomplishments. For example:

---

5. Checklist adapted from the 3M guide, page 77. See note 2.

To: Jim Sharp
From: Joan Henreid
Re: Contributions Budget Allocations Meeting Summary
Date: October 15, 19——

In our meeting of October 14 we agreed to fund last year's contributions fully this year. In addition, we decided to modify Foundation policy guidelines to permit local subsidiaries to recommend contributions to organizations in their areas and causes they believe deserving. We set aside $11,000 this year for these purposes:

- $3500 for The Greater Midvale Girl Scout Council, the first approved pilot project under the new guidelines. Our three Midwestern divisions will make the contribution jointly, and <u>we will need to have a check ready to be delivered no later than Wednesday of next week.</u> If you anticipate any problem with getting the check request (attached) through accounting procedures in time, will you please let me know?
- $7500 for further consideration next week. The proposals from our New England and Texas subsidiaries received favorable discussion at the meeting. But we need further information before committing ourselves to the awards.

We also agreed to continue funding multiyear projects for at least the next five years.

Except for these departures, the budget will remain as approved by you and Stan, in accordance with the meeting's consensus.

cc: Stan Clements
       Henry Coleman
       Brad Holtzman

ARRANGING LARGE OR DISTANT MEETINGS

Arrangements for large or distant meetings are similar to those we have already discussed. But they are on a larger scale and can become complex. They may involve arranging for facilities over several or many days. They may involve handling arrangements and accommodations for out-of-town participants and for guests and spouses. Detailed instruction for this kind

Survival Tip: A Secretary's Role

Don't come down with a bad case of aloof executivitis when you have to organize a meeting; that is, don't decide that you should leave everything to your secretary. A good secretary is often far more efficient at these jobs than many executives: after all, secretaries handle such details routinely. But if the meeting has been assigned to you, keep a close watch on every particular. If some detail causes a glitch, nobody will remember that your secretary set up the meeting. They will remember that it was *your* meeting.

This is not to say that you should not use your secretary's skills effectively. Just don't be out to lunch when it's time to check the details.

of meeting is beyond the scope of this book. We can, however, offer the following Guidelines to help you, should such an assignment come your way. Additional tips are embedded in the Appendix at the end of this chapter, which provides a sampling of the complex communications that a large meeting can generate.

GUIDELINES

Arranging a Major Meeting

1. *Overall, be prepared.* Arm yourself with a checklist and a time-and-action calendar, and remember to check every item and all its details at least twice—personally, if you can manage it. Remember also to keep your temper and to anticipate changes in plans.

2. *Begin early; call widely.* Begin to make the arrangements at the earliest possible moment. If the dates are not yet certain, try to pin down several tentative dates to check with the purveyors of the services and facilities you will need. Call suppliers of meeting rooms, food, tours, amenities, and services, and check the tentative times with them. If you are fairly certain of your dates, ask essential suppliers to block out those times and reserve them briefly until you can get back to them with a confirmed date.

3. *Confirm everything in writing.* Confirm in written detail every arrangement you make for facilities or services and ask for a confirmation from the supplier as well. Be sure also to confirm your invitations to the participants in writing.

Keep copies of the memos you write and the confirmations from suppliers, including their cost estimates and any understandings about what will be supplied when. File all these for reference when it is time to pay the bills. If the meeting is a large and important one, and especially if it is a recurring one, build a postmortem procedure into the process. In your file keep notes on which things and which suppliers worked well and which didn't.

4. *Delegate as much as you can, but check on it yourself.* If you are delegating the arrangements to an assistant or your secretary, plan time at every stage to go over every detail: menus, bathroom facilities, tours for spouses, timing, access to telephones, materials (including pencils and paper) and their distribution, provision for taking messages—in short, everything. And make sure somebody calm and competent is detailed to deal with problems that arise the day of the meeting when you are occupied with the meeting itself.

AUTHENTIC BUSINESS PROBLEMS

1. Write an agenda.

   The following memo is reproduced from Chapter 7. The writer, whom we call Denise Jones, derived the memo from decisions taken at a meeting of the Consumer Marketing Group at her retailing conglomerate.

   a. Study the situation outlined in the memo and the decisions taken and write an agenda for that meeting, an agenda Denise Jones might have used to obtain those results.

   b. Then write a memo to your instructor, explaining the thinking behind your agenda.

```
To:      John Sealand [SVP, Marketing, Glotz's Depart-
         ment Stores, Inc]
From:    Denise Jones [Director of Consumer Marketing]
Subject: Budget, Fall Harvest Sale
Date:    July 17, 19—


As you know, last year's Fall Harvest promotional
event was not as well attended as we had hoped. Nor
did the sales justify what we spent on its promotion.
We would like to recommend a change in the amount of
money being spent on the event this year, as well as
a major change in the allocation of the dollars.

BACKGROUND
Last year's budget of $0,000,000 was allocated in
this way:

Direct mail                $000,000
Newspaper inserts          $000,000
Broadcast effort           $000,000

RECOMMENDATIONS
• Allocate $1 million to this year's budget.
• $450M for a newspaper insert (preprint). To be
  run in major city newspapers in our various mar-
  kets on Sunday, October 17, 76 pages, 4 color,
  consisting of promotional merchandise from every
```

department in the store, specific items to be cleared
with the merchants involved and presentation in line
with the fall nature of the promotion.
- $300M for direct mailing of some of the material
  from the newspaper insert.
- $250M for broadcast support of the print pieces.

ANALYSIS
1. The bulk of the money should be spent on the newspaper insert because, according to our latest marketing survey, this is currently the best way to
   reach our buying-oriented customers.
2. We can cut our normal budget for direct mail in
   half since we now have a system that enables us to
   identify the most productive portion of our credit
   customer list. We should send only to the 30% that
   research shows are most likely to respond.
3. Using portions of the newspaper insert for the
   mailing will not only result in substantial printing savings, but will give the additional reinforcement advantage of repetition.
4. Further reinforcement should come from the broadcast component, which will be devoted solely to
   the support of the printed matter. It will alert
   customers when to look for the print pieces, where
   they can be found, and will provide reminders of
   the sale as it progresses.
5. The $1 million total represents a 20% decrease
   from last year's event. That could cause some ap-
   prehension on the part of the merchants that they
   are not receiving adequate support for this promotion.

To speak to their concerns:
- The united focus of this campaign plus the new
  direct mail system should result in maximum benefit from our resources.
- But if we decided to increase the total allocation, we would recommend adding approximately
  $100M to the direct mail effort to catch the
  next most likely responders on the list and another $100M to the broadcast effort to support
  the print program more fully.

The numbers in this memo are only approximate. Different allocations could be made based on discussions
with Jim and Martin, which we should have promptly.
   If you could let me have your response by Tuesday,
I would be able to set up the necessary meetings in
time for the publication deadline.

2. Plan a large meeting.

Here is the situation:

The sales force of Southern Manufacturing, Inc., has been having a difficult time getting their products delivered after they have sold them. When their problem came to the attention of the president, J. P. Fortinbras, he suggested to the vice president in charge of operations, L.R. Calpe (for whom you work as first assistant), that a regional meeting be held on one of three dates in March—the 12th, 17th, or 30th—to straighten the matter out. On January 5, you were assigned to set up the meeting.

Although the main office of the company is in Milwaukee, the sales office is in Miami, and that is where the meeting is to be held—at the Sunshine Plaza, if they can handle it on any of the three dates. At Southern Manufacturing, such meetings are traditionally held all day with a morning session, lunch, afternoon session, and dinner. For the after-dinner speaker, the president has suggested Reginald T. Dulleart, the president of the trade association. Mr. Dulleart is an expert on inventory control and order fulfillment.

Those who would attend the meeting include (in addition to the Miami sales executives): the production managers, quality control managers, and plant managers of all the plants in the Southern Division. Southern Manufacturing has plants in Pensacola, Florida; Little Rock, Arkansas; Huntsville, Alabama; and Memphis, Tennessee.

a. Work out a communications plan for the project. Decide who needs to be contacted when and what needs to be written to whom; and set up an order in which the communications should be taken care of. You do *not* need to write the actual letters and memos, but do indicate who should be copied on each.

b. Write the confirming communication to the participants. Be sure to include an annotated schedule of the projected sessions.

CHAPTER APPENDIX:
Communications to Organize a Major Meeting

A large meeting is complicated and so are the communications needed to organize one. To understand how to handle the complex communications for such a meeting, consider the following scenario and the typical written material it generated.

THE SITUATION. In May of last year, Sara Miles, Director of Corporate External Affairs at Cordright Enterprises, Inc., went to a meeting of the machine tool association to which her company belongs. At lunch she sat next to her old friend Peter Brigham, who had just been promoted to Vice President for External Affairs at his company, Conrad-Leste.

After lunch, when Miles and Brigham talked about the positions their companies would take in the afternoon discussions, they found that their companies held the same point of view on most of the major issues. Like most American machine tool companies, theirs had been experiencing heavy competition from the Japanese. But unlike many of the companies in the association, theirs had neither restructured nor attempted to out-source their production by buying components or manufacturing items abroad in countries where wages are lower. Although both companies are large and their dues contribute heavily to the maintenance of the trade association, they often found themselves outvoted by those members whose aims and corporate structures are somewhat different. Both Miles and Brigham could see the advantages of their companies' making common cause on some of these issues.

Miles suggested that Brigham might bring his staff to Cordright for a visit. The two External Affairs staffs might put their heads together and come up with a strategy. They would try to influence the trade association members to vote in ways that would be more beneficial to the industry than the present set of policies.

Brigham liked the idea, and was particularly interested in talking to Charles Wheatley, his new counterpart at Cordright, whom he had not yet met. Miles agreed to speak to Wheatley and try to set up the meeting.

THE WRITTEN MATERIAL. Making the arrangements for the meeting that was eventually (and successfully) held generated the material reproduced on the following pages.

```
Sara Miles' Log

May 23          Reported to Wheatley on actions taken at association
                meeting; also talked to CW about the possibility of
                a meeting between Peter Brigham and our staff; CW
                favorably disposed to inviting Conrad-Leste people
```

here; would like to see some tentative dates and a list of possible topics.

June 8   Staff meeting: Talked with CW about October dates for Conrad-Leste meeting, but speaking engagement will take him out of the country until the first week in October. Will discuss dates with Brigham and get back to CW.

June 24   Talked with Brigham; he and staff believe October or November dates workable for Conrad-Leste.

June 28   Phone conversation with Gerry Klinger, at Peter Brigham's request, to discuss meeting dates and agenda. Memo to CW re decision about dates and agenda. Have discussed with CW possibility of inviting Hank Southern, Vice President for External Affairs at Klemrud, here in the city; he is interested in the outsourcing issue, and Klemrud might be a valuable ally. CW agreed.

July 12   November dates confirmed and entered on CW calendar. Invitation letters to Brigham, and two staff members (Klinger and Allbright) he wants to bring, drafted and in tickler file for mid-September signing by CW.

September 15 Letters out to Brigham, Klinger, and Allbright. Asked Jan to call Sharp's secretary with suggestions for lodging and to advise on flight and ground transportation scheduling from airport.

September 30 Received 9/28 letter of acceptance from Brigham. Called Hank Southern to invite; he will come if his schedule permits.

October 1   Asked Jan to reserve conference room and executive dining room for November 3 and 4. Met with George [Cordright Executive Chef] to discuss meals for the meeting and menus. Letter of invitation out to Hank Southern to join us for breakfast and first part of meeting.

              Asked Jan to make dinner reservations for 6 at Heritage Casa for evening of November 3 and send confirming letter.

October 7   Confirming memo to George re menus; confirming memo to Mary Beth, Corporate Facilities, for meeting rooms.

October 15	Agenda and memo on meeting arrangements to CW for approvals. CW has invited Cordright's new Director of Manufacturing, Jerrod Schultz; letter drafted from CW to him for CW signature.
	Confirmation letter to Marcel at Heritage Casa for dinner reservations.
October 31	Confirmation letter and agenda out to Henry Southern, Klemrud VP, and Jerrod Schultz, Cordright Director of Manufacturing.
November 3	Asked Jan to check on hotel reservations; confirm arrangements at Heritage Casa by phone. Checked with George on meal arrangements for 11/4. Arrived Heritage Casa 7:15 to greet guests.
November 4	Arrived 8 a.m. to check arrangements. Detailed Jan to take messages, help with guests.
November 7	Wrote summary of meeting for CW; and submitted time-and-action plan to carry out meeting assignments. Sent CZ schedule for convening of next task force meetings through January. Checked to see when he wants to send out copies of meeting summary to all participants.
	Met with Jan to postmortem meeting. Sent thank-you notes to Marcel (Maitre d' Hotel at Heritage Casa), George, Mary Beth Ellinger (Corporate Services).

TO: Charles Z. Wheatley
FROM: Sara Miles
RE: Visit from Conrad-Leste External Affairs Executives

Gerry Klinger called me this afternoon at the request of his supervisor, Peter Brigham. The External Affairs Department at Conrad-Leste is enthusiastic about paying us a visit, and Klinger and I discussed some preliminary steps.

Klinger would like to present a proposal to his management group on Thursday, July 15, so he would <u>need to have some preliminary answers from me by Tuesday morning or Wednesday afternoon of that week at the latest.</u>

Here are the things on which I would need a decision:

Time:	All of October and the first two weeks in November would be a possibility for Conrad-Leste. How would that be for us?

Agenda: They would like particularly to discuss a policy
           stance on outsourcing. Gerry Klinger, who handles
           their Washington program, would probably come, along
           with Brigham and their export sales manager, Karen
           Allbright.

           Brigham also has responsibility for their public re-
           lations, and his group would like to discuss how to
           coordinate a public relations program for whatever
           strategy the meeting group decides to put in place
           on the policy positions.

           In turn, they seem to have good ideas for securing
           commitment to such programs from their operating
           units and they are prepared to make a presentation
           at the meeting about that.

Alex initially suggested something on the order of two days for
the meetings. Klinger didn't seem to think that would be impossible, once we can arrive at an agreed agenda.

I would suggest one day of presentations--some from Cordright,
some from Conrad-Leste--and a time for directed discussion of a
common strategy with the trade association.

Another day might provide time for task force work or for counter-
parts to talk with each other.

cc: Mr. Alex Pierce

                                              September 15, 19—

Mr. Peter L. Brigham
Vice President, External Affairs
Conrad-Leste Corporation
884 Nehantick Plaza
St. Louis, Missouri 00000-0000

Dear Mr. Brigham:

I understand from Sara Miles that you and your staff would be willing to undertake a visit to Cleveland so that Cordright and Conrad-
Leste can compare notes on the issues we anticipate in the
upcoming year in our national trade association meetings.

We are eager to talk with you about working out a position that
would be beneficial to us both; and so I am pleased to extend to
you and the members of your staff our invitation to join us for
dinner on Thursday, November 3, and for meetings on November 4.

If you will let Sara know the names and titles of those staff members you would like to bring, I will write to them to extend my personal invitation to join us.

I look forward to seeing the agenda that Sara and Gerry Klinger are working on; and I very much look forward to meeting all of you.

Please let me know if there is anything we can do to help with your arrangements.

Sincerely,

Charles Z. Wheatley
Executive Vice President
for Administration and
Executive Affairs

cc: Sara Miles

September 24, 19—

Ms. Karen Allbright
Export Sales Manager
Conrad-Leste Corporation
884 Nehantick Plaza
St. Louis, Missouri 00000-0000

Dear Ms. Allbright:

At Peter Brigham's suggestion, I am pleased to invite you to join him and Gerald Klinger in a visit to Cordright on November 3 and 4. At dinner on the 3rd and in a day of meetings on the 4th, we will discuss national trade association policy positions and other common issues concerns for both our companies.

I have asked Sara Miles, our Director of Corporate External Affairs, to contact you about details for the meetings.

I very much hope you will be able to join us, and I look forward to welcoming you in November.

Sincerely,

Charles Z. Wheatley

cc: Mr. Peter Brigham
     Ms. Sara Miles

[Gerald Klinger received an identical letter.]

September 30, 19—

Mr. Gerald R. Klinger
Director, National Programs
Conrad-Leste Corporation
884 Nehantick Plaza
St. Louis, Missouri 00000-000

Dear Gerry:

Attached are materials and an agenda for our meetings on Thursday, November 3, and Friday, November 4. In the informational packets are materials which describe Cordright, a list of who we are on this staff and what we do, and a map of the downtown Cleveland area, with the Cordright headquarters building, your hotel, and the restaurant where we will convene Thursday evening highlighted.

We will begin with dinner, at 7:30 on Thursday evening, at the Heritage Casa Restaurant, 616 Fourth Street. That is just a couple of short blocks from your hotel. (As I understand your arrangements, you will stay at the Largish Urban Plaza. You will arrive in Cleveland, on Deluxeair Flight #408, at 5:20 p.m.) The 7:30 dinner hour should give you plenty of time to get into Cleveland from the airport and get registered at your hotel. I will meet you at the restaurant.

As you will note, Hank Southern, Vice President for External Affairs for Klemrud, Inc., will join us, at Chuck Wheatley's invitation, for breakfast on the 4th. When I talked with Peter last week, he said that he would find that addition entirely agreeable; so we have scheduled a discussion on the outsourcing problem at that time to take advantage of Hank's being there.

The meeting ends on Friday at 4:00. Then we have scheduled some light refreshments before your departure at 4:30, which should give you enough time to get to the airport on a busy Friday evening for your flight home.

Do call if you have any questions or comments, or if I can be helpful in any way with your arrangements. We are very much looking forward to seeing you, Peter, and Karen Allbright.

Sincerely,

Sara Miles
Director, Corporate External Affairs

cc: Peter Brigham
bcc: Charles Z. Wheatley

[Karen Allbright received an identical letter.]

October 7, 19—

TO: Mary Beth Ellinger, Corporate Services
FROM: Jan Hensley
RE: Reservations for 17th Floor Conference Room, November 4

This will confirm our telephone conversation of this morning.
Please reserve the 17th Floor Conference Room from 8:30 to 4:30 on
November 4. We will need seating for 15, but no audiovisual equip-
ment.

Please charge the room's use to Charles Wheatley's departmental
budget.

Thank you.

cc: Sara Miles

October 7, 19—

TO: George Sauverre [Executive Chef, Cordright]
FROM: Sara Miles
RE: Meals for November 4 meetings with guests from Conrad-Leste

Attached are the menus and schedules we agreed upon in our conversation on Wednesday for breakfast, lunch, and an afternoon tea.

As we agreed, breakfast will be served; but lunch will be buffet,
except for dessert, which your servers will pass.

We will also need soft drinks, coffee, and tea for 15 in the 17th
floor conference room for both morning and afternoon sessions.

Please let Jan know if you should have questions.

cc: Jan Hensley

Conrad-Leste visit

Menus

Breakfast (8:30 a.m., Executive Dining Room)

Orange juice and fresh-fruit cup
Scrambled eggs with sautéed mushrooms

Crisp bacon and ham slices
Hash brown potatoes
Homemade wheat bread
Butter
Fruit preserves
Homemade prune Danish
Coffee
Tea

Lunch (12:15, Executive Dining Room, Parlor A)

Washington chowder
Entrees from the Main Dining Room Buffet (including rib-eye beef
and fresh sea scallops or a seafood casserole)

Dessert: Ice cream, strawberries with raspberry sauce, George's
chocolate cake, George's pumpkin pie with spiced cream

Afternoon Tea (3:30 p.m.)
Miniature French pastries
Fruit and cheese board
Coffee
Tea
Soft drinks

To: Charles Wheatley
From: Sara Miles
Ext. # 1234
Date: 10/15/--

RE: Attached agenda for your approval, Conrad-Leste meetings,
       November 4, 19——

I would appreciate having your comments on the agenda and attached
materials as soon as possible so that I can send those by express
mail this afternoon to St. Louis.

If you would like modifications of any of the other plans, that
can easily be arranged, and, indeed, even the agenda can go to St.
Louis as a tentative agenda for revision by telephone.

Attached are:

- a tentative agenda for November 4;
- materials that I intend to send for each guest;
- a schedule of events (with guest lists attached);
- logistics and menus

The guests for this meeting--Peter Brigham, Karen Allbright, and Gerry Klinger are now confirmed--are expected to arrive Thursday, November 3, on Deluxeair Flight #408, which leaves St. Louis at 2 p.m. and arrives in Cleveland at 5:20 p.m. They will stay at the Largish Urban Plaza.

As you will note, I have included a map in their information packets, with Cordright's headquarters, the hotel, and the Heritage Casa Restaurant highlighted. I have made reservations for 12 at the Heritage Casa for 7:30 p.m. (subject to your confirmation of these plans). My letter to Peter Brigham (attached) asks them to meet us at the restaurant. I will be there early to greet them.

On Friday, November 4, we will convene for breakfast here in the Executive Dining Room at 8:30 a.m. We have structured the agenda so that we can have a discussion of outsourcing during breakfast, when Hank Southern has said he would like to attend.

I have attached a letter for your signature, letting Hank know our plans and inviting him to sit in on other sessions as well. We might want to invite Jim McCord to come to those he would be interested in as well.

I will also ask Saul Penner and Bob Kline to sit in on the pertinent sessions for their areas, and I have made the head count for breakfast and lunch sufficiently loose to accommodate them--or anyone else you would like to include--for those meals.

I have also attached a letter to Jerry Schultz from you, as well as memos from you to Pierce, Penner, Kline, and Zwick, inviting them to sit in on some sessions.

The Conrad-Leste people are scheduled to leave on Friday afternoon, on Deluxeair Flight #412, which leaves Cleveland at 5:45 and arrives in St. Louis at 7:15. I have set refreshments and adjournment for 4 p.m. so they can leave by taxi at 4:30.

I would be glad to answer any questions you might have.

Meeting: Conrad-Leste and Cordright Issues Meeting

November 4, 19—

<u>AGENDA</u>

8:30   <u>Breakfast (Executive Dining Room)</u>

      Introductions   Sara Miles

Breakfast discussion: problems with
national trade association policies
on outsourcing

Special guest: Hank Southern, Vice
President, External Affairs, Klemrud,
Inc.

9:30   Convene (Conference Room, 17th Floor)

9:45   Welcome   Charles Z. Wheatley
        Cordright philosophies and organization
        Meeting focus: How Conrad-Leste and
        Cordright can work together effectively
        to influence association policy changes

        Conrad-Leste philosophies and
        organization   Peter Brigham

10:00-
10:45   How we are perceived in domestic and
        global markets
            Conrad-Leste programs   Karen Allbright
            Cordright programs   Alex Pierce

10:45-
11:15   National Trade Association Programs
        and Their Funding
            Conrad-Leste priorities   Jerry Klinger
            Cordright priorities   Charles Wheatley

11:15-
12:00   Sales Program Responses
            Conrad-Leste programs   Karen Allbright
            Cordright programs   Saul Penner

12:00   Break

12:15   Buffet Luncheon: Executive Dining Room

1:15   Reconvene, Conference Room, 17th Floor

1:15-
2:00   Discussion of issues positions and
        appointment of ad hoc task forces to
        recommend strategies

2:00-
2:45   Task Force Meetings

```
2:45-
3:15   Task Force Reports
       Summation: What specific programs
       should the two companies carry out
       cooperatively?

       What priorities and target dates for
       program completion should be set?          Charles Wheatley
                                                   Peter Brigham


3:15-
4:00   Free time (Wheatley/Brigham meeting
       in CW office)


4:00   Refreshments and Adjournment
```

Conrad-Leste Meetings
November 4, 19—
Participants

Conrad-Leste Corporation, St. Louis, Missouri

Peter Brigham, Vice President, External Affairs
Gerry Klinger, Director, National Programs (Washington)
Karen Allbright, Export Sales Manager

Klemrud, Inc., Cleveland

Henry A. Southern, Vice President, External Affairs
James G. McCord, Director, Southern Regional Programs

Cordright Enterprises, Inc., Cleveland

Charles Z. Wheatley, Executive Vice President for
Administration and External Affairs
Alex J. Pierce, Operating Vice President, Public Relations
and Urban Affairs
Saul A. Penner, Vice President, Export Sales
Robert G. Kline, Vice President, Domestic Sales
Hans M. Zwick, Associate Corporate Counsel
Jerrod M. Schultz, Vice President and Director of Manufacturing
Sara Miles, Director, Corporate External Affairs

M. Marcel Dutourd
Maitre d'Hotel
The Heritage Casa
616 Fourth Street
Cleveland, OH 00000

Dear Marcel:

This will confirm the reservations we agreed upon by telephone on Monday for dinner for six people at 7:30 on Thursday evening, November 3. The reservations should be held and the dinners billed in the name of Charles Wheatley, Vice President for Administration and External Affairs, Cordright Enterprises, Inc., 1233 Nonomen Blvd., but sent to my attention at the same address.

As we discussed, our party will be seated in a private dining room; but we would like to order from your regular menu.

Should you have questions, please call my secretary, Jan Hensley, or me.

Thank you for your help with the arrangements.

Sincerely,

Sara Miles

10/21/—

TO: Alex J. Pierce
        Saul A. Penner
        Robert G. Kline
        Hans M. Zwick
        Jerrod M. Schultz

FROM: Chuck Wheatley

RE: Meetings with Conrad-Leste External Affairs Department

On Friday, November 4, members of Conrad-Leste's staff will visit us for meetings on common policy issues objectives for the upcoming year. As I know you are aware, our national trade association has taken positions on a number of trade and tax issues over this past year that have been troubling to old-line companies such as ours and Conrad-Leste. The trade association position on outsourcing is a particular problem.

What we hope is that we can review all of the issues we expect to confront over the next year or two and come up with some common goals and some cooperative programs.

Attached is a tentative agenda. We hope you will be able to join us for as many of these sessions as your own work schedule permits, but we hope that you will make a particular effort to attend those that touch on policy issues which affect your responsibilities.

We will begin with breakfast at 8:30 in the Executive Dining Room and convene for the first session in the Conference Room at 9:30. Lunch is at 12:15 in the Executive Dining Room, and we will say goodbye to our guests with some light refreshments at 4:00 that afternoon.

Please let Sara (4484) know whether or not you will be able to join us and for which sessions. Luncheon arrangements are sufficiently flexible that we could accommodate you easily if you need to make a late decision about coming to lunch. Just let Lila know if you can find you can make it.

Look forward to seeing you there.

October 15, 19——

Mr. Henry A. Southern
Vice President, External Affairs
Klemrud, Inc.
5555 Commanche Avenue
Cleveland, OH 00000-0000

Dear Hank:

As Sara Miles has discussed with you, our department here at Cordright and members of the External Affairs Department at Conrad-Leste will meet on November 4 to discuss policy issues of concern to both companies. The major issue--outsourcing--is one that I know you have a particular interest in and, I understand from Sara, one that you are particularly knowledgeable about.

If your schedule permits, we would be delighted to have you join us for breakfast on November 4 and the first part of the meeting, which will deal with outsourcing.

You also would be very welcome to stay for any other part of the agenda that you might find of interest.

I hope you will be able to join us.

Sincerely,

Charles Z. Wheatley

October 15, 19—

Mr. Jerrod Schultz
Vice President and Director of Manufacturing
Cordright, Inc.
Town and Country Road
P.O. Box 8888
Cleveland, OH 00000-0000

Dear Jerry Schultz:

I'm sorry that your schedule last Tuesday did not permit us to meet, but I am delighted to welcome you as Cordright's new Director of Manufacturing. As soon as you can see your way clear to spending a couple of hours with us here at headquarters, do let me know, and we'll try to get you oriented to some of our issues. Perhaps lunch one day next week?

Unquestionably, your work will plunge you very quickly into Cordright's major issue--the outsourcing problem. I have asked our Director of Corporate External Affairs, Sara Miles, to call you in a week or so and make herself available for a briefing meeting at your convenience.

Sara has also suggested that you might find it helpful to attend a meeting that we have scheduled for November 4 with the External Affairs Department of Conrad-Leste. As you may be aware, policy at the national trade association has not gone to our liking or to Conrad-Leste's for some time, and we want to meet and talk about how we might persuade other members of the association to take a position that both our companies would find more beneficial than the present policy.

Sara will tell you about the arrangements, but I hope your busy first weeks will let you find time to join us.

I look forward to meeting you.

Sincerely,

Charles Z. Wheatley

October 31, 19——

Mr. Henry A. Southern
Vice President, External Affairs
Klemrud, Inc.
5555 Commanche Avenue
Cleveland, OH 00000-0000

Dear Hank:

Attached is a copy of our tentative agenda for meetings with members of the External Affairs Department of Conrad-Leste here at Cordright headquarters on Friday, November 4.

I understand from Sara that you will join us for breakfast. That is scheduled to begin at 8:30 here in our Executive Dining Room, on the 18th Floor.

As I indicated in my earlier letter to you, the discussion on outsourcing is scheduled during breakfast, and we are pleased that you will be able to give us the benefit of your experience with the issue.

I'll be a bit late arriving, because I have an early appointment; but one of the staff will be able to contribute Cordright's point of view to that discussion. And I hope that you will be able either to stay for part of the first few sessions or perhaps to join us later in the day.

Perhaps Jim McCord would like to be with us for some of the discussions that center on his areas of responsibility. Those sessions are, I believe, scheduled mainly during the morning. If he and you would like then to join us for lunch, we'd be delighted to have you.

Please let Sara Miles (314-4484) know which sessions you expect to attend and whether you can come for lunch.

I'll look forward to seeing you Friday.

Sincerely,

Charles Z. Wheatley

October 31, 19—

Mr. Jerrod Schultz
Vice President and Director of Manufacturing
Cordright, Inc.
Town and Country Road
P.O. Box 8888
Cleveland, OH 00000-0000

Dear Jerry:

I'm delighted that you will be able to join us for dinner on Thursday, November 3, and for meetings with members of the Conrad-Leste external affairs staff on November 4.

Dinner is scheduled for 7:30 p.m. at the Heritage Casa Restaurant, 616 Fourth Street. (I have enclosed a map, with the Cordright headquarters building and the restaurant highlighted, for your information.)

I have also enclosed a tentative agenda, subject to change if need be, and I would be pleased to have your comments by telephone should you wish to offer any.

Those coming from Conrad-Leste include: Peter Brigham, Vice President for External Affairs; Gerry Klinger, Director, National Programs (Washington); and Karen Allbright, Export Sales Manager.

I am sorry that we still have not had a chance to get together, but everybody I talk to is extremely pleased to have you on board, and I hear nothing but good things. If your Friday evening plans could accommodate a late meeting with me after the Conrad-Leste guests leave, we could sit down and get you oriented to some of our other issues.

Just call my secretary, Lila Powell, and let her know what you would find convenient. I look forward to seeing you on Friday.

Sincerely,

Chuck Wheatley

November 7, 19—

TO: George Sauverre

FROM: Sara Miles

RE: Conrad-Leste Meeting

My thanks--and Chuck's--to you and all of your staff for the out-standing job you did for us during the meetings with Conrad-Leste executives last week. As usual, your meals were superb: the pump-kin pie got raves. Moreover, several guests commented on how smooth and unobtrusive the service was and how quickly and effi-ciently we moved through the meal periods. Please let everyone on your staff know how very much we appreciate the extra effort they clearly made to help us entertain our guests.

You did us proud.

November 7, 19—

TO: Mary Beth Ellinger, Corporate Services

FROM: Sara Miles

RE: Conrad-Leste Meeting

Chuck has asked me to add his thanks to mine for the efficient way in which you and your staff handled the facilities preparation for our meetings with Conrad-Leste executives on Friday.

The rooms were ready on time, everything was in place, and every-thing worked perfectly. The call we made for extra chairs Don an-swered promptly, and he handled the whole call so unobtrusively that the meetings were not at all interrupted.

Please thank Don, Jack, and Linda for us, for all they did to provide such professional support for those meetings.

And thanks to you for a terrific job of coordinating: Jan says
she's never before worked on a meeting with anybody who made it
all go so smoothly. We appreciate your efforts.

cc: John R. Bridges [Vice President for Corporate Services]

WRITING TO SPEAK EFFECTIVELY

EXECUTIVE SUMMARY

Effective business speaking and effective business writing share the same principles:

Consider your audience in light of your purpose.

- Focus on what you are trying to get across.

- Empathize with your audience.

For oral presentations, follow the principles and adapt the planning strategies you used to produce effective recommendation memos and sales letters.

For formal speeches, add to those techniques the planning for an expository essay.

   The oral component in both presentations and speeches should only intensify your reliance on the principles:

- Plan your talk for a *specific* audience.

- Begin with an empathetic and orienting introduction.

- Engage your audience so they interact with you; be lively.

- Develop your purpose and support it in the central portion.

- Close with an action request and relate to your audience as you conclude.

- Make sure to prepare thoughtfully for the question period.

   Because many people have difficulty with aural comprehension:

Be brief. Be simple. Be clear.

- Simplify your syntax, your diction, and your information; develop no more than three main points.

- Share the structure of your talk.

- Repeat everything you want remembered.

- Use visuals wherever appropriate.

For a job interview, also apply the principles: purpose and empathy. Research the job, with attention to the employer's needs. Decide: What about your character, your qualifications, and your experience makes you a good fit for the position? Rehearse the interview to discover ways you can get this vital information across to your audience, the interviewers.

Survey any group of business managers. Ask them what skill their subordinates most need to improve in, and they will say: public speaking, oral presentation. Ask them about themselves and you will get much the same reply. Oral presentations might have been invented by some malicious business deity for the scourging of the faithful. Confronted with the necessity to speak before a group, brisk and able women grow withdrawn and silent, CEOs get edgy, and strong men weep. And not altogether without reason. The stakes are often high. The talents that make a good executive and those that make a good public speaker do not always coincide. And the pitfalls can be many and deep.

Even so, the essentials of business speaking are not complex, and you are already familiar with them. *Effective business speaking and effective business writing share the same principles.* After all, rhetoric was the art of persuasive speaking long before it was applied to persuasive writing.

PRINCIPLES OF EFFECTIVE BUSINESS SPEAKING

You should not be surprised to find that this axiom is at the heart of effective business speaking:

Consider your audience in light of your purpose.

The purpose principle and the empathetic principle derived from this axiom are even more central to business speaking than to business writing. Every successful oral presentation has a specific purpose. You may wish to:

- Persuade your listener to approve your recommendations.
- Persuade a customer to buy your product or service.
- Increase your company's prestige.
- Get yourself a job.

Whatever your purpose, keep it uppermost in mind both as you plan and as you make your presentation.

Focus on what you are trying to get across.

To achieve your purpose, you will need to persuade your audience. To persuade your audience, first analyze them as specifically as possible. What do I know about these people? What should appeal to them? What might irritate them? What should they find persuasive? How would I feel in their place? Then both prepare your presentation and present it so as to appeal to your audience's particular sensibilities.

Empathize with your audience.

STRATEGIES OF EFFECTIVE BUSINESS SPEAKING

With those principles as the foundation, the strategies you have learned for effective business writing throughout this text will also help you in your business speaking. Use the writing strategies, for example, to structure your oral presentations and speeches.

- Begin each with an empathetic or orienting introduction.
- Develop your purpose and support it in the central portion.
- Conclude with an action request.

You will also find other familiar writing strategies useful. In business speaking as in business writing:

Be brief. Be simple. Be clear.

Useful for writers, these cautions are even more important for speakers. Most people have more difficulty understanding what they hear than what they read. Simply to have your listeners understand you, you *must* be brief, simple, and clear.

A SPECIAL STRATEGY FOR BUSINESS SPEAKERS

Besides the writing strategies, for business *speakers* we will add one more:

Be prepared.

In business there is no such thing as an effective extemporaneous presentation. Business executives judge. And they want facts—hard evidence to support what you're telling them. You can't provide such support without extensive preparation. Nor can you provide the smoothness, economy, and persuasiveness that business values. So be prepared.

These principles and strategies hold for any business speaking you may be asked to do. But in this chapter we will emphasize just three major kinds of business speaking: oral presentations, formal speeches, and job interviews.

SECTION A: *Effective Oral Presentations*

WHAT ORAL PRESENTATIONS DO

Oral presentations come in many varieties. They can be internal—to present budgets, products, strategies, plans, or solutions to perceived problems. Or they can be external—given, for instance, at trade shows, annual board meetings, industry conventions, and press conferences.

INTERNAL ORAL PRESENTATIONS

Here are some typical examples of internal presentations:

- David N. recently gave a presentation for his project group. He explained the new specifications of a government licensing agency and recommended design changes that would permit his company's product to fulfill the requirements.
- Shirley F. wrote a memo detailing her investigation of the unemployment-compensation structure of the states within which her large company does business. She suggested ways to reduce this tax burden and was subsequently asked to present her report to a senior management group.
- Every year, at the annual sales meeting, Marjorie O. introduces her company's new line of products to the sales staff.

What these widely diverse internal presentations have in common is their fundamental resemblance to a recommendation memo. In Chapter 7, we defined the recommendation memo:

> Its purpose is to report on or bring about action. . . . Through it you should support and facilitate decision making by presenting:
>
> - Clearly stated judgments and recommendations.
> - Support—in the form of clearly demonstrated data. . . .
>
> The entire process must take account of both the implications for your company and its goals for their project at hand.

This is also a good definition for the substance of an internal oral presentation.

EXTERNAL ORAL PRESENTATIONS

Just as internal oral presentations resemble recommendation memos, external oral presentations resemble sales letters—though less obviously. These presentations and sales letters share a common purpose: to interest the audience in a particular product or service and to build goodwill for the company. Consider these representative examples:

- Jesse B. introduces a new product to the press.
- At a trade show, Ruth C. describes a security problem that has been troubling a large number of computer file systems and reports on a solution that will be incorporated into a forthcoming product of her company.

The sales motive, openly expressed in most sales letters, is usually implicit in external oral presentations.

An internal oral presentation may not be exactly an oral recommendation memo, and an external presentation is not quite like an oral sales letter. But the relationship is close enough for you to apply what you know about such memos and letters to *whatever* oral presentation you may be assigned.

HOW TO GO ABOUT MAKING AN ORAL PRESENTATION—INTERNAL OR EXTERNAL

To make an oral presentation, follow the steps you would take to write a recommendation memo.

1. Think through the problem.
2. Search out the relevant data. (A review of business research methods on pages 215–226 in Chapter 8 might be helpful here.)
3. Turn the data into information by considering it in terms of the problem and *your* company's present situation. You might ask yourself the following questions:

   - What do these facts or numbers imply for *my* company?
   - What significance does that implication have for my company's goals and objectives?
   - How can this data be used on this project to help my company
     —continue a favorable trend?
     —correct an unfavorable trend?

4. Study and evaluate the information and decide on your recommendations.
5. Decide what information will best support your recommendations.
6. Organize so as best to develop your ideas and support your recommendations. Consider how you will handle:

   - Statement of purpose (and support).
   - Recommendation(s) (and support).
   - Request for approval to implement the action (and support).

Allow plenty of time for this preparatory work. The most admired business speaker we know offers this rule of thumb: *One hour of preparation time for every five minutes of presentation.*

CONSIDER YOUR AUDIENCE

The steps suggested above will help you prepare the substance of an effective talk, but they do not take into account the fact that your presentation will be oral, that you will be addressing—and facing—a real, breathing audience. Here's where sales techniques (albeit implicit) come into your preparations.

MAKE YOUR OPENING EMPATHETIC. Before you get to your introductory statement of purpose or, if you are especially clever, *while* you are getting to it, take a moment to orient your audience, to relate to them in a personal way. Let each person experience you as one human being talking to another. Briefly touch on something light, something topical, or something personal, if it's only about the weather. Make reference to something you all share: tell an inside joke (if you're sure there's no harm in it). Then make a quick transition—connected, if possible, to the purpose of your presentation—and set up the structure of your talk. (See the "Be Simple" section below for a detailed discussion of a setting-up-the-structure technique.)

BE AWARE OF YOUR LISTENERS. Because of the oral nature of your presentation, the number of points you can make effectively is severely limited. Research has determined that an audience cannot hold more than three points comfortably in mind at one time. Extra ideas need to be subordinated to the major points. But too many subordinations lessen the impact of them all. To be persuasive, therefore, select your support carefully—even strategically. How?

Think people: psychology, politics, hierarchy. Ask yourself who exactly will attend your presentation. If it's an external meeting, what sort of people will be there? What do you know about that group? Do you know anything about any particular individuals likely to attend? Who are the movers and shakers among them? What can you find out about the way they are likely to approach your topic? Are there any sensitive areas in your material? Are there any controversies surrounding it which you should be aware of?

If you are to give your presentation at an internal meeting, you are likely to know most of your audience personally or by reputation. When you think about what you plan to say, consider how it is likely to be received by them—especially the ranking members who will have to approve your recommendations. Accentuate what *they* will consider the positive. Your time is limited. So eliminate—as far as possible, or perhaps until the question period—what they will consider the negative.

For example, does J. B. Houlihan gnash his teeth at the thought of cost overruns? Then, for goodness' sake, don't highlight cost overruns in your presentation. Concentrate on the potential cost savings. But be sure to prepare a well-supported answer in case Houlihan decides to grill you on the subject.

In other words, when you choose your points and the data to support them, be sensible. Given what you know of your topic, the situation, and the individuals in your audience, decide:

- Which supporting ideas are sure to sell?
- Which have a fighting chance of selling?
- Which are a lead-pipe cinch to be rejected?

Think and choose accordingly. Your choice is important. It could be the making of your presentation.

REMEMBER YOUR AUDIENCE AS YOU CONCLUDE. Make your audience feel they have heard *something* when you've finished your presentation. Don't just end. Conclude. An audience is least comfortable with the ending where the presenter says, with a self-deprecating shrug, "Well, I guess that's all."

Instead, sum up. Where appropriate, repeat the options. Phrase your recommendations in their most persuasive form. End with a final action request. Let your listeners know what you want them to do—even if it is only to think about what you have said. Then say thank you and sit down.

Or open the proceeding for questions. If you have caught your audience's attention and interest, they will want to participate. Anticipate probable questions, and prepare ahead for them so you can answer confidently. Listen carefully to your questioners. You need to catch all the nuances so that you can speak to what is *really* intriguing or disturbing them.

BE BRIEF

Business people joke about their short attention spans. But there's a good bit of truth in the joke, because business executives are nearly always pressed for time and their time is valuable. A *successful* oral presentation is a *short* presentation.

WHEN YOUR PRESENTATION IS STRICTLY SCHEDULED. Sometimes brevity is simply a requirement. More often than not, you are assigned a limited time in which to make your presentation. Be rigidly disciplined about adhering to the time allotted.

WHEN THE UNFORESEEN ARISES. What's more, the limits imposed on an oral presentation can be tricky. They may not stretch beyond the time originally scheduled for you—even though other agenda items have eaten up the time or a ranking executive has made last-minute changes in the agenda.

It is, therefore, wise to design your presentation to run slightly *under* your time allotment if at all possible. Then, if other agenda items or other speakers run over, you won't find yourself squeezed out with time only to present half your important ideas. To prepare for such emergencies, figure

Meeting the Risks of a Question Period

The most direct way for your audience to interact with you and your material is to ask questions and be answered. A question period can be persuasive. It is also a time of some risk.

The Risk of Tough Questions

There is, of course, the risk of tough questions. But if you have prepared well, you should welcome such questions. They will give you the opportunity to fill in the blanks your audience missed and also to present additional support for points on which you have not yet persuaded them. In preparing for your talk, try to anticipate where such difficult spots might be. Confer with a colleague or an intelligent outsider. Such consultation may reveal questionable links in your reasoning that you are too close to recognize.

The Risk of the Difficult Questioner

A more formidable risk comes in fielding the queries of those who monopolize the discussion, distract attention from the subject, or ride their own hobbyhorse without actually asking any questions at all. Occasionally you may even have to face a hostile questioner. Whether such questioners behave this way to show off in front of colleagues and superiors, have their own axes to grind, woke up grumpy, or are simply not very bright, they can weaken the audience's impression of your presentation if you do not keep them under control.

Handling the grandstander. You cannot control the questions, but you can control the time when questions will be permitted. Say, for example:

- "I'm sorry to interrupt, but our time is short and I see there are a number of other questions." Or: "I'm sorry to interrupt, but I want to be sure we have time to cover . . ."

- "That's a good question. I think what you're asking is [give your own interpretation]. And my answer to it is . . ."

With this strategy* it doesn't matter whether you actually understand the long-winded question or not. The idea is to come close to the questioner's point and turn it into a question you feel comfortable answering—or even would *like* to answer.

Handling the hostile questioner. If you face hostile interrogators, again you cannot control the questions. But the answers, at least, are yours. If you begin to feel angry—and you well might, because hostility breeds hostility—do not show your temper. Few gifted souls can erupt into righteous anger and turn it to their own (or even their company's) account. So stick to charm. And if that's too much to manage in face of the onslaught, stick to impeccably polite manners.

Handling hostility in external presentations. Remember that you are not required to answer all questions. When the query is off the subject or out of bounds—whether it's personal or about the company you represent—just smile and say, "It wouldn't be appropriate for me to comment on that." Then

---

*Not recommended if the questioner is a person of rank in your company.

make a remark that will get the discussion back on track again. And you need not volunteer information. Often a simple *yes* or *no* will do.

Handling hostility in internal presentations. If the presentation is an internal one and the hostile questioner outranks you, the situation is delicate and doubly risky. If you know the answer, answer. If the answer would be too long or detailed, or would derail the rest of your presentation, try something like:

> "It's difficult to give you a short answer to that. But perhaps you might like to look at the data sheets when we have finished our presentation."

Don't fake it. If you don't know the answer, say:

> "I'm sorry. If I understand your question, I don't know the answer, but I'll check and get back to you."

If you don't want to answer, or if the questioner's pressing questions are not constructive or won't contribute to the knowledge of the rest of your audience, say:

> "That's a good question. But another way of looking at it might be . . . [turn the question into one you want to answer]."

But what if your data has not been sufficiently persuasive? What if you sense that your questioner isn't convinced and doesn't really want to be bothered with the facts? If the rank is very high—say, the CEO—and it's clear you're not going to please no matter what the answer (and it happens), retreat.* But retreat on your own terms. Say:

> "Well, clearly we have not addressed your concerns. We'll rework this and get back to you."

Keep cheerful and smile, and you'll retreat in good order and live to fight another day.

Be prepared. The best way to handle hostile questions—internal or external—is to be prepared. Ask a colleague who knows something about your subject to play devil's advocate and think up every possible *nasty* question. Then prepare answers for all those unpleasant contingencies and rehearse. Even just rehearsing the answers to hostile questions can be wearing. But it's far better to suffer anxiety ahead of time and be ready to answer a zinger than to have to field it cold. Besides, think how smooth you'll look if you don't break stride answering a mean question. That shows you can think on your feet.

Worth the Risks

Whatever the possible risks, question periods are clearly worth them. They give you necessary feedback. They let you correct misconceptions and explain what hasn't been understood. And they let you relate to each person in your audience as one human being to another.

---

*Caution: Before you retreat, be sure your questioner is not simply challenging to test your conviction about your recommendations. If you think that's what's happening, stick to your guns for one more barrage, and then you can retreat if necessary.

out ahead what *could* be cut if necessary. Mark that on your speaking notes so that you will be ready to rise to the occasion in a way that won't make it necessary to scuttle the heart of your presentation. *Be prepared.*

WHEN YOU CAN SET YOUR OWN TIME. Even when your presentation time is yours to choose, brevity is a good idea. There are absolute limits to how long you can command the attention of busy minds with many responsibilities. Think in terms of 15 minutes. If you've been assigned 20 or 30 minutes, use the rest of the time for questions. Leave your audience wanting more.

BE SIMPLE

In Chapter 2 we cited research to demonstrate the importance of simplicity in business writing. Business speaking adds a whole new dimension to this guideline. Most people comprehend more easily when they can see something than when they merely hear it. This fact argues for using visual aids (a topic we discuss later). More significantly, it underlines the need for verbal simplicity just to achieve plain understanding.

Set out your ideas in language an eighth-grader could understand. This is no insult. Professional media consultants advise pitching language and concepts in oral presentations at the seventh-to-eighth grade level. This advice is based on research that shows what kind of language and organization is most easily and efficiently grasped by the human brain.

The following Guidelines come from a senior executive whose presentations are renowned for their elegant simplicity. During a long and distinguished career, he has made hundreds of highly regarded presentations to the captains of American industry, business, and finance. So skilled is he that he is widely believed to be able to explain an international interest-rate swap to a kindergartener—and, with the same presentation, to a CEO in the same audience.

■■■■■■■ **GUIDELINES** ■■■■■■■

Be Simple

- You can never make your presentation too simple.
- Businesspeople are used to concentrating, but even the most attentive listener—however bright—can keep track of only about three concepts at one time.
- Details are even harder to retain. Your presentation will be the most effective when it is the most simple. Leave out detail; but have it available in case you're asked.
- Practice with an audience *unfamiliar* with your topic. If someone who knows nothing about the subject understands your presentation, it will communicate to your actual listeners. If your test audience doesn't understand something, go back to your desk and simplify.

- No big words. No buzzwords.
- Don't complicate matters—ideas, syntax, or diction—to show how smart you are. Your audience will judge how smart *you* are by how well *they* comprehend what you are trying to tell them. This is true no matter how smart or highly ranked your audience is.
- Limit your statistics. Simplify information. Think about it in terms of what you would have to do to get it on a bumper sticker. You can provide details later in a backup handout sheet.
- Even if you know your audience is sophisticated, bright, and savvy, or very experienced, don't make your presentation—either the visuals or the oral parts—any more complex. If such a group gets itchy, they will tell you with body signals. Then don't complicate the presentation; just pick up the pace. You can never be too simple.

BE CLEAR

Clarity is essential when the stakes are high. No matter how terrific your plan, no matter how cleverly you have solved your business problem, if you can't make it clear you will not persuade. Busy executives assume that an idea is inadequate if the presentation is inadequate.

GET RIGHT TO YOUR POINT. Catching on with one's ears alone is very difficult for most people. But listeners, like readers, process what they can anticipate. There is a good deal of truth in the public speaker's adage:

- Tell 'em what you're gonna tell 'em.
- Tell 'em.
- Tell 'em what you've told 'em.

So get right to the point. Put your thesis—ordinarily, your recommendations—right up front. You might begin, for example, by saying:

> "The consumer research department has just completed an analysis of data that we have gathered over the last five months. Those numbers show that we could double sales in five years *if we moved into the Southwest market with three operations by 1997.*" [Recommendation in italics]

SHARE THE STRUCTURE OF YOUR TALK. To further help your audience understand your oral presentation, make the structure immediately clear. Thus, in your introduction, along with your empathetic reaching out and your statement of purpose, find a way to suggest your plan of approach.

You might actually outline your talk verbally. Continuing the example about the Southwest market, for instance, you could add:

> "The consumer research department has just completed an analysis of data that we have gathered over the last five months. Those numbers show that we could double sales in five years if we moved into the Southwest market with three operations by 1997. *Today we want to (1) show you what the numbers say; (2) suggest how we think we should proceed; and (3) offer you a tentative timetable for carrying out the program.*"

And don't hesitate to use similar numerical listings throughout your presentation. Your audience will understand and appreciate what you have to say far better if they always know where they are.

Or you could outline your presentation visually. Use a projected visual (see the computer sidebar) or scratch or rough out an outline on a chalkboard or flip chart. But don't distribute handouts until after the presentation. (If you do, you might lose your audience, because they will be reading the sheets instead of listening to you.)

REPEAT AND SUMMARIZE AS YOU GO.   To insure your audience's comprehension, don't forget the last line of the adage: "Tell 'em what you've told 'em." Introduce each new point by summarizing what has gone before. Approaching the final point, the advocate of the Southwest market, for example, might say:

> "We have seen how the figures point to a $000,000,000 increase in sales in only five years in a newly opened Southwest market, and we have discussed the advantages of openings in Dallas, Salt Lake City, and Phoenix. Now let's turn to the chart to see what the numbers suggest for a timetable for this move."

Repeat everything you want remembered.

In addition, look at your audience and read them as you speak. Sometimes you'll notice heads nodding. Or you may sense that people are losing track. Remember, what you say is not nearly as important as what your audience actually takes in. So repeat in a more lively way when you suspect someone has missed a point or has ceased to follow your argument. And, of course, be sure to summarize at the close, as you make your final call for action.

USE VISUALS WHEREVER APPROPRIATE   Since it is the aural aspects of a talk that make comprehension difficult, the best way to remedy the problem is to add a visual component to your presentation. And research shows that it works. Chester K. Guth and Stanley S. Shaw, for example, discovered that one group of sales representatives remembered only 10% of a presentation three days later; but the group who heard the same material with visual aids remembered 67%.[1] Furthermore, the more complex your information, the more useful the visual. A well-versed computer engineer we know says, "Every technical presentation I've ever seen used visuals."

Whatever medium you decide to use—flip charts, overheads, overlays, slides—visuals are powerful tools. Use outlines to signify structure; use tables to present figures; use graphs to show complex relationships (see Chapter 10). And colorful graphics and pictures spur enthusiasm at sales-incentive or marketing meetings.

"Tonight, we're going to let the statistics speak for themselves."

From *Do You Want to Talk About It?* by Edward Koren, © 1968 by Edward Koren. Published by Pantheon Books, New York.

WITH VISUALS TOO: BE SIMPLE. Follow the same rule of simplicity when you construct your visuals. For example, if you illustrate your oral presentation with a table, never work with more than *three columns* or *four lines*. You can add or drop a column in successive visuals, but highlight more than three columns or four lines at a time and you defeat your purpose entirely.

---

1. *How to Put On Dynamic Meetings.* (Reston, VA: Reston Publishing, 1980): 47.

KEY YOUR TALK TO YOUR VISUALS.   Many successful speakers, particularly when addressing technical subjects, make visuals central to their presentations rather than simply illustrative. To make this kind of presentation, open with an overall outline visual. Continue with visuals that break up the main structure into subpoints. Key your notes as well as your pictures and graphics to these subpoints. (See the computer sidebar for information on software helpful for this technique.)

But, when you use visuals this extensively, be especially careful not to let them come between you and your audience. Keep them covered or turn off the projector when you are not using them so the audience can concentrate on what *you* are saying. And when you do use visuals, keep looking at and focusing your attention on the audience as much as possible.

USE PROGRESSIVE VISUALS.   No matter how complex your material, keep the content of the screen, flip chart, overhead, or chalkboard simple. The point is: Don't risk having your audience's mind wander around the total display of your data. They might reach conclusions you don't want them to reach. You want to make sure the point that gets made is the point you *want* made.

Computer Aids for Your Oral Presentations

A number of software programs are designed to assist your presentations. With these software programs you can produce:

- Paper visuals for the overhead projector.
- Transparent overlays, if your printer is so equipped.
- 35mm slides by using special services.

You can make outlines and graphics. If you use overlays or slides, you can also have a paper copy to distribute to your participants for note taking.

Some programs (MORE, for example) practically construct the visual for you. You choose the format and supply the material. Other programs, such as PowerPoint, permit you to make the visuals yourself with the aids supplied by the program. They also supply accompanying speaker's notes. The former offers the advantage of ease; the latter, of flexibility. Many successful oral presentations have been made with both types.

To do so, you will need to control the order in which the audience perceives the data. So focus your visual on just those items you want them to concentrate on.

Start with one axis, and build on that foundation as your visuals progress. This strategy keeps the viewers from having to switch mentally from one basis to another. It can also be effective in showing the progression of your data. Keeping your basic visual, add or subtract lines or columns as you go. But don't add too much. Don't let your graphs or charts get too busy.

Let's suppose, for example, that you want to present a plan to double your firm's profits in five years. You will want to analyze the components of the profits and then show how to control specific items to arrive at the profit targets. One way to present such a plan *simply* and persuasively, without confusing the audience, is to follow the steps shown in Figure 15.1.

A word of warning. Be sure your audience can see your visuals clearly and can read them with understanding.

- Sometimes a room is too light for slides or overlays to be clearly visible.
- Sometimes an overhead image is distorted by window or room light.
- Sometimes the chalkboard or the flip chart is at the wrong angle or too far away for viewers to make it out.
- Sometimes an exhibit is too cluttered to be taken in during the brief time it's displayed.

Plan ahead so you can avoid these and similar problems. People become irritable if they have to strain to see or understand. Too often in business this irritation transfers over to your project—and even to your own reputation.

On the other hand, you will garner much credit if your visual presentation is clear, well coordinated, and professional. Capture your audience with wit and charm, and they're yours.

SECTION B: *Effective Speech Writing*

Businesspeople give speeches at civic group lunches and charity banquets. They speak at trade convention dinners and before local, state, and national business groups. They give talks at industry or intra-industry meetings. They serve on panels concerned with all sorts of currently important topics.

You may be asked to speak at such an occasion yourself. Or if you are inexperienced in business, it is more likely that you will be asked to write

1. Construct a grid—like this.

Year	1	2	3	4	5
Sales					
Cost of Sales					
Gross Profit					
Selling, General & Admin.					
Pre-Tax					

2. Now fill in the vertical column under Year 1.

Year	1	2	3	4	5
Sales	100				
Cost of Sales	70				
Gross Profit	30				
Selling, General & Admin.	20				
Pre-Tax	10				

3. Show the horizontal column for the Sales line.

   "Let's look at the sales projection over the next five years. Note the 10% constant growth."

Year	1	2	3	4	5
Sales	100	110	121	133	146
Cost of Sales					
Gross Profit					
Selling, General & Admin.					
Pre-Tax					

4. "Now let's compare Sales to Gross Profit and Cost of Sales." (Show only the 1st, 3rd and 5th years.)

Year	1	2	3	4	5
Sales	100		121		146
Cost of Sales	70		85		102
Gross Profit	30		36		44
Selling, General & Admin.					
Pre-Tax					

5. Now show Gross Profit, years 1–5.

Year	1	2	3	4	5
Sales					
Cost of Sales					
Gross Profit	30	33	36	40	44
Selling, General & Admin.					
Pre-Tax					

6. Show Selling, General and Administrative, the full horizontal line.

Year	1	2	3	4	5
Sales					
Cost of Sales					
Gross Profit					
Selling, General & Admin.	20	20	22	23	23
Pre-Tax					

7. "We show a constant growth in Sales of 10%, and a constant growth in Cost of Sales of 10%. Gross Profit also shows a constant growth of 10%."

Year	1	2	3	4	5
Sales	100	110	121	133	146
Cost of Sales	70	77	85	93	102
Gross Profit	30	33	36	40	44
Selling, General & Admin.					
Pre-Tax					

8. "We cannot control Cost of Sales, but with a constant growth in Sales of 10%, we can control expenditures for Selling, General and Administrative."

Year	1	2	3	4	5
Sales	100	110	121	133	146
Cost of Sales	70	77	85	93	102
Gross Profit	30	33	36	40	44
Selling, General & Admin.	20	20	22	23	23
	20%	18%	18%	17%	16%
Pre-Tax	10	13	14	17	21

FIGURE 15.1: A Progressive Visual

a speech for someone further up the hierarchy who has been asked to speak. In either case, here's the place to put to use everything you've learned about rhetoric and composition. In fact, it would not be wrong to define such a speech as *a spoken expository essay enhanced by audience interaction.*

CREATING A SPOKEN EXPOSITORY ESSAY

The purpose of business talks of this sort is mainly to instruct or persuade, but also to entertain. You represent your company well if you give your audience—or the audience of the speaker for whom you write—enough to ponder so as to make them glad they came. To do so, whether you write for yourself or for someone else, compose your speech much as you would compose an expository essay (the sort of essay commonly studied in a college freshman composition course). Focus it on an interesting central point, a thesis. By developing your thesis with sound and interesting support, you will persuade the audience to give serious thought to your points.

PREWRITE

Where do you find this thesis and support? Try the techniques for inventing reviewed on page 8. Or use your computer and run through the strategies discussed on pages 60–63.

You will most probably be given a topic. It might well be your answer to a variation of one of these questions, which are typical:

- What are the major issues confronting us all?
- What do you think is going to happen to the economy?
- What are your prognostications for the month? The year? The decade? The near term? The midterm? The out years?
- What are your suggestions for solving this particular current problem?
- Where do you stand on this current controversial issue?
- How is this new state budget [national law, world event, environmental contingency, etc.] going to affect our industry? Our community? Our interests? (A specific topic on this question might be: "How the political reapportionment mandated by the latest census will work out in our area and what it will mean for the funding of projects in your industry.")

Or if the engagement is to serve on a panel, the topic could be more general. It could be anything from sexual harassment in the workplace to health-care delivery services. But in that case you, or the person for whom you write, will probably have been chosen to represent a particular point of view on the subject.

If the invitation is to chair a charitable function, the topic for the short introductory speech would be a comment on the particular area the charity serves. (The National Council of Christians and Jews, for instance, might expect a few remarks on civil rights.)

Whatever the topic:

- Think about it, ask about it, research it.
- Decide what aspects of it would most appeal to the particular audience.
- Brainstorm it through free-writing or listing, whichever works better for you.
- Derive your thesis and support from your brainstorming.
- Structure your support so as to make your thesis most convincing.
- Write your plan. (If you will be speaking yourself, you may wish to work from a detailed outline rather than a finished text.)

WRITE AND REVISE

To write and revise your draft, you could not do better than to adapt the suggestions given in Chapter 1:

- Follow your plan (but change it as needed), and support your purpose in paragraphs. State each supporting or amplifying point clearly in a sentence (or heading) at or near the beginning of your paragraphs (or paragraph clusters).
- Be sure to demonstrate and/or develop each point concretely and specifically.
- Write in your own voice or that of your speaker. Write directly to your audience. Picture them as you write. What will interest them? What will persuade them?
- As you write, don't hesitate to work *recursively,* to pause and rethink and even revise as you go along.
- When you finish your draft, check your work for *clarity, unity,* and *coherence.* Edit as necessary. (For assistance, see pages 33–35, 65–67.)
- Reconsider your work. Try to read it as your audience will hear it. Revise as necessary.
- Correct errors and problems with syntax (sentence structure) or diction (word choice).

ENHANCING YOUR SPEECH WITH AUDIENCE INTERACTION

Following this advice should give you a good composition. But a speech is not just a composition. The immediate presence of the audience and the oral quality of the medium present challenging differences.

RELATE FAVORABLY TO YOUR AUDIENCE

In the first few minutes, members of the audience decide how comfortable they are with speakers and even judge how much respect or trust they are willing to give them and their ideas. Since audiences relate to a speaker one way or another, your aim as speaker is to make the relationship a good one—right from the start.

SPEAK FROM NOTES. If at all possible, do not read your speech. Have a conversation with your audience. You can rely on well-prepared notecards. Here's how:

- Triple-space your notes in speech-writer typeface[2] or print them clearly on each card. Use only one side.
- Turn your cards into a detailed outline of your speech: only one major point to a card.
- To give yourself confidence, make sure every phrase absolutely essential to your speech is on these cards—whether or not you ever actually have to refer to it. These essentials include:
—Your introduction.
—Your conclusion.
—Important transitional sentences as you move to new points.
—Effective turns of phrase.
—Key memory cues.

THE SPEECH

A good part of audience judgment is based on the personal presence of the speaker and the characteristics of delivery, subjects beyond the scope of this text (though see the Guidelines on page 427). But much also depends on what the speaker says.[3]

BEGIN EMPATHETICALLY. The introductory portion of your speech is crucial. Effective speakers almost invariably reach out to their audiences at this point—personally, emotionally, through the urgency of the topic, or imaginatively. You may want to try some of the following techniques that have proved successful.

Relating personally. Some speakers aim to identify with their audience. In so doing, they not only establish an intimacy but are often subtly flattering. Nadine Jackson-Smith, Communications Consultant

---

2. An oversized type font that makes speech text and notes easy to read.

3. You can study exactly what effective speakers say. Each month the best speeches given by North Americans are published in a journal called *Vital Speeches of the Day*. Before you write your first speech, you might want to look at the latest volume. The quotations in the following paragraphs have been selected from business executives' speeches recorded in Volume 55 (1988–89).

and Chief Public Information Officer, Washington State Department of Licensing, for example, uses this technique in her keynote address to a support-staff training conference (Washington State Attorney General's Office):

> . . . I am pleased to be with you today, because it brings back memories of my first real job. I worked as a secretary at the University of Washington and my office was located in the same wing as the Assistant Attorney General for Student Affairs.
>
> I was in awe of the support staff, all women. My father is a lawyer, so I was used to them; but these women really were role models for me. . . . To a young secretary just starting out, these women somehow seemed so professional, so sure of themselves. They were also rather snooty and so we weren't friendly. Yet, they were unwitting mentors for me, as I observed the way they went about their duties, the way they carried themselves; and I learned from them. (55:145)

This kind of personal opening has become fairly conventional. In fact, Robert J. Haugh, for instance, in using this strategy, feels it necessary to stress his sincerity. Haugh, Chairman and CEO of the St. Paul Companies, reminds his Minnesota Trial Lawyers Association audience that he too has a legal background and gets in a compliment as well:

> THANK YOU—I am very pleased to be here. That is the standard thing—for speakers to say—because it's not only polite—but they're expected to say something like that. But—my pleasure is indeed REAL—and SPECIAL—for two reasons.
>
> First—I am complimented—that you want to hear the St. Paul Companies' perspective—on issues that concern you. Second—as a lawyer myself—I am happy to appear before members of a profession—that is absolutely ESSENTIAL—to a free—and healthy—society. (55:152)

Relating emotionally.   Many effective speakers begin by telling a humorous or poignant anecdote. After all, if you can get your audience to join you in laughter or if you can touch them, you have them won. Beware of sentimentality, of course. But when you use a heart-tugging story appropriately, your audience can identify with you emotionally. John W. Johnstone, Jr., Chairman, President, and CEO of the Olin Corporation, uses such a narrative to good effect in addressing a White House Conference on getting the private sector involved in the war on drugs. He begins:

> On a sweltering night this past July, Everne Johnson was enjoying some fresh air outside of her housing project in South Norwalk, Connecticut. The 26-year-old woman was 8 months pregnant, and despite the poverty that surrounded her, she had high hopes that her own baby would grow up to enjoy a happy and fruitful life.

> She never got the chance to see her baby. Everne and another resident of the housing complex, 18-year-old Shawn Clemens, were gunned down in a hail of machine gun fire. . . . Norwalk police are still investigating this crime, but they believe that it involved a turf war between drug dealers from New York City and Fairfield County. There is no evidence that Everne or Shawn were involved with drugs. They were simply caught in the crossfire of a vicious, drug-related crime. (55:325)

A joke that goes well can also be especially warming. Nevertheless, we advise you to exercise caution before you begin in this way. A joke that falls flat falls very flat, and it can even prove offensive. You also have to be very sure of your audience before telling a story that is even a little off-color. David S. Tappan, Jr., Chairman and CEO of the Fluor Corporation, makes this caveat explicit when he begins a speech before an American Bar Association meeting by saying, ". . . You won't hear any tired, old lawyer jokes from me." As a rule of thumb, introduce with a funny story *only*:

- If you have the special energy and skill needed to put such a story over.
- If the story fits the audience.
- Especially, if the humorous story or the witty remark leads directly to or enhances what you really want to say.

Morton Egol, of Arthur Anderson, had to go back a few centuries to find a witty opening suitable for his talk on government accountability for the International Consortium of Government Financial Management, meeting in England:

> Four hundred years ago, Richard Hooker, a philosopher in Elizabethan England, said: "He that goeth about to persuade a multitude that they are not as well governed as they ought to be, shall never want for attentive and agreeable listeners."
>
> The mere fact that 400 years later I can travel across an ocean that Mr. Hooker never crossed, and repeat this saying to an international group of government officials from 31 countries, who knowingly chuckle at it, is proof enough of its enduring truth. (55:149)

Relating through the urgency of the topic. The speaker says the subject is so urgent that "you and I have to talk about it together *right now*." This technique is similar to identifying personally with the audience. But the speaker does not claim "we are inherently alike," but rather "we are here to work on this urgent problem together." Lawyer Fulton Haight adopts this strategy in discussing medical malpractice lawsuits with the Congress of Neurological Surgeons:

Good morning, ladies and gentlemen. It is a pleasure to have the opportunity to address you this morning. As I began to prepare this talk, it quickly became apparent that you don't need either humor or sympathy, you need help. So if I may, I will dive right in with my analysis. (55:180)

Relating imaginatively. Other effective speakers stir an imaginative response in their audience by opening with an anecdote or quotation analogous to their point. The trick here is that the analogy must be pertinent. The audience identifies when they sense the pertinence. For example, Robert A. Ferchat, President of Northern Telecom Canada, begins his talk about the role of chaos in stimulating business creativity and innovation with an analogy to the space program:

Good morning. Just 20 years ago this summer, the world was celebrating the first man on the moon. Imagine. Already, 20 years. It seems somehow impossible that it can be that long since Neil Armstrong took his walk.

Imagine, too, the dismay in the space program in 1961 when President Kennedy kicked the space race into high gear with his announcement that the U.S. would put a man on the moon by the end of the decade. Nothing like the boss setting impossible goals to set off a few shock waves in the ranks.

I wasn't there, but I suspect those shock waves created many chaotic times for the people involved. . . . But out of that chaos came success—not only in the great mission of which Kennedy spoke, but also in spin-off technologies that are fundamental to our way of life today. (55:727)

CONCLUDE MEMORABLY. Build your speech to its conclusion. And make that conclusion compelling. It's what your audience will best remember and what they will carry away with them. Be sure to restate your thesis in its most convincing form. The most effective speeches conclude with a resounding request for agreement, commitment, or action, often in inspiring words, sometimes wittily phrased, frequently including a quotation. Often, the speakers invite their audiences into their thinking with rhetorical questions. For example:

Tom Siddon, Canadian Minister of Fisheries and Ocean, addressing the International Business and Investment Exposition on the subject of free trade:

The wave of the future is not constrained to regeneration; it is the liberation of the enterprise of free nations, free men and free women. Together on the North American Continent, we Canadians and American neighbours are riding with the tide of the future. (55:224)

Peter L. Scott, Chairman and Chief Executive of the Emhart Corporation, addressing the Arthur W. Page Society:

I hope I have stimulated you . . . maybe I've provoked you . . . certainly, I think, I've challenged you. I also recognize that I have asked you to stick your necks out and take risks. Is it my right to do this?

Let me close by answering it this way . . . As CEO's, we suffer no shortage of advice on how to be leaders. Some of it's relevant, most of it's common sense, some of it is naive. It all comes down to a philosophy of life. Nearly 90 years ago, Teddy Roosevelt said it better than I can. He said in a speech . . . and I paraphrase.

It is far better to dare mighty things . . . to win glorious triumphs . . . even endure some failures . . . than to be only those poor spirits who never taste victory, or suffer death because they live in a gray twilight zone of no risk safety. (55:126)

C. William Gray, Vice President of Human Resources, B. F. Goodrich, addressing the Machinery and Allied Products Institute on the health-care crisis:

Let's form partnerships with others involved in this problem to find solutions that are in everyone's best interest. For example. . . .

We have our work cut out for us. Let's get on with the job and take the steps necessary now to help solve this health-care crisis. (55:387)

B. M. Thompson, Executive Vice President of Phillips Petroleum, addressing the Coalition for Responsible Waste Incineration:

Twenty years from now will our fear of risk have buried us beneath a mountain of trash? I don't think so. Not if science, industry, the government and the public begin now to establish an integrated waste management system.

. . . Together, we can truly say good riddance to our wretched refuse. Thank you for the opportunity to share my views. (55:687)

Using a circular structure. A circular structure to a speech offers the opportunity to conclude with a particularly satisfying sense of closure. With this sort of organization, you begin with a striking quotation, metaphor, bit of rhetoric. You explain your subject in terms of this analogy, echo it verbally once or twice throughout the speech, and conclude with a final reference to it.

At the end of his speech, Morton Egol, for instance, returns to the Hooker quotation with which he began and uses it effectively:

No doubt, however much progress is made, Richard Hooker's admonition will continue to be regarded as testimony to the inevitable friction between government and the governed. . . .

Consider the quote again not as a joke, but with a sense of what can be accomplished in the future where enlightened political leaders use the power of information in the interest of innovation and accountability: "He that goeth. . . ."

It may be too much to ask, to visualize a world in which that quote is a testimony to man's ability to govern himself; but it is the world we need to create, if we are going to meet the challenges of the next millennium. (55:152)

And having summed up his suggestions for the "big role . . the private sector can play . . . in combatting drug abuse," John W. Johnstone, Jr., uses a circular structure to bring the audience back to the tragic consequences of a drug-ridden society with which he began:

If we are truly allowed to employ these tools in an effective manner, we will be able to cut deeply into substance abuse. True, we might never see the day when we can proclaim America drug-free, but we can measure our progress in lives saved and lives redeemed. If you don't think that amounts to much, ask the families and friends of people like Everne Johnson, Shawn Clemens and Mary Boucher-Javery. (55:327)

■ SPEECH WORKOUT ■

1. Closely analyze two of the quoted introductions. Point out the strategies used by the speaker. Evaluate them and explain your assessment.
2. Closely analyze two of the quoted conclusions. Point out the strategies used by the speaker. Evaluate them and explain your assessment.

HOW TO HANDLE THE AURAL CHALLENGE

An audience for a speech is likely to be larger, less specialized, and often less vitally interested than an audience for an oral presentation. The room is also frequently larger, and often there is the further distraction of a meal. In such circumstances, audience comprehension problems are intensified. All the suggestions for ensuring that your audience understands thus become doubly important when you give a speech.

BE BRIEF. BE SIMPLE. BE CLEAR. Remember especially to:

- Keep your speech short and lively.
- Let your audience anticipate your ideas.
- Give (or hint at) your thesis early on.
- Share the structure of your talk with the audience; and remind them of that structure as you move from point to point.
- Reinforce important ideas through repetition.

- Be especially careful to clarify transitions from one idea to another, because your audience must follow your argument here or become lost.
- Summarize as needed throughout; and be sure to bring it all together at the end.

CONSIDER A THREE-PART ORGANIZATION. A three-part structure seems to have become conventional.[4] American audiences have learned to anticipate it; and, therefore, material organized in this way is clearer to them.

■ **GUIDELINES** ■

Delivery

Here are some pointers to remember as you give your address:

1. Your own state of mind is crucial. It's infectious. If you are enthusiastic, excited about your material, and have a high level of energy, your audience will catch your enthusiasm.
2. Be sure you can be heard throughout the room. Have the microphones adjusted properly for you before you begin. Project your voice. Be careful especially with the ends of phrases or sentences. (If you have a tendency to swallow your words, practice not doing so well before the day of your speech.)
3. Public speaking is performing. Put color in your voice. Think about the words as you say them. Give them the appropriate emphasis. Vary your tone and your pitch appropriately. Don't rush.
4. Have a trusted colleague listen to you rehearse (or tape-record a rehearsal) to discover if you are burdened with speech mannerisms such as "And uh," "You know," and "Okay?" If you use such expressions habitually, try hard to break the habit. They can be irritating to an audience.
5. Read your audience. Be alert for signs that they are becoming bored, confused, mad, or dead. Watch eye contact and body English. Pay attention to ambient noises—chairs creaking, people coughing, paper rattling, pens tapping. Should you notice such signs:

   - Liven up your presentation. Say something a bit startling; ask a question; move about; skip over the duller matter and get more quickly to the good stuff.
   - Summarize or repeat any important material they may have missed while dozing.

---

4. Almost all the business executives quoted in the *Vital Speeches* volume used a threefold structure. Interestingly enough, however, they did not all use the same organization: Some presented their thesis and used three points to support it, and others counted their thesis as one of their three points.

WRITING A SPEECH FOR SOMEONE ELSE

Your supervisor or your supervisor's supervisor has accepted an invitation to speak. Considerations for public relations or politics within the industry made this "an invitation not to be refused." Yet this is your company's busy time, and the invited executive is one of the busiest during this period. Though the impression made by the speech will be important, it is very far from number one on the executive's must-do list. In short, you've been asked to write the speech.

HOW TO BEGIN   **MAKE A SCHEDULE.** Start just as soon as you get the assignment. Speech writing for someone else takes time. Time for conferral. Time for many drafts. Time for comments and approvals by many people. Think it through. Set up a tentative schedule. Then you can show your savvy by arriving at your first interview with the invited speaker with your draft schedule (marked "draft schedule") in hand.

INTERVIEW THE SPEAKER. When you write a speech for someone else, that person *may* have some idea of what he or she wants to say. Or *may not*. You will have to interview skillfully and sensitively to find out—especially if the speaker's rank is high. What does he or she want to get across in this speech? Take careful notes. Were any guidelines suggested by the inviting group? Are there any speeches you might look at that the speaker especially admires?

When the speaker has few ideas. Try to sense the executive's needs. It may be that he or she hasn't got an idea in the world on the topic. Such a situation is not uncommon—especially if the speech is for an activity outside the business. Executives want the speech to be good, to be well written, and to say something important. But they haven't time to think about what it should say. That's your job—this is one of those "please handle" assignments we told you about.

If you sense that this is the case, having sounded the executive out as far as you could on the subject, tactfully ask if there is someone else you might speak to about it or some reading you might do. And make note of any suggestions offered. Then propose that you do some preliminary research and get back later with an outline and a tack to take.

COMPOSE THE   As for the actual writing process, for the most part follow the approach you
SPEECH   use when writing a speech for yourself. Of course, you must write this speech out in full, even if the speaker chooses to give it with notecards. In that not very usual case, he or she will make cards (or ask you to make cards) from your fully written speech. But as for structure, format, and content, you should find that the advice in this chapter continues to be useful.

You will want to protect your speaker from criticism or embarrassment. A caution or two are thus in order.

- Adopt a modest tone in the introduction. The higher the rank of your speaker, the greater the need for modesty. The very importance of the position that got your executive the speaking engagement may tend to intimidate the audience. In a 1989 speech, John G. Smale, then Chairman of the Board and Chief Executive of Procter & Gamble, having suggested that he will speak about public policy, offers a modest disclaimer for himself and an attractive—and topic-appropriate—pride in his company when he says:

  > I speak not because I have all the answers. I am not a lawyer or an economist. But I hope I can bring to this discussion a useful perspective. My perspective naturally grows out of my own experience. But it grows as well out of the hard-won values of a company that has successfully served its owners—and the public interest generally—for 151 years. (55:330)

- Be especially careful with the humor you include. Ask yourself, could that funny opening story offend any part of the public? An ethnic or professional group? Women? The elderly?
- Study the implication of your language. A busy executive may take your speech and use it—jokes and all—without considering the ramifications. So *you* consider them before you give her or him the speech.
- Test for embarrassing tongue twisters by reading the entire speech aloud before you submit it.

A public mistake can be devastating—especially if the speaker is prominent in her industry, a leader in his field. Be cautious. The speaker's reputation depends on you.

SECTION C: *Effective Job Interviewing*

The most important oral communication you may ever undertake in your business career is, of course, a job interview. And you should prepare for it as carefully as you would construct an oral presentation or write a speech.

Job interviewing is a two-sided undertaking. It should provide information for the applicant and information for the employer, so that a mutual decision can be made. As director of the interview, the company representative is—and should be—firmly in charge. But you'd be surprised at how much control you, the applicant, can have over the exchange of information.

PREPARING FOR THE INTERVIEWS

By careful preparation, you can almost always be sure that you will find out what you need to know about the position and that the interviewers will learn what you want them to know about you.

RESEARCH

Research the job for both purposes:

- To gain the knowledge you need to ask the questions that will help you decide about the position.
- To find out what you will want the interviewers from this specific business to know about you. You will also find that some familiarity with what your interviewer may tell you about the nature of the job will help you respond more intelligently. (Besides, coming in prepared in this way would impress most interviewers with your interest and diligence.)

WHAT DO YOU NEED TO KNOW? You need to know everything you can learn about the company, the industry or sector to which it belongs, what's going on with them currently, and what is on the horizon for them. You also need to find out as much as you can about the particular job you are applying for: What exactly do people holding such a position do—at that company and elsewhere? What salary do they make and what is the salary for comparable positions?

WHERE CAN YOU FIND THE INFORMATION? The best source of information is still word of mouth. So follow every lead you hear of, but cautiously evaluate all such data in terms of how knowledgeable your informants are. The library can be helpful too.

Sources. These sources are likely to prove useful:

- *People you know in the company.* Friends in business or in that industry. Lawyers and journalists also are often quite knowledgeable about local business affairs.
- *The company's annual report.* Call the public relations department and ask for one. Or check the business department of a large metropolitan library for *Compact Disclosure* services (see page 217).
- *The New York Times Index* or *The Wall Street Journal Index.* To find everything currently newsworthy, check the listing for your company's name, industry, and product.
- *Current Department of Labor publications.* These can also be useful—and they contain comparative salary information by industry.

Don't neglect such preparation. This interview is at least as crucial as a college exam.

| REHEARSE

DISCOVER WHAT YOU WANT TO GET ACROSS. After you've gathered all the information you can, you will need to decide exactly what you want to get across to your interviewers. Review your résumé, the letter you sent to the company, and any other relevant credentials (a portfolio of your work, for instance). Thoughtfully consider them in terms of what you have learned about the job. Decide:

> What about your character, your qualifications, or your experience makes you a good fit for the position?

Jot down your answer in list form. For each point, also jot down the facts that support it. For example:

```
The job description says the position requires ini-
tiative--After a series of muggings last year on our
campus, I organized an escort service and got it
authorized.
```

Think about it some more and revise your list until you're happy with it—and really believe it. That's important. Your belief in yourself and "the fit" is what will convince your interviewers.

TRY IT OUT. Now that you've learned what you want the interviewers to know about you, figure out how you will get it across. Practice answering questions typically asked and see where you can fit in the points on your list. Here are some typical questions:

- What can you tell us about yourself?
- How did you happen to choose this career?
- Why would you like to work here?

Interviewers also frequently derive questions from your résumé. They usually have it in front of them as they talk with you. Some will inquire about interesting points on it ("How did you happen to minor in Philosophy?" "Tell me about the exhibition where your painting won a ribbon"). So practice getting what you want to say into answers to that sort of question, too.

Practice. When you have your ideas in hand, rehearse with a trusted friend—an especially useful idea if your friend has had some business experience.

| CONCLUDING
| QUESTIONS
| AND SUMMARY

One final preparation. Almost invariably before your interview is over, you will be asked if you have anything more you would like to ask or add. You probably still have some questions about the company, and here is the place to ask them. But again, you should come prepared. Here is the sort of questions that show appropriate concern:

- What do you see as the career path for this position?
- Is there a good potential for growth here?
- What do you like most about this company? Least?
- What view does senior management take of the growth potential of this department?

Phrase your questions politely and with respect, but don't hesitate to ask a penetrating question. What questions should you avoid? You probably shouldn't inquire too closely about benefits until after the job is offered.

CLOSING SUMMARY. We hope you will have managed to cover all that you want the company to know about you by the conclusion of the interview. But it's a good idea to prepare and practice a statement summarizing how you think you can be useful to the company and expressing your appreciation. You might make such a remark as you rise to leave.

FACING YOUR INTERVIEWERS

If you are interviewed by companies large enough to have a personnel department, you will almost certainly have at least two interviews: one with personnel people and another one or two with people in the department where you would be working.[5] The personnel representative may interview you on campus or at the company. The second interview may follow after a preliminary decision about you has been made, or it may be scheduled on the same day (almost surely so if you are making an out-of-town visit). The departmental interviewers make the decision. The purposes of the two kinds of interviews are not the same. The basic difference is that while the departmental people are looking at you to see if they can fit you in, the personnel staff is observing you to see if they should screen you out.

THE PERSONNEL DEPARTMENT INTERVIEW

The job of the personnel department is to make the first cut. They cut on the basis of rather conventional criteria. In the first place, they check for the education and experience the position requires. Their inquiries here, however, are necessarily general. Often they are just working from a job description. For this interview, therefore, be sure that you can demonstrate in detail how you meet the specified criteria. Or, if you do not completely meet them, come prepared to offer substitute qualifications or to show why your qualifications should be considered satisfactory. If your explanation

---

5. If you apply to a smaller concern, your interview will probably be the kind we call departmental.

is good enough, you might even be able to turn a shortcoming to your advantage. For example, if you fell a bit short of the company's preferred 3.5 GPA, you might show you were able to achieve a 3.3 even though you were required to work nights to pay your way through college.

Another job of personnel department interviewers is to check candidates for general conformity to their corporate culture. They watch for the qualities listed in the sidebar on page 434. Courteous, well-groomed, well-spoken people are valued in most businesses.

The interviewers also want to find out if you are healthy, reliable, and sensible. Sometimes they even pose trick questions for this purpose. They might, for example, ask, "Would you expect to give your job your entire, undivided attention?" The question is meant to screen out fanatics or the dishonest. The answer they are looking for is something like this: "Of course, I would be willing to devote that sort of attention to my work during periods of emergency. But ordinarily I have responsibilities also to my family and friends, and I would expect to go on living a balanced life." Answer all their questions thoughtfully and truthfully , and rely on your own common sense.

THE DEPARTMENTAL INTERVIEW

Personnel people usually want to find someone clearly in the business mainstream, but the departmental interviewers are looking for someone who stands out. They are hoping to hear you say something that shows you have a special viewpoint on—or analytical ability for—the sort of problems they need to solve in that job. How do you show them? Pay close attention. Empathize with your interviewers. Be sensitive to what they are looking for. Be truthful in your answers, but phrase them so that the interviewers will see that you understand what they are looking for.

Let's say, for instance, that you're applying for a job in public relations. The personnel people will probably pass you on to a departmental review if you say nothing tactless or unguarded. But you will need to let the departmental interviewers understand that you know how to handle a delicate situation smoothly and that you can think on your feet. If they ask you a difficult question, you've got to come back with a smooth reply.

Suppose you are asked: "Are you a people person?" You might reply:

"Yes, I think I am. I like very much having contact with people. I enjoy working with others, rather than alone."

If the question came from a personnel interviewer, you might let the answer stand right there. For the departmental interviewers, however, you might choose to build a bridge that will get you over to what *you* want to emphasize. For example, you might say:

"Yes, I think I am. I like very much having contact with people. I enjoy working with others, rather than alone. *But if you are asking me*

Company Manners

We like to think that important decisions about hiring are made on the basis of a rational comparative assessment of the qualifications of an applicant. And, doubtlessly, most of those who must decide try to make their decisions in this way. But human nature being what it is, the interviewer's impressions of a candidate are often crucial—particularly the first impression. You thus disregard your appearance, your manners, and your mannerisms at your peril. We can't guarantee that the advice given below will get you the position. But you will not lose out on a position by following it.

Manners and Mannerisms

- Be prompt. (Arrive about 10 minutes ahead of time so that you are sure not to be late and so you will have a few minutes to gather your thoughts.)
- Look your interviewer in the eye.
- Smile.
- Shake hands firmly.
- Sit when you are invited to do so, but not before.
- Sit comfortably, but don't slouch.
- Try not to fidget.
- Don't smoke.
- Don't eat—unless you are invited to join your interviewer in a cup of coffee or tea.
- Don't chew gum.
- Watch for signs the interview is coming to a close. And shake hands again as you leave.
- Other than that—be yourself!

Your Appearance

- Dress like the people whose ranks you want to join: business executives dress conservatively.
- Appear clean and well groomed. Your hair should be newly trimmed and neatly combed; your nails clean and cared for. (It's odd how many people notice nails.) Do not wear a heavy scent.
- *Women:*
  —It is no longer mandatory to wear a suit; on the other hand, a skirt and jacket are the one outfit that is *always* right.
  —Wear a skirt in any case. (You can wear slacks later, if you find that the corporate culture approves them.)
  —Wear stockings and sensible shoes (no sneakers; no sandals).
  —No matter what fashion decrees—and even in a fashion-forward industry—do not wear miniskirts, plunging necklines, masses of ruffles, wild prints, or heavy or extreme jewelry.
- *Men:*
  —Wear a jacket and tie.
  —Be pressed and polished. But be comfortable in your clothes. It is best to wear new clothes once or twice before the interview.
  —Be newly shaved; if you wear a beard or mustache, be sure it is neatly trimmed.

Your Speech

- Be confident, but not cocky.
- Say *nothing* derogatory.
- If asked for information that might reflect badly on a former employer or an earlier interviewer, say that you don't know much about that.
- Don't evaluate somebody else's performance or character—even if your interviewer seems to be inviting such comment.
- Don't gossip. Your interviewer will assume that if you are careless with information about another company, you will be so with theirs.
- Don't be embarrassed if your tongue gets tangled or you misspeak. Just catch your breath, back up, smile, and do it again, right.

if I like everyone I meet—of course, I don't. Not *everyone*. But for a PR person, it seems to me the challenge is to handle the situation smoothly whether you like the people or not." [Bridge in italics]

FINDING THE FIT; MAKING THE MATCH. The departmental people, those who will make the final decision, are, like you, looking for a fit: they are looking for a person whose interests and skills—current and potential—fit the job they need done.

Perhaps equally important, they are looking for a person whose way of looking at the world fits their own. It's a well-known but little-discussed fact that people tend to hire themselves. They are naturally drawn to people who share their values, people they are comfortable with. And here is where empathy comes in again. Sometimes empathetic identification *seems* harder when the interviewer is of a gender, race, religion, or social class different from your own. And perhaps, at first, these superficial differences might offer a barrier. But real empathy, from one human being to another, should see you through.

Our advice again, then, is: Empathize with your interviewers. Be sensitive to what they are looking for. Be yourself. But show that part of yourself that will best fit into the demands of the particular job and of the particular corporate community. If you find it easy to empathize with the people in the department, the fit is probably good. Chances are that this would be a good position for you, and that your interviewers will think so too.

▬▬▬▬▬ AUTHENTIC BUSINESS PROBLEMS ▬▬▬▬▬

1. Prepare and present an oral presentation using:
   - The information and material you gathered for the report you wrote for Chapter 9.
   - Or the material you gathered for your case study in the Focus Segment on Individual Business Problems.
   - Or material you have garnered in one of your other courses.
   - Or material you are currently working on professionally.
2. Find a partner to act as interviewer, and rehearse an interview with the company you addressed your cover letter to in Chapter 11.

FOCUS:
Collaborative Business Problems and Assignments

MANAGEMENT TEAMS

One great strength of the corporate model is that it can assemble experts from a variety of fields into teams to make the best use of their individual strengths. The whole becomes greater than the sum of its parts. This Segment's case studies are designed to give you experience with real business problems, working in the configuration of a *management team*.

COLLABORATIVE WRITING

As these typical assignments suggest, management-team problems involve complex communications and usually written documents. Teams collaborate on the writing; but not in the way you might think. As Barbara Couture and Jane Rymer write in analyzing a Wayne State University study of 400 business professionals:

> "Collaboration" usually does not involve producing a document with a group. Rather it typically represents simple interaction—either before or after drafting.[1]

The study found that businesspeople often write important documents after a planning discussion, then revise after receiving feedback. Special assignments, like those this Segment proposes, are sometimes handled by group planning, with individuals writing and a team member acting as editor to coordinate the project. Your group may want to try these methods too.

SUGGESTIONS FOR COMPLETING THE ASSIGNMENTS

1. Take on the identity of a company team or task force member. Choose your position and, insofar as is possible, *become* that person. Think from that point of view, as that person would be likely to think in helping to solve the problem for the company.

2. Do not feel that you have to hold many full-scale team meetings with formal agendas and Robert's Rules of Order to carry out the assignments.

   The method of operation for a typical business management team is highly pragmatic, and yours can be too. For example, one team might hold an initial meeting to assess the problem and parcel out assignments. Then they might conduct the entire project by phone, with one

---

1. "Interactive Writing on the Job: Definitions and Implications of 'Collaboration,'" in Myra Kogen, ed., *Writing in the Business Professions* (Urbana, Ill.: National Council of Teachers of English, 1989): 74.

person functioning informally as a coordinator of the final report. Another team might wish to meet briefly every few days to check on how the work is progressing and to make needed adjustments.

3. Take a portion of the overall assignment to work on yourself.
4. Keep in touch with your team members between meetings; consult with them in small groups or in quick one-to-one meetings in the halls or over lunch.
5. Contribute what you are committed to contribute to the effort, on time and in professional form—typed, proofed, and signed, with proper copies.
6. Get together to plan the final report so that every member can contribute expertise and research findings.
7. Throughout the project, if you are efficient and effective in your individual work and contribute to the overall product, you will carry out the spirit of the assignment in the manner of a real business team or task force.

ASSIGNMENT ONE: THE SINISTER TEDDY BEAR
(Communications for a Product Recall)

For purposes of this assignment, assume the identity of one of the employees of either Slade's or Toybears, Inc. Operating from that point of view, work with your own team to come up with a solution to the problem that will satisfy the consumer safety issue, the legal compliance issue, the profit and loss issue for both companies, and the customer relations problem for Toybears, Inc. Prepare a report for your CEO, using the information provided and making whatever recommendations you feel should be made to carry out a sensible strategy.

THE SCENARIO   **PROBLEM AT SLADE'S.** In late January of 19——, a customer walked into the toy department of Slade's, a large downtown department store, to return a Christmas present that she had bought there for her three-year-old nephew. The toy she wanted to return was a teddy bear, called Phurry Bear. The woman was concerned because, in watching her small nephew hug his Christmas present, she had noticed what looked like a headless pin protruding from the bear's abdomen. She had taken the bear, squeezed it herself, and extracted two more of the pinlike objects. The alert sales clerk, Lani Stewart, made a refund, apologized to the customer, and then called the store's general counsel in the administrative offices.

The general counsel, Sara Elizabeth Brevard, who is herself the mother of two small daughters, collected several of the bears from stock, took them back to her office, and cut them open. She also cut open the returned bear and found four or five more of the headless pins. She found no pins in the bears from the stock shelves. Nevertheless, she was worried, and she called in Jim Jacobs—the headquarters lawyer in charge of product safety at Slade's parent company. They began an investigation.

They eviscerated more bears. In one of them, they found several pins. In all, they discovered that, on average, one out of five of the bears in a random stock sample had pins in it.

CONSUMER PRODUCT SAFETY COMMISSION (CPSC) NOTIFIED. Because the two lawyers believed that a young child could be injured by being cut or by ingesting one of the metal slivers, they considered the risk serious enough to be reportable to the Consumer Product Safety Commission. Accordingly, they made that report and notified the toy's supplier, Toybears, Inc., that they had done so. The supplier manufactures bears both in this country and abroad, but the Phurry Bears were made under license in an Asian factory, for import and sale in the United States.

The Consumer Product Safety Commission will investigate, and if it deems the problem a *substantial product hazard,* it may require that Toybears "recall" the bears and replace or modify them. The recall procedure is commonly accompanied by considerable publicity, because the CPSC guidelines require it. The problem must be widely publicized to reach consumers who might be exposed to the hazard.

TOYBEARS, INC., NOTIFIED. When the Slade's lawyers called Toybears, Inc., they reached Nell Leighton—the administrative assistant to Toybears' CEO, John Houghton. At that time, Houghton was in Europe on another buying trip, but his assistant reached him by telephone, and he told her that he would divert his travel schedule to Hong Kong and visit the factory where the Phurry Bears are manufactured. He would investigate and call her with his findings.

THE SOURCE OF THE PROBLEM. When Houghton looked into the overseas process, he discovered that the stuffing for the bears had been purchased from small jobbers, who collect and buy clean waste material from the manufacturing process used to produce cotton flannel for men's shirts. During the brushing process that produces the characteristically soft, slightly napped flannel, fine metal tines from the roller brushes sometimes break off and fall into the waste material. Although the jobbers who bought this waste for resale claim that their cleaning process removes any metal pieces with a magnet, obviously that process had proved ineffective.

THE BEAR. Toybears sold 1.2 million Phurry Bears to Slade's and another 400,000 to other stores across the company. Phurry Bear is a chubby little bear with large, appealing brown eyes and a black leather nose. Slade's and other stores featured him in many pre-Christmas promotions, and the bears have sold well. In fact, they have already accounted for about 35% of Toybears' Christmas sales. Christmas revenues make up more than 60%

of a total year's business for a company like Toybears, so the stakes are large.

Toybears' *wholesale cost* per bear from the foreign supplier was $3.50. With shipping, warehousing, etc., the *landed cost* was $6.00. Toybears, Inc., sold the 1.2 million bears to Slade's at a *delivered cost* of $9.00 per bear. Prices to other customers who bought fewer were between $9.50 and $10. The *bear retails* for about $18.00.

| THE COMPANIES | **TOYBEARS, INC.** Toybears, Inc., was founded six years ago by its present CEO, John Houghton. It is a closely held corporation. Its products, stuffed toy animals, have met with great success, and its present annual sales exceed $_____. Houghton had worked for a large toy importer before he founded Toybears, and he invested in the business all of an inheritance and some money borrowed from his father-in-law. This is the first year he expects to turn a substantial profit—largely because of landing the huge order for Phurry Bears from Slade's Department Stores. He is eager for this relationship with Slade's to expand, because Slade's itself, as the largest department store in its rural three-state region, is potentially a good repeat customer. In addition, Slade's was bought last year by Annexa, Inc., a large chain of department stores that operates in nine states. It is common for buyers throughout stores in the chain to exchange ideas during their seasonal market meetings in New York, so if the Phurry Bear promotion is successful, word could spread through the Annexa chain and Houghton's business could increase dramatically. |

Personnel at Toybears, Inc., include the following:

John Houghton, Chairman and CEO. Houghton is 43, a kind and decent man, the father of two daughters and one son. His children are all teenagers, and he is an attentive father. The family has always been intimately involved in the business. In fact, Ellen Houghton, John's wife, designed the first prototype of Phurry Bear.

Larissa Harris, Partner in Nedick and Klotter, the law firm that serves as Toybears, Inc.'s outside counsel. Educated at a large Eastern law school, Harris came to Nedick and Klotter four years ago. She accepted the job because she thought that working in a large firm with corporate clients would give her an opportunity to deal with a wide variety of legal situations and be good experience toward deciding whether or not she would like to specialize further. Lately she has handled a number of product liability cases for the firm, and she is particularly interested in this case.

Joe Lugarno, Manager of Shipping Services for Toybears, Inc. Joe has worked for the company since it was founded and is intensely loyal to Houghton. Joe is an ambitious young man who believes the job at Toybears will grow as he continues to learn. He has enrolled in business management classes at his local university extension, and, methodical and orderly by nature, he personally keeps meticulous records of Toybears, Inc.'s inventory and shipments. He should be able to tell his team when the bears in question were received in his shipping room, from what supplier they came, and in what condition they were shipped out to the customer. He also knows what shipments are still due to arrive from the supplier in question, and he has already taken steps to isolate these particular products for further examination when they arrive. He will instruct the four shipping clerks who report to him that they are not to fill any future orders for these toys without his express knowledge.

Nell Leighton, Administrative Assistant to Houghton. Nell attended Wilsboro College in Wilsboro, Ohio, where she majored in business. When she moved to New Jersey, where Toybears, Inc., is located, she held several temporary jobs in other importing and manufacturing businesses; but last year she met Ellen Houghton at a toy fair, and Ellen was impressed with Nell's ideas for toy marketing. When John decided that his heavy travel schedule required him to find some help with marketing and administration, Ellen remembered Nell and recommended her to John as a candidate for the assistant's job. Nell feels fortunate to have a chance to learn the business from the ground up, and she is eager to prove her worth to the company.

Additional Toybears, Inc., scenario. The first thing Nell Leighton did was to call Larissa Harris, who told Nell some disturbing things.

- Neither Slade's nor Toybears, Inc.'s other retail customers would like to be associated with having sold a toy that might bring harm to a child, but *the responsibility belongs principally to Toybears, Inc.* So far, there have been no known injuries; but if a child *should* be injured, Toybears, Inc., could have considerable liability exposure. This would be particularly true if it could be shown that the company had known about the hazard and had *failed to warn* those who could be injured.

- Toybears, Inc., *could* stonewall, taking the position that the defective bears found among Slade's inventory were just an isolated incident. But the Slade's attorneys have already reported the incident to the Consumer Product Safety Commission, which has begun an investigation. At the end of the investigation, which could take some time, the CPSC will make a determination as to whether the defect constitutes a *substantial product hazard.* The Commission may then order a *recall* and a replacement or modification of the product for each consumer. Any penalties that might ultimately be imposed by the Commission would take serious account of whether or not the company had cooperated to protect the safety of consumers.

- At this point, it is not known whether any other wholesale customers have returned bears because of defects, so Joe Lugarno, who manages the shipping department for Toybears, Inc., will have to investigate his returns records.

- Also at issue is how Toybears, Inc., will respond to Slade's. Slade's will of course expect that Toybears will make some adjustment for defective bears to cover their returns, and how this delicate customer relations problem is handled could determine whether or not Slade's continues to buy from Toybears, Inc., in the future.

The assignment. *Handle* this for your CEO. He wants your team to assess the situation and, by the time he returns, have a memo on his desk that will enable him to make a decision to limit the damage. You need to assess the possible damage to your company in all respects—*monetary cost* as well as *business reputation.* Make sure that he has *all* the information he will need to make a decision. And make sure that you recommend what you think best. Do any research necessary (start at the library) to understand what the requirements of the CPSC might be, and use the information given here to construct your strategy. The relationship with Slade's, an important customer, is riding on your handling of this problem. And you need to find out whether any other stores that are Toybears customers have had any problems as well. For the company's sake, however, take care not to publicize the problem too widely in the early stages of your project until you know all the facts.

Since this is a legally delicate problem, you will need to be in touch with your company's counsel at every stage of your investigation; and since anything you write down could turn up as evidence in a regulatory or court proceeding, you will want to measure every written word.

Write whatever communications you believe necessary, both internal and external, to handle the problem. These might include, but not be restricted to:

- Reports to your outside or in-house counsel.
- The full report, with recommendations and cost analyses, to your CEO.
- A memo to the person in charge of your inventory to ask for information.
- Letters to Slade's and/or other suppliers.
- Letters or calls to the CPSC, etc.

You have also had a call from the local paper, which has got wind of the situation from somebody in one of Slade's stores and wants to talk with you. Decide how you will handle that (will you think it necessary to coordinate what you say with Slade's?), and report what you do to your CEO.

SLADE'S. For more than 60 years, Slade's has been the principal department store in the medium-size Southern city where its founding family is a pillar of the community. Last year, Slade's was acquired by Annexa, Inc., a large retail holding company based in Dallas. Annexa operates nearly 300 stores in nine Southern and Southwestern Sunbelt states.

The states immediately surrounding Slade's home city are relatively rural. Because Slade's draws customers from the entire three- or four-state area, it does a substantial business. Last year, its annual sales were probably $_____, though there is no hard evidence for that, since Annexa does not report the sales of its divisions.

Slade's is an institution. Generations of brides have bought their gowns and their trousseaux there; families have furnished their households from Slade's and clothed their children. For many years, Slade's has functioned almost as a community center, hosting civic luncheons and visiting dignitaries, and presenting a biennial world's fair of crafts. Additionally, it has for many years been an important contributor to both charitable and arts organizations in every community in which it operates stores.

For many women, a day of shopping and lunch in Slade's tearoom is a weekly ritual. Slade's customers are loyal and trust the store to provide high-quality merchandise and to stand behind everything it sells. The store has long maintained a testing laboratory that screens fabrics for such things as flammability and durability. In short, Slade's functions as a responsible corporate citizen and is proud of its reputation as a community institution and benefactor.

Personnel at Slade's include the following:

Sara Elizabeth Brevard, Slade's corporate counsel, has lived in Slade's flagship city all her life. She attended a prestigious Southern law school, and Slade's is her second career job. She began her career in one of the city's elite corporate law firms, then came to Slade's 10 years ago to be its corporate counsel, a job that has a wide range of responsibilities for Slade's compliance with the laws. Four years ago, she began her family, and she now divides her time between Slade's corporate offices, on the seventh floor of the downtown flagship store, and her suburban home. She is particularly committed to toy safety, because many years ago a cousin's young child choked to death on a small part that had come loose from an inexpensive wooden toy. She reports to Si Cohen.

Jim Jacobs, the Annexa lawyer assigned to product liability issues, is a liberal by persuasion. In college he was active in many liberal and consumer protection causes. But he has had many years' experience in handling product liability issues for a large corporation, and he is acknowledged to be a good lawyer. His careful attention to the legal aspects of product safety in the merchandise Annexa stores sell is one reason that the company has never lost a major liability lawsuit. He and Annexa are justifiably proud of that record. He reports to the Senior Vice President for Law at Annexa's corporate headquarters.

Si Cohen is CEO of the Slade's division of Annexa. Each Slade's store has its own manager, but Cohen is responsible for the flagship store and all the regional branches. Because the present retail climate in the flagship city is becoming increasingly competitive, Slade's has been asked by Annexa to cut personnel costs wherever possible, so Slade's does not have a public relations officer presently. Cohen and Sara Brevard share these responsibilities.

Cohen is good at public relations, quick-witted and personable, able to think on his feet. But he likes to be thoroughly briefed on a subject before he has to speak about it. He has a quick temper, and nothing irritates him more than to be inadequately prepared for a public encounter. The Phurry Bear publicity *could* turn out to be a positive thing for Slade's image, and Cohen is smart enough to understand that. But he knows also that much will depend on how the situation is handled, so he wants to be in full command of facts and plans for dealing with the problem *before* he talks to the media.

He also does *not* want to have to absorb heavy losses because of Phurry Bear returns, and he wants quick reimbursement from Toybears, because cash flow is important in retailing results, and he is determined to turn in to Annexa a good profit and loss statement for the fourth quarter. He likes the Annexa management, and he wants to retain his 12-year post with Slade's. He does not want a highly public problem that seems to be out of control.

John Luce is the manager of Slade's downtown flagship store. He started his career selling menswear during his summer and Christmas vacations from college and has worked his way up to store manager. He reports to Si Cohen. John is a born retail manager—charming, affable, popular with his employees, and well known in the city's business community. His name is frequently in the paper, because he is a member of the mayor's advisory committee on youth. Although he is ambitious, he would not want to become a divisional manager for any other Annexa division, because his heart and aspirations are all with Slade's and the city in which it operates. He would like to advance to Cohen's job eventually, but he does not have further ambitions.

Lani Stewart, the sales clerk on the floor who took back the first suspect Phurry Bear, is actually a Slade's buyer-in-training. She grew up in a Midwestern city, attended Williams College, then went to New York to attend the Tobe Coburn School of Retailing and interned at Saks Fifth Avenue. Last year she married David Stewart, whose family runs a printing business in Slade's home city, and they came back to start their home and family. Because she was involved in the problem from the beginning, and because the two women are personal friends, Sara Brevard has kept her involved as the situation has unfolded, and she has continued to work with Sara and Jim on the project. Moreover, Lani worked on the original Phurry Bear promotion plans, so she has a particular stake in seeing that that highly successful promotion does not end in disaster. Her career could be damaged by association with such a debacle. Furthermore, she is fond of David's many small nieces and nephews, and she gave Phurry Bears to several of them for Christmas. She is involved in the problem from many standpoints. She reports to a buyer, who reports to a divisional merchandise manager, who reports to an operations manager, who reports to Cohen.

The assignment.   Cohen has instructed Brevard, Stewart, Luce, and Jacobs to take whatever immediate action is necessary to cover legal liability and regulatory requirements, to report these to him, and to come up with a plan both to deal with the situation and to turn this lemon into lemonade for Slade's. He has told the team that he will do whatever they ask of him in the way of radio and television appearances or press interviews to explain the situation to Slade's customers.

Hint: Because the slivers in the bears are made of metal, a stock clerk in the toy department suggested half-jokingly last week that what was needed was an X-ray machine. Why, she said, you could tell your customers to take their bears to the airport and have them X-rayed to see if they had slivers. Or, she said, we could X-ray bears and offer to exchange bears without slivers for bears that X-ray "positive." What do you think of her idea?

ASSIGNMENT TWO: SOUTH AFRICA
(Communications to Handle a Moral Dilemma)

The political situation in South Africa is longstanding, complex, and controversial. Although major change took place in the early 1990s, it is likely that political and social strife will continue.

HISTORY OF THE PROBLEM

In 1986, the U.S. Congress passed The Comprehensive Anti-Apartheid Act. That legislation imposed economic sanctions on South Africa to pressure its government to repeal the apartheid policy that oppressed its majority black population. With the Act in effect, American companies disinvested and divested their South African holdings.

For a number of years before the sanctions were imposed, American corporations, universities, and other institutions found themselves under pressure to divest their portfolios of holdings that operated in South Africa or did business with South Africa. This pressure presented a dilemma for companies that had found South Africa a source of materials or investment opportunity or for whom South Africa had been or could be a lucrative market.

In 1990, South African President F. W. de Klerk and his government set in motion the legislative changes to end apartheid. In April of 1991, the European Economic Community lifted economic sanctions.

The U.S. sanctions legislation passed in 1986 provided that sanctions would end when five conditions were met. By the summer of 1991, the South African government had met the five conditions. On July 10, President Bush announced that U.S. sanctions also would be lifted.

THE CURRENT PROBLEM. Nevertheless, with or without international economic sanctions, political and social strife are likely to continue in South Africa. And because the world economy is growing increasingly interdependent both politically and economically, the situation in South Africa will continue to have quite a real and immediate impact for American business.

Even with sanctions lifted, opinion in the United States is likely to continue to be sharply divided. Some groups continue to oppose dealing with South Africa. Others believe that because most American firms doing business in South Africa before sanctions were imposed subscribed to the Sullivan Principles (a set of operating guidelines that ensured decent working conditions), the jobs that American firms provided for black South Africans were important opportunities for economic advancement and eventual economic and political empowerment.

This controversy would certainly be likely to affect the two companies modeled in this business problem simulation.

THE ASSIGNMENT

For this assignment, you and your team members will take on the problem posed by the corporate situation set out in the company descriptions on pages 449–452. Nobody would wish to pretend that the problems you will face in handling this assignment are simple. Whatever your own views in the controversy, your job in this exercise will be to make prudent decisions for the mythical company you work for. Your principal aim should be to write the necessary communications to deal with the problem as it applies to "your" company. You may end up communicating decisions and offering recommendations that run counter to your own feelings. You need not agree with the decisions that seem prudent to your task force.

Your job is to set out the problem and to write, clearly and correctly (according to good, standard business practice), the letters, reports, memos, statements, policies—*whatever you decide is required*—to position your company to its best advantage.

You will need to read national press accounts, to find the material you will need—both for the background and for the factual bases of your reports and other communications. Many of your (soon-to-be) business colleagues are struggling right now with these or similar problems.

The following hints should be helpful:

- You may find it useful to *look at the annual reports of several large banks* if you draw First Bigmonia Corporation or of several medium-size manufacturers who export if you draw Sharp Industries.
- *Pay attention to the structure of the corporation you are working with.* The structure will dictate what kinds of distributions you have to indicate for your communications, and may influence some of the decisions you make.
- *Pay attention to business protocol,* and be sure you accord due courtesies (by informing those who need to know and by listing people according to their proper ranks). Observing the necessary business courtesies can have an important bearing on whether your recommendations are well or badly received and on whether your supervisor is pleased and congratulated for the good job you have done or is embarrassed.
- *Pay attention to proper dates and chronologies.* Show a decent regard for *confidentiality* where it is necessary, and be sure that anything sensitive you write down has no more than a limited distribution. Widely distributed corporate communications can—and often do—become the source of embarrassing leaks. Be careful. Decide what should be confidential and mark it so.

ESSENTIAL COMMUNICATIONS. You and your group must decide what communications documents are necessary or useful. Be sure to include, however, at least:

- One comprehensive report or background memo with appropriate graphic support. Or
- One graphic presentation.
- A variety of other communications—such as memos, letters to shareholders, statements, policy statements, press releases, press contingency statements, internal announcements, meeting agendas—whatever is needed to do the job.

A FINAL CAVEAT. Again, your aim is *not,* repeat *not,* to make a moral decision or judgment. Your managers will have to make a business decision or a moral decision that will dictate a business decision. Your job is to take care of the communications to make your managers aware of the probable situations, as well as of the public policy and public relations implications of what they do. Do what is prudent for your company. The difficult part of the problem is to come up with a practical public policy stance—and to communicate it well—one that will permit you to stay in business and still operate as a decent, responsible corporation. Don't forget, as you craft your programs, that the first duty of the organism is survival.

THE
COMPANIES

SHARP INDUSTRIES, INC. Sharp Industries, located in Greencastle, Indiana, is a medium-size manufacturer of surgical instruments and appliances. Sharp sells to hospitals in the United States and in many overseas markets. Sales are $68 million annually.

The problem. An indispensable component of the stainless-steel items you manufacture is a rare metal mined in South Africa. You cannot make your most important product lines without it. South Africa is not only the principal source of the metal; it is the cheapest and the only *reliable* source. The metal is also mined in Zambia and in the Soviet Union, but neither trades strategic metals with Western nations; and the only way you can procure the supplies you need is to buy them through intermediaries—at a very high cost relative to your present prices.

Your sales increased only slightly over the last year, and you are going to have unimpressive results to announce at the end of your fiscal year. Your earnings have not been strong, and the security analysts who follow your industry's stocks are watching you closely.

Japanese competitors have been invading your markets; and they can buy the metal from Zambia, because Zambia does trade with Japan. If you have to buy your metals from countries other than South Africa, you face having to raise your prices. You stand to lose as much as 10% of your market share if you have to raise prices.

Claude Smoothly, your senior vice president in charge of sales and marketing, has been in South Africa for a month; and he reports that he is close to persuading a group of hospitals there to contract for a large, long-term supply of your instruments. This would open an important new market for you.

The Sharp Industries Annual Shareholders' Meeting will take place on June 20, 19——, at 11 a.m., at the company's headquarters auditorium, at Highfall and Main Streets, in Greencastle, Indiana. All shareholders of record are invited to attend.

The Ecumenical Church Alliance Against Apartheid, a coalition that includes both church groups and major hospitals, has decided that 25 members of their coalition will buy one share each of your stock, so as to be able to attend your annual meeting and introduce a shareholder resolution requiring that the company do no sourcing, direct or indirect, in South Africa. The coalition is, of course, unaware of the market you would like to develop in South Africa.

It is almost certain that your company can defeat the resolution, but the Indianapolis newspapers usually cover your annual meeting, and your CEO is worried that because South African sourcing is still controversial, too much publicity might affect the company's image in the medical and hospital communities.

He is also worried about a meeting, scheduled for June 25 in New York, with your industry's security analysts. He would like the annual meeting to go smoothly, and he does not want either the sourcing or market issue to become a focus of questions there.

The personnel. Key personnel include John T. Hackett, President and CEO; Marianna Caustic, Senior Vice President and Chief Financial Officer; Sloan R. Smith, Director of Manufacturing; and Howard M. Flackery, Vice President for Public Relations and Public Affairs.

The communications. Your problem is to deal with the necessary preparations for the upcoming shareholders' meeting, First, let your top managers know what the situation is. Then let them know what preparations have been made, and what the expected outcome is. If you need to hold meetings, write the agendas for the meetings and report on the results. *Provide all necessary communications, both internal and external,* to plan for all eventualities to permit the corporation's meeting to go smoothly so that the company can emerge with as little adverse publicity as possible.

It is likely that John T. Hackett will preside at the annual meeting. You may need memos to inform him and other officers about the possible exposure on the issue. You may wish to report on what other companies have done to handle similar problems. You may need a statement, or you may decide that no statement is best. Think the matter through, and make your best judgment.

Hint: Start with a work plan and questions: What must we find out? Who should find out what? How should information be reported and to whom and by what dates? What communications must be prepared? List them. Make a time-and-action calendar.

FIRST BIGMONIA CORPORATION. First Bigmonia Corporation is a bank holding company with dual headquarters in Kansas City, Missouri, and Mobile, Alabama. Its two main subsidiary companies, The Bigmonia Corporation and The Mobilia Corporation, are engaged in banking and bank-related financial services. First Bigmonia's total assets are $17.7 billion.

The Bigmonia Corporation's principal subsidiary, Bigmonia Bank and Trust Company, N.A., provides personal, commercial, trust, and institutional banking services through 200 full-service banking offices in 24 Missouri cities and towns. It also maintains offices in New York City and Zurich. Retail banking is conducted primarily through the statewide branch network, but other services are provided to corporations and institutions across Missouri, the Southeast, the nation, and the world.

The Mobilia Corporation, which has a total of 117 offices in Alabama, also provides a full range of banking services. The First Mobilia Bank of Mobile is the corporation's lead bank.

The merger of First Bigmonia and The Mobilia Corporation became effective on December 12, 1985. First Bigmonia and Mobilia are about equal in size and in assets. Both First Bigmonia and Mobilia have large pension plans. First Bigmonia's pension assets are managed by different pension investment management firms than are Mobilia's. First Bigmonia's pension investment portfolio includes no South African investments, either direct or indirect.

However, First Mobilia Bank's pension plan is managed by a pension investment management firm which has placed the plan's investments in the stocks of some U.S. corporations that have investments in South Africa. If the pension plan has to divest itself of these investments, the portfolio could be reduced in value (with an accompanying loss for the pension plan's participants, who are the employees of First Mobilia).

The Trust Department of First Mobilia has also invested their clients' money in companies that have investments in South Africa, and some of their accounts hold direct investment in South African gold mines.

The problem. Sylvia E. Brusque, First Bigmonia's loan officer, has found out that the Church Movement Against Apartheid has 50 members who have purchased one share of stock each, in order to be eligible to attend the stockholders' meeting. The group intends to submit a shareholder proposal that would "require Bigmonia's directors to divest all interests, direct or indirect, in South African companies."

To complicate matters further, it is known that Henrietta Bigmonia, a member of Bigmonia's founding family, who herself still owns a large number of shares, is a member of the Church coalition and intends to be at the meeting. Henrietta is an extremely wealthy woman. She is eccentric and colorful, and she is famous for attending the annual meetings of companies in which she owns stock. Whenever she attends a meeting, she makes news, and both the local and national media cover her. Henrietta has seen fit to call a friend who is a reporter on the largest newspaper in Kansas City to announce that she will attend the meeting and will personally introduce the shareholder resolution.

Although your management believes there will be no problem with defeating the resolution, in some companies where this kind of thing has happened, such resolutions have received as much as 20% of the vote; and this alone is likely to make news.

The company would like to avoid publicity over this matter, especially since it would like to make some measured, carefully considered changes in the operations of Mobilia, which it has just acquired in the last year of a merger.

Notoriety is not good for a banking corporation's image; and if customers (both consumer and business) begin to choose up sides on such an issue, the corporation can only lose.

Your problem is to deal with the necessary preparations for the upcoming shareholders' meeting. First, let your top managers know what the situation is. Then let them know what preparations have been made, and what the expected outcome is. If you need to hold meetings, write the agendas for the meetings and report on the results. *Provide all necessary communications, both internal and external,* to plan for all eventualities and to permit the corporation's meeting to go smoothly so that the company can emerge with as little adverse publicity as possible.

The personnel.   Key personnel include T. Gordon Titan, Chairman and Chief Executive Officer, First Bigmonia Corporation; Anthony M. Hatch, Chairman and CEO, First Mobilia Bank; James E. Meddler, President and CEO, First Bigmonia Bank and Trust Company; Sylvia E. Brusque, Chief Loan Officer, First Bigmonia Bank; and Ernesto Emilio Fiduciat, Vice President, Trust Department, First Mobilia Bank, and Secretary, First Bigmonia Corporation.

The communications.   You must decide what communications you will need. You may need such things as a statement for your CEO to make at the annual meeting, a press release, or a set of questions and answers to be used to prepare your officers for the questions they may get both from shareholders during the meeting and from the press afterwards. It is likely that T. Gordon Titan will preside at the annual meeting, which, after all, is the annual meeting of the holding company.

You may need memos to inform your CEO and your corporate secretary about the possible exposure with respect to some of the company's investment holdings. You may also wish to remind your CEO or other officers who will help to plan the annual meeting about the extent of the bank's involvement in South African investments. That is, you may want to make a graphic presentation that would show percentages of investment either for the officers or for them to use to explain the extent of the holdings at the meeting.

Make up any additional facts you need. You may decide that the best thing to do is to make no apologies and no public statements on the matter of the South African investments. Think the matter through.

Note: The Annual Meeting of Shareholders of First Bigmonia Corporation will be held at 10 a.m. on June 20, 19——, in Room 301A of the Kansas City Hotel, Kansas City, Missouri. All shareholders are invited to attend.

ASSIGNMENT THREE: A CORPORATE TAKEOVER
(Communications for an Anti-Takeover Strategy)

This assignment has two parts. The first one will help you to find out something about the issue of a corporate takeover. In the second part, you will work on a strategy to protect your company and to deal with the kinds of issues that arise in the course of a corporate takeover.

**PART ONE:
THE ISSUE**

Compile a short lexicon of takeover terms. Try such items as:

arbitrager	white knight
golden parachute	white squire

greenmail

two-tier front-end load;
   two-tier offer

creeping tender offer

Pac-man defense

poison pill (*also* cyanide capsule)

sale of the crown jewels

scorched earth

shark repellent

corporate raider

bridge loan

the whole is greater than the sum
   of its parts

hostile takeover

friendly takeover

acquisition

merger

restructuring

Hint: Forbes, Time, and *Business Week* all published articles dealing with such terms shortly before May 10, 1985. There may also have been more recent articles, and, in addition, you will find definitions for such terms in news accounts of corporate takeover battles.

THE ASSIGNMENT. Write a (tactful) cover memo to your CEO, who needs precise definitions of these terms but who will almost certainly know rough definitions of some or most of them. Your supervisor, who reports to the CEO, asked you to prepare the list.

PART TWO: AN ANTI-TAKEOVER STRATEGY

Now consult *The New York Times* and/or *The Wall Street Journal* indexes for 1988. You will find almost daily news about large corporate takeovers, because 1988 set a record both in numbers of takeovers and in dollars tendered.

THE ASSIGNMENT. Choose a company, collect as many articles about its takeover fight as you can find, and photocopy them for your team. *Study the articles and use the information in them as the basis for a set of communications—both internal and external—that you might need to generate if you worked for the target company in the course of the takeover.*
   Among the communications you may need to write are:

- Periodic announcements to your employees about the progress of the takeover and its implications for their job security; they will be understandably worried.
- Press statements or background information sheets for the press, which will be asking for information.

Hint: Be very careful with these communications. There are extremely strict Security and Exchange Commission (SEC) rules about what a publicly held corporation must and/or may disclose during the course of a takeover. The SEC also takes a very dim view of rumors that could be thought to have emanated from a takeover target. A corporation must exercise extreme care to see that such rumors are not given wide currency or attributed to the company itself. Because such rumors can affect stock prices and leave a company and its management open to charges of stock manipulation, control of rumors is a serious business. If you are writing drafts of such documents, be sure either to seek legal help from a friendly corporate lawyer who knows or to find out how to consult SEC disclosure regulations. *The New York Times* and *The Wall Street Journal* should be good sources for such information as well. Check their indexes.

The press is very likely to want information about the structure of your company—what businesses it operates (if it is diversified), where it operates, how many subsidiaries it has, what its sales and profits (or losses) were last year, etc. You may want to put together such information to have it readily available for use by company spokespersons or as a quick reminder to your senior managers if they have to make public statements in pressured situations. For example:

- Questions and answers about the progress of the takeover; what measures your company is taking to combat the hostile tender offers, if the takeover is hostile; when your board is expected to meet; when another statement may be forthcoming.
- Memos on staffing needs; information to employees about the strict necessity for keeping their work confidential and not commenting on the takeover to outsiders; clarification of misleading information or rumors to employees.
- Drafts of advertisements or other messages to shareholders, recommending to them their board's position and suggesting to them how the management believes their stock should be voted in any proxy fight.
- Biographical information on senior managers or board members; information about outside counsel being used by the corporation, etc.
- Internal requests, from department to department, for information that might be pertinent to the managers carrying on the fight. Such things might include accounting reports, sales analyses of subsidiaries, reports on accounts receivable, reports on current company financing, etc.
- A plan for restructuring the company to avoid the takeover. (Many of the news stories you find will contain information about restructurings as company defense measures. Use that information as the basis for your restructuring plan.)

After you study your chosen company and its situation, decide what communications you need to produce for, say, a week's worth of activity. Do not produce more than 10 documents; but one of them should be either a report or a recommendation memo that summarizes the position of the company at the end of the week you have chosen.

For purposes of the assignment, choose identities for a team of three to five managers to handle this problem. Draw the names of your team and their positions from the news accounts you research for your company.

If your news accounts show an outcome (either a takeover or a maneuver on the part of the target company that has avoided the takeover), factor this situation into your communications.

ASSIGNMENT FOUR: A CORPORATE RESTRUCTURING
(A Short Report and an Evaluation)

In June of 1982, you were the beleaguered senior vice president for finance and planning of International Harvester, a company that was then the nation's largest manufacturer of large farm machinery but, because of recessionary pressures, was very possibly facing bankruptcy.

PART ONE: A BRIEF REPORT

Using the data included in the article from the June 7 edition of *The Wall Street Journal* reproduced on page 210, write a brief report to the International Harvester Board, recommending the three measures your financial team has decided on to keep the company afloat. Pretend that none of these measures had yet been adopted and that you have them among your options to recommend. Date your report *June 1, 1982.*

Do *not* simply reproduce the article. Use the data carefully as you turn it into information and recommendations and set it out in the form of a short report. Don't overlook explanations of the problems, but assume that your board will have knowledge of the business and of financial strategies and will not need to have everything explained. On the other hand, be clear about what you recommend for the company and why.

Bear in mind that this assignment is *not the same* as the earlier, simpler recommendation memo you wrote based on this information. For this assignment, you should add supporting material as appendixes.

PART TWO: AN EVALUATION MEMO

Now research what has happened to International Harvester since 1982 and, in light of the information you find, evaluate the recommendations your report makes. Be honest, and set out the evaluation in another memo to the present IH board, dated with the current date.

ASSIGNMENT FIVE: REPOSITIONING PRODUCT LINES
(A Short Report on a Marketing Strategy)

On Wednesday, February 1, 1989, the business section of *The New York Times* ran a story about Xerox Corporation. On that day, the company announced an important marketing strategy.

According to the *Times* story, "a recent book, *Fumbling the Future,* [by] Douglas K. Smith and Robert C. Alexander, discussed many problems that

Xerox faced in trying to develop and market a personal computer in the 1970's and early 1980's. . . . According to a Xerox executive who asked not to be named, the book was widely read by company managers and was used . . . by a special mid-level management task force of the company's young managers."

THE ASSIGNMENT

Imagine that you and your classmates were members of the team of young managers appointed to that midlevel management task force. We don't know what the task force's actual assignment was, but for purposes of this exercise, *assume* that *your assignment is to study the company's product lines and their market positions and make recommendations to senior management.*

Use the material in the news account (*and* the Smith/Alexander book, if you wish) to write a report on *your* task force "findings" and to recommend a market strategy. Structure your report as Chapter 9 directs, and write any additional communications you would consider necessary to carry out your task force assignment.

Be sure to include both the essential components of a report *and* whatever optional parts your task force considers useful to buttress your report's recommendation.

Hint: The New York Times and other publications carried large Xerox ads around the time of the restructuring announcement. These ads described Xerox product lines and provided illustrations of many. You could also gain additional information from a Xerox annual report or from Xerox sales brochures.

PAINLESS USAGE GUIDE (PUG)

U sage rules are not absolute, and even experts disagree on a surprising number of points. In some respects, business usage is more conservative and traditional than academic usage. Our aim in this Guide is to present acceptable business usage.[1]

This section is not intended as an exhaustive manual of style. It is rather a quick ready reference designed to resolve some of the questions your business practice will be most likely to pose.[2]

Abbreviations

Usage experts disagree on whether to use periods with abbreviations. The trend is toward omitting the period. The following examples represent conservative business usage.

Use periods

- in titles with proper names:

  Ms., Mrs., Mr., Messrs.
  Adm., Gen., Lt., Sgt.
  Pres., Gov., Sen., Rep.
  Dr., Prof.
  Sr. (Sister), Fr. (Father), Rev. (Reverend, The Reverend)
  Fr. (Frau), Frl. (Fraulein), Hr. (Herr)

---

1. Widely accepted usage guides you might also want to consult include the following:
   The Chicago Manual of Style
   The New York Times Style Manual
   The Harper Dictionary of Contemporary Usage
   Webster's Ninth New Collegiate Dictionary
   Webster's Dictionary of English Usage
   Fowler's Modern American Usage
   The American Heritage Dictionary
   The AP (Associated Press) Style Manual
2. If we have missed a problem that causes you or your colleagues particular agony, write to us at HarperCollins, and we will try to include your item in the PUGs of future editions.

                                                        B.S.N. and S.H.S.

Mlle. (Mademoiselle), Mme. (Madame), M. (Monsieur)
Sra. (Senora), Sr. (Senor), Srta. (Senorita)

- in company structures:

Br., Bros., Co., Corp., Ltd., Inc.

- in other cases:

f.o.b. (free on board) or F.O.B.
U.S. (United States)
P.M. or p.m.

Omit periods

- in abbreviations of the names of Government agencies: FBI, CIA, HUD
- in radio or television call letters: WKRP, WNRK, CBS, NBC
- in acronyms (initials that spell a pronounceable word): NATO, AIDS, VISTA
- in other (miscellaneous) uses: COD
- in geographic directions: NE, NW, SE, SW
- in the standard postal abbreviations for states: NY, OH, PA, etc.

Experts disagree

m.p.h. (miles per hour)	mph
r.p.m. (revolutions per minute)	rpm
M.B.A. (Master's in Business Administration)	MBA
Ph.D. (Doctor of Philosophy)	PhD
ft., yd. (foot, feet, yard)	ft, yd

If an abbreviation falls at the end of a sentence, regular punctuation prevails. But do not use two periods in a row, of course. Do not space between the period at the end of an abbreviation and the final punctuation mark.

Shall we come at 6 P.M.? It's already 6 P.M.

Identify all abbreviations. Write the title fully the first time it occurs, together with the letters in the abbreviation. In all subsequent references abbreviate. Either of the following styles is acceptable.

Mr. Jenkins took over the DPW (Department of Public Works) in December. The DPW now employs 400 people.

Mr. Jenkins took over the Department of Public Works (DPW) in December.

Accept/Except

Accept means "to take or receive." *Except* means "with the exclusion or exception of."

We **accept** everything **except** personal checks.

Adjectives Used as Adverbs. See Good/Well and Bad/Badly

Advice/Advise

Advice (like *ice*) is a noun. *Advise* is a verb.
John's **advice** is worth taking. I **advise** you to take it.

Affect/Effect

Affect and *effect* are both nouns and verbs. As verbs, they have similar—though not identical—meanings. *Affect* means "to influence." *Effect* means "to bring about."

How did Marjorie's speech **affect** you?
They lowered taxes to **effect** economic change.

Effect, when used as a noun, means "result." *Affect,* less often used as a noun, means "emotion."

The price change had little economic **effect.**
His face was expressionless; there was absolutely no **affect.**

Aggravate/Irritate

Irritate means "to annoy." *Aggravate* means "to make worse an already bad situation."

Try not to **irritate** your supervisor before you request a
    raise.
His supervisor's irritation was **aggravated** by his request for
    a raise.

All Ready/Already

Each of these expressions has its own meaning. They are not interchangeable. *All ready* means "completely prepared." *Already* refers to time.

She had **already** prepared her talk, so she was **all ready** for the
    conference.

If you are still in doubt, test to see if you can break the expression to add words. If you can, you know to write *all ready.*

> We are **all** of us **ready.**

All Together/Altogether

These two expressions have different meanings and are therefore not interchangeable. *All together* means "collectively, everyone at one time or place." *Altogether* means "completely."

> **All together** now—pull!
> Your proposal is **altogether** unacceptable.

If you are still in doubt, test to see if you can break the expression to add words. If you can, then you know to use *all together.*

> **All** of us **together** now . . .

Anxious/Eager

Both words refer to anticipation, but *anxious* implies a worried, fearful anticipation and *eager* refers to a joyful and enthusiastic anticipation.

> Cheryl was **anxious** about her interview next Tuesday and was
>   **eager** for that day to be over.

Anybody, Anyone, Everybody, Everyone, Somebody, Someone

All of these words are singular and therefore take singular verbs and are replaced by singular pronouns.

> **Is** anyone here? **Has** everybody come? Someone **is** still missing.
>   We'll wait until everyone **arrives.**
> Did anybody lose **her** purse?

A tricky problem occurs when the individual(s) referred to by these words are of unknown or mixed gender. The old rule that advised using a masculine pronoun (*he, him, his*) in this case is no longer acceptable. It is best, therefore, to avoid the follow-up pronoun construction if you can. It is not yet standard usage to follow up with a plural pronoun (*they, them, their*). But when you see no other way around the difficulty, we think the plural construction or even *he or she* preferable to the all-purpose masculine usage. (See also Chapter 2, pages 47–49, and **He, She . . .**)

Apostrophe Use

The apostrophe (') has two functions: (1) to replace the missing letters in contractions and (2) to indicate possession.

1. Use the apostrophe to punctuate contractions.

cannot = can't; has not = hasn't; do not = don't; would not = wouldn't; he is = he's; we have = we've; it is = it's; they are = they're; will not = won't; we would = we'd

2. Use an apostrophe to signify ownership by adding it *after* the person(s) or thing(s) the object(s) belong(s) to. Add an *s after* the apostrophe if the word is singular or has a non-*s* plural. You do not need to add an *s* if the plural already has one.

John's briefcase; a house's chimney; a dog's tail; a woman's magazine; the houses' chimneys; the dogs' tails; women's magazines

Note: Don't confuse the contraction *it's (it is)* with the possessive pronoun *its.* (See page 473.) The possessive pronoun never has an apostrophe.

Its fur was mussed.

As/Like

As and *like* both convey the idea of comparison. In speaking and in informal writing they are increasingly used interchangeably, but many careful writers frown on the use of *like* to introduce a clause.

FROWNED ON: The plan is proceeding like it should.
PREFERRED: The plan is proceeding as it should.

They also recommend avoiding the use of *like* to mean *as if* or *as though.*

AVOID: It looks like we're going to meet the quota.
USE: It looks as though [*or* as if] we're going to meet the quota.

Assure/Ensure/Insure

All of these words have the sense of providing sureness, certainty. *Assure* carries the idea of promise; it is frequently used to suggest avoiding worry or concern. *Ensure* means "to make certain." *Insure* almost always refers to the business of paying to protect the value of life or property.

I **assure** you that the loan will be okayed on time.
This pass will **ensure** your admittance to the trial.
We tried to **insure** our property in California.

Bad/Badly

Bad is an adjective, qualifying nouns and pronouns. **Badly** is an adverb, qualifying verbs. Be careful not to confuse them. Many find the following nonstandard usage offensive.

NONSTANDARD: Terry types bad.

CORRECT: Terry is a bad typist. Terry's typing is bad. Terry types badly.

You need to make an exception, however, for verbs of feeling or sense. "I feel *badly*" means that there is something wrong with my sense of touch. "I feel *bad*" means that I am not well. "I smell *badly*" means that I have an impaired sense of smell. "I smell *bad*" means, in the words of Dr. Samuel Johnson, noted more for his lexicographical skills than his personal hygiene, "I stink."

Beside/Besides

Beside means "at the side of." *Besides* means "furthermore" or "in addition to."

I like to work **beside** you. **Besides,** I have no other office.

Biannual/Biennial/Bimonthly/Biweekly

These words are confusing. Modern dictionaries show all except *biennial* with more than one meaning—either "every two . . ." or "twice a . . ." The only safe advice is to avoid using the *bi-* words entirely. Say instead, "once every two years" or "every two months," "twice a week" or "every two weeks."

A *biennium,* however, is a two-year period, so you're in no danger of being unclear if you use that term.

Bring/Take

You *bring* something *here.* You *take* something *there.*

Take George a copy of the report, please, and **bring** me back that envelope he's been holding for me.

Can/May

Can indicates ability. *May* indicates permission.

I **can** easily drive to Brooklyn tomorrow, if my supervisor says I **may.**

Capital/Capitol

The only time you use *capitol* is when you refer to the center of government, the building itself. (The federal Capitol is capitalized; the others are in lowercase.) Otherwise use the word *capital.*

We visited the **Capitol** when Congress was in session.
That is a **capital** idea.
I should reinvest my **capital.**
He committed a **capital** crime.
Do we need **capital** letters?
Is Austin the **capital** of Texas?

Capitalization

Use capital letters only when absolutely necessary. There are a number of occasions when they are necessary.

1. Capitalize beginnings of sentences and most lines of verse.
2. Capitalize the proper names of particular persons, places, dates, or things. Leave general categories in lowercase.

   Last Thursday, Arbor Day, we drove our Chevrolet Impala to see Uncle James and my three aunts in South Dakota. Though I almost failed Geography 101, I enjoyed the geography of the region.
   The South has always been noted for its hospitality, but birds fly north in the spring.
   According to my résumé, I majored in history and English and minored in Spanish.

3. Capitalize the pronoun *I* and the interjection *Oh* or *O*.
4. Capitalize important words in titles of works. Do not capitalize articles, conjunctions, or prepositions of less than five letters unless they are the first or last word of a title or subtitle.

   How to Run Better Business Meetings: A Reference Guide for Managers

   Do not capitalize the *the* before a periodical title unless the article is part of the title.

   the *Los Angeles Times*
   The Wall Street Journal

5. Capitalize personal titles and titles of high office.

   Mr. and Mrs. Abercrombie met the Secretary of State and his private secretary.

6. Capitalize adjectives derived from proper nouns.

   French pastry, Russian roulette, Spanish lace, English literature

7. Capitalize corporate titles if your company's house style does so. Do not capitalize otherwise.

John Harper has served as senior vice president of three Fortune 500 companies.

Connie Wong, Executive Vice President of Cordright, will conduct the meeting.

Cite/Sight/Site

Cite, sight, and *site* are unrelated words that happen to be pronounced the same.

I can **cite** the article in the zoning laws that prohibits a construction **site** from being filled up with rubbish and becoming a distasteful **sight.**

Colon Use

The colon (:) signifies "namely," "to wit," "that is," or "Let me explain" and is used to introduce examples or to set up explanations.

The following instances are typical: the Jones matter, the Alphonse case, and the O'Hara fiasco. (The colon here may be translated as "namely.")

None of this is cheap: the container alone costs $4000. (Translate this colon as "that is.")

Colons are also used in the following technical ways:

- Following the salutation of a formal letter: Dear Ms. Ferrara:

- To separate hour and minutes (9:45); volume and page of a periodical (*Business Week* 16: 197); and place of publication and publisher (New York: HarperCollins).

You may use a capital letter after a colon when a full sentence follows; always use a capital when a question follows.

The question must be asked: What can be done?

Comma Use

A comma (,) signifies a pause, but not a full stop, within a sentence. Though fewer are better with commas, use them to promote clarity. They can make a difference.

Mr. Vanover, our CEO has been arrested.

Mr. Vanover, our CEO, has been arrested.

1. *Use commas to isolate parenthetical, extraneous, or interrupting elements.* Surround any interrupting material with commas to set it off

from the rest of the sentence. (Always use a pair of commas for such interruptions unless one side is already identified by some other mark of punctuation or the beginning of the sentence.) Use commas to set off:

- Interrupting phrases: *Perspiring noticeably,* Jan Douglas, *Amalgamated's counsel,* presented, *or tried to present,* their case to the examining board.

- Introductory or interrupting clauses: *When the meeting was over,* we set out for Pittsburgh and our other eastern cities.

  Or: We set out, *when the meeting was over,* for Pittsburgh and our other eastern cities.

  Note: You need *not* use a comma when this sort of clause comes at the sentence's end: We set out for Pittsburgh *when the meeting was over.* (The clause is not considered an interrupter here.)

- Nonessential *who, which* clauses: John Clancy, who represents this district in Congress, spoke for an hour.

  Note: To tell whether to use a comma, ask yourself whether the clause is necessary for the meaning you intend. Take, for example: John saw the banker who was standing in the corridor. If your point is that John saw the banker, then the fact that the banker was standing in the corridor is only parenthetical—a bit of additional, though nonessential, information—and you would use commas:

  NONESSENTIAL: John saw the banker, who was standing in the corridor.

  But if you want to distinguish one banker from another, then the clause becomes essential to your meaning and you should not use commas.

  ESSENTIAL: John saw the banker who was standing in the corridor [walk over and speak to the banker in the doorway].

- Interrupting words: *Therefore,* Harry returned, and brought the papers with him, *nevertheless.* He had, *however,* lost some of them.

  Note: Business frequently uses an "open" style, which eliminates commas around interrupting words.

2. *Use a comma to separate the clauses of a compound sentence when the second clause is introduced by a coordinating conjunction (but, and, nor, for, or yet).* Unless such a sentence is very short. insert a comma after the first clause, before the conjunction. (Remember, however, that in business usage sentences are often very short.)

The ticker was a half hour behind the market, but they did not close it down.

Caution: Do NOT use a comma between main clauses that are not also separated by a coordinating conjunction (*and, but, or*). Such sentences require a full stop, that is, a semicolon or a period.

The ticker was a half hour behind the market; however, they did not close it down.

It is also wiser to use a semicolon for this central separation if you have used commas within the clauses.

3. *Use commas to separate parts of a series.* The comma is optional before the final conjunction.

We bought stocks, bonds, and certificates of deposit.

4. *Use commas in certain technical situations.*

- Between the day and year in dates: Sunday, December 7, 1941.

- Between places in addresses: Philadelphia, Pennsylvania.

- Between names and titles or degrees: Patrick Sanders, Jr., or Jane Killane, PhD.

- To divide numbers of more than three digits, separating them into groups of three: 1,233,987; 6,345 (6345 is also acceptable).

- After the complimentary close or the salutation in informal letters:

Yours truly,
Dear Mrs. King,

Using a comma after the salutation is mainly for personal correspondence. Business prefers the colon.

Complement/Compliment

Complement means "to complete, fill out, bring to fulfillment." *Compliment* means "to give praise to."

Statistics should **complement** your presentation.
Sara **complimented** Jonathan on his fine work.

Continual/Continuous

Continual means "repeated over and over, but with pauses or breaks." *Continuous* means "without interruption." Drumbeats are *continual.* Droning is *continuous.*

Their **continual** bickering was a problem.
The **continuous** downpour stopped all construction.

Council/Counsel/Consul

Council is a noun that means "a group of advisors or people who deliberate."

The city **council** is in session every Thursday.

Counsel, as a noun, means both "advice" and "attorney."

James had been our in-house **counsel** for years, and we always
found his **counsel** on tax problems helpful.

Counsel, as a verb, means to give advice.

When you **counsel** your clients, remember their economic problems.

A *consul* is a foreign service officer.

Stop by and see the Brazilian **consul** if you need a visa.

Councilor and *counselor* are preferred spellings, although *councillor* and *counsellor* are also correct. *Counselor* can also be a synonym for "attorney."

Criteria/Criterion

The singular form is *criterion;* the plural is *criteria.* Say "the criterion is" and "the criteria are."

Dangling Modifier

A dangling modifier is a modifier that is not clearly hitched to the word it modifies, sometimes with confusing or unintentionally humorous results.[3]

INCORRECT: Ancient and battered, Callahan picked up his briefcase.
CORRECTED: Callahan picked up his ancient and battered briefcase.

INCORRECT: A traditional dish for Chanukah, the whole office staff
will enjoy including potato latkes at their holiday party.
CORRECTED: At their holiday party, the whole office staff will enjoy
including potato latkes, a traditional dish for Chanukah.

---

3. E. B. White, the dean of American stylists, wrote: "When you say something, be sure you have said what you mean to say. The chances that you have done so are only fair."

The word being described (modified) must be clearly identified and be placed as close as possible in the sentence to the modifier. Watch out for this kind of dangler too:

AMBIGUOUS: Because of the death of Alfred Jones, he asked for a delay.

CLEAR: Because of the death of Alfred Jones, Smith asked for a delay.

Though not strictly speaking a dangling modifier, the ambiguity in cases like this can be embarrassing or, as in this instance, grisly.

Data

Data comes directly from Latin, where it is the plural form of *datum* and would therefore take a plural verb. The singular form is now rarely used in English, however; and the distinction has largely been discarded in contemporary business usage. Follow the current practice and use *data* with a singular verb.

His **data was** easy to understand.

Double Negative

In theory, negative words cancel each other out and turn a statement positive. In practice, double negatives are considered an especially troublesome error and should be avoided.

NONSTANDARD: No one never came. (Literally means "Somebody always came.")

CORRECT: No one ever came.

Eager. See Anxious/Eager

Effect. See Affect/Effect

Elicit/Illicit

Elicit means "to draw out." *Illicit* means "illegal" or "not allowed."

Try to **elicit** more information from that witness.
She was engaged in the **illicit** manufacture of alligator belts.

Emigrate/Immigrate

Migration is "moving from one place to another." "Migrate to" a place is *immigrate.* "Migrate from" a place is *emigrate.*

> Stanislaus Warshafski **emigrated from** Poland in 1923. He
>   **immigrated to** the United States.
> Stanislaus Warshafski was an **emigrant from** Poland. He was an
>   **immigrant to** the United States.

Eminent/Imminent

These words have little in common but their sound. *Imminent* means
"about to occur, immediately forthcoming." *Eminent* is related to *preemi-nent* and means "distinguished, well respected."

> The board room is not available because of the **imminent** arrival of
>   the **eminent** diplomat Dr. Soong.

Everybody, Everyone. See Anybody, Anyone, Everybody . . .

Farther/Further

Farther and *further* both mean "to a greater degree or extent," but the use
of *farther* is usually reserved for actual distance in space which can be
measured.

> Is Cleveland or Cincinnati **farther** from Columbus?
> I changed my opinion upon **further** consideration.

Fewer/Less

Fewer is used with number. *Less* is used with quantity.

> There were **fewer** than six people on the sign-up sheet.
> There was **less** noise tonight.
> We had hoped for **fewer** cases of DWI (driving while intoxicated)
>   this year.
> We had hoped there would be **less** DWI this year.

With *fewer,* you can count the number of cases. *Exception:* You can use *less*
with a number when it refers to a collective sum ("*less* than 30 years old"
or "a salary *less* than $25,000").

Fragments

A fragment is a portion of a sentence that is punctuated as if it were a
sentence.

> Though it is not a sentence.
> Which was a surprise.

Occasionally, an experienced writer employs a fragment effectively.

> What's wrong with nondiscrimination, with simple fairness? **Two things really.** [William Raspberry]

But in general, fragments—like all structural errors of the sentence—can be distracting to readers and are best avoided.

Gender. See Chapter 2, pages 47–49; **Anybody, Anyone . . . ;** and **He, She . . .**

Girl, Lady, Woman

A *girl* is a female child. The term should not be used to refer to anyone old enough to be employed.

Lady is a social term. It is not useful in the business world.

Appropriate designations for an adult female in business include *woman, businesswoman,* or *business person.*

Good/Well

Good is an adjective, qualifying nouns and pronouns. *Well* is an adverb, qualifying verbs. Be careful not to confuse them. Many find the following nonstandard usage offensive.

NONSTANDARD: Terry types good.
CORRECT: Terry is a good typist. Terry's typing is good. Terry types well.

He, She; Him, Her; His, Hers

All these words denote an antecedent of specific gender. Problems arise when the subject is of mixed or unknown gender. Since the traditional rule of using the masculine term in such cases is now widely considered offensive, it is better to avoid the problem altogether and rephrase with a plural subject:

NOT THIS: The American worker is interested in his health benefits.
BUT THIS: American workers are interested in their health benefits.

In the rare cases where the plural simply cannot be used, *his or her* or *he or she,* though awkward, is acceptable.

> The American worker is interested in his or her health benefits.

(See also Chapter 2, pages 47–49, and **Anybody, Anyone . . .**)

Hopefully

Technically, the sentence "Hopefully, Jane will finish the contract tomorrow" means that Jane will finish the contract full of hope. But what the writer really means (and should say) is "I hope Jane will be able to finish the contract tomorrow."

Although the *hopefully* construction is becoming more widely accepted, it is still not standard practice, and you would do best to avoid it.

I/Me

Confusion between *I* and *me* occurs usually when the pronouns are compounded ("my wife and me" or "my wife and I"?). To know the right word, make the *I* or *me* stand alone and let your ear decide. For example, you wouldn't say "Mrs. Jannings asked *I* to attend the dinner," but you would say "Mrs. Jannings asked *me* to attend." So you know that the proper usage is "Mrs. Jannings asked my wife and *me* to attend the dinner." A similar test:

INCORRECT: I think me should be sent to California. (Of course not!)
CORRECT: I think I should be sent to California.
CORRECT: I think Helen and I should be sent to California.

If ... Were

When *if* or *as if* or *as though* is used to express a condition that does not exist or a situation that is only wished for or desired, the subject is followed by *were:*

If the world **were** flat . . .
John led the meeting **as if** he **were** president.
John **wished** he **were** president.

Imply/Infer

The speaker or writer *implies* (suggests, hints). The listener or reader *infers* (draws his or her own conclusions).

He **implied** that he was rich by mentioning that his wife had left her sable coat in the Rolls-Royce.
We **inferred** from his remarks that he was rich.

Individual

The word *individual* carries with it the sense of singleness, of separate entity. It should not be used synonymously with a word as general as *person.* Avoid using such expressions as "Elmer Jackson was the individual who applied for the job."

Elmer Jackson was the **person** who applied for the job.

Infer. See **Imply/Infer**

Insure. See **Assure/Ensure/Insure**

Irregardless/Regardless

Irregardless is not a word.

Irritate. See **Aggravate/Irritate**

Its/It's

It's, a contraction meaning "it is" or "it has," should not be confused with the possessive *its.*

The marketing department has broken **its** fax machine, but **it's** not within our budget to repair it.

Lay/Lie

The verb *lie* (meaning "to recline") does not take an object.

The elderly judge can **lie** on the couch in his office during a court recess.

The verb *lay* means "to put" and always takes an object.

Lay your coat down. **Lay** your bets.

Lay and *lie* sometimes confuse people because their forms are irregular and because *lay* is also the past tense of *lie.*

Today I **lie** down. Yesterday I **lay** down.

The past tense of *lay* (the one that means "to put" and always takes an object) is *laid.*

Yesterday I **laid** my book down and then I **lay** down for a nap.

Less/Fewer. See **Fewer/Less**

Lets/Let's

Lets means "allows." *Let's* means "let us."

> Becky **lets** the intern borrow her word processor.
> **Let's** try to get there early.

Loose/Lose

Lose rhymes with *whose* and means "misplace." *Loose* rhymes with *goose* and means "unconfined" or "unrestrained."

> Because the handle was **loose,** Herman was afraid he would **lose** his briefcase.

Majority/Plurality

Majority means more than half the total number. But if more than two numbers make up the total, there may be no number greater than half, and hence no majority. The largest number then is called a *plurality.*

As is the case with most collective nouns, *majority* takes a singular verb when the group acts as a unit and a plural verb when the members act separately.

> The **majority is** determined to defeat the bill.
> The **majority disagree** about how to do it.

May. See **Can/May**

Media/Medium

Media is the plural form of *medium.* Television *is* a *medium* of communication. So is radio. So is the newspaper. They *are* all communications *media.* It is incorrect to say "The *media is* treating the President harshly." Say rather, "The *media are* treating the President harshly."

Misplaced Modifier. See **Dangling Modifier**

Myself (Herself, Himself, etc.)

Myself is not correctly used in place of *I* or *me.*

> INCORRECT: Ms. Brown took Larry and myself to lunch.
> CORRECT: Ms. Brown took Larry and me to lunch.
> INCORRECT: Larry and myself went to lunch with Ms. Brown.
> CORRECT: Larry and I went to lunch with Ms. Brown.

The *-self* words are correctly used in the following sentences.

> I hurt myself on that broken file drawer.
> I myself took Larry to lunch yesterday. He paid for lunch himself on Tuesday.

Negative. See **Double Negative**

Neither . . . Nor

Neither . . . nor can be used only when referring to two elements. When both elements are singular, the verb is singular.

> Neither **she** nor her **secretary is** in today.

When both elements are plural, the verb is plural.

> Neither **stocks** nor **bonds are** worth buying today.

When one element is singular and the other is plural, the verb agrees with the closer one.

> Neither the union **representatives** nor **management was** prepared for the meeting.
> Neither **management** nor the union **representatives were** prepared for the meeting.

None

None is considered singular when it means "not one."

> **None** of the secretaries **has** gone to lunch yet.

However, when *none* means "not any"—and it usually does—the plural is used.

> **None** of the two hundred victims **were** from our town.

Nothing

Nothing always takes a singular verb.

> **Nothing** but pain and injuries **has** plagued him all season.

Numbers

Under most circumstances, spell out numbers from one through nine and write larger figures (13; 874; 69,998,303) in numerals. As a rule, show dates and times (December 2, 1931, at 2:40 a.m.) in numerals. If you must begin a sentence with a number, it is usually best to spell it out.

Only

The placement of *only* can alter the meaning of a sentence. Note the following:

> **Only** Paula borrowed the typewriter. (No one else borrowed it.)
> Paula **only** borrowed the typewriter. (She returned it.)
> Paula borrowed **only** the typewriter. (She didn't borrow anything else.)
> Paula borrowed the **only** typewriter. (There was just one typewriter available.)

Only should not be used as a conjunction.

> DON'T USE: He wanted to address the group, *only* he had a sore throat.

Instead use *but* or whatever conjunction seems appropriate.

Parallelism, Faulty

Whenever you use parallel constructions, it is important to make sure that the parallel elements are syntactically alike. Parallel structure is especially important when you choose to bullet the separate elements.

> The real estate deal fell through because
>
> - the buyer couldn't get financing,
> - the title had a defect, and
> - the seller had second thoughts.

Awkward, sometimes even ludicrous, effects result from faulty parallelism.

> AWKWARD: The real estate deal fell through
>
> - because the buyer couldn't get financing,
> - the seller having had second thoughts, and
> - a defect in the title.

Practicable/Practical

Practicable means "capable of being put into practice"—that is, "feasible." *Practical* means "sensible, useful." It is the opposite of "theoretical."

> The committee took a **practical** approach and developed a **practicable** plan.

Precede/Proceed

Precede means "to go before." *Proceed* means "to continue or go forward."

> The chairman **preceded** the speaker as the group **proceeded** to the head table.

Principal/Principle

Principal means "first" or "head" or "most important." It can also refer to a sum of money that earns dividends.

> Steinmetz took a **principal** role in uncovering the fraud.
> A **principal** can be considered the CEO of a school.
> She lived on the interest and did not have to use the **principal** in her account.

A *principle* is a rule by which a person lives or by which an organization is conducted.

> Loyalty to her employees was her guiding **principle.**

Proceed. See **Precede/Proceed**

Quite/Really/Very

Quite, really, and *very* are intensifiers; that is, they are meant to emphasize the adjective or adverb they qualify and make it stronger. They are so overused, however, that in most cases it is questionable whether they achieve that end. Like exclamation points, they can add a gushy rather than an emphatic quality.

> LESS EFFECTIVE: Elston Partridge, our CEO, is really [quite, very] well known.
> STRONGER: Elston Partridge, our CEO, is well known.

Really/Real

Real and *really* are not interchangeable. Use *real* only when you want to ascribe reality to something.

> My pearl came from a real oyster.

Avoid using *real* as an intensifier in business writing.

> COLLOQUIAL: Mrs. Hogan was real impressed with your credentials.
> CORRECTED: Mrs. Hogan was really impressed with your credentials.

Usually it is more effective to eliminate the qualifier altogether.

BETTER: Mrs. Hogan was impressed with your credentials.

(See also **Quite/Really/Very**)

Reason is because

Avoid this construction. Write instead: "The reason is *that . . .*"

> **The reason** we should avoid writing this construction **is that** it is not accepted by conservative business writers.

Regardless. See **Irregardless/Regardless**

Run-on Sentences

A run-on sentence is a group of words that contains more than one main (independent) clause but is punctuated (incorrectly) as if it were a single sentence.

RUN-ON: Our stock had an exceptional day it went up 12 points.
CORRECTED: Our stock had an exceptional day. It went up 12 points.
CORRECTED: Our stock had an exceptional day; it went up 12 points.

Substituting a comma for the period or the semicolon in the edited versions would be as incorrect as the first example.

Semiannual/Semimonthly/Semiweekly

Semiannual means "happening or appearing twice a year." *Semimonthly* means "twice each month." *Semiweekly* means "twice a week."

> Our newsletter will appear **semiweekly,** on Tuesdays and Fridays.

(See also **Biannual**)

Semicolon Use

A semicolon (;) joins two or more closely related clauses when no coordinating conjunction (such as *and, but, or, nor, yet, for,* or *so*) is used. It is particularly valuable when a connective that is ordinarily followed by a comma (*therefore, however, indeed, nevertheless*) is present.

> Marcia has always been capable and bright; she understands the most complex material almost as soon as she reads it.

> Marcia has always been capable and bright; furthermore, she understands the most complex material almost as soon as she reads it.

Use a semicolon as a strong comma to separate elements in a compound sentence or in a series when one or more of those elements contain commas.

> I substituted for Joe at the Chamber of Commerce meeting; and sitting at my table were representatives of Procter & Gamble, Milacron, U.S. Shoe Corp., and some lesser-known companies.
>
> Most memorable among the delegates were a ruddy-faced, round-bellied, heavy-breathing man from one of the breweries; an elderly woman in a fantastic pink hat, representing a chain of boutiques, who spoke intelligently and well; and an attractive, well-tailored woman of about my age with an interesting smile.

Note: A semicolon indicates a full stop—much as a period does. Be careful NOT to use it as a substitute for a comma, but confine your use of it to the two situations just outlined.

Sentence Fragments. See **Fragments**

Set/Sit

Set takes an object. *Sit* does not take an object. You cannot *sit* something; you must *set* it.

> **Set** the books on that chair, and **sit** over here with us.

She/He; Her/Him; Her/His. See **He, She . . .**

Sight/Site. See **Cite/Sight/Site**

So/So That

So stands alone or unites with *and* when it expresses a consequence of some action.

> Mike had an accident, and **so** he will have to rent a car.

So is followed by *that* when it means "in order that."

> He needed a ride **so that** he could get there by Friday.

Spelling

Because the spelling of English words does not always coincide with the way they are pronounced, the only sure method is to memorize the spelling of individual words and determine to look up the rest. Nevertheless, you may find a number of rules helpful:

Double Vowels

These rules, which will probably have a vaguely familiar ring from your early schooldays, can still be of use when you can't remember which way to order vowels.

1. For most double vowels:

    Rule: When two vowels go walking,
    The first one does the talking.

    p*ea*ch, b*oa*t, p*ou*r

    Exceptions: Diphthongs such as *ou* and *oi* and the *i*-and-*e* combination.

2. For *i* and *e* combinations:

    Rule: *I* before *e*
    Except after *c*.
    Or when sounding like "ay,"
    As in *neighbor* and *weigh*.

    fr*ie*nd, bel*ie*f, ach*ie*ve, rec*ei*ve, th*ei*r

Adding Suffixes That Begin with Vowels (-ed, -ing, -able, and so on)

1. For words that end in *e*:

    Rule: Drop the *e* before adding the suffix. The reason is that the final vowel *e* serves to keep the central vowel sound long, and the vowel in the suffix will serve the same purpose.

    mope, moping, moped. Chris sat around and **moped.**

2. For final accented words that do NOT end in *e*:

    Rule: Double the final consonant before adding the suffix. The reason is that the double consonant prevents the vowel in the suffix from turning the central vowel sound long. The doubling thus keeps the vowel sound short.

    mop, mopping, mopped. Chris **mopped** the floor.

3. For words that end in *y*:

Rule: Change *y* to *i* and add the suffix. When the suffix is *-s*, change it to *es*.

vary, varied, varies

Exceptions: (a) Keep the *y* when the suffix is *-ing: varying*
(b) Keep the *y* when forming the plural of a proper noun: *Murphys*

Combined Words

Rule: Words formed by combining two words retain all the letters of both words, even if a letter repeats.

roommate, withheld, overrule

Words formed by adding a prefix retain all the letters of both prefix and base, even if a letter repeats.

misspell, unnatural, interracial, dissatisfied

After the Rules

Unfortunately, English has a number of common words whose spellings cannot be worked out by the rules. If you habitually misspell any of these, it is important to locate them. Test yourself on the accompanying list of commonly misspelled words. Memorizing the spelling of any that are troublesome to you will save much dictionary time.

absence	comparative	inoculate	principle
accept	conscious	intelligence	privilege
accommodate	decision	judgment	psychology
achieve	definite	knowledge	receive
acknowledged	describe	library	recognize
acknowledgment	description	maintenance	rhythm
advertisement	difference	millennium	science
alleged	effect	necessary	separate
analogous	embarrass	neighbor	shining
argument	environment	ninety	similar
assistance	especially	ninth	society
athlete	exercise	occasionally	studying
beautiful	experience	occurring	succeed
beginning	familiar	opportunity	supersede
believe	February	parallel	surprise
benefit	forty	personal	thoroughly
business	fourth	persuade	traveling
characteristic	friend	planned	Tuesday
circumstances	hoping	possession	usually
committee	immediately	presence	Wednesday

Stationary/Stationery

Stationary means "not moving, remaining in one place." *Stationery* refers to paper, cards, and envelopes used to correspond by note or letter.

> The cabinets were **stationary.** We ordered imprinted **stationery** in two sizes.

Than

In order to decide what pronoun to use following *than,* mentally complete the thought. For example, which do you mean?

> Alice wanted the position more **than he** [did].
> Alice wanted the position more **than** [she wanted] **him.**

Than is always used in this comparative way. Do not confuse it with *then,* which usually indicates time.

That/This

This and *that* and their plurals, *these* and *those,* refer to, point to, or substitute for *specific* objects or persons.

> This memo. Those memos. That letter. Those letters. Letters such as these.

Avoid using these words to signify "all this" or "all that I have just said."

> VAGUE: We could purchase the options, wait to see what happens, and then make our final decision. This would be feasible.
> CLEARER: **This plan** would be feasible.

Their/There/They're

Their and *theirs* are possessives. They express the idea of "belonging to."

> This is **their** furniture. The house is also **theirs.**

There can be used as an introductory word or as a word to indicate place.

> **There** can be only 12 members. **There's** no reason to involve more people. Only the 12 members were **there.**

They're is a contraction of *they are. There's* is a contraction of *there is.*

> **They're** leaving to pick up **their** notes which they left **there** overnight. **There's** no doubt that **they're theirs.**

Then. See **Than**

To/Too/Two

Errors in using these words are probably the result of carelessness rather than lack of understanding. Watch for them when you proofread. *Two* is always a number. *Too* means "also" and "overly" or "excessive." In other situations, *to* is the correct spelling.

> The **two** workers walked **too** far **to** go **to** the bank and back **to** the plant **too.**

Try and/Try to

Do not substitute *try and* for *try to*. Although this construction is often heard in conversation, it is better avoided in writing.

> COLLOQUIAL: We should try and remember the way back.
> PREFERRED: We should **try to** remember the way back.

Unique

Since *unique* means that the idea or thing it describes is the only one in the world, such expressions as "very unique" or "the most unique" are excessive and should be avoided.

Used to

Never write *we use to* or *we didn't used to*. Write *we used to* and *we didn't use to*.

> We **used to** enjoy homemade ice cream, but we **didn't use to** make it in large quantities because no one **used to** have a freezer.

Very. See **Quite/Really/Very**

Well. See **Good/Well**

When/Where

When and *where* should not be used after *is* to form a definition.

> FROWNED ON: A production breakdown is where at least two lines operate at only half capacity.
> CORRECTED: A production breakdown is a slowdown in which . . .
> FROWNED ON: A hole in one is when a golfer sinks the ball with one driving stroke.
> CORRECTED: A hole in one occurs when a golfer . . .

Where . . . at

At is usually not needed after *where.*

> INCORRECT: Where's it at?
> CORRECT: Where is it?

Who/Whom

Who is used as the *subject* of a sentence or clause. So is *whoever. Whom* and *whomever* are used as *objects.*

> **Who** is your best worker? Your best worker is **whoever** can be relied on most in an emergency.
>
> The person to **whom** the responsibility has been given is not always the person **whom** you would most want to rely on.
>
> We asked **who** had been here longest. He is the one **whom** we wanted to interview.
>
> We will present the keys to **whoever** wins the raffle.

In the last sentence, the entire clause *whoever wins the raffle* is the object of the preposition *to,* but *whoever* is the subject of *wins.*

The language is changing, and the distinction between these forms may become obsolete. In fact, some careful writers have already abandoned the *whom* form. Professor Richard A. Lanham, whom we quote in Chapter 2, writes: "Who is kicking who?" The bottom line: In your business writing, make the conservative choice and use the correct form for the sentence structure—or recast your sentence to eliminate the problem.

Who's/Whose

Who's means "who is" or "who has." *Whose* is a possessive form.

> We know **whose** tapes are being pirated, but we don't know **who's** doing it.

It is now acceptable to use *whose* with inanimate objects.

> The report deals with companies **whose** CEOs earn more than a million dollars a year.

Would have/Would of

Would have is correct. Don't write *would of.*

> NONSTANDARD: I would of come earlier.
> CORRECT: I would have come earlier except for a last-minute call.
> CORRECT: I would've come earlier.

The same rule applies to *could have* (or *could've*) and *should have* (or *should've*).

Your/You're

Your is a possessive. *You're* is a contraction of *you are*.

You're always leaving **your** coat on that chair.